Artificial Intelligence, Digital Learning, and Leadership:

Redefining Higher Education

George Ngwacho Areba
Kisii University, Kenya

Billiah Nyamoita Gisore
Kisii University, Kenya

Evelyn Wanjiru Njurai
Kisii University, Kenya

IGI Global
Publishing Tomorrow's Research Today

Vice President of Editorial	Melissa Wagner
Managing Editor of Acquisitions	Mikaela Felty
Managing Editor of Book Development	Jocelynn Hessler
Production Manager	Mike Brehm
Cover Design	Phillip Shickler

Published in the United States of America by
IGI Global Scientific Publishing
701 East Chocolate Avenue
Hershey, PA, 17033, USA
Tel: 717-533-8845
Fax: 717-533-8661
Website: https://www.igi-global.com E-mail: cust@igi-global.com

Library of Congress Cataloging-in-Publication Data

Names: Areba, George, 1978- editor. | Gisore, Billiah, 1972- editor. | Njurai, Evelyn Wanjiru, editor.
Title: Artificial intelligence, digital learning, and leadership : redefining higher education / Edited by George Ngwacho Areba, Billiah Gisore, Evelyn Njurai.
Description: Hershey, PA : IGI Global Scientific Publishing, [2025] | Includes bibliographical references and index. | Summary: "Each chapter of this book presents a critical examination of how AI and digital tools are being leveraged to enhance educational processes, while also addressing the ethical concerns and leadership imperatives that arise as institutions shift from traditional to modern learning systems"-- Provided by publisher.
Identifiers: LCCN 2024060582 (print) | LCCN 2024060583 (ebook) | ISBN 9798337300252 (hardcover) | ISBN 9798337300269 (paperback) | ISBN 9798337300276 (ebook)
Subjects: LCSH: Artificial intelligence--Educational applications. | Education, Higher--Web-based instruction. | Educational leadership. | Education, Higher--Effect of technological innovations on.
Classification: LCC LB1028.43 .A785 2025 (print) | LCC LB1028.43 (ebook) | DDC 370.78/563--dc23/eng/20250210
LC record available at https://lccn.loc.gov/2024060582
LC ebook record available at https://lccn.loc.gov/2024060583

British Cataloguing in Publication Data
A Cataloguing in Publication record for this book is available from the British Library.

Editorial Advisory Board

Table of Contents

Detailed Table of Contents

AI age. It requires the learning researchers to delve into exploration and involve other education stakeholders. Methods used were partial literature review plus qualitative assessment of teaching methods in the period of AI. The study targeted curriculum and instruction designers, policy maker, administrators, educators including stakeholders passionate in teaching and learning in modern times of AI and furtherance of sustainable development in Kenya and environs.

This chapter discusses the evolving Artificial Intelligence (AI) landscape in Higher Education. AI is the new development that affect pedagogy and learning outcomes in higher education. This chapter examines AI as a key component in the delivery of curriculum. It aims to guide institutions of higher learning to adjust to fit into possible changes and not be swayed by AI wave that has gathered momentum globally. The institutions of higher learning should prepare stakeholders of a future that will require shrunk office spaces. Further, there is need for adoption and use of such technologies within the confines of known rules and regulations that ensure zero compromise on quality of teaching, learning, learning outcomes and productivity.

Integration of digital techniques like learning management systems and artificial intelligence has revolutionized teaching methodologies. Blended learning models, combining face-to-face instruction with online components, foster dynamic learning experiences and democratize access to resources, promoting flexibility and inclusivity. In Kenya, digital adoption in higher education has surged, enhancing accessibility and efficiency in instructional and administrative processes. Digital tools facilitate active learning, collaboration and personalized learning, transforming traditional instructional methods and promoting student engagement and motivation. The flipped classroom model supported by digital technologies, encourages active learning and critical thinking. Effective tutor training is crucial for integrating digitization, focusing on developing digital competencies and pedagogical skills. Although challenges persist, the digital era offers opportunities for enhancing teaching and learning, making education more accessible.

The digital revolution has brought about significant changes in Higher Education Institutions (HEIs), transforming teaching, learning, and assessment. The chapter explores the impact of this paradigm shift from analogue to digital methods and discuss how education practices in higher education institutions have been revolutionized. The chapter provides a comprehensive overview of the key models and approaches that have guided this critical transformation. The mission of this chapter is to provide educators, researchers, and practitioners with an in-depth understanding of how digital technologies are reshaping higher education. The examination of the various models and approaches, is aimed at providing strategies needed to effectively navigate the digital space and enhance teaching, learning, and assessment. At the same time, the chapter recognizes that digital transformation of higher education comes with its own set of concerns and challenges. The best practices have also been suggested in the chapter.

Open and Distance E-Learning (ODEL) is transforming higher education in East and South Africa by addressing barriers to access and inclusivity. Accelerated by the COVID-19 pandemic, ODEL supports educational continuity and lifelong learning. Evolving from 19th-century correspondence courses, ODEL now leverages internet access, Learning Management Systems (LMS), mobile technology, and artificial intelligence, aligning with the UN Sustainable Development Goals (SDGs). Key challenges include the digital divide, cultural and language barriers, and resource limitations. Strategies include leveraging mobile technology, low-cost solutions, and policy enhancements. Future AI and virtual reality advancements promise further improvements, fostering a more equitable educational landscape.

The rise of online open electives has transformed education, shifting from traditional classrooms to virtual platforms due to technological advancements and improved accessibility. This shift fosters a culture of continuous learning globally, accommodating diverse schedules and overcoming geographical barriers. Demographic trends, such as the globalization of education and the growing emphasis on lifelong learning, highlight the inclusive nature of online open electives. This study utilizes the Measure of Online Communication Attitude (MOCA) to explore online communication attitudes across different demographic groups, focusing on gender, age, and locality. Conducted from January to April 2023, Bayesian statistical analyses were employed to assess psychological dimensions. Results reveal nuanced gender differences in self-disclosure, apprehension, miscommunication, social connection, and ease. Psychological similarities were found among different age groups, with slight variations observed in apprehension and miscommunication across rural, semi-urban, and urban localities.

Collaboration in education is significant for many reasons such as it enhances learning experience, develops deeper understanding and improves skill level. In academia, collaborative practices helps the educators as connecting with different people can help them learn and share teaching strategies and resources. The present report highlights the collaborative practices of higher education institutions with research organizations and industry. It also defines the challenges and issues that happen while collaborating with external partners along with difference of goals between academia and industry. In addition to this, discussion is also included regarding the impact of collaboration on innovation and research capabilities. Therefore, from the study it has been found out that global collaboration assist the higher education institutional students to build diverse skills which are crucial for their career or profession.

Education is the most powerful weapon that can be put to use to change the world and requires a good head and a good heart for its effectuality. Higher education is an umbrella encompassing all types of education as provided by universities, technological institutes, teacher training colleges and normally intended for students who have completed secondary education and have an educational objective of acquisition of a title, a grade, certificate, or diploma of higher education. Higher education is facing a myriad of challenges that are impacting negatively towards its progress and performance. To forestall such, transformational leadership has been touted as a game changer that when applied can be beneficial in aiding higher education recourse and adopt a trajectory geared towards its betterment. The chapter highlights key components that transformational leadership impacts to cause necessary changes and realignments: training of leaders, financial management, collaboration partnerships, technology, inclusivity and diversity, and innovation.

Academic work is a significant factor in mental health and academic performance of university students. Mental health challenges can impede academic success. Academic performance and mental health wellness have an interactive relationship. The top two mental health issues faced by College Students include anxiety and depression. This chapter will focus on how the two disorders with high comorbidity can impede the academic success of students. Anxiety and depression are major predictors of academic performance among university students. Students with the two disorders are likely to lose interest in learning and therefore, perform poorly in class. There is often a positive correlation between anxiety and depression and poor academic performance by university students. The two disorders among university students have been established to be on the rise besides other mental health problems that students experience while in campus, leading to poor academic performance and failure to transit to graduation.

Foreword

In the rapidly evolving landscape of higher education, the intersection of technology, leadership, and pedagogy has brought about unprecedented transformations. At the forefront of these changes is the advent of Artificial Intelligence (AI) and digital learning tools, which have not only reshaped teaching methods but also redefined the very structure of knowledge dissemination and acquisition. This book, Artificial Intelligence, Digital Learning, and Leadership: Redefining Higher Education, explores the significant impacts of AI and digital innovation on higher education in Kenya and beyond, offering insights into the challenges, opportunities, and ethical considerations that accompany this shift.

As Higher institutions globally navigate the transition from analogue to digital learning environments, the need for adaptive leadership and innovative strategies have never been greater. The first chapter, Leveraging Artificial Intelligence Tools for Learning in Higher Education in Kenya, delves into the transformative potential of AI in enhancing educational outcomes. It underscores the necessity of aligning technology with local contexts to create relevant and impactful learning experiences.

The ethical implications of AI in education are thoroughly examined in chapters such as Intrigues of Artificial Intelligence in teaching and Learning in the modern times; Artificial Intelligence: Ethics and Academic Integrity in Higher Education. As AI becomes an integral part of academic processes, questions surrounding integrity, fairness, and the responsible use of technology are increasingly pressing. These discussions are crucial in ensuring that AI is harnessed to elevate learning without compromising the values that higher education upholds.

The book also addresses the broader, systemic changes brought about by the digital revolution, such as Transition from Analogue to Digital Technology: Examining Teaching, Learning, and Assessment in Higher Education in Kenya and Fostering a Conducive Open and Distance E-Learning (ODEL) Environment in the 21st Century in Higher Learning Institutions. These chapters highlight how digital learning has enabled more flexible, accessible, and equitable educational opportunities, particularly in regions where traditional models of education have faced significant barriers.

Furthermore, the role of leadership in guiding these transformations cannot be understated. Transformational Leadership in Higher Education and Innovative Synergies Collaborating with Industry, Research Organizations, and Global Institutions in Higher Education provide a roadmap for educational leaders to foster collaboration, innovation, and resilience in the face of rapid technological advancements.

Finally, the well-being of students remains a core concern amidst these changes. In Mental Health and Academic Performance among University Undergraduate Students: Depression and Anxiety, the mental health challenges that often accompany the pressures of modern academic life are addressed, reminding us that the future of education must be as much about supporting students' mental and emotional needs as it is about technological advancement.

As you journey through the chapters of this book, you will encounter a comprehensive exploration of how AI, digital tools, and visionary leadership are reshaping the higher education landscape. The future is one of promise and complexity, and it is our collective responsibility to ensure that the transformation of higher education serves to empower learners, educators, and institutions alike.

With this, I invite all leaners, educators, policymakers, and institutional leaders to engage deeply with the ideas presented in this book, and to consider how they might inform and inspire their own approach to education and learning in the 21st century.

Mzee Awuor

Administration, Planning and Finance (DVC), Human Centered Computing,-Kisii University, Kenya

Preface

In the rapidly evolving landscape of higher education, technology has become the driving force behind revolutionary changes in teaching, learning, and leadership. The intersection of artificial intelligence (AI), digital learning platforms, and innovative leadership practices has created opportunities and challenges that are reshaping education systems around the world. This book, *Artificial Intelligence, Digital Learning, and Leadership: Redefining Higher Education*, explores these dynamic developments globally. By examining various aspects of AI's integration into education, it provides valuable insights into the transformative power of technology in academic environments. The book presents a critical examination of how AI and digital tools are being leveraged to enhance educational processes, while also addressing the ethical concerns and leadership imperatives that arise as institutions shift from traditional to modern learning systems.

The first chapter, *Leveraging Artificial Intelligence Tools for Learning in Higher Education in Kenya*, sets the stage by exploring how AI tools are enhancing both the teaching and learning experiences in Kenyan universities. This chapter delves into practical applications of AI in education, showing how it can improve access, efficiency, and engagement in the learning process.

Building upon this, *Intrigues of Artificial Intelligence in teaching and Learning in the modern times* focuses on the ethical considerations that come with AI integration, particularly in preserving academic honesty. As AI systems become more sophisticated, so too do the methods for circumventing them, raising important questions about maintaining integrity in digital learning environments.

Chapters three and four, *Artificial Intelligence: Ethics and Academic Integrity in Higher Education* and *Transition from Analogue to Digital Technology: Examining Teaching, Learning, and Assessment in Higher Education in Kenya* further explore the complexities of using AI in education. They highlight both the potential benefits and the ongoing challenges of applying AI to academic settings, offering balanced perspectives on the opportunities and risks inherent in these technological advances.

The shift from traditional to digital education is at the heart of *From Analogue to Digital Revolution - Transformed Teaching, Learning, and Assessment in Higher Education:* This chapter explores how the digital revolution has not only changed the methods of teaching and learning but also redefined assessment practices, fostering a more dynamic and interactive approach to higher education.

In a broader context, *Fostering a Conducive Open and Distance E-Learning (ODEL) Environment in the 21st Century in Higher Learning Institutions in East and South Africa* investigates the role of open and distance learning platforms in transforming access to education. This chapter offers a regional perspective on how digital learning is breaking down traditional barriers and providing more inclusive opportunities for students across East and South Africa.

With the rise of online learning, *Virtual Classrooms and Communication Behavior: A Bayesian Statistical Study Across Demographic Groups* explores how these digital platforms offer innovative learning spaces that transcend the physical classroom. This chapter discusses the implications for curriculum design, student engagement, and knowledge delivery in the online space.

Collaboration plays a critical role in educational advancement, and *Innovative Synergies: Collaborating with Industry, Research Organizations, and Global Institutions in Higher Education* showcases how partnerships between educational institutions and external organizations drive innovation. These collaborations not only enhance research but also open up new opportunities for students and institutions alike.

Leadership in this evolving landscape is equally important, and *Transformational Leadership in Higher Education* examines the role of visionary leaders in guiding institutions through these transitions. Transformational leadership is essential for fostering the agility and adaptability required in a constantly changing educational environment.

Finally, *Mental Health and Academic Performance among University Undergraduate Students: Depression and Anxiety* addresses an often-overlooked aspect of education – the mental well-being of students. As the pressure of academic performance and digital integration increases, so too does the need for institutions to support students' mental health. This chapter offers insights into the relationship between mental health and academic success, urging leaders to take proactive steps to ensure student wellness.

This book provides an informed overview of how AI, digital learning, and leadership are shaping the future of higher education. It offers a rich blend of theoretical perspectives and practical insights, making it a valuable resource for educators, administrators, and policymakers alike. As we move forward, it is clear that embracing technological innovations, while staying grounded in ethical considerations, will be key to creating a higher education system that is not only advanced but also inclusive and sustainable.

Chapter 1
Leveraging Artificial Intelligence Tools for Learning:
Academic Integrity and Ethics in Higher Education in Kenya

Edwin Okumu Ogalo
Institute of Educational Development, Aga Khan University, Tanzania

Fredrick Mtenzi
Institute of Educational Development, Aga Khan University, Tanzania

ABSTRACT

The emergence of Large Language Models like ChatGPT has come with the promise to transform education. However, its advent has ushered in a new era of unprecedented opportunities and ethical challenges. This paper explores the dynamic nexus between artificial intelligence, ethics, and academic integrity in higher education. The study involved a theoretical review that largely utilized secondary data utilizing up-to-date methodical and meta-analysis of literature assessments and personal reflections on the practical application featuring ChatGPT's use among master's students at Aga Khan University. The study revealed that artificial intelligence tools have the potential to improve pedagogy and promote learning. However, it presents significant ethical concerns associated with maintaining academic integrity, including the risk of plagiarism, the stifling of critical thinking, and data privacy. The study recommends a balanced, responsible approach, supported by clear guidelines, ethical frameworks, and ongoing research to explore benefits of artificial intelligence.

DOI: 10.4018/979-8-3373-0025-2.ch001

INTRODUCTION

In today's fast-paced digital era, the convergence of artificial intelligence and education has emerged as a critical area of exploration. The discourse around artificial intelligence just gained significant momentum, yet artificial intelligence has long been at the forefront of technological advancements and educational innovations. The use of artificial intelligence has its roots in the foundational work of Alan Turing in the 1950s. It has continuously evolved, with generative artificial intelligence standing out as a notable subset. This subset of artificial intelligence concentrates on generating novel content such as text, pictures, audio, and synthetic data by leveraging deep learning models to "learn" from raw data and generate novel outputs (Anantrasirichai & Bull, 2022).

The advent of the COVID-19 pandemic has hastened a shift to the use of technology in education. The urgent need to strengthen the education sector in the face of such pandemics has necessitated this shift, prompting a widespread move to online teaching and learning platforms to enhance resilience. This transition has, in turn, spurred a reassessment of how information technology is used in education, with artificial intelligence emerging as a prominent digital technology in the 21st century (Pandey & Pal, 2020). Advancements in artificial intelligence and information and communication technology have been used in the Global North to enrich education. However, African nations like Kenya are still struggling to fully harness the potential of artificial intelligence (Kolog et al., 2022).

In Kenya, artificial intelligence is increasingly being adopted in higher education. Some of the recent studies can underscore this to illustrate the trend. For instance, research by Jepkemoi et al. (2024) demonstrates how adopting generative artificial intelligence tools like ChatGPT can potentially improve teaching and learning practices in higher learning institutions. Similarly, another study by Wanjiku Wang'ang'a (2024) unveils the potential benefits of generative artificial intelligence among university students in Kenya but acknowledges some limitations. These studies reflect a growing interest in artificial intelligence utilization within Kenyan higher learning institutions. Additionally, the Kenyan government's curriculum reforms emphasize digital literacy (KICD 2017). These reforms aim to integrate Information and communication technology into the national education system and recognize cutting-edge technologies like artificial intelligence to equip learners with digital skills and enrich their learning experiences. However, challenges such as equity concerns and ethical dilemmas regarding data privacy and algorithmic bias must be resolved to ensure artificial intelligence's responsible and equitable integration into education (Kiemde & Kora, 2022; UNESCO, 2021).

In higher education, the use of artificial intelligence presents both opportunities and challenges concerning academic integrity (Yeo, 2023). As generative artificial intelligence models become more advanced, they may offer new avenues for academic dishonesty, such as plagiarism during assessments. This raises concerns among educators and administrators and calls for measures to effectively detect and prevent such practices while ensuring fair assessment of students' work. Despite the numerous risks and ethical concerns associated with artificial intelligence in education within developing countries, the potential benefits justify further exploration of optimal approaches for integrating artificial intelligence technologies into teaching and learning practices (Wall et al., 2021).

The main objective of this paper therefore is to explore the intersection between artificial intelligence ethics and academic integrity in higher education in Kenya. It examines the opportunities and challenges presented by using artificial intelligence and offers insights into the responsible and equitable use of artificial intelligence in higher education.

BACKGROUND

Artificial intelligence has become ubiquitous in modern society. It has seamlessly integrated into many facets of daily life, particularly in accessing information online (Williamson & Eynon, 2020). The definition of artificial intelligence has transformed considerably over time. A study by Chassignol et al. (2018) emphasizes that the literature offers a diverse range of definitions for artificial intelligence, accentuating its dynamic nature. One foundational and influential definition is rooted in the Turing Test, which posits that artificial intelligence involves machines' ability to interact with humans in a manner indistinguishable from human interaction, with success determined by a binary criterion (Turing, 1950).

Pioneering researcher Marvin Minsky further defined artificial intelligence as the capacity of machines to perform tasks that typically require human intelligence (Fogel, 2022; Minsky, 1961). As the field advanced, artificial intelligence was increasingly understood through the lens of the symbolic school of thought, which defines it as the manipulation of symbols, where the most basic symbols correspond to physical entities (Santoro et al., 2021). More contemporary definitions emphasize artificial intelligence's function in addressing cognitive challenges akin to human intelligence, including learning, problem-solving, and pattern recognition (Korteling et al., 2021).

According to Y. Jiang et al. (2022), artificial intelligence is defined as the theory and development of computer systems that can perform tasks normally requiring human intelligence, such as visual perception, speech recognition, decision-making, and language translation. Similarly, OpenAI (n.d.) describes Artificial intelligence as systems that perform tasks typically requiring human intelligence, such as language understanding and image recognition, with the ability to learn from data, improve over time, and generalize from experience using machine learning and neural networks.

EVOLUTION OF ARTIFICIAL INTELLIGENCE IN EDUCATION

Artificial intelligence has experienced significant evolution, transitioning from a nascent concept to a sophisticated technology that now holds a crucial role in various domains, including education (Roll & Wylie, 2016). The concept of artificial intelligence has its roots in the mid-20th century, a period marked by rapid advancements in mathematics, logic, and computer science (Zhao et al., 2023). The formal inception of artificial intelligence as a field of study is often traced back to the Dartmouth Conference in 1956, where pioneers like John McCarthy, Marvin Minsky, Nathaniel Rochester, and Claude Shannon came together to discuss the potential of creating machines that could simulate aspects of human intelligence (Adiguzel et al., 2023; McCarthy et al., 1956). This conference laid the groundwork for artificial intelligence research, focusing on symbolic reasoning and the development of algorithms that could solve problems akin to human thought processes.

Early artificial intelligence research was dominated by symbolic artificial intelligence, where machines were programmed with explicit rules to perform tasks like theorem-proving and puzzle-solving (McCarthy, 2022; Simon, 1995). Notable early artificial intelligence systems included the Logic Theorist and the General Problem Solver, which demonstrated the feasibility of using machines to perform logical reasoning (Newell & Simon, 1956). However, these early systems were limited by their inability to handle the vast variability and complexity of real-world situations, leading to the first artificial intelligence winter in the 1970s, a period of reduced funding and interest due to the failure of artificial intelligence to meet the high expectations set by early enthusiasts (Crevier, 1993; Ouyang & Jiao, 2021).

Despite these setbacks, studies on artificial intelligence continued to advance, particularly with the development of machine learning and neural networks in the 1980s and 1990s (Toosi et al., 2021). These approaches marked a shift away from rule-based systems towards data-driven models that could learn from experience (Shaik et al., 2022). The resurgence of artificial intelligence during this period was fueled by advancements in computational power, the availability of large datasets, and the development of more sophisticated algorithms, laying the foundation for the next major leap in artificial intelligence, that is the development of Large Language Models (LLMs) (Zhao et al., 2023).

Large Language Models (LLMs)

Large Language Models (LLMs) represent a significant advancement in the field of artificial intelligence, particularly in the domain of natural language processing (NLP) (Nazi & Peng, 2024). Large Language Models are neural network-based systems trained on extensive text datasets (Jing & Xu, 2019; Kucharavy, 2024). This training enables them to generate human-like text, comprehend context, and execute a range of language-related tasks effectively. The development of LLMs was greatly facilitated by the introduction of the Transformer architecture by Vaswani (2017), which revolutionized NLP by allowing models to process entire sequences of text in parallel, thereby improving both efficiency and accuracy.

The Generative Pre-Trained Transformer (GPT) series, particularly GPT-3, is one of the most prominent examples of LLMs. GPT-3, developed by OpenAI, contains 175 billion parameters and can generate text that is often indistinguishable from that written by humans (Brown, 2020). The ability of GPT-3 to perform tasks such as translation, summarization, and content creation with minimal input has made it a powerful tool across various domains, including education.

The evolution of LLMs has continued with the development of even more advanced models, such as GPT-4 and Google's Gemini, which are designed to be more interactive and context-aware, offering personalized and nuanced responses (Google AI, December, 2023; OpenAI, 2023, March). These models have found applications not only in content generation but also in complex problem-solving tasks, such as software engineering, where LLMs are used for code generation, debugging, and optimization (Hou et al., 2023). This ability of LLMs to understand and generate code, as well as their capacity to learn from diverse datasets, underscores their potential to transform industries, including education.

Chatbots and Artificial Intelligence in Education

The integration of artificial intelligence into education has been significantly accelerated by the development of chatbots and artificial intelligence-powered educational tools (Ratnam et al., 2023). Chatbots such as ChatGPT, which utilize large language models (LLMs), have gained prominence as virtual assistants capable of answering questions, providing explanations, and offering personalized tutoring (OpenAI, 2023, March). These tools mark a considerable advancement in the delivery of instructional content, promising more interactive and adaptive learning experiences.

Natural Language Processing (NLP) technologies are integral to various educational applications, particularly in assessment and content creation. Artificial intelligence systems leveraging NLP have been employed for automated grading, thereby reducing educators' workloads (Gupta et al., 2021). Additionally, platforms like Duolingo utilize NLP to craft interactive language lessons, harnessing artificial intelligence's capability to understand and process human language (Zerkowska, 2024). However, these advancements also bring forth concerns about the accuracy of automated grading, the ethics of artificial intelligence-generated content, and potential language barriers in artificial intelligence-human interactions (Pappachan & Rahaman, 2024).

In recent years, the impact of large language models (LLMs) on education has expanded significantly. Tools such as OpenAI's GPT-4, Google's Gemini, Bing AI, Gamma, and Phind offer advanced language understanding and content generation capabilities. These models are utilized in various educational settings, from personalized tutoring to the creation of detailed academic content, enhancing learners' engagement with complex subjects (Bahroun et al., 2023). For instance, Gemini and Bing AI provide contextualized responses and refined outputs, improving research and study experiences (Leite, 2024). Phind on the other hand is designed to accelerate learning in technical fields like programming (Phind, n.d.). Gamma AI aids in generating presentations and visual content, enhancing the learning experience in various subjects (Gamma, 2023). Despite their benefits, these tools raise concerns about academic integrity, plagiarism, and the ethical use of AI-generated work.

Other Artificial Intelligence Tools Used in Education

Artificial intelligence in education extends far beyond the use of chatbots. As Tapalova and Zhiyenbayeva (2022) argue, artificial intelligence-powered systems are increasingly being utilized to create personalized learning pathways, adapt content to individual students' needs, and provide real-time feedback. For instance, artificial intelligence-driven adaptive learning platforms can analyze student performance and adjust the difficulty of tasks to ensure learners progress at a suitable pace (Dutta et al., 2024). This personalized approach to education has the potential to address diverse learning needs, promoting inclusivity and improving educational effectiveness.

In higher education, as Hadi et al. (2024) opine, artificial intelligence is also revolutionizing administrative tasks, such as grading and admissions, allowing educators to dedicate more time to teaching and research. In Kenya, where higher education is rapidly expanding, artificial intelligence could play a key role in addressing challenges related to resource allocation and promoting educational equity.

Artificial intelligence tools in education offer solutions to various pedagogical challenges. One significant innovation is Virtual Teaching Assistants (VTAs), which are artificial intelligence-driven systems that enhance instructor support and foster a sense of community among online learners (Talwar, 2023). A prime example is IBM Research's Jill Watson SA, which facilitates personalized interactions and strengthens connections in distance education (Goel, 2020). Research by AlGerafi et al. (2023) demonstrates that VTAs significantly improve student engagement and learning outcomes in higher education, showcasing their value as complements to traditional teaching methods.

Another key artificial intelligence application in education is adaptive learning systems, which use advanced algorithms to monitor student performance and adjust instructional content based on individual learning needs (Colchester et al., 2017; Gligorea et al., 2023). Platforms like DreamBox Learning Math and Carnegie Learning's Cognitive Tutor Algebra I illustrate this approach by providing tailored math instruction and AI-driven algebra tutoring (Chee & Sanmugam, 2023). Although these systems enhance teaching efficiency and student outcomes, challenges related to equity and potential overreliance on technology, especially regarding access to resources, persist.

Intelligent tutoring systems offer another major artificial intelligence-driven innovation, providing personalized, real-time feedback to support student learning (Yufeia et al., 2020). These systems offer guidance on grammar, structure, and content, transforming the assessment process. Tools like Grammarly and QuillBot also assist students by improving writing quality, grammar, and style, further personalizing the learning experience. Additionally, Turnitin is a widely used artificial intelligence-based plagiarism detection tool. It ensures academic integrity by checking the originality of student submissions (Jebadurai et al., 2023). These tools help maintain high academic standards, though concerns remain regarding the reliance on artificial intelligence, particularly in monitoring and detecting potential biases.

Artificial intelligence-powered proctoring tools enhance exam security by monitoring remote test environments and detecting potential cheating attempts through advanced behavior analysis (Oravec, 2022). Tools such as ProctorU, ExamSoft with ExamMonitor, Honorlock, Respondus Monitor, and Proctorio use artificial intelligence to track students' movements, facial expressions, and screen activities, flagging suspicious behaviors like looking off-screen, talking, or using unauthorized devices (Booc et al., 2023). These systems help uphold academic integrity in online exams by automatically identifying potential violations, though they also raise concerns about privacy and the possibility of artificial intelligence misinterpreting normal behaviors as suspicious. These technologies increase efficiency and immediacy in education. However, they also raise concerns about artificial intelligence biases, privacy risks associated with surveillance, and the digital divide, as equitable access to reliable internet connectivity remains a significant issue.

Transformative Applications of Artificial Intelligence in Education

The incorporation of artificial intelligence in education covers a broad spectrum of uses, from personalized learning environments to automated assessment tools. Recent studies have concentrated on the integration of artificial intelligence in education, emphasizing its significance in improving learning experiences (Jaiswal & Arun, 2021). The integration of artificial intelligence has revolutionized traditional teaching and learning methods, offering innovative solutions that cater to individual student needs, streamline administrative tasks for educators, and create more inclusive learning environments (Iweuno et al., 2024; Rane et al., 2023). This tailored approach helps address diverse learning styles and paces, promoting better engagement and understanding among students.

The integration of artificial intelligence in education has evolved significantly over the past decades. Initially, artificial intelligence applications in education were limited to simple computer-assisted instruction and basic tutorial systems. As technology advanced, so did the complexity and capabilities of artificial intelligence systems (Chen et al., 2020). As Guo et al. (2021) opine, the development of intelligent tutoring systems marked a significant milestone, providing more sophisticated and adaptive learning experiences. In recent years, the role of artificial intelligence in education has grown, encompassing natural language processing, data analytics, and machine learning, creating more dynamic and interactive learning environments (Bahroun et al., 2023). The continuous growth and innovation in artificial intelligence technologies promise further enhancements in academic practices and outcomes (Chen et al., 2020). Artificial intelligence systems can be categorized into several systems, as discussed below:

Personalized Learning Environments

Personalized learning environments, powered by artificial intelligence adapt to individual student needs, boosting engagement and enhancing learning outcomes. These systems use algorithms and data analytics to analyze student data to provide tailored content and feedback, ensuring that each learner's pace and style are accommodated (Zawacki-Richter et al., 2019). These tools use data analytics to adapt lessons in real-time, providing additional support where students struggle and advancing when they show proficiency. Tools such as intelligent tutoring systems and adaptive learning platforms exemplify this trend, offering tailored feedback and learning pathways that accommodate diverse learning styles and paces (Forum, 2023; UNESCO, 2021).

These artificial intelligence-driven environments support differentiated instruction, enabling teachers to effectively cater to diverse student populations. Onesi-Ozigagun et al. (2024) found that adaptive learning platforms employ artificial intelligence algorithms to assess students' strengths and weaknesses and adjust the curriculum, accordingly, offering customized learning experiences that address each student's learning style. Additionally, Graepel (2022) posits the efficacy of artificial intelligence-driven personalized learning platforms in improving student engagement and performance. The study highlighted that artificial intelligence systems could identify learning gaps and suggest appropriate interventions, thereby fostering a more supportive learning environment.

Automated Assessment Tools

Artificial intelligence has been essential in creating automated assessment tools that greatly simplify the evaluation process. Utilizing natural language processing (NLP) and machine learning (ML) techniques, these tools can grade essays, offer feedback, and identify instances of plagiarism (Shaik et al., 2022). By automating these tasks, educators can reduce their workload while offering students timely feedback, which is essential for their academic growth.

A recent study by Latif and Zhai (2024) demonstrated that fine-tuning domain-specific artificial intelligence models like ChatGPT using data tailored to specific tasks can enhance the automatic scoring and grading of students. This improvement is attributed to ChatGPT's extensive training in vast online language resources, such as Wikipedia and academic journals. The study highlighted that ChatGPT's capacity to process large volumes of data ensures consistent and objective grading, addressing a common challenge faced by human graders.

Thus, incorporating artificial intelligence into automated assessment tools marks a major leap forward in education, promising to improve the quality and efficiency of evaluations while supporting educators and benefiting students.

Intelligent Tutoring Systems

Intelligent Tutoring Systems (ITS) represent a pivotal application of artificial intelligence in education. These computer-based systems are meticulously designed to emulate the personalized interaction typical of a tutor-student relationship, providing customized instruction and feedback, customized to meet each learner's individual needs (Mousavinasab et al., 2021). Intelligent Tutoring systems can harness the capabilities of artificial intelligence to adapt dynamically to the learner's progress, offering a highly individualized learning experience. Additionally, they operate by simulating one-on-one tutoring, delivering personalized guidance and feedback based on the learner's interactions. Intelligent Tutoring Systems can diagnose student errors, suggest hints, and adjust the complexity of tasks instantly, thereby creating an adaptive learning environment (Lin et al., 2023).

Some studies underscore the efficacy of Intelligent Tutoring Systems in improving educational outcomes. For instance, comprehensive meta-analysis studies conducted by Alam (2023) and Lee et al. (2024) substantiate the positive impact of Intelligent Tutoring Systems on student performance. The findings reveal that students who engage with Intelligent Tutoring Systems demonstrate superior learning outcomes compared to their peers who receive traditional instruction. The evidence from these studies highlights artificial intelligence's transformative potential in enhancing educational practices' effectiveness through integrating Intelligent Tutoring Systems in learning environments.

Benefits of Artificial Intelligence in Education

The convergence of Artificial Intelligence and education marks a pivotal moment in the evolution of pedagogical practices. Studies by Bahroun et al. (2023), Haider (2023), and Mustafa (2023) underscore the transformative potential of Artificial Intelligence in reshaping conventional educational paradigms. Integrating Artificial Intelligence in education offers immense benefits, including personalized and adaptive learning experiences, immersive technologies for interactive instruction, streamlined administrative tasks to empower educators, and democratized access to quality education on a global scale. This symbiotic relationship between technology and pedagogy enhances human capabilities rather than replacing them, ultimately resulting in a more efficient and inclusive learning environment (Markauskaite et al., 2022).

Artificial intelligence -Driven Data Analytics

Artificial intelligence-driven data analytics is a critical benefit of artificial intelligence in education. This is because it can process and analyze vast amounts of data efficiently. These software solutions utilize artificial intelligence to automate and improve data analysis tasks. They employ advanced technologies like machine learning, natural language processing (NLP), and predictive analytics to process and interpret data, extract insights, and generate predictions or recommendations (Rane et al., 2024). The advanced analytics tools offer crucial insights into student performance and learning patterns, helping educators refine and enhance their teaching strategies. Artificial intelligence systems can identify trends and patterns that might not be immediately apparent to educators by collecting and analyzing large volumes of data (Pedro et al., 2019). This information can help make data-driven decisions, such as pinpointing students who might require extra support or modifying teaching strategies to better address classroom needs (Amer-Yahia, 2022).

Insights into Student Performance

Artificial intelligence-driven data analytics enable educators to gain a comprehensive understanding of student performance by tracking a wide range of metrics that include test scores, attendance, participation, and engagement levels during lessons. When this data is analyzed, educators can identify students who are struggling and may need additional assistance, as well as those who are excelling and might benefit from more advanced material (Jamal, 2024). This focused strategy guarantees that every student receives the necessary support to thrive.

Furthermore, artificial intelligence systems can deliver immediate feedback, enabling educators to promptly respond to learning gaps and adjust their teaching strategies accordingly. For instance, artificial intelligence-driven analytics can predict students' future performance based on their current and past data, enabling early interventions that can prevent potential issues before they become significant problems (Ahmad et al., 2023).

In addition, artificial intelligence-driven data analytics can aid teachers in their professional growth. Since these tools can provide insights into which teaching methods are most effective, they can help educators refine their instructional practices and improve overall learning outcomes. As noted by Celik et al. (2022) and Pedro et al. (2019), artificial intelligence's ability to provide detailed feedback on teaching performance is invaluable for continuous improvement in learning.

Administrative Efficiency

Artificial intelligence has significantly enhanced administrative processes in learning institutions. Once time-consuming tasks, such as scheduling, grading, and managing student records, can now be automated (Haderer & Ciolacu, 2022). This automation enables educators to reclaim valuable time, allowing them to focus more on teaching and interacting with students. For instance, artificial intelligence-powered systems can automatically assess assignments and exams, delivering instant feedback to students and lightening the workload for teachers (Srinivasa et al., 2022). Additionally, artificial intelligence can help in scheduling classes, and meetings, and even predicting student enrollment trends, thereby optimizing resource allocation (Aytaç, 2024).

Immersive Learning Experiences

Artificial intelligence can significantly enhance learning experiences by utilizing technologies such as virtual reality (VR), augmented reality (AR), and generative artificial intelligence tools to make them more engaging and immersive. These technologies recreate real-world scenarios, offering students practical experience in a safe and controlled setting. VR tools can create fully immersive environments where students engage with 3D models and simulations, such as medical students practicing surgeries or engineering students assembling virtual machinery (H. Jiang et al., 2022). AR overlays digital information onto the real world, enabling students to view and interact with virtual objects within their actual environment, which is particularly useful in subjects like biology where AR can help visualize anatomical structures in 3D (Chystaya et al., 2022). These can improve comprehension of the concepts in the respective subject areas.

Generative artificial intelligence tools, such as ChatGPT and DALL-E, are also enhancing immersive learning experiences by generating realistic text, images, and simulations, providing interactive and dynamic content. ChatGPT, for example, can act as a virtual tutor, offering personalized explanations and answering questions in real-time, which helps students explore topics in greater depth and clarify doubts immediately (Javaid et al., 2023). Additionally, generative artificial intelligence tools can produce personalized learning materials designed to meet individual needs, including interactive problem sets or simulations that target specific areas where a student requires improvement.

The use of immersive technologies and generative artificial intelligence tools has been shown to significantly enhance student engagement and retention. Immersive experiences engage multiple senses, offering a more comprehensive grasp of the subject and making learning both more enjoyable and memorable. The interactive nature of these technologies keeps students motivated and interested, leading to better retention of information (Almusaed et al., 2023).

Support for Special Education

Artificial intelligence offers significant advantages for special education by delivering customized support to students with disabilities (Hopcan et al., 2023). Artificial intelligence-powered tools can aid students with visual or hearing impairments, learning disabilities, and other special needs. Speech-to-text and text-to-speech applications are particularly beneficial for students with dyslexia or other reading challenges during their learning journey. Similarly, artificial intelligence-driven applications can translate spoken language into sign language for students with hearing impairments, thereby improving accessibility and inclusion (Almufareh et al., 2023).

Fostering Global Collaboration

Artificial intelligence facilitates global collaboration by breaking geographical barriers and connecting students and educators worldwide. Translation tools powered by artificial intelligence can enable students to communicate and collaborate on projects with peers who speak different languages (Kessler, 2018). Additionally, artificial intelligence can facilitate the creation of global virtual classrooms, enabling students from diverse backgrounds to learn collectively, share experiences, and gain a broader perspective (Markauskaite et al., 2022).

Theoretical Framework

Several theoretical frameworks can be used to anchor this study and connect the key variables arising from the integration of artificial intelligence into higher education in the Kenyan context. These variables include technological adoption, pedagogical strategies, content delivery, and academic integrity, all critical to understanding the ethical implications of using artificial intelligence tools like ChatGPT in academic settings. Other frameworks that could be considered include the Davis (1989) Technology Acceptance Model (TAM), which explores user acceptance of new technologies, and Constructivist Learning Theory, which emphasizes learners actively constructing knowledge through interaction with tools and resources.

However, the Technological Pedagogical and Content Knowledge (TPACK) framework by Mishra and Koehler (2006) is particularly relevant to this study as it offers a comprehensive approach to understanding the intersection of technology, pedagogy, and content knowledge in learning. TPACK provides a clear framework for exploring how educators can effectively integrate artificial intelligence tools into their teaching while upholding ethical standards and ensuring academic integrity. This aligns with a study by Thomas (2024), which underscores the importance of balancing technological innovation with sound pedagogical practices and subject-matter expertise, making TPACK an ideal framework for addressing the complexities of artificial intelligence use in education.

METHODOLOGY

PRISMA-Based Literature Review

This study utilizes a systematic literature review approach following the PRISMA (Preferred Reporting Items for Systematic Reviews and Meta-Analyses) guidelines. The approach enables the examination of recent research trends and explores the intersection of artificial intelligence, ethics, and academic integrity in higher education. The SCOPUS and EBSCOHost databases were used as the primary data source, with searches conducted using the keywords "artificial intelligence," "ethics," and "academic integrity" over the period from May to July 2024. The PRISMA methodology applied in this study comprised four essential stages: identification, screening, eligibility, and inclusion.

Identification Stage

In this phase, all pertinent research articles from the SCOPUS and EBSCOHost databases were collected. The search utilized specific keywords to maintain relevance to the study's objectives. Additionally, the search was restricted to articles published within the past two years to incorporate the latest research trends and advancements in the field. This preliminary search resulted in a substantial collection of articles.

Screening Stage

After identification, the screening stage involved filtering the initially identified articles based on predefined inclusion and exclusion criteria. The focus was on journal articles and conference proceedings written in English to maintain the quality and accessibility of the selected literature. Additionally, the scope was refined to include only articles that directly pertain to higher education, ethics, and artificial intelligence. This stage was crucial in narrowing down the vast pool of articles to those most relevant to the study. Articles that did not meet these criteria, such as those unrelated to higher education or not addressing ethical concerns, were excluded from further consideration.

Eligibility Stage

The selected articles underwent additional scrutiny to confirm their relevance to the ethical implementation of artificial intelligence in upholding academic integrity within higher education institutions. This process was done manually, with each article being meticulously reviewed for alignment with the study's theme. The abstracts, methodologies, and findings were thoroughly examined to assess their pertinence. Articles that did not explicitly address the ethical implications of artificial intelligence in higher education or failed to offer substantial insights into maintaining academic integrity were excluded at this stage.

Inclusion Stage

The inclusion phase involved a detailed examination of the articles deemed eligible from the previous stage. These articles were analyzed to extract pertinent information related to the authors, study objectives, methodologies, and findings. This comprehensive data extraction process captured all relevant details for subsequent analysis. The selected articles were then discussed in-depth, with particular emphasis on aligning their findings with the overarching objectives of the study. This analysis elucidated the nexus between the various study outcomes and the specific goals of the research, providing a cohesive understanding of how each article contributed to the broader context of the study.

Analysis and Discussion

The extracted data were systematically reviewed, concentrating on how each study's findings correspond with the main objectives of this meta-analysis. This method ensured that the discussion stayed focused and relevant, emphasizing key insights and drawing meaningful conclusions that supported the primary goals of the research. This rigorous and methodical approach was employed to achieve a nuanced understanding of the relationship between artificial intelligence, ethics, and academic integrity in higher education, utilizing the most current and pertinent literature in the field.

Exploring Personal Experience Using Generative Artificial Intelligence Tools

Personal experiences using artificial intelligence tools, particularly ChatGPT were also explored to corroborate the findings from the meta-analysis of literature. This exploration focused on how Master's students at Aga Khan University - Institute of Educational Development, East Africa, utilized ChatGPT in their academic activities, including assignments, research work, and the development of research proposals and dissertations.

DATA COLLECTION

Academic Assignments

To understand the impact of ChatGPT on completing academic assignments, detailed logs and reflections were maintained throughout the coursework. Each instance of ChatGPT usage was documented, noting the type of assignment, the nature of assistance provided by ChatGPT (for instance, idea generation, essay structuring, literature suggestions), and the perceived effectiveness of the tool. The reflections also included critical evaluations of the artificial intelligence-generated content for accuracy, relevance, and academic integrity.

Research Work

The utilization of ChatGPT in research work was examined by documenting its role in literature review processes, research design, and data analysis. Specific attention was given to how ChatGPT assisted in summarizing articles, identifying key themes, and suggesting research gaps. Personal experiences and reflections on using ChatGPT for formulating research questions and hypotheses were also recorded. Additionally, an empirical study was conducted where ChatGPT was used to facilitate physics learning in a secondary school in Kenya. The impact of ChatGPT on learner engagement, motivation, and academic performance in physics was observed and documented.

Academic Writing: Proposals and Dissertations

The use of ChatGPT in writing research proposals and dissertations was explored through detailed logs of its contributions to document structuring, argument refinement, and ensuring logical coherence. The reflections included assessments of ChatGPT's proficiency in academic language and style and its impact on the overall quality of the writing. Critical evaluations were conducted to ensure that artificial intelligence-generated content was used as a guide rather than a substitute for original thought.

Data Analysis

The collected data were subjected to thematic analysis to identify patterns and trends in the usage of ChatGPT. The analysis focused on the perceived benefits and challenges of using ChatGPT in different academic contexts. Key themes included efficiency, quality of work, enhancement of understanding, and ethical considerations.

Ethical Considerations

Throughout the study, ethical considerations were prioritized. The study adhered to responsible artificial intelligence usage guidelines, emphasizing the importance of academic honesty and the critical evaluation of artificial intelligence-generated content.

Findings Synthesis

The findings from the personal experience exploration were integrated with data from the literature review to offer a thorough overview of the use of artificial intelligence tools in academic settings. The synthesis involved comparing theoretical insights with practical experiences, highlighting how artificial intelligence tools can be effectively utilized in higher education. Key recommendations for leveraging ChatGPT's strengths and mitigating its limitations were formulated to guide both educators and students.

RESULTS AND DISCUSSION

Overview of Publication Trends

From May to July 2024, the analysis identified a total of 18 relevant documents, with 13 published in 2024 and 5 in 2023. This analysis highlighted publication trends and the sources contributing to the research during this period. The increasing number of publications from 2023 to 2024 reflects a growing interest and research activity in the field of artificial intelligence in education and its implications. This trend indicates an escalating focus on understanding and integrating artificial intelligence technologies within educational settings, addressing ethical concerns, and exploring the potential benefits and challenges associated with artificial intelligence tools like ChatGPT.

Types of Publications

The study involved analyzing book chapters, articles, conference papers, and reviews. This demonstrates strong involvement in both primary research and academic discussions. The diversity in publication types, including book chapters and conference reviews, reflects a wide array of contributions to the field.

Table 1. Document Specifications in Inclusion Criteria

No.	Author(s)	Study Objectives	Study Results
1.	Dhruv et al. (2024)	To evaluate AI-generated solutions at high school, college, and graduate levels based on fulfillment, presentation, and helpfulness.	There is a risk of bias against those with real efforts.
2.	Butson R. & Spronken-Smith R. (2024)	To explore AI and its implications for research in higher education: a critical dialogue.	The study identifies complex tensions between the efficiency provided by AI and the ethical concerns it raises in academic research through a structured dialogue.
3.	Gaumann N. & Veale M. (2024)	To evaluate how current legislation on academic integrity specifically those targeting contract cheating and essay mills applies to AI-powered services.	The study finds that current academic cheating laws may unintentionally apply to general-purpose AI services like ChatGPT, creating challenges in distinguishing between legitimate educational support and cheating.
4	Michels S. (2023)	To explore how AI and generative technologies can enhance content delivery, promote active learning, and improve academic and professional outcomes for students.	AI technologies can enhance the clarity and engagement of educational content and facilitate more active learning, allowing instructors to focus on higher-level educational outcomes.
5.	Sanchez et al (2024)	To identify and discuss the ethical implications and challenges of adopting AI technologies in urban planning.	While AI holds potential benefits for urban planning, its adoption raises significant ethical concerns around bias, privacy, lack of equity and transparency, and risks of misinformation.
6.	Pokkakillath S. & Suleri J. (2023)	To explore the potential of ChatGPT in enhancing education through instant feedback, personalized learning experiences, and 24/7 availability.	ChatGPT holds significant promise for revolutionizing education but further research is needed to fully understand its impact and determine effective integration methods.
7.	Luo (2024)	To explore how university students navigate trust-building with their teachers in an AI-mediated assessment landscape.	Students experience a relatively low level of trust towards their teachers due to issues like a lack of two-way transparency and communication of GenAI policies from a punitive perspective.
8.	Crawford et al (2024)	To evaluate the impact of AI chatbot usage on university students' academic performance, social interactions, psychological well-being, and sense of belonging.	While AI chatbots can positively impact student performance, their use is associated with negative effects on social support, psychological well-being, and sense of belonging.
9.	Papyshev G. (2024)	To investigate the contrasting sentiments of research postgraduate students in public policy towards the use of generative AI technologies in their research, teaching, and learning practices.	The study identified both positive and negative sentiments towards generative AI, highlighting the need for adaptable academic policies, discipline-specific AI training, and tailored AI systems.
10.	Montoya-Cantoral, et al (2023)	To analyze the institutional policies established in the intellectual property regulations of universities concerning the use of artificial intelligence in academic work.	The key finding of this study is that, to date, higher education institutions have not established any intellectual property regulations or a code of ethics to govern the use of artificial intelligence in academic production.

continued on following page

Table 1. Continued

No.	Author(s)	Study Objectives	Study Results
11	Şenocak et al. (2024)	The main objective of this study is to investigate the complex interplay between generative artificial intelligence (AI) and human intellect in academic writing and publishing. It aims to examine the implications of using generative AI tools in educational and academic integrity contexts, critique the 'publish or perish' culture in academia, and address the legal and ethical challenges associated with authorship, ownership, and copyright laws related to AI-generated content.	The integration of generative AI in academic writing necessitates a systemic reevaluation of academic practices and the development of new mechanisms to identify and regulate AI use to ensure adherence to academic integrity and ethics. The study underscores the importance of transparent reporting and suggests innovative AI-inclusive strategies to adapt to the transformative impact of generative AI in various information-processing domains.
12	Kumar, et al (2024)	to explore the intersection of academic integrity and artificial intelligence (AI), particularly focusing on the implications of large language models (LLMs) like OpenAI's GPT-3 on academic integrity. The study aims to outline the stages of development in algorithmic writing technologies and provide recommendations for educators on how to uphold academic integrity in the face of these advancements.	the evolution of AI and algorithmic writing technologies will significantly impact the understanding and conceptualization of academic integrity. Educators will need to progress through three stages: awareness, detection and support, and eventually, the adoption or integration of these technologies into pedagogical strategies. The study offers recommendations for pedagogy and policy to help educators navigate these changes.
13.	Dahal, B. (2024)	To provide an evidence-based overview of academic integrity in Nepal, exploring its historical context, current practices, and instances of academic misconduct from the 1950s to the 2020s.	The study emphasizes the growing importance of integrating ethical considerations in the use of AI within higher education. This intersection is critical to ensure that AI-driven tools and analytics uphold the values of academic integrity, preventing new forms of academic misconduct and fostering a culture of ethical behavior among students and educators.
14	Qadhi, et (2024)	To quantify and characterize the current research trends and critically assess the discourse on ethical AI applications within higher education.	The study identified three thematic clusters—ethical frameworks and policy development, academic integrity and content creation, and student interaction with AI. While AI offers significant benefits for educational advancement, it also presents challenges that require vigilant governance to maintain academic integrity and ethical standards.

continued on following page

Table 1. Continued

No.	Author(s)	Study Objectives	Study Results
15	Yusuf, et al (2024)	To examine the usage, benefits, and concerns of generative Artificial Intelligence (GenAI) in higher education from a multicultural perspective, addressing the gap in existing research regarding its impact and concerns across different cultures.	The study revealed a high level of awareness and familiarity with GenAI tools among participants from 76 countries, with many having prior experience and intending to continue using these tools primarily for information retrieval and text paraphrasing. There is a strong correlation between cultural dimensions and respondents' views on the benefits and concerns related to GenAI, emphasizing the need for ethical guidelines and robust policies that address cultural expectations to ensure the responsible use of GenAI in enhancing learning processes.
16	Crawford, et (2023)	To explore how educators can leverage AI tools like ChatGPT to create supportive learning environments that foster good character among students. The study aims to propose strategies for integrating AI in a way that enhances academic integrity, character development, and authentic assessment, rather than viewing AI solely as a threat to educational standards.	While AI tools like ChatGPT can be misused for academic dishonesty, they also have significant potential to enhance learning outcomes when used ethically. The study underscores the importance of leadership in guiding the ethical use of AI, promoting character development, and implementing authentic assessments to support deeper and more effective student learning.
17	Perkins, (2023)	To explore the academic integrity considerations associated with students' use of Artificial Intelligence (AI) tools, specifically Large Language Models (LLMs) such as ChatGPT, in formal assessments. The study examines the evolution of these tools and highlights the potential educational benefits they offer, including teaching writing and composition, facilitating co-creation between humans and AI, supporting English as a Foreign Language (EFL) learners, and improving Automated Writing Evaluations (AWE)	The primary concern regarding the use of LLMs by students lies in the potential for these tools to generate original, coherent text that can evade detection by current technological methods and trained academic staff. This poses significant academic integrity challenges for Higher Education Institutions (HEIs). The study concludes that it is not the mere use of AI tools by students that constitutes plagiarism or a breach of academic integrity, but rather the transparency and clarity of their use as defined by the academic integrity policies of the respective HEIs. These policies need to be updated to address the future use of these tools in educational settings.
18	Acosta-Enriquez et al (2024)	To assess the knowledge, concerns, attitudes, and ethics regarding the use of ChatGPT among Generation Z university students in higher education in Peru	The study found that higher education students' knowledge and positive attitudes toward ChatGPT do not necessarily lead to its effective adoption and use. The significant predictors of ChatGPT use were perceived ethics (B = 0.856) and student concerns (B = 0.802). These findings indicate the importance of addressing ethical concerns through comprehensive training programs, guidelines, and policies to promote the responsible use of AI tools like ChatGPT in educational settings

SYNTHESIS OF META-ANALYSIS AND PERSONAL REFLECTIONS FINDINGS

Emerging Themes and Discussion

Ethical Concerns and Academic Integrity

From the literature identified for this study, it can be observed that the use of artificial intelligence in higher education still raises significant ethical concerns and challenges to academic integrity. The findings from the meta-analysis reveal that studies such as Gaumann & Veale (2024) and Butson & Spronken-Smith (2024) identify critical issues, such as the unintended application of academic cheating laws to general-purpose artificial intelligence services and the complex tensions between artificial intelligence's efficiency and ethical implications. Furthermore, Acosta-Enriquez et al. (2024) highlight that knowledge and positive attitudes toward ChatGPT do not guarantee its effective and ethical use. Personal reflections confirm the necessity of establishing clear guidelines and policies to mitigate misuse and ensure responsible artificial intelligence deployment. The need for ethical frameworks that address the emerging challenges associated with artificial intelligence tools is evident, reinforcing the call for comprehensive training programs and policies.

Generative artificial intelligence tools, such as ChatGPT, have become integral to higher education, and their presence is expected to endure. As a result, these technologies continue to shape educational practices in these institutions. Higher learning institutions therefore need to develop and implement policies that ensure their ethical use amidst concerns about academic integrity breaches. Established clear guidelines will foster transparency, and institutions can leverage the benefits of artificial intelligence while addressing potential risks related to academic dishonesty and privacy. Proactive policy development and targeted training for educators and students will help integrate artificial intelligence effectively into learning environments. Consequently, this will help uphold the core principles of academic integrity while embracing the advancements that artificial intelligence offers.

Enhancing Pedagogy and Learning Experiences

Artificial intelligence tools are proving valuable in enhancing pedagogy and learning experiences. Studies like Pokkakillath & Suleri (2023) support the notion that artificial intelligence can improve content delivery, foster active learning, and address pedagogical challenges. Acosta-Enriquez et al. (2024) also suggest that while artificial intelligence can facilitate personalized learning, it is crucial to balance its use with traditional methods. Personal reflections on using artificial intelligence tools like ChatGPT for solving complex problems further affirm artificial intelligence's potential to provide clear, step-by-step explanations and support educational processes. Learners can use generative artificial intelligence tools like ChatGPT as study companions, helping with personalized and immersive learning experiences. However, the effectiveness of artificial intelligence tools is contingent on their integration into well-designed pedagogical frameworks.

Challenges and Limitations

Despite the benefits, there are notable challenges and limitations associated with artificial intelligence in education. The meta-analysis identifies concerns such as bias, privacy issues, and negative perceptions (Sanchez et al., 2024; Crawford et al., 2024). For instance, Crawford et al. (2024) report that while artificial intelligence chatbots can enhance academic performance, they might negatively affect social support, psychological well-being, and a sense of belonging. Personal reflections highlight artificial intelligence's limitations in addressing complex problems and stress the importance of cross-verifying artificial intelligence-generated information with traditional resources. The challenge of maintaining academic integrity amidst the growing use of artificial intelligence tools necessitates updated policies and practices. Additionally, the negative impact of artificial intelligence chatbots on social support and psychological well-being (Crawford et al., 2024) points to the need for a balanced approach to integrating artificial intelligence into education.

Multidisciplinary and Collaborative Approaches

The study emphasizes the value of multidisciplinary and collaborative approaches in exploring artificial intelligence's educational role. The diversity of interdisciplinary contributions to the meta-analysis reflects a broad interest in artificial intelligence's applications. Studies like those by Yusuf et al. (2024) and Bozkurt (2024) highlight the necessity for ongoing research and dialogue across various academic disciplines. Personal reflections also highlight the critical role of collaboration in the successful integration of artificial intelligence tools into teaching and learning practices. They suggest that cross-disciplinary efforts are vital for advancing artificial intelligence in education. Such collaboration will equip both educators and learners with the necessary skills to navigate an environment increasingly saturated with artificial intelligence technologies, ensuring that they are well-prepared to thrive in a world where these tools are an everyday reality.

Practical Applications and Recommendations

Both the meta-analysis and personal reflections provide practical recommendations for integrating artificial intelligence into education effectively. Key recommendations include using artificial intelligence for instant feedback and personalized learning experiences. Pokkakillath & Suleri, (2023) view artificial intelligence as a supplementary tool rather than a replacement for traditional teaching methods and enhancing artificial intelligence literacy among educators and students. Additionally, the insights from personal reflections on using ChatGPT in higher learning institutions underscore the need to leverage artificial intelligence to support, rather than replace, conventional teaching strategies. This balanced approach is critical for maximizing artificial intelligence's benefits while addressing its limitations.

Directions for Future Research

The study recommends that the impact of artificial intelligence on critical thinking skills in higher learning institutions be investigated particularly through controlled studies comparing student essays written with and without artificial intelligence assistance. These studies can evaluate the depth of analysis, use of evidence, and originality of arguments to determine whether artificial intelligence hinders or enhances critical thinking skills. The research should also explore how artificial intelligence tools can be leveraged to enhance research skills.

Furthermore, understanding student and educator perceptions of artificial intelligence in education is vital. Research can be conducted with students and tutors to reveal their attitudes toward using artificial intelligence for academic work, including perceptions of fairness, learning benefits, potential risks associated with artificial intelligence use, and best practices for incorporating artificial intelligence ethically.

CONCLUSION

This study involved meta-analytic and reflective synthesis which incorporates findings from the meta-analysis and personal reflections to provide a comprehensive understanding of artificial intelligence's role in higher education. It revealed that while artificial intelligence offers opportunities for enhancing pedagogy and learning experiences, it also presents significant ethical concerns and challenges related to academic integrity. The findings also underscore the importance of multidisciplinary collaboration and continuous exploration of artificial intelligence's evolving role in education. The study therefore recommends a balanced, responsible approach, supported by clear guidelines, ethical frameworks, and ongoing research to effectively explore artificial intelligence's benefits while mitigating its limitations and risks.

REFERENCES

Acosta-Enriquez, B. G., Arbulú Ballesteros, M. A., Arbulu Perez Vargas, C. G., Orellana Ulloa, M. N., Gutiérrez Ulloa, C. R., Pizarro Romero, J. M., Gutiérrez Jaramillo, N. D., Cuenca Orellana, H. U., Ayala Anzoátegui, D. X., & López Roca, C. (2024). Knowledge, attitudes, and perceived Ethics regarding the use of ChatGPT among generation Z university students. *International Journal for Educational Integrity*, 20(1), 10. DOI: 10.1007/s40979-024-00157-4

Adiguzel, T., Kaya, M. H., & Cansu, F. K. (2023). Revolutionizing education with AI: Exploring the transformative potential of ChatGPT. *Contemporary Educational Technology*, 15(3), ep429. https://doi.org/https://doi.org/10.30935/cedtech/13152. DOI: 10.30935/cedtech/13152

Ahmad, K., Iqbal, W., El-Hassan, A., Qadir, J., Benhaddou, D., Ayyash, M., & Al-Fuqaha, A. (2023). Data-driven artificial intelligence in education: A comprehensive review. *IEEE Transactions on Learning Technologies.*

Alam, A. (2023). Harnessing the Power of AI to Create Intelligent Tutoring Systems for Enhanced Classroom Experience and Improved Learning Outcomes. In *Intelligent Communication Technologies and Virtual Mobile Networks* (pp. 571–591). Springer. DOI: 10.1007/978-981-99-1767-9_42

AlGerafi, M. A., Zhou, Y., Oubibi, M., & Wijaya, T. T. (2023). Unlocking the potential: A comprehensive evaluation of augmented reality and virtual reality in education. *Electronics (Basel)*, 12(18), 3953. DOI: 10.3390/electronics12183953

Almufareh, M. F., Tehsin, S., Humayun, M., & Kausar, S. (2023). Intellectual disability and technology: An artificial intelligence perspective and framework. *Journal of Disability Research*, 2(4), 58–70. DOI: 10.57197/JDR-2023-0055

Almusaed, A., Almssad, A., Yitmen, I., & Homod, R. Z. (2023). Enhancing student engagement: Harnessing "AIED"'s power in hybrid education—A review analysis. *Education Sciences*, 13(7), 632. DOI: 10.3390/educsci13070632

Amer-Yahia, S. (2022). Towards AI-powered data-driven education. *Proceedings of the VLDB Endowment International Conference on Very Large Data Bases*, 15(12), 3798–3806. DOI: 10.14778/3554821.3554900

Anantrasirichai, N., & Bull, D. (2022). Artificial intelligence in the creative industries: A review. *Artificial Intelligence Review*, 55(1), 589–656. DOI: 10.1007/s10462-021-10039-7

Aytaç, Z. (2024). Using Artificial Intelligence Tools in Higher Education. In *Innovation in the University 4.0 System based on Smart Technologies* (pp. 164–175). Chapman and Hall/CRC. DOI: 10.1201/9781003425809-11

Bahroun, Z., Anane, C., Ahmed, V., & Zacca, A. (2023). Transforming education: A comprehensive review of generative artificial intelligence in educational settings through bibliometric and content analysis. *Sustainability (Basel)*, 15(17), 12983. DOI: 10.3390/su151712983

Booc, N. B., Sobremisana, K., Ybañez, A., Tolosa, R., Ladroma, S., & Caparoso, K. (2023). Artificial intelligence-powered calculator application usage in mathematics summative assessments. *Iconic Res. Eng. J*, 6(10), 446–474.

Brown, T. B. (2020). Language models are few-shot learners. *arXiv preprint arXiv:2005.14165.*

Butson, R., & Spronken-Smith, R. (2024). AI and its implications for research in higher education: A critical dialogue. *Higher Education Research & Development*, 43(3), 563–577. DOI: 10.1080/07294360.2023.2280200

Celik, I., Dindar, M., Muukkonen, H., & Järvelä, S. (2022). The promises and challenges of artificial intelligence for teachers: A systematic review of research. *TechTrends*, 66(4), 616–630. DOI: 10.1007/s11528-022-00715-y

Chassignol, M., Khoroshavin, A., Klimova, A., & Bilyatdinova, A. (2018). Artificial Intelligence trends in education: A narrative overview. *Procedia Computer Science*, 136, 16–24. DOI: 10.1016/j.procs.2018.08.233

Chee, K. N., & Sanmugam, M. (2023). *Embracing Cutting-edge Technology in Modern Educational Settings*. IGI Global.

Chen, L., Chen, P., & Lin, Z. (2020). Artificial intelligence in education: A review. *IEEE Access : Practical Innovations, Open Solutions*, 8, 75264–75278. DOI: 10.1109/ACCESS.2020.2988510

Chystaya, Y., Poyade, M., Rea, P. M., & McCorry, O. (2022). Application of AR and 3D technology for learning neuroanatomy. In *Medical Visualization and Applications of Technology* (pp. 147–180). Springer. DOI: 10.1007/978-3-031-06735-8_5

Colchester, K., Hagras, H., Alghazzawi, D., & Aldabbagh, G. (2017). A survey of artificial intelligence techniques employed for adaptive educational systems within e-learning platforms. *Journal of Artificial Intelligence and Soft Computing Research*, 7(1), 47–64. DOI: 10.1515/jaiscr-2017-0004

Crawford, J., Allen, K. A., Pani, B., & Cowling, M. (2024). When artificial intelligence substitutes humans in higher education: The cost of loneliness, student success, and retention. *Studies in Higher Education*, 49(5), 883–897. DOI: 10.1080/03075079.2024.2326956

Crawford, J., Cowling, M., Ashton-Hay, S., Kelder, J. A., Middleton, R., & Wilson, G. S. (2023). Artificial Intelligence and authorship editor policy: ChatGPT, Bard Bing AI, and beyond. *Journal of University Teaching & Learning Practice*, 20(5), 1. DOI: 10.53761/1.20.01.01

Crevier, D. (1993). *AI: the tumultuous history of the search for artificial intelligence*. Basic Books, Inc.

Dahal, B. (2024). Academic Integrity in Nepal. In *Second Handbook of Academic Integrity* (pp. 95–115). Springer Nature Switzerland. DOI: 10.1007/978-3-031-54144-5_192

Davis, F. D. (1989). Perceived usefulness, perceived ease of use, and user acceptance of information technology. *Management Information Systems Quarterly*, 13(3), 319–340. DOI: 10.2307/249008

Dhruv, A., Saha, S., Tyagi, S., & Jain, V. (2024, May). Investigating the Transformative Impact of Generative AI on Academic Integrity Across Diverse Educational Domains. In 2024 2nd International Conference on Advancement in Computation & Computer Technologies (InCACCT) (pp. 87-92). IEEE. DOI: 10.1109/InCACCT61598.2024.10551108

Dutta, S., Ranjan, S., Mishra, S., Sharma, V., Hewage, P., & Iwendi, C. (2024). Enhancing Educational Adaptability: A Review and Analysis of AI-Driven Adaptive Learning Platforms. 2024 4th International Conference on Innovative Practices in Technology and Management (ICIPTM)

Fogel, D. B. (2022). Defining artificial intelligence. *Machine Learning and the City: Applications in Architecture and Urban Design*, 91-120.

Forum, W. E. (2023). How AI can transform education for students and teachers. https://www.weforum.org/agenda/2023/05/ai-accelerate-students-holistic-development-teaching-fulfilling/

Gamma. (2023). *Gamma AI: Transforming presentations with AI-generated content.* https://gamma.app

Gaumann, N., & Veale, M. (2024). AI providers as criminal essay mills? Large language models meet contract cheating law. *Information & Communications Technology Law*, 33(3), 1–34. DOI: 10.1080/13600834.2024.2352692

Gligorea, I., Cioca, M., Oancea, R., Gorski, A.-T., Gorski, H., & Tudorache, P. (2023). Adaptive learning using artificial intelligence in e-learning: A literature review. *Education Sciences*, 13(12), 1216. DOI: 10.3390/educsci13121216

Goel, A. (2020). AI-powered learning: making education accessible, affordable, and achievable. *arXiv preprint arXiv:2006.01908.*

Google, A. I. (December, 2023). *Introducing Gemini AI.* https://youtu.be/jV1vkHv4zq8

Guo, L., Wang, D., Gu, F., Li, Y., Wang, Y., & Zhou, R. (2021). Evolution and trends in intelligent tutoring systems research: A multidisciplinary and scientometric view. *Asia Pacific Education Review*, 22(3), 441–461. DOI: 10.1007/s12564-021-09697-7

Gupta, P., Yadav, D., & Dey, R. (2021). AI Diagnosis: Rise of AI-Powered Assessments in Modern Education Systems. *Transnational Marketing Journal*, 9(3), 625–633.

Haderer, B., & Ciolacu, M. (2022). Education 4.0: Artificial intelligence assisted task- and time planning system. *Procedia Computer Science*, 200, 1328–1337. https://doi.org/https://doi.org/10.1016/j.procs.2022.01.334. DOI: 10.1016/j.procs.2022.01.334

Hadi, M. U., Al Tashi, Q., Shah, A., Qureshi, R., Muneer, A., Irfan, M., Zafar, A., Shaikh, M. B., Akhtar, N., & Wu, J. (2024). Large language models: a comprehensive survey of its applications, challenges, limitations, and future prospects. *Authorea Preprints.*

Haider, J. (2023). Revolutionizing Education: Integrating Artificial Intelligence through an Interdisciplinary Lens. *Journal of Environmental Science and Technology*, 2(1), 141–150.

Hopcan, S., Polat, E., Ozturk, M. E., & Ozturk, L. (2023). Artificial intelligence in special education: A systematic review. *Interactive Learning Environments*, 31(10), 7335–7353. https://doi.org/https://doi.org/10.1080/10494820.2022.2067186. DOI: 10.1080/10494820.2022.2067186

Hou, X., Zhao, Y., Liu, Y., Yang, Z., Wang, K., Li, L., Luo, X., Lo, D., Grundy, J., & Wang, H. (2023). Large language models for software engineering: A systematic literature review. *arXiv preprint arXiv:2308.10620.*

Iweuno, B. N., Orekha, P., Ojediran, O., Imohimi, E., & Adu-Twum, H. T. (2024). Leveraging Artificial Intelligence for an inclusive and diversified curriculum. *World Journal of Advanced Research and Reviews, 23*(2), 1579-1590. https://doi.org/https://doi.org/10.30574/wjarr.2024.23.2.2440

Jaiswal, A., & Arun, C. J. (2021). Potential of Artificial Intelligence for transformation of the education system in India. *International Journal of Education and Development Using Information and Communication Technology*, 17(1), 142–158.

Jamal, S. (2024). *Applications of Predictive and Generative AI Algorithms: Regression Modeling*. Customized Large Language Models, and Text-to-Image Generative Diffusion Models.

Javaid, M., Haleem, A., Singh, R. P., Khan, S., & Khan, I. H. (2023). Unlocking the opportunities through ChatGPT Tool towards ameliorating the education system. *BenchCouncil Transactions on Benchmarks. Standards and Evaluations*, 3(2), 100115.

Jebadurai, D. J., Dheenadayalan, L. R., Jawahar Rani, K., & Chandrasekaran, S. (2023). Relevancy of Artificial Intelligence in Education: A Conceptual Review. *Journal of Informatics Education and Research*, 3(2).

Jepkemoi, B., Mulwa, P. K., & Mwanda, S. O. (2024). Influence of ChatGPT Affordances on Adaptive Learning Experiences among Undergraduate Religious Education Teacher Trainees at the University of Nairobi, Kenya. *Canadian Journal of Educational and Social Studies*, 4(1), 25–35.

Jiang, H., Vimalesvaran, S., Wang, J. K., Lim, K. B., Mogali, S. R., & Car, L. T. (2022). Virtual reality in medical students' education: Scoping review. *JMIR Medical Education*, 8(1), e34860. DOI: 10.2196/34860

Jiang, Y., Li, X., Luo, H., Yin, S., & Kaynak, O. (2022). Quo vadis artificial intelligence? *Discover Artificial Intelligence*, 2(1), 4. DOI: 10.1007/s44163-022-00022-8

Jing, K., & Xu, J. (2019). A survey on neural network language models. *arXiv preprint arXiv:1906.03591.*

Kessler, G. (2018). Technology and the future of language teaching. *Foreign Language Annals*, 51(1), 205–218. DOI: 10.1111/flan.12318

KICD. (2017). Basic Education Curriculum Framework. https://kicd.ac.ke/wp-content/uploads/2017/10/CURRICULUMFRAMEWORK.pdf

Kiemde, S. M. A., & Kora, A. D. (2022). Towards an ethics of AI in Africa: Rule of education. *AI and Ethics*, 2(1), 35–40. DOI: 10.1007/s43681-021-00106-8

Kolog, E. A., Devine, S. N. O., Egala, S. B., Amponsah, R., Budu, J., & Farinloye, T. (2022). Rethinking the implementation of artificial intelligence for a sustainable education in Africa: Challenges and solutions. In *Management and Information Technology in the Digital Era* (Vol. 29, pp. 27–46). Emerald Publishing Limited. DOI: 10.1108/S1877-636120220000029003

Korteling, J., van de Boer-Visschedijk, G. C., Blankendaal, R. A., Boonekamp, R. C., & Eikelboom, A. R. (2021). Human-versus artificial intelligence. *Frontiers in Artificial Intelligence*, 4, 622364. https://doi.org/doi. DOI: 10.3389/frai.2021.622364

Kucharavy, A. (2024). From Deep Neural Language Models to LLMs. In *Large Language Models in Cybersecurity: Threats, Exposure and Mitigation* (pp. 3-17). Springer. DOI: 10.1007/978-3-031-54827-7_1

Kumar, R., Eaton, S. E., Mindzak, M., & Morrison, R. (2024). Academic integrity and artificial intelligence: An overview. Second Handbook of Academic Integrity, 1583-1596.

Latif, E., & Zhai, X. (2024). Fine-tuning ChatGPT for automatic scoring. *Computers and Education: Artificial Intelligence*, 6, 100210.

Lee, J., Hicke, Y., Yu, R., Brooks, C., & Kizilcec, R. F. (2024). The life cycle of large language models in education: A framework for understanding sources of bias. *British Journal of Educational Technology*, 55(5), 1982–2002. DOI: 10.1111/bjet.13505

Leite, B. S. (2024). Generative Artificial Intelligence in chemistry teaching: ChatGPT, Gemini, and Copilot's content responses. *Journal of Applied Learning and Teaching*, 7(2). https://doi.org/https://doi.org/10.37074/jalt.2024.7.2.13

Lin, C.-C., Huang, A. Y., & Lu, O. H. (2023). Artificial intelligence in intelligent tutoring systems toward sustainable education: A systematic review. *Smart Learning Environments*, 10(1), 41. DOI: 10.1186/s40561-023-00260-y

Luo, J. (2024). A critical review of GenAI policies in higher education assessment: A call to reconsider the "originality" of students' work. *Assessment & Evaluation in Higher Education*, •••, 1–14.

Markauskaite, L., Marrone, R., Poquet, O., Knight, S., Martinez-Maldonado, R., Howard, S., Tondeur, J., De Laat, M., Shum, S. B., & Gašević, D. (2022). Rethinking the entwinement between artificial intelligence and human learning: What capabilities do learners need for a world with AI? *Computers and Education: Artificial Intelligence*, 3, 100056. DOI: 10.1016/j.caeai.2022.100056

McCarthy, J. (2022). Artificial intelligence, logic, and formalising common sense. *Machine Learning and the City: Applications in Architecture and Urban Design*, 69-90.

McCarthy, J., Minsky, M. L., & ML, N. (1956). Rochester, and CE Shannon (1955). *Proposal for the 1956 Dartmouth Summer Research Project on Artificial Intelligence*.

Minsky, M. (1961). Steps toward artificial intelligence. *Proceedings of the IRE*, 49(1), 8–30. DOI: 10.1109/JRPROC.1961.287775

Mishra, P., & Koehler, M. J. (2006). Technological pedagogical content knowledge: A framework for teacher knowledge. *Teachers College Record*, 108(6), 1017–1054. DOI: 10.1111/j.1467-9620.2006.00684.x

Montoya-Cantoral, E., Espinoza-Suarez, S. M., Acra-Despradel, C., Mamani-Calcina, J., Ponce-Aranibar, M. P., Villalba-Condori, K. O., & Cardona-Reyes, H. (2023, September). Analysis of Institutional Policies on the Use of Chat GPT in Peruvian Universities. In *2023 XIII International Conference on Virtual Campus (JICV)* (pp. 1-4). IEEE. DOI: 10.1109/JICV59748.2023.10565652

Mousavinasab, E., Zarifsanaiey, N., & Niakan Kalhori, R., S., Rakhshan, M., Keikha, L., & Ghazi Saeedi, M. (. (2021). Intelligent tutoring systems: A systematic review of characteristics, applications, and evaluation methods. *Interactive Learning Environments*, 29(1), 142–163. DOI: 10.1080/10494820.2018.1558257

Mustafa, D. (2023). Smart classrooms, bright minds: The intersection of education and artificial intelligence. *Journal of Environmental Science and Technology*, 2(1), 150–158.

Nazi, Z. A., & Peng, W. (2024). Large language models in healthcare and medical domain: A review. *Informatics (MDPI)*, 11(3), 57. DOI: 10.3390/informatics11030057

Newell, A., & Simon, H. (1956). The logic theory machine—A complex information processing system. *IEEE Transactions on Information Theory*, 2(3), 61–79. DOI: 10.1109/TIT.1956.1056797

Onesi-Ozigagun, O., Ololade, Y. J., Eyo-Udo, N. L., & Ogundipe, D. O. (2024). Revolutionizing education through AI: A comprehensive review of enhancing learning experiences. *International Journal of Applied Research in Social Sciences*, 6(4), 589–607. DOI: 10.51594/ijarss.v6i4.1011

Open, A. I. (2023, March). *GPT-4 Developer Livestream [video]*. https://www.youtube.com/watch?v=outcGtbnMuQ

Open, A. I. (n.d.). *Artificial intelligence*. https://openai.com

Oravec, J. A. (2022). AI, Biometric Analysis, and Emerging Cheating Detection Systems: The Engineering of Academic Integrity? *Education Policy Analysis Archives*, 30(175), n175. https://doi.org/https://doi.org/10.14507/epaa.30.5765. DOI: 10.14507/epaa.30.5765

Ouyang, F., & Jiao, P. (2021). Artificial intelligence in education: The three paradigms. *Computers and Education: Artificial Intelligence*, 2, 100020. DOI: 10.1016/j.caeai.2021.100020

Pandey, N., & Pal, A. (2020). Impact of digital surge during Covid-19 pandemic: A viewpoint on research and practice. *International Journal of Information Management*, 55, 102171. DOI: 10.1016/j.ijinfomgt.2020.102171

Pappachan, P., & Rahaman, M. (2024). Conceptualising the Role of Intellectual Property and Ethical Behaviour in Artificial Intelligence. In *Handbook of Research on AI and ML for Intelligent Machines and Systems* (pp. 1–26). IGI Global.

Papyshev, G. (2024). Situated usage of generative AI in policy education: Implications for teaching, learning, and research. *Journal of Asian Public Policy*, •••, 1–18. DOI: 10.1080/17516234.2024.2370716

Pedro, F., Subosa, M., Rivas, A., & Valverde, P. (2019). Artificial intelligence in education: Challenges and opportunities for sustainable development.

Perkins, M. (2023). Academic Integrity considerations of AI Large Language Models in the post-pandemic era: ChatGPT and beyond. *Journal of University Teaching & Learning Practice*, 20(2). Advance online publication. DOI: 10.53761/1.20.02.07

Phind. (n.d.). *Phind: AI-powered search for developers.* https://phind.com

Pokkakillath, S., & Suleri, J. (2023). ChatGPT and its impact on education. *Research in Hospitality Management*, 13(1), 31–34. DOI: 10.1080/22243534.2023.2239579

Qadhi, S. M., Alduais, A., Chaaban, Y., & Khraisheh, M. (2024). Generative AI, Research Ethics, and Higher Education Research: Insights from a Scientometric Analysis. *Information (Basel)*, 15(6), 325. DOI: 10.3390/info15060325

Rane, N., Choudhary, S., & Rane, J. (2023). Education 4.0 and 5.0: Integrating artificial intelligence (AI) for personalized and adaptive learning. *Available atSSRN* 4638365. DOI: 10.2139/ssrn.4638365

Rane, N., Choudhary, S., & Rane, J. (2024). Artificial Intelligence-driven corporate finance: enhancing efficiency and decision-making through machine learning, natural language processing, and robotic process automation in corporate governance and sustainability. *Natural Language Processing, and Robotic Process Automation in Corporate Governance and Sustainability (February 8, 2024).* https://doi.org/https://doi.org/10.48185/sebr.v5i2.1050

Ratnam, M., Sharma, B., & Tomer, A. (2023). ChatGPT: educational artificial intelligence. *International Journal, of advanced trends in computer science and engineering, 12*(2). DOI: 10.30534/ijatcse/2023/091222023

Roll, I., & Wylie, R. (2016). Evolution and revolution in artificial intelligence in education. *International Journal of Artificial Intelligence in Education*, 26(2), 582–599. https://doi.org/DOI 10.1007/s40593-016-0110-3. DOI: 10.1007/s40593-016-0110-3

Sánchez, O., Castañeda, K., Vidal-Méndez, S., Carrasco-Beltrán, D., & Lozano-Ramírez, N. E. (2024). Exploring the influence of linear infrastructure projects 4.0 technologies to promote sustainable development in smart cities. *Results in Engineering*, 23, 102824. DOI: 10.1016/j.rineng.2024.102824

Santoro, A., Lampinen, A., Mathewson, K., Lillicrap, T., & Raposo, D. (2021). Symbolic behaviour in artificial intelligence. *arXiv preprint arXiv:2102.03406*.

Şenocak, D., Bozkurt, A., & Koçdar, S. (2024). Exploring the Ethical Principles for the Implementation of Artificial Intelligence in Education: Towards a Future Agenda. In Transforming Education With Generative AI: Prompt Engineering and Synthetic Content Creation (pp. 200-213). IGI Global.

Shaik, T., Tao, X., Li, Y., Dann, C., McDonald, J., Redmond, P., & Galligan, L. (2022). A review of the trends and challenges in adopting natural language processing methods for education feedback analysis. *IEEE Access : Practical Innovations, Open Solutions*, 10, 56720–56739. DOI: 10.1109/ACCESS.2022.3177752

Simon, H. A. (1995). Artificial intelligence: An empirical science. *Artificial Intelligence*, 77(1), 95–127. DOI: 10.1016/0004-3702(95)00039-H

Srinivasa, K., Kurni, M., & Saritha, K. (2022). Harnessing the Power of AI to Education. In *Learning, teaching, and assessment methods for contemporary learners: pedagogy for the digital generation* (pp. 311–342). Springer. DOI: 10.1007/978-981-19-6734-4_13

Talwar, P. (2023). *The Strategic Use of Virtual Teacher Assistants to Increase Faculty Engagement and Job Satisfaction*. Trident University International.

Tapalova, O., & Zhiyenbayeva, N. (2022). Artificial intelligence in education: AIEd for personalised learning pathways. *Electronic Journal of e-Learning*, 20(5), 639–653. DOI: 10.34190/ejel.20.5.2597

Thomas, A. P. (2024). Balancing Innovation and Integrity: Addressing Concerns of AI in Classroom Environments. https://scholarworks.gvsu.edu/gradprojects/451

Toosi, A., Bottino, A. G., Saboury, B., Siegel, E., & Rahmim, A. (2021). A brief history of AI: How to prevent another winter (a critical review). *PET Clinics*, 16(4), 449–469. https://doi.org/https://doi.org/10.1016/j.cpet.2021.07.001. DOI: 10.1016/j.cpet.2021.07.001

Turing, A. M. (1950). Computing Machinery and Intelligence. https://redirect.cs.umbc.edu/courses/471/papers/turing.pdf

UNESCO. (2021). *Artificial intelligence in education: Guidance for policy-makers*. https://unesdoc.unesco.org/ark:/48223/pf0000374802

Vaswani, A. (2017). Attention is all you need. *Advances in Neural Information Processing Systems*.

Wall, P., Saxena, D., & Brown, S. (2021). Artificial intelligence in the Global South (AI4D): Potential and risks. *arXiv preprint arXiv:2108.10093*.

Wanjiku Wang'ang'a, A. (2024). Consequences of Artificial Intelligence on Teaching and Learning in Higher Education in Kenya: Literature Review. *East African Journal of Education Studies*, 7(1), 202–215. DOI: 10.37284/eajes.7.1.1718

Yeo, M. A. (2023). Academic integrity in the age of artificial intelligence (AI) authoring apps. *TESOL Journal*, 14(3), e716. DOI: 10.1002/tesj.716

Yufeia, L., Salehb, S., Jiahuic, H., & Syed, S. M. (2020). Review of the application of artificial intelligence in education. *Integration (Amsterdam)*, 12(8), 1–15.

Yusuf, A., Pervin, N., Román-González, M., & Noor, N. M. (2024). Generative AI in education and research: A systematic mapping review. *Review of Education*, 12(2), e3489. DOI: 10.1002/rev3.3489

Zerkowska, A. M. (2024). PERSONALIZED LANGUAGE LEARNING IN THE AGE OF AI. Leveraging Large Language Models for Optimal Learning Outcomes.

Zhao, W. X., Zhou, K., Li, J., Tang, T., Wang, X., Hou, Y., Min, Y., Zhang, B., Zhang, J., & Dong, Z. (2023). A survey of large language models. *arXiv preprint arXiv:2303.18223*.

ADDITIONAL READING

Al-Badi, A., Khan, A., & Eid-Alotaibi, . (2022). Perceptions of learners and instructors towards artificial intelligence in personalized learning. *Procedia Computer Science*, 201, 445–451. DOI: 10.1016/j.procs.2022.03.058

Baskara, R. (2023). Exploring the implications of ChatGPT for language learning in higher education. *Indonesian Journal of English Language Teaching and Applied Linguistics*, 7(2), 343–358. https://doi.org/http://dx.doi.org/10.21093/ijeltal.v7i2.1387

Benke, E., & Szőke, A. (2024). Academic Integrity in the Time of Artificial Intelligence: Exploring Student Attitudes. *Italian Journal of Sociology of Education, 16*(Italian Journal of Sociology of Education 16/2), 91-108.

Dempere, J., Modugu, K., Hesham, A., & Ramasamy, L. K. (2023). The impact of ChatGPT on higher education. *Frontiers in Education*, 8, 1206936. DOI: 10.3389/feduc.2023.1206936

Gallent Torres, C., Zapata-González, A., & Ortego-Hernando, J. L. (2023). The impact of Generative Artificial Intelligence in higher education: A focus on ethics and academic integrity. *RELIEVE.Revista ELectrónica de Investigación y EValuación Educativa*, 29(2), 1–19.

Khatri, B. B., & Karki, P. D. (2023). Artificial Intelligence (AI) in Higher Education: Growing Academic Integrity and Ethical Concerns. *Nepalese Journal of Development and Rural Studies*, 20(01), 1–7. DOI: 10.3126/njdrs.v20i01.64134

Moya, B., Eaton, S., Pethrick, H., Hayden, A., Brennan, R., Wiens, J., & McDermott, B. (2024). Academic Integrity and Artificial Intelligence in Higher Education (HE) Contexts: A Rapid Scoping Review. *Canadian Perspectives on Academic Integrity, 7*(3).

Pratama, M. P., Sampelolo, R., & Lura, H. (2023). Revolutionizing education: harnessing the power of artificial intelligence for personalized learning. *Klasikal: Journal of education, language teaching and science, 5*(2), 350-357.

Rawas, S. (2024). ChatGPT: Empowering lifelong learning in the digital age of higher education. *Education and Information Technologies*, 29(6), 6895–6908. DOI: 10.1007/s10639-023-12114-8

Sullivan, M., Kelly, A., & McLaughlan, P. (2023). ChatGPT in higher education: Considerations for academic integrity and student learning. https://doi.org/https://doi.org/10.37074/jalt.2023.6.1.17

Wiredu, J. K., Abuba, N. S., & Zakaria, H. (2024). Impact of Generative AI in Academic Integrity and Learning Outcomes: A Case Study in the Upper East Region. *Asian Journal of Research in Computer Science*, 17(7), 214–232. DOI: 10.9734/ajrcos/2024/v17i7491

KEY TERMS AND DEFINITIONS

Academic integrity: Ensuring that artificial intelligence tools do not facilitate cheating or plagiarism. It also includes developing policies and practices to maintain honesty and originality in students' academic work.

Artificial intelligence: The development of computer systems that can perform tasks typically requiring human intelligence, such as problem-solving, decision-making, language understanding, and pattern recognition.

ChatGPT: An advanced language model developed by OpenAI, designed to generate human-like text based on the input it receives. It can engage in conversations, provide explanations, answer questions, and assist with a variety of language-related tasks.

Data Privacy: The protection of personal information collected, stored, and processed by artificial intelligence systems especially safeguarding student data used by artificial intelligence tools from unauthorized access, misuse, or breaches.

Ethics: The moral principles governing the use of artificial intelligence technologies in higher education, ensuring that they are used responsibly, fairly, and without causing harm.

Generative Artificial Intelligence: Artificial intelligence systems that can create new content, such as text, images, or audio, based on the data they have been trained on.

Higher Education: Refers to how artificial intelligence tools can be leveraged to enhance learning, teaching, and administrative processes within Kenyan higher education institutions, aiming to improve educational outcomes and operational efficiency.

Large Language Models (LLMs): A subset of artificial intelligence, trained on vast amounts of text data to understand and generate human-like language.

Machine Learning: A branch of artificial intelligence that focuses on systems that can learn from data and improve their performance over time without explicit programming.

Plagiarism: It is the potential for students to use artificial intelligence-generated content without citation poses new challenges to maintaining academic integrity in higher education.

Chapter 2

Intrigues of Artificial Intelligence in Teaching and Learning in the Modern Times

John M. Onyango Yambo
Kisii University, Kenya

ABSTRACT

This chapter addressed intrigues of Artificial Intelligence (AI) in teaching and learning in the modern times. This study was guided by the Situated Learning Theory (SLT). Situated knowledge or situated learning was at the onset propagated by Brown, Collins and Dugud (1989) and later elaborated by Lave and Wenger (1991). Despite of the unavoidable circumstantial changes occasioned by AI, it looked at predictive models in teaching and learning, policies for AI in teaching, Neo-predictive models in Instruction and knowledge acquisition and automated learning in the current AI age. It requires the learning researchers to delve into exploration and involve other education stakeholders. Methods used were partial literature review plus qualitative assessment of teaching methods in the period of AI. The study targeted curriculum and instruction designers, policy maker, administrators, educators including stakeholders passionate in teaching and learning in modern times of AI and furtherance of sustainable development in Kenya and environs.

DOI: 10.4018/979-8-3373-0025-2.ch002

INTRODUCTION

Artificial Intelligence (AI) has become a new norm. Historically, according to Pradipta (1999); Lave and Wenger, (1991) AI has been a division of Science with a concern of aiding machines to find answers to compound issues, problems in a more human-like fashion in society. It commonly involves adoption-of characteristics from human-like intelligence, and using them as algorithmic program in a computer amiable manner (Pradipta, 1999). A more flexible or cost-effective approach can be taken depending on the necessitated established situation, which determine how artificial the intelligent behavior look to be (Panigrahi & Joshi 2020).

During the interval between 17th and 19th century, as put forward by Anyoha (2017:7), the term "computer" has the same connotation as human calculator in various work sections since there was no equivalent in the planet doing calculation in an autonomous way (Host, 2021). Furthermore, the studies by Anyoha (2017) revealed that Alan Turing's innovation in recent computer science in 1940s, the word "computer" became bit by bit isolated from its original anthropological meaning and alternatively turned to be a manipulative machine with universal purposes. The term "artificial intelligence" was very first propagated by John McCarthy in 1956 in an scholarly presentation (Anyoha, 2017:6; Forman, Udvaros & Avornicului 2023), which has now various definitions presently. One such simple definition was that AI is the simulated human intelligence by computers or machines which are programmed to support as humans do and mimic humans' do (Panigrahi & Joshi 2020).

Successively according to Host (2021) human beings are surviving in a world where technical promotion is progressing rapidly with a faster-than-ever rate including an abundance of information and data being created and stored (Annuš, 2024) . It has been estimated that the worldwide data volume reached 59 zettabytes in 2020 and was projected to 149 zettabytes in 2025 (Forman et al. 2023; Host, 2021). In this regard, 1 zettabyte equals to enormously 1021 bytes. It is no doubt that we have arrived at an age of big data where AI combined with big data opens up many opportunities that would be controlled for the human brain to cognitively process (Forman et al. 2023).

Generally, AI including related AI-enabled technologies have been advanced in the recent past. Their popularity plus invention, as put forward by the work of Annuš (2023) are increase in popularity presently to assist human life and modify human innovative advancement. As much as the global Education for Sustainable Development (ESD) has been concerned with promising conduct that advance a sustainable progression, Forman et al. (2023) added that approaching the period of envisaged climate change, technological advancement and change has established considerably (Yambo, 2023). The contemporary technological innovation, ChatGPT has forced generative artificial intelligence into the public domain since late 2022, where many education researchers and stakeholders have asked whether AI digital technology offers real opportunities (Annuš, 2023). According to Forman et al. (2023), it can assist in connecting the many peripheral learners, like those with disabilities, or those from linguistic and cultural minority communities (Yambo, 2023). Furthermore, the work of Panigrahi and Joshi (2020) alluded that it can alleviate the provision of more individualized learning and allow for more flexible school scheme which can also be used to overcome boundaries of place and time to create desired learning outcome and expected experiences (UNESCO, 2023).

BACKGROUND

The wake of AI use in educational institutions and in administration has been not new phenomenon. In America, according to the U.S. Department of Education (2023: 9) historically revealed that a wide cultural consciousness of AI can be traced back to the occasion of 1968 film "2001: A Space Odyssey"—where by the "Heuristically-programmed ALgorithmic" computer, (HAL) converses with astronaut Frank. HAL assisted Frank to pilot the journey through space, a job that Frank could not have done own. Nevertheless, according to Friedman, Blair, Walker and Roschelle (2021), when Frank eventually went outside the spacecraft, HAL took over the control, and this did not end well for Frank. HAL displayed human-like behaviors, such as thinking, talking, and acting. Like all applications of AI, HAL can assist humans but also presents unforeseen risks—especially due to the fact that AI explains in different ways and with different limitations than masses do. (U.S. Department of Education, 2023; Friedman et al.2021). While considering the idea of "human-like. This brings in the concept of AI which is useful because it can be a script for the idea that computers now have capabilities that are very different from the capabilities of early education technology applications used in schools then (Annuš, 2024).

With the increase and improvement in technology, as alluded by Maslej et al (2023); Annuš, (2023) the use of Chat-bots, Smart-boards, ChatGPT educational applications has been able to converse with students and teachers, to co-pilot how activities unfold in classrooms, and take actions that impact students and teachers more broadly (Forman, 2023). There are both opportunities to do things much better than we did in the past and risks that must be anticipated and addressed are not few. The human-like shorthand is not always useful, however, because AI processes information differently from how people process information (Annuš, 2024). When educators and administrators gloss over the differences between people and computers, according to Maslej et al (2023); Holmes and Porayska-Pomsta (2022) they may frame policies for AI in education that miss the mark. Care and precision is therefore necessary in the making of the needed practical AI policies (Sagar, 2020).

Automation and robotics are found to be useful for teachers as well as organizational leaders. The work of Panigrahi and Joshi (2020) pointed out that the improvement and application of intelligent robots will emancipate teachers of colleges and universities from daily, repetitive, mechanical and ordinary work. According to Maslej et al (2023), this could provide them with opportunity so that they can have more time for professional knowledge acquisition, ability transformation and inventive teaching designs. Additionally, automation and robotics, as prescribed by Sagar (2020) provide intelligent support for the creation of gold courses in colleges and universities (Panigrahi & Joshi, 2020).. This fully release the creative vigour of lecturers of universities and tutors of colleges. Studies by Maslej et al (2023) on the other hand, reiterated that AI can help to explore the teaching characteristics and laws of colleges and universities in the new era, and explore new teaching and learning methods in colleges and universities (Jin, Gao, & Yin 2022).

Theoretical Framework

The Situated Learning Theory (SLT) guided this study. Situated cognition or situated learning was first defined by Brown, Collins and Duguid (1989); later expounded by Lave and Wenger (1991). Since then, it has had an important effect on educational thinking and outcomes. SLT has emerged as an alternative to dominant, cognitive perspectives on learning. SLT, or at least elements of it has emerged as a possible vehicle for invigorating the understanding of, and preparations for, how knowledge is developed and organized within workplaces (Brown et al. 1989; Motteram, 2013). SLT holds that knowledge should be delivered in a reliable context. Beginning learners should be involved in authentic settings of daily practice, applying knowledge, and making use of artifacts in predicting learning outcomes (Lave & Wenger, 1991).

This theory therefore, led researchers like Brown et al. (1989) to reason that acquisition of education can only be important if it is incorporated in the social and physical context (Motteram, 2013). They pointed out that formal learning is often quite defined from authentic activity performed by professional persons in their everyday work (Lave & Wenger, 1991). In other words, students' activities, particularly in classroom settings, are usually isolated from the ordinary influence of the culture (Brown et al. 1989). Furthermore, Lave and Wenger (1991) explicated that learning take place when individuals are members of the communities, in which they are used to and at the same time participate actively in the transmission, reproduction, and improvement of practice knowledge about agents, activities, and artifacts. They also believed that to know is to be capable of taking part with the requisite potentiality in the complex web of relationships among citizenry and activities (Shaltry, 2013; Motteram, 2013).

The SLT however, had some limitations which were explained by (Forman et al. 2023) who argued that situative theorists ignore issues of race, class, gender, and other cultural and personal complexities. In schools, students with diverse abilities may not be able to participate meaningfully in particular systems of practice. Additionally, it was contended by Mills (2013) that the situative perspective was silent on the issue of resistance in communities, in which tools and activities may be unfair or dysfunctional in nature (Jackson, 2024). SLT consequently suggests that learning is experienced and mediated through relationships with community members or within a community of practice (Lave & Wenger, 1991). Here a community of practice or group members jointly share and develop practices, learn from their interactions with group members, and gain opportunities to develop individually, professionally, or intellectually (Mills, 2013).

SLT therefore, as supported by Kozulin (2003) stresses the opportunities for students to reveal their abilities and talents. Research done by Schoenfeld (2013) equally revealed that it can provide students with a learning environment that mirrors the culture and tools that are cast in the same mold as those used in real life situations (Kozulin 2003; Cleveland, 2011; Schoenfeld, 2013).

AUTOMATED LEARNING IN THE AGE OF AI

When dealing with automated learning, the U.S. Department of Education (2023) referred to AI as mechanization based on associations (Holmes & Porayska-Pomsta, 2022). During the time computers automate reasoning based on associations in data (or associations deduced from expert knowledge), two shifts fundamental to AI occur and shift computing beyond accepted educational technology. Additionally, Walton Family Foundation (2023) added that automation assists capturing data to *detecting patterns* in data while Maslej, et al. (2023) alluded that AI provide access from instructional resources to automating decisions about instruction and other educational processes. By so doing, according to U.S. Department of Education (2023) AI will be able to detect patterns and automating decisions which are leaped in the level of responsibilities that can be delegated to a computer system, hence automation take place. On the contrary, research done by Holmes and Porayska-Pomsta (2022) revealed that the process of developing an AI system may lead to bias in how patterns are detected and unfairness in how decisions are automated. In this regard therefore, educational systems must govern their use of AI systems to avoid nay form of biasness. As empasised by Walton Family Foundation (2023) this report described opportunities for using AI to improve education, recognizes challenges that would arise, and develops recommendations to guide further policy development on the automation of learning in schools.

In the era of AI learning, the work of Dirican (2015) who dealt more with the impacts of robotics opined that AI and machine learning techniques provide a new perspective for business applications in the twenty-first century. Most people expect AI to play a key role in company management and educational institutions. In America, the U.S. Department of Education (2023) equally contended that the process of mounting an AI system may not only lead to prejudice in how patterns are sensed and partiality in how judgement are automated (Dirican, 2015). In this regard, educational systems must regulate their use of AI systems especially in automating learning.

A current study by Walton Family Foundation (2023) prescribed that many precedence for improvements to teaching and learning are still unmet. Educators are searching technology-enhanced approaches to address these priorities that would be safe, effective, and scalable. According to Zacamy and Roschelle (2022) educators marvel if the rapid advances in technology in everyday lives could help. Nearly all educators use AI-powered services in their routine lives, such as voice assistants in their homes; tools that can correct grammar, complete sentences, and write essays; and automated trip planning on their phones, hence make life easier. More educators are actively exploring AI tools as they are newly released to the public for use (Walton Family Foundation 2023).

Ordinarily, automated learning and use of AI, according to Holmes and Porayska-Pomsta (2022) may enable achieving educational priorities in better ways, at scale, and with lower costs involved. Addressing varied unfinished learning of students due to the pandemic is a policy priority, and AI may improve the adaptivity of learning resources to students' strengths and needs (U.S. Department of Education (2023). automated learning also improves teaching profession which should be a priority, and via automated assistants or other tools, AI may provide teachers greater support. According to Dirican (2015) AI may also enable teachers to extend the assistance they offer to individual students when they run out of time in schools (Zacamy & Roschelle, 2022). Developing resources that are receptive to the knowledge and experiences students bring to their learning—their community and cultural assets—is of importance, and AI may enable greater customizability of curricular resources to meet local and international needs (Holmes & Porayska-Pomsta, 2022).

The more new technological knowledge increase, Panigrahi and Joshi (2020) noted that AI-based automated tests do not only allow for repair, but also for intelligent test generation. Furthermore, Annuš (2024) found that international research results confirmed that the use of student analytics and tools for educational data mining have assisted most students in reviewing their accomplishments, anticipating more support and attention required by students, aiding their teachers in devising supportive interventions, and enhancing existing courses or curricula in schools. For example, machine learning techniques were utilized to automatically boost user and group models by observing the previous behaviour of students and supplying training examples for forecasting future activities (Forman et al. 2023).

Research by Göksel and Bozkurt (2019) reiterated that the use of automated assessment systems was seen as important mainly by university teachers, which could also mean automated improvement of theses and dissertations. According to Lilja (2018) the primary school teachers use of chatbots and predictive models have taken a back seat. However, they ranked higher for secondary school and university lecturers. Likewise, in Sweden, experiments have been made using neural networks to check essay-based texts (Lilja, 2018). Additionally, Prashanta (2020) opined that genetic programming which is an machine-controlled method for creating a working computer program from an ordinarily high-level problem statement of the kind of work which is supposed to be done and automatically creates a computer program to solve the problem in learning institutions (Göksel & Bozkurt, 2019).

Generally, it has been considers imperative to differentiate between the methods of AI and automation learning system. The work of Yannick, Tim and Sven (2022) reported that nowadays AI systems work with automated learning methods which are equally used in education. Accordingly, these are the cognitive systems. According to Holmes and Porayska-Pomsta (2022). automated learning has been a distinct portion of AI and used with artificial neutral networks (Lilja, 2018). Furthermore, studies done by Terstegen Lennings, Suchy, Schalter and Suarsana (2018) equally reiterated that the construction of the artificial neural networks can have not the same levels of complexness (Yannick et al. 2022). In this case, when the complexity of the structures of the network is very high, the methods are called deep learning (Terstegen et al. 2018). Deep learning according to Terstegen et al. (2018);Yannick et al. 2022) isolate the section of machine learning from AI even in teaching and learning. Here the application of deep learning involves the training of neural networks where there are different conceptualisation available like (un) supervised learning or reinforcement learning in school (Lilja, 2018).

In automated learning, according to Xiong (2023) AI will increase the productivity of leaders, teachers and managers by taking over some automated, mechanical, and administrative activities (Forman et al. 2023). These tasks generally correspond to the challenging aspects of leadership even in teaching. With time therefore, many people worry that AI will change the workforce, especially those simple and automated jobs including learning and absorbing new information and technology. According to Yannick et al. (2022) AI technology and techniques will be rapidly updated as required to give ease in teaching and learning by employing the latest technology to help users manage teams and set strategic direction. In this aspect, managers and educators should continue to learn, have hands-on, improve and accept new AI tools (Terstegen et al. 2018).

In the higher institutions of learning, academic leaders and principals as put forward by Majed (2019) should embrace automating internal procedures and tasks that goes with it. Institutions should start to perceive how to mechanize the internal operations and processes needed by the business affiliated to the third-party computer system (Xiong, 2023). Educators should handle AI as cooperation and create ways to accomplish desired intention. According to Yannick et al. (2022) automated teaching and learning application, especially machine vision and natural language processing, could be used to make up self-service computer system that supply cognitive advancement automation in schools, this would allow administrators and teaching staff to deal with complex multistage procedures more effectively (Terstegen et al. 2018).

Moreover, computer learning systems can envision many transaction (Majed, 2019). In this way, the work Xiong (2023); Forman et al. (2023) pointed out that teachers could visually compare each simulate strategy and choose the most suitable approach for their organization and institutions appropriately. Adopting machine learning technologies can save time and money for leaders, employees, and enterprises altogether (Yannick et al. 2022). Administrators with strong soft power can better accomplish their teams and cultivate an environment of precise cooperation to achieve their goals in schools (Majed, 2019).

While automating learning, according to Xu, Dainoff, Ge and Gao (2022) leaders were given more opportunities which could try a wide range of innovative application through research of their own preference, such as scheming a schoolroom computing device that could well handle their areas of specializations. Additionally, the work of Shaltry (2013) teachers had to adopt their own classroom and teaching identities and create detailed websites with blogs, videos, images, and imagined showcases of their future students' examinable work. In learning institutions, there has been various decisions made on academic work. Consequently AI could aid in making decisions on learning. Research done by Xu et al. (2022) on transformation to human action with AI articulated that there is an urgent need in using a human-centric thinking to adopt AI in decision-making duties both in schools and in organizations (Terstegen et al. 2018). According to Xu et al. (2022) the analysis found that the conformation of human-AI produced lower trust as compared to others. Furthermore, no configuration was found in which AI as a colleague was able to produces lower trust than human beings (Shaltry, 2013).

AI AND RETRIEVAL OF ESSENTIAL EDUCATION CONTENTS

Retrieval of information has been significant in schools and organizations. According to Maya and Charles (2018) the expectation would be that students build on the base of knowledge they create in school, one important characteristic of this base would be that of their sufficiently representative of all the ways they could choose to build on and retrieve information (Subirana, Bagiati & Sarma 2017). In schools generally, according to Somar and Jianwei (2021) when students are exposed to many fields of human undertaking through coupling core concepts with necessary content, education can allow children to study the different manageable life and career paths so that they may eventually make informed decisions as to which endeavors they would be best suited for in life (Maya & Charles, 2018).

When considering storage and retrieval of information, Subirana, Bagiati and Sarma (2017) contended that the content must be reconsidered either as for short or long term. This has been on the basis of society's new connection with information (Somar & Jianwei, 2021) . Education stakeholders, according to Arbesman (2013) also found that the storage of information was scarce for most of human history, but became plentiful with the mass production of books. Through acquisition of personal computers, as alluded by Somar and Jianwei (2021) there became an abundance of resources and access to manipulate information as well. The work of Subirana et al. (2017) any simple piece of information can be found quickly online, and powerful computational tools are easily accessible for retrieval of essential information. In addition, the evidence by Arbesman (2013) suggested that individuals forget academic content at the rate of 50% every two years and that what was known in a given field changes over time such that a foreseeable fraction of what is learned in school will be outdated by the time it would be retrieved as useful in a professional setting (Subirana et al. 2017).

Retrieval of information aids the provision of quality education systems. According to UNESCO (2023) the very quality education have to enable learners to continuously adapt their competencies, ability to retrieve important and useful information while continuously acquiring and even developing new ones in schools. These competencies as suggested by Arbesman (2013) are diverse in scope; ranging from core skills, content knowledge, cognitive skills, soft skills, to occupational skills. They enable teachers to meet a complex demand or carry out a complex activity or task successfully (Somar & Jianwei, 2021). retrieved information can be referred to in a time of need and even more effectively in a certain contexts. Their typologies and methods are as diverse as the entities—countries, organizations and individuals—that define them (Bialik & Fadel, 2015).

While using AI in the retrieval of useful contents, Simonton (2000) suggested that the main way to reach these goals was to restructure knowledge around core concepts and content must be modernized as well. One way to approach this, according to Arbesman (2013) was to eradicate portions of the curriculum that are outdated where educators take away the non-load-bearing blocks without decreasing the construction, thereby keeping the essential structure for future use. Considerably, it is possible to remove more information while the goal is to store what is needed most for future retrieval. In addition, Barnett and Ceci (2002) indicated that valuable contemporary topics should be added to the classic content to update its relevance. Finally, the way content is taught should be restructured, making use of new educational as well as professional tools be efficient to retrieve important information (Simonton (2000).

In retrieval of information, Boyle (2017) suggested that the incorporation of virtual reality (VR) and augmented reality (AR) in educational contexts which has opened new opportunities for immersive and interactive learning experiences was key. In this regard, Arbesman (2013) opined that understanding these fundamental milestones was essential for grasping the trajectory of AI in education and appreciating the diverse range of applications that have molded the field. Furthermore, collaboration between educational institutions, technology developers, and professional development providers, as put forward by Siemens (2005) was essential to create tailored programs that cater to the diverse needs of educators in recovery of pertinent information. By prioritizing professional development, educators can harness the full potential of AI to improve teaching practices and advance learning outcomes, ensuring a seamless transition to AI enhanced educational environments (Miailhe & Hodes, 2017). As AI technologies permeate educational settings, it is essential to assess their implications on pedagogy, retrieval of academic information, student engagement, and the overall learning experience (Siemens 2005). Furthermore, Cimpian and Salomon (2014) argued that, even if extrinsic information is known, it is not readily accessible by the mental shotgun that people use to retrieve information (Dirican, 2015).

Recovery of information according to Miailhe and Hodes (2017) are useful for improvement. Due to noted ambiguity in AI retrieval of information it is crucial for business and education leaders to first understand what AI can do in application, including its potentialities and limitations in reclamation of information (Cimpian & Salomon, 2014). In terms of capabilities, AI can be categorized as 3 different types from low to high capabilities as follow: Artificial Narrow Intelligence (ANI), Artificial General Intelligence (AGI) and Artificial Super Intelligence (ASI) (Miailhe & Hodes, 2017). Additionally, Bialik and Fadel (2015) reiterated that, in terms of universality of utilization, ASI is still far away from reality and is hypothetically fictional, while AGI has just achieved some theoretical foundations in recent years

(Cimpian & Salomon, 2014). However, ANI has been the most extensively used and has achieved tremendous successes in different business sectors (Miailhe & Hodes, 2017).

The research by Somar and Jianwei (2021) pointed out the questions of design in a more open way with the aim to collect more open data as possible with the marginal impact of bias in the responses and to retrieve abundant data for the different magnitude (Miailhe & Hodes, 2017). In dealing with information retrieval, some used keywords in the database of AI creators. In the existing studies by Tran et al., 2019), for example were, AI also referred to as artificial neural network, machine intelligence, machine learning, deep learn and robotic as terms used in retrievals or search.in education the key words are used to refer to many bibliometric studies which were useful for retrieval important data (Hallinger & Chatpinyakoop, 2019).

NEO-PREDICTIVE MODELS IN CURRENT TEACHING AND LEARNING

AI teaching materials have been linked to others in their predictive context. Studies by Baker, Esbenshade, Vitale and Karumbaiah (2022); Englebart (1962) referred to AI models as like financial models: an approximation of reality that is useful for identifying patterns, making predictions, or analyzing alternative decisions in work place. In a typical middle school mathematics curriculum, students use a mathematical model to analyze which of two cell phone plans is better (Baker, et al. 2022). Equally, educational and even financial planners also use this kind of model to provide guidance on a retirement files for workers. In the current usage, according to Zacamy and Roschelle (2022); Baker et al. (2022) AI is a highly advanced mathematical toolkit for building and using models that give accurate envisaged out come. Indeed, in well-known chatbots, multifaceted essays are written one word at a time (Hallinger & Chatpinyakoop, 2019). The underlying AI model prognosticate which next words would probably follow the text written so far; AI chatbots use a very large statistical model to add one likely word at a time, thereby writing unexpectedly coherent essays (Zacamy & Roschelle 2022).

Since teaching and learning involves learners, teachers and parents or guardians, research done by Yambo (2012) reported these key stakeholders are equally challenged in various ways ranging from computer literacy to the use of personalized learning, automated assessment, chatbots, predictive models and intelligent robots among others (Zacamy & Roschelle, 2022Baker et al. (2022)). Due to the fact that some schools are situated in rural settings, suggested that acquiring the needed current predictive models for teaching and learning resources are key though they are posing challenges and some concerns (Hallinger & Chatpinyakoop 2019). In this respect therefore, Forman et al. (2023) recommended that machines, especially those used in teaching have almost the same properties as human intelligence should be encouraged in schools. Consequently, Holmes and Porayska-Pomsta (2022) added that people now live in a world where we cannot tell whether the person we are communicating with is a real person or a (robot) virtual device - think of chat-bots, which can even be used in education to teach students (Forman et al. 2023). According to Annuš, (2023) a concrete and typical example is ChatGPT, one of today's leading artificial intelligence systems, which also has its own potential and threats for education useful teaching and learning. Certainly, these technological developments exhibit that people are witnessing the development of deep learning in science (Göksel & Bozkurt, 2019).

The work of Miller (2017) show that the temporal events is important, in particular that people undo more recent events than more proximal events. For instance, Göksel and Bozkurt (2019) in one of their studies, revealed that participants were asked to act the role of a teacher choosing some examination questions for a task. In one group, the teacher first of all grouped the participants who were told that the students had not yet studied for their examination, while those in the other group, the teacher-second group, were told that the students had already studied for the examination (Göksel & Bozkurt, 2019).. It was found that those in the teacher-second group selected easier questions than those in the first, showing that participants perceived the degree of blame they would be given for hard questions depends on the temporal order of the tasks and predictive ability of AI (Miller (2017). according to Göksel and Bozkurt (2019) this supports the hypothesis that earlier events are considered less mutable than later events (Miller, 2017).

Foretelling models in learning and teaching are increasing in use in the passage of time. According to Gibson, Kovanovic, Ifenthaler, Dexter and Feng (2023) the role of AI in teaching and learning process as many modern fields of inquiry and expression are progressively underpinned and enhanced by computational resources, there is already developing common ground for a unifying framework encompassing AI, learning analytics, educational data mining, machine learning and complexity theory (Tsai et al., 2019). Though according to Dawson et al., (2018) new possibilities for multidisciplinary research on AI in education are rapidly evolving, proposed framework is tentatively, aiming to be expansive and inclusive of existing theories to bridge gaps and explore rather than exclude new ideas (Miller, 2017). The framework is a speculative and suggestive narrative offered primarily as a discussion point and not a definitive answer to all identified challenges of the AI predictive models (Tsai et al., 2019).

Prediction needs skills. When using predictive models, Chen, Xie, Zou and Hwang (2020); Gibson et al. 2023) teachers and instructors need prior knowledge on various predictive education models and patterns. According to Gao et al., (2018) ;

Gibson et al. (2023) predictive models in teaching and learning includes exploring and understanding ideas, images and semantics (Egozi et al., 2011; Ifenthaler, 2010), representing and formulating creative new representations, planning and executing team actions which Wang et al., (2021) opined that assist the team in monitoring and reflecting on progress and achievement (Gao et al., 2018).

Predictive and detection of students work are essential in learning. According to Chen et al. (2020) neural network-related algorithms have been popularly adopted for educational purposes, with frequently used terms such as neural net-work, bayesian network, and network. Such technologies have been found to be applied to tackle various issues, for example, the detection of a student's learning style (García et al., 2007), dropout prediction in e-learning courses (Delen, 2010). Student retention management and prediction of student's mood prediction of students' gaming behaviors (Muldner et al., 2011), improvement of teaching parallel robots (Tan et al., 2012), and detection of students' learning styles are of key importance in schools (García et al., 2008). The work of Chen et al. (2020) found that AI-enhanced digital technology has played an essential role in our daily life, with its great power of changing the way we think, act, and interact. Furthermore, ever since its emergence, AI has developed with success and flourishment, in particular with the emergence of Artificial Neural Networks (ANN) and Deep Learning (DL) (Chan & Zary, 2019).

POLICIES FOR ARTIFICIAL INTELLIGENCE IN TEACHING

Due to the fact that AI is improving faster and announcing societal changes that need effective national policy response. In America, the White House Office of Science and Technology Policy (2022), in addition to broad policies for all sectors of society, education-specific policies are created to address new possibilities and challenges within existing structure that take into consideration federal student privacy laws (Annuš, 2023).

Ordinarily, policies are guidelines that are used in very sector. A report by UNESCO (2023) explained that policy guidance elucidate the techniques used by generative AI and their repercussions for education and learning. It proposes key steps for governments to establish regulations and policy frameworks for their ethical use in all education sectors (Annuš, 2023). The report equally warned that multiplicative AI systems could worsen digital data divides and calls on policy makers to address this matter. Certainly, studies by Maslej, et al. (2023) had it that current ChatGPT models are trained on data from online users which reflect the values and prevailing social customs of the Global North (Annuš, 2023). Many standard initiatives are being developed around AI especially in education sector (Maslej, et al. (2023). In the policy world, according to Forman et al. (2023) the open letter calling for all AI laboratories to pause the training of AI systems more powerful than GPT-4, signed by tech experts and published in March 2023, seemed to precipitate the policy response (Annuš, 2023; Forman et al. 2023). This part of the policy, according to Pedró, Subosa, Rivas and Valverde (2019) made UNESCO to react by calling on its member states to adopt safeguards and ensure that AI is developed in accordance with ethical principles and respect to human rights as well (UNESCO, 2023).

In teaching and learning, the work of Maslej, et al. (2023) concerning AI in education, noted that the 2023 AI Index Report from the Stanford Institute for Human-Centered AI had documented notable acceleration of investment in AI as well as an increase of research on ethics, including issues of fairness and transparency. Additionally, Holmes and Porayska-Pomsta (2022); Maslej, et al. (2023) reported that ethics is increasing because problems are observed. The ethical problems will occur in education, too hence needs a policy guidance. The Holmes and Porayska-Pomsta (2022) report found a striking interest in 25 countries in the number of legislative proposals that specifically include AI. In the United States, multiple executive orders are focused on ensuring AI is trustworthy and equitable, and the White House Office of Science and Technology Policy has introduced a (Blueprint) that provided principles and practices that helped achieve this goal. These initiatives, according to Maslej, et al. (2023) came up with more policies along with other AI-related policy activities happening in both the executive and legislative branches in the government, would guide the use of AI throughout all sectors of society (Pedró et al. 2019). In Europe, the European Commission recently released similar policy to regulate the usage of AI in education sector, it was a safeguard for both users who are students and the implementer who are teachers and administrators as well while are in the institution (U.S. Department of Education 2023).

The implementation phase has not been free. Since policy implementation require funds, Chen et al. (2020) recommended that policymakers and practitioners are encouraged to propose a suitable strategy to allocate necessary resources so as to support future research and development of the application of AI technologies, particularly deep learning technologies in educational contexts (Maslej, et al. (2023). More effective policies are needed. As put forward by Regona, Yigitcanlar, Xia and Li (2022), education-focused AI policies at the federal, state, and district levels would be required to guide and empower local and individual decisions about which technologies to adopt and use in schools and classrooms (U.S. Department of Education 2023). This should consider what is happening in everyday lives. Many of educators use AI-enabled products because they are often better and more suitable for teaching. For instance, few people want to use paper maps anymore; people find that technology helps in planning the best route to a destination more efficiently and conveniently (Siemens & Long, 2011). In addition, people often do not realize how much privacy they are giving up when they accept AI-enabled systems into their lives hence a policy need. AI will bring privacy and other risks that are hard to address only via individual decision making; additional protections will be needed from a policy perspective (Regona et al. 2022).

According to Annuš (2023) a top policy priority must be establishing human in the loop as a requisite in educational applications, despite contrary pressures to use AI as an alternative to human decision making. On the other, hand, according to Regona et al. (2022) policies should not hinder, creativity, innovation and improvement, nor should they be burdensome to implement especially in schools. The work of Chen et al. (2020) added that society needs an education-focused AI policy that protects civil rights and encourages democratic values in the building, deployment, and governance of automated systems to be used across the many decentralized levels of the American educational system (U.S. Department of Education 2023).

Universally, it has been agreed as pointed out by Annuš (2023) that AI can be utilized to address specific learning encounters in schools and provide targeted interventions for students with diverse needs. This therefore, would contribute to a more inclusive educational landscape (Regona et al. (2022). Policymakers and educators consequently must cooperate to establish guidelines and frameworks that prioritize equity in the deployment of AI technologies in education especially in higher institutions of learning (Siemens & Long, 2011). Policies that regulate the use of AI should be in place. According to Holdren and Smith (2016) creating opportunity to convene an inter-agency panel to determine how AI technology should be coordinated and regulated at the federal level would alleviate some related challenges. The Federal Government must ensure consistent and appropriate policies and regulations for AI usage accordingly. With at least 16 different agencies currently governing sectors of the economy related to AI, uniformity may be difficult to achieve (U.S. Department of Education 2023). Despite these difficulties envisaged, Annuš (2023) reiterated that operational and proactive policies are invaluable for bringing sanity and harmony in learning institutions. Furthermore, these policies need to reviewed periodically depending on the changes and demands that come in use time to time {Holdren & Smith 2016).

RISKS OF AI EXPERIENCED IN TEACHING AND LEARNING

All aspects of life have risks. In education, AI has provided useful insights with related risks that come with it. According to Holmström and Hällgren (2021) AI has penetrated many organizational processes, resulting in a increasing fear that smart machines would soon replace many humans, especially teachers in schools (Gibson et al. 2023).. Furthermore, businesses that rely too much on AI systems also face the risk of collapse (Ye, Shuai, Jun & Shaohui, 2024). Ordinarily, AI has been designed to assist managers in making better judgments in teaching and learning. Another possible risks and fear as envisaged by Gibson et al. (2023) was that of over reliance on AI which would possibly lead to rigid management by leaders and educators. Additionally, Ye et al. (2024) postulated that since artificial intelligence is a machine, it has the potential of malfunction at some point, hence posses a risk. Although the probability of failure is very low, excessive reliance on it would hinder the organization and learning institutions from effectively handling emergency preparedness. Eventually, according to Gibson et al. (2023) contemporary AI is not yet fully integrated into the social environment which includes classroom teaching.

In order to alleviate certain risks in AI usage in education, the work of Holmström and Hällgren (2021) recommended that appropriate budget needs to be set aside because one of the risks for effective use of AI has been scarcity of money. It costs money to adapt various AI tools for various scenarios in learning (Jin et al. 2022). According to Arntz, Gregory and Zierahn (2016) the third generation of AI can break through the biological and social limitations of the creative vitality of teachers in colleges and universities.

Education opens up learners potential. A report by UNESCO (2023) on education, revealed that, given its function to protect as well as facilitate development and learning, education has a special obligation to be finely attuned to the risks of AI – both the known risks and those only just coming into view 'too often, education leaders are ignoring the risks' (Jin et al. 2022:11). Risks in AI come in different forms. In fact, in educational institutions and learning, little assessment exists of those risks. The work of Sagar (2020) posited that education community and stakeholders needs support in understanding them – and measures be put in place to better protect schools from the harms AI could cause. According to UNESCO (2023) many of the risks and harms of AI have been widely reported to the authorities concerned. The risk here was that educators include bias and discrimination as a result of training systems on historic datasets in the institutions. These are serious issues of risks that should give schools and governments good reason to question hyperbolic claims about AI (Arntz et al. 2016). in the sphere of learning, there are also more specific challenges facing education. Some of the challenges concerns the role of teachers and school administrators. As the AI optimists often claim that it won't replace teachers with automated instructors, the pitch has been that AI will save them time, reduce workload, and take on a range of routine tasks (Selwyn, 2017). The risk of mechanizing teaching is that AI will demand additional forms of labour. According to Jackson (2024) educators will be required to adapt their pedagogic approaches to work with automated technologies to aid their work in schools. As teachers might not be replaced by robots, but AI could robotize the role of the human teacher by doing their lesson planning, preparing materials, providing feedback to students, and assessing assignments in real time (UNESCO, 2023).

The work of Jackson (2024) pointed out that one critical consideration in the integration of AI in education was the potential impact on equity and inclusivity. While AI has the capability to personalise learning experiences, there is a risk of intensifying existing educational disparities if not enforced thoughtfully (Arntz et al. 2016). As privacy and confidentiality becomes a matter of concern, when AI systems collect and analyze sensitive student data, there has been a heightened risk of privacy breaches and unauthorized access (Floridi & Taddeo, 2016). By combining principles of fairness and transparency into the design and evaluation of AI algorithms in educational institutions, stakeholders can mitigate the risk of continuing societal biases within educational systems (UNESCO, 2023, Floridi & Taddeo, 2016).

SOLUTIONS AND RECOMMENDATIONS

A look at the future projection, several anticipated trends in AI and education are poised to shape the landscape of learning (Jackson 2024; Russel & Norvig, 2010). Continued advancements in natural language processing, machine learning, and adaptive algorithms are expected to enhance the potentiality of AI-driven educational tools (Russel & Norvig, 2010).

In using models incorporated with AI the work of Khosravi et al. (2022) suggested that the centre of the AI is a model. In the Learning carefulness is needed that models align to the learning which is envisioned that they are not too narrow. Now, based on the needs of teachers (as well as students and their families/caregivers), Jackson 2024 added another layer to the criteria for good AI models: the need for explain-ability (Khosravi, et al. 2022). A number of AI models can acknowledge patterns in the world and do the right action, but they cannot always explain why (Jackson 2024). For instance, how they arrived at the connection between the pattern and the action. This lack of explainability will not suffice for teaching (Russel & Norvig, 2010). This is because teachers would need to know how an AI model analyzed the work of one of their students and why the AI model suggested a particular tutorial, resource, or next step to the student (Baker et al. 2022).

The governments should provide more specialized training for AI usage. According to Holdren and Smith (2016) even private sector and academic stakeholders should have clear consensus that effectively governing AI and AI-related technologies requires a level of technical expertise. Numerous public and private organizations and institutions have recommended increasing expertise.

Additionally, Stanford University's One Hundred Year Study of Artificial Intelligence (AI100) recommended that policy makers "define a path toward accruing technical expertise in AI at all levels of government (Baker et al. 2022:14). in this regard, effective governance of AI usage requires more experts who understand and can analyze the interactions between AI technologies, programmatic objectives, and overall societal values effectively (U.S. Department of Education 2023).

FUTURE RESEARCH

The impact and influence of AI and automation both in education and industry should be checked carefully. This has been because AI is currently shifting computing beyond conventional educational technology. In teacher training institutions, more emphasis should be put in AI technology and how it is evolving with time (Maslej, et al. 2023). Since AI is providing access from instructional resources in teaching to automating decisions about instruction and other educational processes, according to UNESCO (2023) clear and current pragmatic policies need to be put in place for any eventuality. More studies on the teachers' level of AI and teaching automation should be done to alleviate the situation so as to meet the Education for Sustainable Development (ESD) goals for quality teaching and Learning in the modern times.

CONCLUSION

Education managers should not ignore the risks and limitations of using AI tools, they still should regard AI as one of their employees and avoid relying on AI to draw conclusions. Educationists must consider more human and social factors when making the final educational choice. This study offers cardinal materials to better understand of fundamental issues in AI which will be beneficial to AI Education practitioners and scholars. This study helps scholars recognize important institutions and countries plus regions that have made significant contributions to AI education research for further collaborations or scientific exchanges. Governments, should budget for more funds to cater for the use of AI in education and automation in teaching and learning.

REFERENCES

Annuš, N. (2023). Chatbots in Education: The impact of Artificial Intelligence based ChatGPT on Teachers and Students. *International Journal of Advanced Natural Sciences and Engineering Researches*, 7(4), 366–370. DOI: 10.59287/ijanser.739

Annuš, N. (2024). Education in the Age of Artificial Intelligence. *TEM Journal. 13(1) 404-413*, ISSN 2217-8309, DOI: DOI: 10.18421/TEM131-42

Anyoha, R. (2017). *The History of Artificial Intelligence.* [Online] Available at: https://sitn.hms.harvard.edu/flash/2017/history-artificial-intelligence/

Arbesman, S. (2013). *The half-life of facts: Why everything we know has an expiration date*. Penguin.

Arntz, M., Gregory, T., & Zierahn, U. (2016), *The Risk of Automation for Jobs in OECD Countries: A Comparative Analysis.* OECD Social, Employment and Migration Working Papers, No. 189, OECD Publishing, Paris.

Baker, R. S., Esbenshade, L., Vitale, J., & Karumbaiah, S. (2022). Using demographic data as predictor variables: A questionable choice. https://doi.org/DOI: 10.35542/osf.io/y4wvj

Barnett, S. M., & Ceci, S. J. (2002). When and Where Do We Apply What We Learn? A Taxonomy for Far Transfer. *Review of Research in Education*, 24, 61–100.

Bialik, M., & Fadel, C. (2015). *Meta-Learning for the 21st Century: What Should Students Learn?* Center for Curriculum Redesign.

Boyle, B. (2017). Virtual Reality and Augmented Reality in Education. Retrieved from https://www.westpoint.edu/sites/default/files/inlineimages/centers_research/center_for_teching excellence/PDFs/mtp_project_papers/Boyle s_17.pdf

Brown, J. S., Collins, A., & Duguid, P. (1989). Situated Cognition and the Culture of Learning. *Educational Researcher*, 18(1), 32–42. DOI: 10.3102/0013189X018001032

Chan, K. S., & Nabil, Z. (2019). Applications and Challenges of Implementing Artificial Intelligence in Medical Education: Integrative. *JMIR Medical Education*, 5(1), e13930. https://preprints.jmir.org/preprint/13930. DOI: 10.2196/13930

Chen, X., Xie, H., Zou, D., & Hwang, G. (2020). Application and theory gaps during the rise of Artificial Intelligence in Education. *Computers and Education: Artificial Intelligence*, 1, 100002. DOI: 10.1016/j.caeai.2020.100002

Cimpian, A., & Salomon, E. (2014). The inherence heuristic: An intuitive means of making sense of the world, and a potential precursor to psychological essentialism. *Behavioral and Brain Sciences*, 37(5), 461–480. DOI: 10.1017/S0140525X13002197

Cleveland, B. W. (2011). Engaging Spaces: Innovative Learning Environments, Pedagogies, and Student Engagement in the Middle Years of School. In *Unpublished Ph.D. Thesis*. Faculty of Architecture, Building and Planning, the University of Melbourne., https://pdfs.semanticscholar.org/e602

Dawson, S., Poquet, O., Colvin, C., Rogers, T., Pardo, A., & Gasevic, D. (2018). *Rethinking learning analytics adoption through complexity leadership theory*. ACM., DOI: 10.1145/3170358.3170375

Delen, D. (2010). A comparative analysis of machine learning techniques for student retention management. *Decision Support Systems*, 49(4), 498–506. DOI: 10.1016/j.dss.2010.06.003

Dirican, C. (2015). The impacts of robotics, artificial intelligence on business and economics. *Procedia: Social and Behavioral Sciences*, 195, 564–573. DOI: 10.1016/j.sbspro.2015.06.134

Egozi, O., Markovitch, S., & Gabrilovich, E. (2011). Concept-based information retrieval using explicit semantic analysis. [TOIS]. *ACM Transactions on Information Systems*, 29(2), 1–34. DOI: 10.1145/1961209.1961211

Englebart, D. C. (1962). Augmenting human intellect: A conceptual framework. SRI Summary Report AFOSR3223. https://www.dougengelbart.org/pubs/augment-3906.htm

Floridi, L., & Taddeo, M. (2016). What is Data Ethics? *Philosophical Transactions. Series A, Mathematical, Physical, and Engineering Sciences*, 374(2083), 20160360. DOI: 10.1098/rsta.2016.0360

Forman, N., Udvaros, J., & Avornicului, M. S. (2023). ChatGPT: A new study tool shaping the future for high school students. *International Journal of Advanced Natural Sciences and Engineering Researches*, 7(4), 95–102. DOI: 10.59287/ijanser.562

Friedman, L., Blair Black, N., Walker, E., & Roschelle, J. (2021). *Safe AI in education needs you.* Association of Computing Machinery blog, https://cacm.acm.org/blogs/blog-cacm/256657-safe-ai-in-education-needs-you/fulltext

Gao, J., Galley, M., Li, L., Brain, G., Brockett, C., Celikyilmaz, A., Cheng, Y., Dolan, B., Fung, P., Gan, Z., Lee, S., Li, J., Li, X., Liu, B., Madotto, A., Majumder, R., Papangelis, A., Pietquin, O., Quirk, C., … Zhang, Y. (2018). Neural approaches to conversational AI question answering, task-oriented dialogues and social chatbots. *ArXiv.Org*.

García, P., Amandi, A., Schiaffino, S., & Campo, M. (2007). Evaluating Bayesian networks' precision for detecting students' learning styles. *Computers & Education*, 49(3), 794–808. DOI: 10.1016/j.compedu.2005.11.017

García, P., Schiaffino, S., & Amandi, A. (2008). An enhanced Bayesian model to detect students' learning styles in Web-based courses. *Journal of Computer Assisted Learning*, 24(4), 305–315. DOI: 10.1111/j.1365-2729.2007.00262.x

Gibson, D., Kovanovic, V., Ifenthaler, D. Dexter, S. & Feng, S. (2023). Learning theories for artificial intelligence promoting learning processes DOI: 10.1111/bjet.13341

Göksel, N., & Bozkurt, A. (2019). Artificial Intelligence in Education: Current Insights and Future Perspectives. In Sisman-Ugur, S., & Kurubacak, G. (Eds.), *Handbook of Research on Learning in the Age of Trans humanism* (pp. 224–236). IGI Global. DOI: 10.4018/978-1-5225-8431-5.ch014

Hallinger, P., & Chatpinyakoop, C. (2019). A bibliometric review of research on higher education for sustainable development, 1998–2018. *Sustainability (Basel)*, 11(8), 2401. DOI: 10.3390/su11082401

Holdren, I., & Smith, M. (2016). "Preparing for the Future of Artificial Intelligence," Executive Office of the President, National Science and Technology Council, 2016. https://www.whitehouse.gov/sites/default/files/whitehouse_files/microsites/ostp/NSTC/preparing_for_th e_future_of_ai.pdf

Holmes, W., & Porayska-Pomsta, K. (Eds.). (2022). *The ethics of artificial intelligence in education*. Rutledge. ISBN 978- 0367349721 DOI: 10.4324/9780429329067

Holmström, J., & Hällgren, M. (2021). AI management beyond the hype: Exploring the co-constitution of AI and organizational context. *AI & Society*, •••, 1–11.

Host, A. 2021. *Amount of information globally* 2010-2024. [Online] Available at: https://www.statista.com/statistics/871513/worldwidedatacreated/#:~:text=Amount%20of%20information%20globally%202010%2D2024&text=The%20total%20amount%20of%20data,ever%2Dgrowing%20global%20data%20sphere

Ifenthaler, D., Masduki, I., & Seel, N. M. (2011). The mystery of cognitive structure and how we can detect it: Tracking the development of cognitive structures over time. *Instructional Science*, 39(1), 41–61. DOI: 10.1007/s11251-009-9097-6

Jackson, E. A. (2024). *The Evolution of Artificial Intelligence: A Theoretical Review of its Impact on Teaching and Learning in the Digital Age*, ZBW – Leibniz Information Centre for Economics, Kiel, Hamburg https://hdl.handle.net/10419/280893

Jaspars, J. M., & Hilton, D. J. (1988). Mental models of causal reasoning. In *The social psychology of knowledge* (pp. 335–358). Cambridge University Press.

Jin, X., Gao, Q., & Yin, J. (2022). Research on Teaching Paradigm Reform of "Student Development as the Center" under the Background of New Liberal Arts [J]. *The Economist*, 2 (2): 186.

Khosravi, H., Shum, S. B., Chen, G., Conati, C., Tsai, Y.-S., Kay, J., Knight, S., Martinez-Maldonado, R., Sadiq, S., & Gašević, D. (2022). Explainable artificial intelligence in education. *Computers and Education: Artificial Intelligence*, 3, 100074. Advance online publication. DOI: 10.1016/j.caeai.2022.100074

Kozulin, A. (2003). *Vygotsky's Educational Theory in Cultural Context*. Cambridge University Press. [ed] DOI: 10.1017/CBO9780511840975

Lave, J., & Wenger, E. (1991). *Situated Learning: Legitimate Peripheral Participation*. Cambridge University Press., DOI: 10.1017/CBO9780511815355

Lilja, M. (2018). *Automatic Essay Scoring of Swedish Essays using Neural Networks*. Uppsala University.

Majed, S. (2019). The role of leadership soft skills in promoting the learning entrepreneurship. *Journal of Process Management.Nuclear Technology*, 7(1), 31–48.

Maslej, N., Fattorini, L., Brynjolfsson, E., Etchemendy, J., Ligett, K., Lyons, T., Manyika, J., Ngo, H., Niebles, J. C., Parli, V., Shoham, Y., Wald, R., Clark, J., & Perrault, R. (2023). *The AI index 2023 annual report. Stanford University: AI Index Steering Committee*. Institute for Human-Centered AI.

Maya, B., & Charles, F. (2018). Knowledge for the Age of Artificial Intelligence: What Should Students Learn? Center for Curriculum Redesign. https://curriculumredesign.org/wp-content/uploads/CCR-Meta-Learning-FINAL-Nov.-17-2018.pdf

Miailhe, N., & Hodes, C. (2017). The Third Age of Artificial Intelligence. *Field Actions Science Reports*, •••, 6–11.

Miller, T. (2017). Explanation in Artificial Intelligence: Insights from the Social Sciences. DOI: https://www.researchgate.net/publication/317821828DOI: 10.1016/j.artint.2018.07.007

Mills, N. (2013). Situated Learning through Social Networking Communities: The Development of Joint Enterprise, Mutual Engagement, and a Shared Repertoire. *CALICO Journal*, 28(2), 345–368. DOI: 10.11139/cj.28.2.345-368

Motteram, G. (2013). *Innovations in Learning Technologies for English Language Teaching*. British Council. Available online also at. [ed], https://www.teachingenglish.org.uk/sites/teacheng/files/C607

Muldner, K., Burleson, W., Van de Sande, B., & VanLehn, K. (2011). An analysis of students' gaming behaviors in an intelligent tutoring system: Predictors and impacts. *User Modeling and User-Adapted Interaction*, 21(1–2), 99–135. DOI: 10.1007/s11257-010-9086-0

Panigrahi, A., & Joshi, V. (2020). Use of Artificial Intelligence in Education. *The Management Accountant Journal*, 55(5), 64–67. DOI: 10.33516/maj.v55i5.64-67p

Pedró, F., Subosa, M., Rivas, A., & Valverde, P. (2019). *Artificial intelligence in education: challenges and opportunities for sustainable development*. UNESCO.

Pradipta, K. D. (1999). *Artificial Intelligence Lecture Notes for Bachelor of Technology in Computer Science and Engineering & Information Technology Department of Computer Science and Engineering & Information Technology*. Veer Surendra Sai University of Technology Burla.

Prashanta, K. P. (2020). *Lecture Notes on Artificial Intelligence*. College of Engineering and Technology.

Regona, M., Yigitcanlar, T., Xia, B., & Li, R. Y. M. (2022). Opportunities and adoption challenges of AI in the construction industry: A PRISMA review. *Journal of Open Innovation*, 8(45), 45. Advance online publication. DOI: 10.3390/joitmc8010045

Roschelle, J., & Teasley, S. (1995). The construction of shared knowledge in collaborative problem-solving. In O'Malley, C. (Ed.), *Computer-supported collaborative learning* (pp. 69–97). Springer-Verlag. DOI: 10.1007/978-3-642-85098-1_5

Russel, S., & Norvig, P. (2010). *Artificial Intelligence: A Modern Approach*. Prentice Hall.

Sagar, R. (2020). Open-AI *releases GPT-3, the largest model so far*. Analytics India Magazine. https://analyticsindiamag.com/open-ai-gpt-3-language-modelv/

Schoenfeld, A. H. (2013). "Reflections on Problem Solving Theory and Practice" in *The Mathematics Enthusiast*, 10(1) Article 3. Available online also at: https://scholarworks.umt.edu/tme/vol10/iss1/3

Shaltry, C. (2013). "Situated Learning with Online Portfolios, Classroom Websites, and Facebook" in *Tech Trends*, 57(3). doi: , N. (2017). *Education and Technology: Key Issues and Debates*. Bloomsbury Publishing.DOI: 10.1007/s11528-013-0658-9.Selwyn

Siemens, G. (2005). Connectivism: A Learning Theory for the Digital Age. *International Journal of Instructional Technology and Distance Learning*, 2(1), 3–1.

Siemens, G., & Long, P. (2011). Penetrating the Fog: Analytics in Learning and Education. *EDUCAUSE Review*, 46(5), 30–32.

Simonton, D. K. (2000). Creative Development as Acquired Expertise: Theoretical Issues and an Empirical Test. *Developmental Review*, 20(2), 283–318. DOI: 10.1006/drev.1999.0504

Somar, A., & Jianwei, L. (2021). Impact of Artificial Intelligence on Management and Leadership in Research & Developmen. A Case Study of Thermo Fisher Scientific. Karlskrona Sweden

Subirana, B., Bagiati, A., & Sarma, S. (2017). On the Forgetting of College Academics. *Ebbinghaus Speed*, (68), 1–12.

Tan, D.-P., Ji, S.-M., & Jin, M.-S. (2012). Intelligent computer-aided instruction modeling and a method to optimize study strategies for parallel robot instruction. *IEEE Transactions on Education*, 56(3), 268–273. DOI: 10.1109/TE.2012.2212707

Terstegen, S., Lennings, F., Suchy, O., Schalter, K., & Suarsana, D. (2018). *Leistung & Entgelt Arbeits- und Betriebsorganisation kompakt - Künstliche Intelligenz in der Arbeitswelt der Zukunft – Ansichten und Standpunkte*. Joh. Heider Verlag GmbH.

Tran, B. X., Latkin, C. A., Vu, G. T., Nguyen, H. L. T., Nghiem, S., Tan, M.-X., Lim, Z.-K., Ho, C. S. H., & Ho, R. C. M. (2019). The current research landscape of the application of artificial intelligence in managing cerebrovascular and heart diseases: A bibliometric and content analysis. *International Journal of Environmental Research and Public Health*, 16(15), 2699. DOI: 10.3390/ijerph16152699

Tsai, Y.-S., Poquet, S., Gašević, D., Dawson, S., & Pardo, A. (2019). Complexity leadership in learning analytics: Drivers, challenges, and opportunities. *British Journal of Educational Technology*, 50(6), 2839–2854. DOI: 10.1111/bjet.12846

UNESCO (2023). Education in the age of artificial intelligence. UNESCO Courier, 7 place de Fontenoy, 75352 Paris 07 SP, France UNESCO 2023.

U.S. Department of Education, Office of Educational Technology. (2023). *Artificial Intelligence and Future of Teaching and Learning: Insights and Recommendations*, Washington, DC, 2023. https://tech.ed.gov

Walton Family Foundation. (2023). Teachers and students embrace ChatGPT for education. https://www.waltonfamilyfoundation.org/learning/teachers-and-students-embrace-chatgpt-for-education

Wang, D., Ma, X., & Wang, A. Y. (2021). *Human-centered AI for data science: A systematic approach.* http://arxiv.org/abs/2110.01108

White House Office of Science and Technology Policy. (October 2022), *Blueprint for an AI bill of rights: Making automated systems work for the American people.* The White House Office of Science and Technology Policy. https://www.whitehouse.gov/ostp/ai-bill-of-rights/

Xiong, W. (2023). AI and Leadership New Changes of Leadership Under the Development of Artificial Intelligence Business School, The University of Hong Kong, Pokfulam, Hong Kong 999077, China wenjinxiong1998@163.com C. F. Peng et al. (Eds.): MMET 2022, ASSEHR 703, pp. 497–503, 2023. https://doi.org/DOI: 10.2991/978-2-494069-51-0_69

Xu, W., Dainoff, M. J., Ge, L., & Gao, Z. (2022). Transitioning to human interaction with AI systems: New challenges and opportunities for HCI professionals to enable human centered AI. *International Journal of Human-Computer Interaction*, 1(25). Advance online publication. DOI: 10.1080/10447318.2022.2041900

Yambo, J. M. O. (2012). *Determinants of KCSE Examination Performance in SDA Sponsored Schools: A Key to Academic Promotion to the next Level of Learning.* Lambert Academic Publishing.

Yambo, J. M. O. (2023). Dynamics of Teaching in the Era of Climate Change Education. In Sagini, J. K., & Nyatuka, B. O. (Eds.), *Handbook of Research on Climate Change Education for Sustainable Development.* IGI Global., Available at https://www.igiglobal.com/book/handbook-research-climate-change-culture-, DOI: 10.4018/978-1-6684-9099-0.ch013

Yannick, P., Tim, J., & Sven, H. (2022). Artificial Intelligence and its Impact on Leaders and Leadership. 3rd International Conference on Industry 4.0 and Smart Manufacturing www.sciencedirect.com*Procedia Computer Science*www.elsevier.com/locate/procedia

Ye, L., Shuai, W., Jun, L., & Shaohui, Q. (2024). The Innovative Path of Intelligent Teaching in the Age of Artificial Intelligence ICAIE 2023. *AHCS*, 15, 116–124. DOI: 10.2991/978-94-6463-242-2_15

Zacamy, J., & Roschelle, J. (2022). Navigating the tensions: How could equity-relevant research also be agile, open, and scalable? Digital Promise. http://hdl.handle.net/20.500.12265/159

ADDITIONAL READING

Akgun, S., & Greenhow, C. (2022). Artificial intelligence in education: Addressing ethical challenges in K-12 settings. *AI and Ethics*, 2(3), 431–440. DOI: 10.1007/s43681-021-00096-7

Dieterle, E., Dede, C., & Walker, M. (2022). The cyclical ethical effects of using artificial intelligence in education. *AI & Society*. https://link.springer.com/article/10.1007/s00146-022-01497-w Gardner, J., O'Leary, M. & Yuan, L. (2021). Artificial intelligence in educational assessment: "Breakthrough? Or buncombe and ballyhoo?" *Journal of Computer Assisted Learning*, 37(5), 1207–1216. https://doi.org/DOI: 10.1111/jcal.12577

Gray, C. C., & Perkins, D. (2019). Utilizing early engagement and machine learning to predict student outcomes. *Computers & Education*, 131, 22–32. DOI: 10.1016/j.compedu.2018.12.006

Jones, W. A. (2018). Artificial Intelligence And Leadership: A Few Thoughts, A Few Questions. *Journal of Leadership Studies*, 12(3), 60–62. DOI: 10.1002/jls.21597

Kasztelnik, K., & Delanoy, N. (2020). Social Media Utilization with Data Analytics to Support Financial Management Decisions in Canada. SSRN *Electronic Journal*. https://doi.org/DOI: 10. 2139/ssrn.3852321

Kolbjørnsrud, V., Amico, R., & Thomas, R. J. (2016). How artificial intelligence will redefine management. *Harvard Business Review*, 2, 1–6.

Wang, Y. (2021). Artificial intelligence in educational leadership: A symbiotic role of human-artificial intelligence decision-making. *Journal of Educational Administration*, 42(3), 1–31. DOI: 10.1108/JEA-10-2020-0216

Xia, L. (2022). Research on the impact of artificial intelligence on enterprise human resource management. *Enterprise Reform and Management*, 03, 67–69.

KEY TERMS AND DEFINITION

Artificial: That which is made by human beings rather than naturally made. More synthetic and made in imitation of something natural

Artificial intelligence: Artificial Intelligence (AI) is study on hoe to make computers do things that mind can do. This includes many things that are not naturally thought of as intelligent such as moving without bumping into obstacles or gaining information about an environment through vision

AI Techniques: Depict how we represent, manipulate and reason with knowledge in order to solve problems. Knowledge is a collection of 'facts'. To manipulate these facts by a program, a suitable way.

Automated Learning: Automated learning is the process of automating the tasks of applying machine learning to real-world problems. It is the combination of automation and machine learning automated machine learning potentially includes every stage from beginning with a raw dateset to building a machine learning model ready for deployment for work.

Intelligence;: Being mentally able especially to higher developed degree. Having ability to think and understand things clearly and logically . ability to learn facts and skills and apply them.

Policy: Policy is a deliberate system of guidelines to guide decisions and achieve rational outcomes. A policy is a statement of intent and is implemented as a procedure or protocol. Policies are generally adopted by a governance body within an organization.

Teaching and learning facilities: Means all materials designed, built, or installed in support of teaching and learning process

Chapter 3
Artificial Intelligence: Ethics and Academic Integrity in Higher Education

Henry Nyabuto Onderi
Jaramogi Oginga Odinga University of Science and Technology, Kenya

ABSTRACT

This chapter discusses the evolving Artificial Intelligence (AI) landscape in Higher Education. AI is the new development that affect pedagogy and learning outcomes in higher education. This chapter examines AI as a key component in the delivery of curriculum. It aims to guide institutions of higher learning to adjust to fit into possible changes and not be swayed by AI wave that has gathered momentum globally. The institutions of higher learning should prepare stakeholders of a future that will require shrunk office spaces. Further, there is need for adoption and use of such technologies within the confines of known rules and regulations that ensure zero compromise on quality of teaching, learning, learning outcomes and productivity.

INTRODUCTION

The fact that the world is fast experiencing technological advancement cannot be gainsaid. Countries such as China and the United States are leading the pack in this front. The rapid advancement of technology is heavily impacting on higher education globally (Cerviño, & Vera, 2020).

Access to information, study and reference materials is now easier than ever before. At the same time, delivery of lectures in higher institutions of learning can now be done easily from virtually any part of the globe so long as requisite infrastructure is available to users. In most parts of Africa, this reality became clearer during the

DOI: 10.4018/979-8-3373-0025-2.ch003

Covid-19 pandemic. Some institutions were able to conduct teaching and examine learners virtually (Maphosa, & Maphosa, 2023).

One of the major highlights of technological advancement is the advent and continuous improvement of computers. Such devices now include desktop computers, laptops, tablets and smartphones. Using these devices and with the aid of the Internet, one is able to be linked to others (be they students or lecturers) wherever they are.

Experts in the technology space continue to make discoveries. This implies that the technology train has already left the station and only those who accept and adapt will cope with the ever-changing information generation, access, dissemination and consumption.

Currently, one of the major conversations in institutions of higher learning revolves around Artificial Intelligence (AI) and its use thereof in pedagogy, tackling assignments and undertaking examinations (Fitria, 2021). This conversation is characterized with questions that touch on ethics and integrity in education. This even as the technology train continues to roll, and the world could be gravitating towards technologies that may be superior to AI.

There is no denying that technology, be it in form of hardware or software is intended to make work easier for human beings. AI is taking its space in enabling computers and machines simulate human intelligence and problem solving capabilities. AI can perform tasks that would otherwise fully require human intelligence or intervention.

Generative AI such Generative-Pre-trained Transformer (ChatGTP), are gaining popularity amongst students. This poses a question on its validity to produce highly competitive and dependable human labour for the future, or if that future will dominantly be driven by AI (Kavlakoglu, Stryker (2024).

Despite AI's world-bending abilities, machines still inferior to the human mind on a host of tasks. Even algorithms built to replicate the function of the human brain – known as neural networks – are relatively unsophisticated compared to the inner workings of our minds (BBC, 2024).

While some institutions of higher on the globe have embraced AI and gone ahead to formulate policies, rules and regulations that govern the use of AI, others are waking up to this reality that they have no option other than adopt and adapt to the new world trend. There are mixed feelings surrounding the use of AI, with concerns that the technology may give users undue advantage over nonusers. This tilts the academic playground in favour of AI users.

The emerging academic landscape in institutions of higher learning cannot overlook the fact that AI is a major factor in delivery of content, taking of class assignments and examinations, and any other possible forms of manipulation that can be undertaken by aid of AI. Not at a time when most AI photo generation, video manipulation and text generator applications are available.

Amidst this AI invasion of issues regarding ethics and integrity of study, research and learning processes, there is need for measures that will guarantee quality of graduates from institutions of higher learning. There is need to understand and appreciate if AI can enhance gamified learning which can make learning more enjoyable, engaging and rewarding, and at the same time guide educators to use of more interactive pedagogical approaches that may precipitate better engagement with learners and achieve remarkable outcomes, within the dictates and confines of higher education as the arena for producing top cream experts for the world.

Additionally, it is imperative to appreciate that AI has a huge bearing on the future of work, with most employers having the luxury of embracing remote working, and university graduates immersing themselves into self-employment, which they can do from the comfort of their homes. Furthermore, institutions of higher learning should prepare their learners and the outside world of a future that will require shrunk office spaces as they known today.

It is therefore critical for actors in the higher institutions of learning environments to not only be ready to accept change but be part of it. They should be at the centre in the formulation of guidelines, rules and policies that govern the use of AI in their institutions. The formulation of those guidelines, rules and policies should be aligned to the constitution, the University Statutes, vision and mission, among other relevant documents.

AI is arguably the main driver of emerging technologies like robotics and big data. Generative AI such as ChatGTP continues to expand the popularity of AI to the extent that no institution of higher learning worth its salt can risk sweeping the idea whose time has come under the carpet (Nah, et al, 2023).

Using own experience and undertaking library research and interviews, the author seeks to delve into this topic with a view of making a contribution towards guiding institutions of higher learning adjust themselves accordingly and not be overtaken or swayed by the AI wave that has already gathered momentum in the world. There is more to gain than to lose when such technologies are adopted and put into use within the confines or known rules and regulations that ensure zero compromise on quality of teaching, learning, learning outcomes and productivity.

BACKGROUND

The development of Artificial Intelligence (AI) has caused a raft of changes in the teaching, learning, assessment and research in higher education. In a study conducted by Moya et al., (2024), that focused on what is known about academic integrity and AI in higher education, the results showed bounded and unbounded ethical implications of AI. The researchers looked at areas such as AI for cheating;

AI as legitimate support; an equity, diversity, and inclusion lens into AI; and emerging recommendations to tackle AI implications in higher education. This chapter seeks to unbundle diverse AI issues affecting higher education, which among others include teaching and learning outcomes, assessment and research. This chapter is an outcome of a library research which discloses that AI can assist in teaching, learning and research despite the ethical and integrity challenges that ought to be surmounted through formulation of policies and guidelines regarding the use of AI use in higher education. Further, the AI landscape is fast evolving and there is need for appropriate policies guidelines in the use of AI in higher education.

Issues/ Controversies

The advent of several forms of AI attracts divided opinion, whether it is an aider of human mind or its replacement. For instance, generative AI such as ChatGTP deliver assignments in a matter of seconds once commanded. Such assignments may take an individual several hours or days to execute. While this may appear to be a fantastic idea, it also possess questions on the place of the human mind and how one's abilities can be assessed/evaluated. Ideally one may hand in an assignment without understanding anything about it since AI did it for him. In light of this, ethical and integrity issues emerge on the kind of graduates that institutions of learning produce and how suitable they would be after studies. AI poses a threat to the book industry, research and access to information to strategic installations and information, to the possible detriment of a nation's security. It is also to a blow to critical thinking and negates creativity as individuals may find it strenuous and unnecessary to critically think, analyze and provide solutions to critical issues affecting the human race.

AI in Administration of Higher Institutions of Learning

As technology advances, the author opines that AI can be used to automate administrative processes, personalizing instruction and predicting academic trends. Institutions of higher learning can use AI in various ways as shown in table 1 below:

Table 1. Use of AI in administration<Tbl_Large></Tbl_Large>

Use	Explanation
Academic data analysis	AI can be applied in various aspects of education such as grades, attendance, standardized test scores and feedback
Personalized teaching	AI makes it possible to personalize teaching and meet the unique and varied needs of each learner.

continued on following page

Table 1. Continued

Use	Explanation
Safety and disaster preparedness	Installation of AI infrastructure such as Closed Circuit Television (CCTV), automated sirens and lighting systems can enhance security in higher institutions of learning.
Financial management	AI use in financial management optimizes administrative processes and identifies opportunities for efficient use of budgets.
Communicating with parents	AI-powered chatbots answer parents' questions, and can schedule meetings, or send reminders about upcoming events and provide updates about the learner's performance.
Timetable optimization	Use of AI in the institutional schedule can be done efficiently and without the need of human intervention. AI takes into account various factors such as teacher preferences; room availability and student needs, and can analyze historical academic performance data.
Logistics mainstreaming	AI can be used to mainstream transport, stores, procurement and other forms of logistics in an institution of higher learning.
Decision making	AI can be used to arrive at worthwhile decisions the institutional administration and management teams for efficiency and effectiveness.
Learner management	AI can be used to monitor attendance, learner attitude and behavior in higher institutions of learning.

Source: Author, 2024

AI as a Teaching and Learning Tool

Institutions of higher learning are investing in AI as a tool of teaching and learning processes. AI can be an innovative learning tool, helping learners improve their writing or study more effectively (Gibony, 2023). Learners can use AI to:

Generate Ideas or Creativity.

Explore how to frame ideas when struggling with outlining information.

Create a formative assessment.

Generate practice questions from the topic.

Practice speech skills for a persuasive argument.

Create study plans.

Assist with note-taking strategies.

Practice providing feedback or education to others that is appropriate and leveled to the intended audience.

Decongest physical classrooms and other teaching and learning spaces. It also enhances and promotes health and safety protocols.

In the author's view, teachers who use AI tools are more likely to have lesser workload on their desk. They are also likely to become popular with students since the technology aids them to deliver content with much ease compared to manual teaching.

In Seven (7) Tools that Help Teachers Work More Effectively, Poth (2013) avers that the benefits of using AI tools in teaching include:

i. Personalized learning: Educators can provide tailored learning experience based on AI-driven analytics that provide valuable insights into learner performance and learning trends. Using this data, AI can instantly adapt leaner learning materials. Educators can then use the information to provide personalized learning experiences, adapting to each learner's strengths, weaknesses and learning pace.

ii. Productivity and efficiency: Educators are responsible for a variety of clerical tasks such as communicating with learners and their families, grading assignments and providing feedback. AI tools can help them to streamline these tasks so that they can have more time for their core mandate, teaching.

iii. Creating and supplementing content: Teachers can use AI to curate a range of educational resources. They can create lessons, activities, assignments, prompts for discussion, and presentations using generative AI tools.

AI in Policies

AI are the technologies that enable machines to act with higher levels of intelligence and emulate human capabilities to sense, comprehend, and act, which are augmented by the ability to learn from experience and adapt over time, according to Kictanet (2013).

It is worth noting that there has been an unprecedented technological innovation on AI driven by increased access to digitised data, unlimited access to computing power, low cost of cloud data storage, and access to internet connectivity.

The rapid pace of development in AI has continued to be dogged by calls for its regulation. There is widespread consensus regarding the possible impact of unregulated AI. This is why governments globally have responded through policymaking to mitigate this risk, *Suleiman, et al., (2024).*

There has been a growing concern in institutions of higher learning regarding the use of text generative AI such as ChatGTP and Bing. Another popular generative AI is Co-Pilot which is integrated within the Microsoft Office suite.

In the author's view, one of the main concerns is that learners may use the AI tools to cheat or plagiarize their written assignments and exams. This, in the immediate and long term may affect the quality of leaners produced by institutions of higher learning that do not regulate the use of AI tools by their learners.

According to a survey of university students by Intelligent.com (2023), nearly one in three students in the US had used a form of AI, such as essay-generating software, to complete their coursework. About one-third of college students surveyed (in a sample size 1000) in the US have utilized the AI chatbot such as ChatGPT to complete written homework assignments, with 60% using the programme on more than half of their assignments.

Some AI tools such as ChapGTP, which are downloadable on gadgets such as mobile phones, laptops and desktops, are capable of imitating human writing. A trial on this app by the author reveals that it offers answers almost real time once given a command. For this reason, some learners may use the tool to do assignments/ tests and hand them in for marking.

It is worth noting that gadgets such as laptops and smartphones are basic requirements for a college/ university learner. These are personal gadgets whose use is difficult to regulate. While some institutions of higher learning have prohibited those gadgets in examination rooms, it is almost impossible to restrict their use during take-away assignments.

During the Covid-19 pandemic, some institutions of higher learning made an attempt to proctor examinations that were done online. This, according to the author, posed a logistical nightmare, with concerns on the credibility and water tightness of such exams to deter malpractice emerging. This is why there are calls for stricter regulations and penalties for academic misconduct involving AI.

Apart from compromising the credibility of tests and assignments, the use of generative AI may lead to a decline in students' writing and critical thinking skills. They become more reliant on automated tools to complete their work Civil, 2023; Warschauer et al., 2023).This, in the author's view, could have a negative impact on the quality of education and harm the students' learning outcomes in the long-term.

Despite the concerns discussed above, it is imperative to appreciate that AI has the potential to revolutionize education. It can enhance the learning experience for learners, by among others, providing a personalized feedback and support to learners, helping them to identify areas of weakness and improve their skills in an adaptive manner. This, in the author's view, calls for universities to come up with policies that can govern, and not abolish AI in its entirety.

AI in Research, Innovation and Development

AI has provided useful tools for research and development. The technology offers multi-faceted, enriching fundamental research methodologies and accelerating product development cycles (Delfino, 2023).

In the author's opinion, AI tools for research are a blessing for researchers based in institutions of higher learning. Research is now easier than ever before due to this interesting turn in the technology space. AI tools for research can help the researcher to discover new sources for literature review or research assignment. These tools will synthesize information from large databases of scholarly output with the aim of finding the most relevant articles and saving researchers' time.

The secret behind the emerging transformation in research and innovation lies in AI's ability to enhance decision-making processes. It is able to make pattern recognition, predictive analytics, and process data. This allows for the rapid identification and resolution of complex problems. The outcome thereof is increased speed of innovation.

The issue of AI in research, innovation and development can also be examined in terms of accuracy. Indeed, most AI tools, just like many other technological innovations such as calculators are more accurate than the human mind since they are automated. Therefore, AI driven research and development contributes significantly to error reduction.

It should be appreciated that human and AI knowledge acquisition methods are not adversaries but complementary players. AI's speed and scale offer unparalleled potential, while human critical thinking and nuanced understanding are essential for interpretation and ethical contemplation (Washington, 2023).

Table 2 shows a comparison between human and AI knowledge acquisition methods:

Table 2. Comparison between human and AI knowledge acquisition methods<Tbl_Large></Tbl_Large>

Parameter	Human knowledge acquisition method	AI knowledge acquisition method
Size	Access is slower and more selective, offering a personal touch.	It can process vast amounts of data, including texts, images, and codes faster.
Efficacy	May take longer, punctuated by the need for sleep, coffee breaks, and existential crises.	Its algorithms can process data faster, and learning and adapting happens on the go.
Understanding	Driven by critical thinking and empathy, can analyze information, weigh evidence, and construct complex interpretations.	Recognizes patterns, identifies correlations, and accurately predicts outcomes.

continued on following page

Table 2. Continued

Parameter	Human knowledge acquisition method	AI knowledge acquisition method
Attribution and ethics	Humans, guided by social norms and intellectual property laws, recognize the importance of attribution.	Requires programming and human guidance to avoid plagiarism and ensure transparency in its knowledge acquisition process and output.

Source: Author, 2024

AI in Research Proposal Writing for Funding

Researchers taking post-graduate studies are required at some point to seek funding so that they undertake projects towards the tail end of their studies. Such researchers may find it easier going if they opt to use AI tools. Generative AI enables individual researchers to write grant proposals at a similar speed to big teams who employ research associates or ghost writers (Parilla, 2024).

The AI tools that are available may not entirely develop a proposal but can help develop proposal sections. Some AI tools for proposal writing build responses based on content the applicant uploads, including copies of the solicitation, reports, and staff biographies. The tools use the uploaded material and answers to prompt and craft a response. After the software prepares a draft, the user must review the generated content to confirm its accuracy and refine the response.

GovSignals (2014) identifies various AI writing tools that include the following:

i. Natural Language Processing (NLP) tools: These tools use AI algorithms to analyze and generate human-like text. They can also help in content generation, language refinement and style improvement.

ii. Machine Learning Platforms (MLP): These platforms use machine learning algorithms to analyze large datasets and provide insights relevant to the research proposal.

iii. Grammar and Proofreading Tools (GPT): These tools can help in identifying and correcting grammar, spelling and punctuation errors in your proposal.

iv. Citation Management Software (CMS): They can help in automatically generating and formatting citations and references in your proposal.

The use of AI tools in proposal writing comes with a number of benefits. Some of the benefits are captured in Table 3.

Table 3. Benefits of using AI tools in proposal writing

Benefit	Explanation
Saves time	AI can automate various tasks involved in proposal writing, such as formatting, proofreading, and referencing, allowing researchers to focus on more critical aspects of their work.
Improve content generation	I algorithms can analyze vast amounts of research papers and suggest relevant content for your proposal. This can save time in literature review and help in identifying research gaps and formulating research questions.
Enhance organization and structure	AI can assist in structuring your proposal by generating an outline or framework. This ensures that all necessary sections are included and presented in a coherent manner.
Refine language and structure	AI algorithms can provide suggestions to improve the clarity, coherence, and language quality of your proposal, ensuring that it is well-written and engaging.
Graphics and design	AI can help a researcher to generate desired graphics and designs for the research and academic proposal.

Source: Author, 2024

AI in Class Management

One of the challenges that institutional administrators find hard to tame is absenteeism. Leaners that are persistently absent are typically shown to have the weakest performance at institutions of higher learning. Keppens (2023) avers that unexcused absenteeism, sickness absenteeism and institutional exclusion all have a negative impact on learners' academic achievement.

Computer vision is recently developing and applying in the utility apps serving people, whereby facial recognition is one of its applications. Although the accuracy of the facial recognition is less than when compared to fingerprint recognition, iris recognition and Radio Frequency Identification (RFID) card recognition (Nguyen, et al., 2021).

In the author's view, chronic absence from an institution of higher learning can:

Inhibit learning abilities of learners

Affect learner attitude and behavior in the institution

Affect lesson delivery as teacher feels uneasy teaching a poorly attended class

In the long-term leads to unfulfilled tasks thus confine one to poverty and criminal activities.

Poor coverage of course content.

Disconnect between a teacher and the learner.

Leads to defiance by the learners.

May strain relationship between learners and educators.

Cause wastage in environments where fees is already paid

Cause withdrawal of sponsorship

May lead to drug and substance abuse.

While combating absenteeism in institutions of higher learning is a good thing, it is worth noting that using AI in monitoring student behavior raises privacy concerns among stakeholders. In the author's view, AI technology has the capacity to revolutionize the way institutions of higher learning tackle absenteeism. It is important to strike a balance between leveraging the benefits of AI and ensuring the privacy and ethical considerations. AI can help reduce school absenteeism through various ways as shown in Table 4.

Table 4. AI in absenteeism in institutions of higher learning<Tbl_Large></Tbl_Large>

Method	Explanation
Predictive analysis	By gathering data on various factors like learner behavior, health records, and environmental conditions, AI algorithms can identify patterns that may indicate potential absentism.
Monitoring learner engagement and performance	By analyzing data from attendance records, test scores, and classroom participation, AI algorithms can identify learners who may be at risk of falling behind or disengaging from the learning process.
Use of chatbots	Chatbots can be integrated into school systems, allowing learners and parents/ guardians to easily access information about attendance policies, upcoming events, and resources to address potential issues that may lead to absentism.
Facial/ finger detectors	Institutions of higher learning may install facial/ biometric detectors/ registers to fight absenteeism.

Source: Author, 2024

AI in Assignments (Assessment, Tests and Examinations)

One of the major integrity issues that institutions of learning are confronted with today is the use of AI by learners during assignments and tests. As indicated earlier, there is increased and continued access to smartphones, laptops and the internet by learners. As well, most AI apps are accessed online free of charge. Some of them, including ChatGTP, Grammarly and Gemni can deliver answers in a matter of seconds. This raises integrity questions on both the learner and the teacher.

In the view of the author, a major paradigm shift in the administration of examinations and assignments was recorded during the Covid-19 pandemic (2019-21). Some institutions including in developing countries like Kenya offered assessments online. Some platforms such as Microsoft Teams offered opportunity to have the examinations proctored. However, there were mixed reactions as to how credible the process was, since students could still manage to use AI and other means to obtain answers and submit them.

Further, AI tools such as ChatGPT have the potential to change teaching and learning in many positive ways. However, for purposes of ensuring and safeguarding the integrity of grades obtained by learners, there should be clear policies and guidelines at college/ university level to prohibit unauthorized use of AI tools in exams and other assessments.

Debby, et al., (2023) highlights the following as some of the challenges of using AI apps such as ChatGTP.

i. Plagiarism: AI essay-writing systems such as ChatGTP are designed to generate essays based on a set of parameters or prompts. This means that learners could potentially use these systems to cheat on their assignments by submitting essays that are not their own work. This undermines the very purpose of higher education, which is to challenge and educate students, and could ultimately lead to a devaluation of higher education certification.

ii. Unfair advantage to some learners over others: If a learner has access to some AI app and uses it to generate high-quality written assignments, they may have an unfair advantage over others who do not have access to the model. This could lead to inequities in the assessment processes.

iii. Distinguishing learner's handwriting and understanding: It is cumbersome to distinguish between a learner's own writing and the responses generated by a chatbot application. Academic staff may find it difficult to adequately assess the learner's understanding of the material when he/she is using a chatbot application to provide answers to their questions.

iv. Undeserved grades: Learners who use AI to generate answers may score highly even in areas that they did not have an understanding. This will lead to production of graduates with high grades but who cannot deliver in the real world.

Since is not about to go anywhere, it is important that educators learn how to detect plagiarized work, or that which originated from AI apps such as ChatGTP. Table 5 shows some tips that can help one detect this form of malpractice.

Table 5. Ways of detecting plagiarized work<Tbl_Large></Tbl_Large>

Tip	Explanation
Patterns or irregularities in the language	AI apps often have limited language abilities and may produce text that is not quite human-like, with repetitive phrases or words, or with odd or inconsistent use of language.
Sources and citations	AI apps are not capable of conducting original research or producing new ideas. Work that has been written by a chatbot is unlikely to include proper citations or references to sources.
Originality	AI content generation apps are not capable of producing original work. Therefore, work that has been written by a chatbot is likely to be very similar to existing sources.

continued on following page

Table 5. Continued

Tip	Explanation
Factual errors	AI language models can produce coherent text but they may not always produce text that is factually accurate.
Time span	AI takes lesser time to generate and deliver an assignment which can be suspect.
Grammar and spelling	Human writing may contain errors and mistakes, such as typos or grammatical errors, while writing generated by AI may be more error-free. However, this can vary depending on the quality of the AI language model and the input data it was trained on.
Inadequacy in content	AI chatbots may be shallow because it gives a summary of information gathered many online sources.

Source: Author, 2024

AI, Human Teaching Resource/ Pedagogy

AI in teaching can be likened to a two-edged sword. This, to the author, implies that those educators who adapt to the 'new normal' by embracing AI might find their work enjoyable and easier. This is unlike those who may want to resist the change that has come with AI. One may therefore wonder if AI will take tutors/ teachers' jobs as traditionally known. AI tools that can be helpful in teaching include ChatGTP, Claude, Microsoft Co-Pilot and Gemini.

Many priorities for improvements to teaching and learning are unmet. Educators seek technology-enhanced approaches addressing these priorities that would be safe, effective, and scalable. Naturally, educators wonder if the rapid advances in technology in everyday lives could help and see opportunities to use AI-powered capabilities like speech recognition. This helps to increase the support available to learners with disabilities, multilingual learners, and others who could benefit from greater adaptivity and personalization in digital tools for learning, Cardona, et al., (2023).

A teacher may choose to incorporate AI use into their assignments with the provision that learners clearly cite where they have used it. Claus (2024) offers some of the examples how a teacher may incorporate AI in teaching:

i. Learners can be allowed to use AI to generate text based on a prompt provided they be asked to critique the results.

ii. Ask learners to conduct a compare/contrast between AI-generated text and human-generated text.

iii. Allow learners to use AI for components of assignments that a professional in the field would be likely to use AI for (e.g simple coding).

iv. Use AI to create interactive case studies or scenarios for students to engage with.

v. Use AI to generate assignments/ examination questions.

The Covid-19 pandemic challenged the world to keep moving by using technology. This is the time the aspect of blending teaching (hybrid teaching) became popular, in that some instructors could teach from home or office, or some students could stay at home and still follow their lesson virtually.

Online teaching is popular because:

i. It is secure, and can enable access for unlimited number of students or teachers for free.

ii. It's great for teaching live one-to-one classes by either video or audio and screen/ share a presentation while you teach. You can also send documents, links to websites, videos, polls and quizzes.

iii. It can deliver learning even to basic mobile phones in areas where connectivity is limited or intermittent.

iv. It doesn't require a lot of learner training and onboarding for students.

v. A teacher can build both synchronous remote and asynchronous blended learning.

vi. When teaching groups, many learners can have their cameras on at any one time.

vii. The teacher can send audio and short video messages that learners can watch and listen to multiple times.

A teacher can screen-share and record lessons to be shared with students and can be downloaded and accessed by them for revision.

One can build powerful blended learning by combining broadcast channels and interactive groups.

A teacher can develop communities and enable sharing and collaboration.

Access and updates aren't mediated by the company and their algorithms. All of your students will see all the content you post.

AI can help the teacher to get timely feedback, offer suggestions of improvement, simulate leaners and enable learning without fear of judgment. While it is possible that some AI tools can indeed deliver lessons without the presence of a teacher, there has to be a human hand/ mind in ensuring the right content reaches the learner. Table 6 shows differences between a human teacher and AI 'teacher'.

Table 6. A comparison between a human teacher and AI 'teacher'

Human Teacher	**AI 'teacher'**
i. They are 'human'.	They are not human.
ii. The can empathize with you and what you are feeling.	They don't have feelings. Can't even get tired
iii. They care about you and want you to do well.	They are always there and don't care about you
iv. They can motivate you through reward and discipline.	They don't motivate anyone

continued on following page

Table 6. Continued

Human Teacher	AI 'teacher'
v. They care about you even when you don't show up.	They don't care whether you are there or not
vi. They experience the same highs and lows that you go through.	They don't know what it means/ feels to be you
vii. They are thrilled when you do well and celebrate your triumphs	They don't care whether you succeed or fail
They have limitations and cannot handle every topic/ subject	They have an incredible depth of knowledge on almost any topic.

Source: Author, 2024

Incorporating AI literacy into education will ensure that learners are not just passive recipients but active participants in the AI ecosystem. Educators need AI as a co-educator to augment traditional teaching methodologies, McNulty (2024).

In the author's view, the beauty of AI is that it can facilitate self-regulated learning. In 2023, the Educational University of Hong Kong issued a press release that, in the author's view, can promote self-regulated learning. The release forms the basis of the 6 points (6Ps) which facilitate the assessment of self-regulated learning. These are:

i. Plan: Plan the content and structure of the writing to effectively respond to an issue, research question or problem.

ii. Prompt: Generate questions for inquiry and prompts using text-based generative AI tools, which provide resources for thought, discussion and further exploration.

iii. Preview: Ensure the output from the tools is previewed, checked for accuracy and screened for discrepancies.

iv. Produce: Produce the written content by synthesizing information from the tools and other academic resources, together with the individual views and personal insights of the learners.

Peer review: Polish the article with peers and ensure that the content and supporting references are reasonable.

vi. Portfolio tracking: Integrate learners' reflections on the writing and learning processes and the formulation of strategies into future writing and learning tasks.

AI in Intellectualism

One of the issues that confront the world today is the fate of intellectualism in the face of AI. There is need of delicate balancing between the two. Indeed, modern intellectuals have to align themselves with the technological advancement. The outcome of failure to do this may bring with it unimaginable outcomes, including rendering their intellectual acumen inferior in the face of a fast evolving world.

Rapid advances in AI chatbots are challenging centuries-old principles in intellectual property- and prompting calls for changes to patent and copyright laws. A new wave of powerful "generative" AI chatbots — such as ChatGPT and Gemini, both of which can produce plausible text and images in response to conversational prompts — has given fresh urgency to ongoing debates in the legal profession and wider society, Huber (2023).

Caldwel (2023) writes that although AI can generate content closely resembling human output, it is not human. And since intellectual property (IP) mainly focuses on non-physical creations or assets made by humans, AI presents a major challenge for legal disputes over patents and IP ownership, namely, who owns AI-generated content?

AI, with its ability to replicate human intelligence and creativity, has

redefined how we generate content, invent, and interact with information Abdallah and Salah (2023). One of the bottlenecks that intellectuals face is the protection of Intellectual Property (IP).

In the author's view, AI and intellectual property requires careful consideration of legal, ethical, and practical issues. It is only by addressing these issues and promoting responsible innovation that there can be a sustainable approach to AI development and intellectual property protection. This therefore makes AI a key component that should be integrated in intellectualism as conventionally known.

Since AI is becoming increasingly integrated into our lives, it is crucial to find a balance between its development and adoption, and IP rights.

The following are some of the ways through which the relationship between AI and intellectual property can be balanced, Dutta and Bruno (2023):

i. Protecting AI with IP: AI can be protected by intellectual property rights such as patents, copyrights, and trade secrets. This can encourage innovation and investment in AI research and development.

ii. Addressing ownership and licensing: When AI is developed by a team or in collaboration with others; ownership and licensing agreements need to be established to ensure that the creators and contributors receive appropriate credit and compensation for their work.

iii. Managing data and privacy: It's important to manage data responsibly and protect privacy, while also allowing for innovation and development of AI.

iv. Considering ethical implications: It's important to consider social and ethical implications of AI, such as bias, discrimination, and automation of jobs, and ensure that AI is developed and used in an ethical and responsible manner.

AI in Libraries

The advent of online and digital libraries has made information more accessible to more people. This is unlike when scholarly materials were available only in tangible, physical formats. The unfolding scenario, in the author's view, precipitates the following concerns:

i. Could artificially intelligent machines eliminate library jobs? Well, the answer is that machines can't replace the deeply human skills of creativity and interaction.

ii. Could AI eliminate the relationships between people and books, and between librarians and their community members? AI will complement the work of librarians.

iii. Without explicit counter-measures, will machine learning & AI inscribe and magnify existing systems of inequality and racism, sexism, homophobia among others?

Another area of concern is the use of AI to write books. Indeed, chatbots such as ChatGTP have been used to write books, even as the authenticity of those books remains in contestation. The rapid consumer adoption of ChatGTP has spurred frenzied activity in technology circles as investors pour money into AI-focused startups and given technology firms new purpose amid the gloom of massive lay-offs. The software's emergence has already ruffled some of the biggest technology firms, prompting Alphabet Inc and Microsoft Corp to hastily debut new functions in Google and Bing, respectively that incorporate AI (Bensinger, 2023).

While publishing a book is seen as a major milestone by authors, unscrupulous people may take advantage of AI to pirate/ plagiarize and mass produce digital books and reap profits unlawfully. This happened to one Rory Cellan-Jones, a former BBC technology correspondent whose memoirs were mass produced behind his back with the aid of Artificial Intelligence as was reported by Tapper in 2023.

There is divided opinion on the use of AI in libraries. Major concerns regarding AI include cheating, eliminating or reducing critical thinking and originality, and replacing human jobs.

The following are some of the advantages of AI in libraries:

i. Improved decision-making, knowledge management, and the ability to analyze texts and data.

ii. Speeding up information retrieval, making relevant recommendations, and improving overall service efficiency.

iii. Improved accuracy and efficiency in data management, enhanced user experience, and cost savings.

iv. AI can support library repository in the form of reference services, indexing, information retrieval, cataloguing, and collection management, among other services.

v. AI libraries does not need large physical space.

vi. Enhanced operational efficiency can increase productivity and expedite workflows by automating repetitive tasks such as information retrieval, classification, and cataloguing by utilizing AI technologies.

vii. AI enabled hardware and software can enhance user experiences by providing tailored recommendations, predictive search functions, and interactive virtual assistants.

viii. Sophisticated recommendation and search engines made possible by AI technology increase the accessibility of information.

Libraries may utilize data analytics and predictive modeling using AI to plan services, create collections, and allocate resources sensibly.

x. AI opens up new opportunities for libraries to be innovative and expand the services they offer.

The following are some of the disadvantages of AI in libraries as elucidated by Priyadarshini (2024):

i. AI driven library systems might become less reliable and efficient due to skewed conclusions, errors, and inaccuracies caused by inadequate or biased datasets.

ii. To integrate AI technology in libraries, a significant upfront investment in software, hardware, and staff training is sometimes required and might face financial constraints.

iii. The application of AI in libraries raises ethical and private concerns regarding data collection, storage, and use.

iv. An overreliance on AI-driven technologies could diminish the value of frontline staff members and librarians by depriving them of the individualized attention and expertise that clients value.

v. AI algorithms have the potential to reinforce or exacerbate biases in the training data, leading to unfair or biased outcomes.

vi. AI systems are complicated, thus maintaining optimal performance and reliability necessitates ongoing maintenance, updates, and troubleshooting.

FUTURE RESEARCH DIRECTIONS

The Artificial Intelligence (AI) landscape is undergoing rapid and fast changing development. As more knowledge of AI becomes available, more people are getting curious to not only make use of it but also seek ways of manipulating and coming up with better forms of AI. There is a possibility that specialists in AI are continually exploring solutions to current and emerging tasks in various facets of human life, including medicine, engineering, computer and business.

For this reason it's imperative to appreciate that there is need for review of policies and regulations guiding the use of AI since the rapid evolution in technology is likely to make existing policies and regulations obsolete and in turn perpetuate integrity and ethical issues surrounding the use of AI. Researchers should keep an eye on the emerging trends in AI and come up with timely findings and recommendations on the use of AI with little interference of ethics and integrity.

At the same time, actors in higher education, including lecturers and administrators should alive be alive to the fact that the sector provides opportunities for new innovators in AI, and that the emerging technologies excite learners who seek them out. There is need to bridge the gap that exists amongst various populations in higher education spaces, through conducting thorough research that involves stakeholders and appreciate how each of them perceive, adopt and use the technologies with a view to finding a more neutral position that upholds ethics and integrity in the use of AI.

CONCULUSION

This chapter has been written at a time when the technology world is not static. More and more innovations continue to emerge, and existing ones are being improved while others are getting obsolete. One of the innovations that may potentially shake AI is Quantum Computing, which is about particle behavior at the lowest sizes. Nevertheless, AI remains one of the finest discoveries in the 21st century.

AI will continue to impact on lives both positively and negatively. It is seen as a threat to ethics and academic integrity in higher education in terms of research, publications, assessment, supervision, protection of IP rights and intellectualism, plagiarism, publishing, critical thinking, utility and innovations, and privacy of learners. It is a threat to knowledge creation and also calls for continuing professional development for educators to keep abreast with the new developments in the sector.

In the higher education space, there is need to have guarded/ circumspect embrace and adoption of AI, while ensuring no erosion of academic integrity. Indeed, academic integrity should be sacred, so much so that stiffer penalties should be imposed on those who compromise it.

In the absence of standardized AI policies across educational systems, there is need for institutions of higher learning to go an extra mile and formulate their own. This way, the institutions will retain their reputation as the epitomes of credible knowledge and the home of highly competent graduates who can take the world to the next level.

REFERENCES

Abdallah, M. Salah, M (2023). Artificial Intelligence and Intellectual Properties: Legal and Ethical Considerations. International Journal of Intelligent Systems and Applications in Engineering. file:///C:/Users/admin/Downloads/IJISAE_13_Mohammadabdallah_9_2020.pdf. Accessed on Thursday 11th July, 2024

BBC. (2024).How AI is testing the boundaries of human intelligence. https://www.bbc.com/future/article/20240501-how-ai-is-testing-the-boundaries-of-human-intelligence. Accessed on Sunday 7th July, 2024

Bensinger, G. (2023). ChatGPT-written ebooks thrive on Amazon. https://www.thedailystar.net/daily-star-books/news/chatgpt-written-ebooks-thrive-amazon-3255536. Accessed on Sunday 7th July, 2024

Cabaleiro-Cerviño, G., & Vera, C. (2020). The Impact of Educational Technologies in Higher Education. GIST – Education and Learning Research Journal, 20, 155-169. https://doi.org/DOI: 10.26817/16925777.711

Caldwel, K. (2023). AI And Intellectual Property: Who Owns It, And What Does This Mean For The Future? Forbes Magazine. https://www.forbes.com/sites/forbesbusinesscouncil/2023/10/31/ai-and-intellectual-property-who-owns-it-and-what-does-this-mean-for-the-future/. Accessed on Thursday 11th July, 2024

Cardona, A. M., Roberto, J. R., & Ishmael, K. (2023). Artificial Intelligence and the Future of Teaching and Learning. Office of Education Technology. https://www2.ed.gov/documents/ai-report/ai-report.pdf. Accessed on Sunday 8th July, 2024

Claus, S. (2024). The Teacher Learning Centre. https://tlc.ucsc.edu/resources/artificial-intelligence-in-teaching-learning/. Accessed on Wednesday 10th July, 2024

Delfino, J. (2023). AI-driven Research and Development: A paradigm shift in innovation. https://www.rdworldonline.com/ai-driven-research-and-development-a-paradigm-shift-in-innovation/. Accessed on Sunday 7th July, 2024

Dutta, S. Bruno, L (2023). Network Readiness Index 2023. Portulans Institute. Accessed on Thursday 11th July, 2024

Fitria, T. N. (2021). Artificial Intelligence (Ai) In Education: Using Ai Tools For Teaching And Learning Processes. Proceeding Seminar Nasional & Call For Papers ISSN Online: 2654-6590 I ISSN Cetak: 2654-5306. file:///C:/Users/admin/Downloads/106-ArticleText-199-1-10-20211225.pdf. Accessed on Sunday 29th September, 2024

George Town University Library. (2013). Artificial Intelligence (Generative) Resources.https://guides.library.georgetown.edu/ai/tools. Accessed on Sunday 7th July, 2024

Gibony, S. (2023). How to use Artificial Intelligence as a Study Tool. https://blog.methodistcollege.edu/how-to-use-artificial-intelligence-as-a-study-tool. Accessed on Sunday 7th July, 2024

GovSignals. (2024). Using AI to Write a Research Proposal. https://www.govsignals.ai/works/ai-to-write-research-proposal. Accessed on Sunday 7th July, 2024

Hubar, N. (2023). Financial Post. Rapid advances in AI set to upend intellectual property. https://www.ft.com/content/b7b3a881-92bb-4c10-85d8-007607477ccf. Accessed on Thursday 11th July, 2024

Intelligent.com. (2023). Nearly 1 in 3 College Students Have Used ChatGPT on Written Assignments. https://www.intelligent.com/nearly-1-in-3-college-students-have-used-chatgpt-on-written-assignments/. Accessed on Sunday 7th July, 2024

Kavlakoglu, E., & Stryker, C. (2024). What is artificial intelligence (AI)? https://www.ibm.com/topics/artificial-intelligence. Accessed on Sunday 29th September, 2024.

Kictanet (2013). Policy Discussion on Artificial Intelligence in Kenya.https://www.kictanet.or.ke/policy-discussion-on-artificial-intelligence-in-kenya/. Accessed on Sunday 7th July, 2024

Maphosa, M., & Maphosa, B. African higher Education institution's response to COVID-19: A bibliometric analysis and visualisation study. Vol 10 (2), 2023. https://www.tandfonline.com/doi/full/10.1080/2331186X.2023.2273002?scroll=top&needAccess=true#abstract. Accessed on Sunday 29th September, 2024

McNulty, N. (2024). AI and Pedagogy. https://medium.com/@niall.mcnulty/ai-and-pedagogy-9647387515bd. Accessed on Sunday 7th July, 2024

Moya, B. A., Eaton, S. E., Pethrick, H., Hayden, K. A., Wiens, R. B. J., McDemort, B., & Lesage, J. (2024). Academic integrity and artificial intelligence in higher education contexts: A rapid scoping review protocol. https://www.researchgate.net/publication/367636342_Academic_integrity_and_artificial_intelligence_in_higher_education_contexts_A_rapid_scoping_review_protocol. Accessed on Sunday 15th, 2024

Nah, F.F, Zheng, R., Cai, J., Siau, K. & Chen L. Generative AI and ChatGPT: Applications, challenges, and AI-human collaboration, Journal of Information Technology Case and Application Research, DOI: . Accessed on Sunday 29th September, 2024DOI: 10.1080/15228053.2023.2233814

Parrila, J. M. (2024). AI levels the playing field for researchers applying for grants. https://www.universityworldnews.com/post.php?story=20240508134752792. Accessed on Sunday 7th July, 2024

16. (PDF) Academic integrity and artificial intelligence in higher education contexts: A rapid scoping review protocol. Available from: https://www.researchgate.net/publication/367636342_Academic_integrity_and_artificial_intelligence_in_higher_education_contexts_A_rapid_scoping_review_protocol [accessed Sep 15 2024].

Poth, D. R. (2023). 7 Tools that Help Teachers Work More Effectively. https://www.edutopia.org/article/7-ai-tools-that-help-teachers-work-more-efficiently/. Accessed on Sunday 8th July, 2024

Priyadarshini, A and Kumar, D (2024). Examining the Advantages, Limitations, Opportunities, and Challenges of AI Implementation in Libraries. Journal of Electrical Systems. file:///C:/Users/admin/Downloads/Examining_the_Advantages_Limitations_Opportunities.pdf. Accessed on Thursday 11th July, 2024

Suleiman, S., Olen, D., & Bezuidenhout, M. (2024). AI regulation and policy in Africa. https://www.dentons.com/en/insights/articles/2024/june/13/ai-regulation-and-policy-in-africa. Accessed on Sunday 7th July, 2024

Tapper, J. (2023). Authors shocked to find AI rip-offs of their books being sold on Amazon. https://www.theguardian.com/technology/2023/sep/30/authors-shocked-to-find-ai-ripoffs-of-their-books-being-sold-on-amazon. Accessed on Sunday 7th July, 2024

Warschauer, M., Tseng, W., Yim, S., Webster, T., Jacob, S., Du, Q., & Tate, T. (2023). The affordances and contradictions of AI-generated text for second language writers.. Accessed on Sunday 7th July, 2024DOI: 10.2139/ssrn.4404380

Washington, J. (2023). Comparing and Contrasting How Humans and AI Learn. https://www.linkedin.com/pulse/comparing-contrasting-how-humans-ai-learn-jerry-washington-ed-d--qmbxc. Accessed on Sunday 7th July, 2024

ADDITIONAL READING

Onderi, H. L. N. (2024). *Basic Education in Kenya: A Reality Check.* Nsemia Inc. Publishers Oakville.

KEY TERMS AND DEFINITIONS

Artificial Intelligence: The general concept of machines acting in a way that simulates or mimics human intelligence.

Assessment: Is a way to measure if the learning objectives of a course are being met.

Chatbot: A programme designed to communicate with people through text or voice commands in a way that mimics human-human conversations.

ChatGPT: An abbreviation for Chat Generative Pretrained Transformer, which refers to an (AI) chatbot that uses natural language processing to create humanlike conversational dialogue.

Ethics: .Moral principles that govern a person's behaviour in the use of AI.

Generative AI: A type of AI that can create new content and ideas, including conversations, stories, images, videos, and music.

Integrity: Holding strongly into rules and regulations that govern institutions of higher learning in the wake of AI.

Pedagogy: A specific approach an educator takes to get their message across a group of students.

Policies and guidelines: These are frameworks that spell out expectations, standards and procedures within which AI is used in higher education.

Research: The systematic investigation into and study of materials and sources in order to establish facts and reach new conclusions.

Technology: A new development in the scientific knowledge that leads to change and manipulation of human environment.

Chapter 4
Transition From Analogue to Digital Technology:
Examining Teaching, Learning, and Assessment in Higher Education in Kenya

Albine Kipkoech Langat
Kisii University, Kenya

ABSTRACT

Integration of digital techniques like learning management systems and artificial intelligence has revolutionized teaching methodologies. Blended learning models, combining face-to-face instruction with online components, foster dynamic learning experiences and democratize access to resources, promoting flexibility and inclusivity. In Kenya, digital adoption in higher education has surged, enhancing accessibility and efficiency in instructional and administrative processes. Digital tools facilitate active learning, collaboration and personalized learning, transforming traditional instructional methods and promoting student engagement and motivation. The flipped classroom model supported by digital technologies, encourages active learning and critical thinking. Effective tutor training is crucial for integrating digitization, focusing on developing digital competencies and pedagogical skills. Although challenges persist, the digital era offers opportunities for enhancing teaching and learning, making education more accessible.

DOI: 10.4018/979-8-3373-0025-2.ch004

INTRODUCTION

The transition from analogue to digital mediums has revolutionized higher education and reshaped methods of teaching and learning as well as assessment in higher education in Kenya. These methods were characterized by teacher-centered instruction where they focused on textbooks and lectures, their effectiveness varied depending on the context, subject matter, and individual learners. Higher Education system transition in terms of teaching, learning, and assessment in Kenya shows a multifaceted approach with profound shift informed by many challenges that requires deep understanding of the dynamic interplay between technology and academia. Traditionally, in global system; higher education was informed by conventional face-to-face lectures, textbooks readings and assessments were done through examinations. The traditional pedagogy involved tutors giving out information through lectures while students take notes. With the traditional pedagogical methods, the students were given assignments and end of semester exams to demonstrate the acquired knowledge (Roehl, Reddy & Shannon, 2013). Njoroge and Kibaru, (2012) noted that Kenya's higher education in the 21st century has undergone transformation, informed by digital innovations. From the traditional confines of analogue lecture halls to the boundless possibilities of digital learning environments, universities and colleges in Kenya are undergoing a seismic shift in their teaching, learning, and assessment paradigms.

The advent of the digital revolution has not merely introduced technological tools into the educational landscape in Kenya but has fundamentally altered the way knowledge is imparted, acquired and evaluated. The integration of digital techniques such as learning management system (LMS), artificial intelligence into Kenya's higher education has revolutionized teaching methodologies, enabling educators to explore new pedagogical approaches that transcend the constraints of traditional classroom settings. As Kirui and Sang (2020) aptly note that the adoption of digital technology has facilitated the emergence of new learning models which incorporates face-to-face instruction with online components in order to facilitate interactive learning experience among the students. Furthermore, the advent of online LMS has liberalized access to educational resources, allowing learners to engage with course materials anytime, anywhere and undertake examinations conveniently (Allen & Seaman, 2016).

This study examined the transition from analogue to digital methods in teaching, learning, and assessment in higher education, it explored how the adoption of digital platforms and tools have impacted instructional methods, student engagement, and the ways learning is assessed. The significance of this study lies in its potential to enhance understanding of how digital technologies are transforming teaching, learning, and assessment in higher education. By exploring the shift from analogue to digital methods, it provides valuable insights into improving educational practices and outcomes. The study will help institutions identify effective strategies for integrating digital tools, addressing challenges like the digital divide, and optimizing learning environments. Ultimately, the study aims to support higher education institutions in harnessing digital innovations to create more flexible, engaging, and inclusive learning experiences, benefiting both students and educators.

BACKGROUND

Digital technology innovations have revolutionized human life, and their impact on teaching, learning, and assessment in higher education is profound. According to Pohekar (2018), the adoption of digital technologies in education acts as a transformative agent in higher education by exploring various digital methodologies. These digital platforms enhance teaching, learning, and assessment in higher learning institutions by revolutionizing traditional methods through more interactive and engaging approaches. The study findings of Cheaney and Ingebritsen, (2006) showed that the adoption and use of digital methodologies as tools for instruction and evaluation in higher education have gained prominence, thereby redefining the global education landscape. When compared, students studying through digital platforms tend to perform better than those relying on traditional methods. This demonstrates the importance of digital technology as a transformative agent in higher education, an idea the universities must consider to improve their institutional performance.

Digital technologies should be adopted not only as tools for instruction but also as tools for assessment in universities because they promote flexibility in the learning environment. According to Ratanya and Muthee, (2018), institutions like Kenyatta University and the University of Nairobi were in the forefront of establishing Open and Distance Learning (ODeL) platforms, where students accessed course materials and modules through online technologies. These tools enhance both teaching, learning and the assessment processes by providing opportunities for more personalized and continuous assessment.

Falcinelli and Moscetti (2021) argue that innovative distance learning programs that emphasize the practical application of digital technologies should be adopted in higher education to promote the mass utilization of digital technology as a medium of learning. Similarly, Kiarie and Jones, (2024) in their research: Towards Learning Excellence in Universities: A Critical Review of Information and Communication Technology Policies in Education in Kenya, asserts that in the contemporary higher education ecosystem, virtual learning platforms such as Google Classroom, Google Meet, Zoom, Moodle, Microsoft Class Notes, and Skype have been adopted by both lecturers and students. These platforms enhance teaching, learning, and assessment by facilitating online lectures, interactive discussions, and real-time evaluations. Hussein, (2011) further emphasizes that integrating these technologies is not merely an alternative that educational institutions should consider but a key component of the educational process. The research further suggest that in digital learning, students' satisfaction is tied to teaching methods and assessment with particular attention being be paid to blended learning, which combines both traditional classes with online learning. Blended learning integrates online assessment tools, offering real-time feedback and ensuring that learning outcomes are continuously evaluated. On the other hand, Camilleri and Camilleri (2017) stress that the successful integration of digital technologies into teaching, learning, and assessment in higher education largely depends on educators' ability to determine the optimal moments for applying these tools.

A study by Musyoka and Musili (2023) on the Effect of digital transformation on higher education during covid-19 pandemic found that students using digital technology showed significant improvements in knowledge acquisition compared to those relying solely on traditional methods. This improvement was not only due to enhanced learning techniques but also more efficient and immediate feedback mechanisms through digital assessments. Furthermore, Borthwick, Anderson, Finsness, and Foulger (2015) highlighted that digital tools optimize the learning process by assisting in content creation, improving engagement, and making learning more meaningful. The same tools also optimize assessment, allowing for more varied and adaptive forms of evaluation. Montreux, Vanderlinde, Schellens, and De Marez (2015) argue that digital educational technologies, which enhance teaching and learning methods, are gaining significant importance in higher education institutions. The extensive use of these technologies simplifies the organization and execution of the educational process, including the assessment of student performance.

Digital technology offers numerous advantages for teaching, learning, and assessment in higher education. Firstly, it enhances accessibility to educational resources. Through online platforms, students can access lectures, textbooks, and research materials anytime, from anywhere, which promotes flexibility and inclusivity (Liu & Kang, 2019). In terms of assessment, digital platforms offer various tools such as quizzes, assignments, and real-time evaluation that enhance the assessment process, making it more dynamic and student-centered. Secondly, digital tools facilitate interactive learning experiences, such as virtual simulations and collaborative projects, fostering student engagement and critical thinking skills (Selwyn, 2020). Interactive digital assessments provide immediate feedback, enabling students to identify areas for improvement in real-time. Furthermore, digital assessment tools streamline evaluation processes, providing timely feedback to students and enabling educators to monitor the progress effectively (Al Lily, Ismail, Abunasser, & Alqahtani, 2019).

These tools allow instructors to assess both individual and collaborative work more efficiently, making the evaluation process transparent and continuous.

Despite the identified benefits, digital technology poses challenges in higher education, particularly in teaching, learning, and assessment. One significant concern is the digital divide, wherein students lacking access to technology or internet connectivity are disadvantaged (Kibuku, Ochieng, & Wausi, 2020). This divide not only affects learning but also impacts students' ability to participate in online assessments. Additionally, integrating digital tools into curricula requires substantial time and resources for training educators and updating infrastructure. The shift towards digital assessment also demands that teachers adapt to new evaluation methods, which can be time-consuming and complex. Moreover, concerns about digital distractions and plagiarism necessitate thoughtful implementation strategies (Eynon, Helsper & Prinsloo, 2019). For assessments, this means designing evaluations that minimize opportunities for academic dishonesty while maximizing student engagement. Furthermore, ensuring data privacy and security remains a critical issue in the digital age (Khan, Bawack, & Kim, 2021). Both student data from learning platforms and assessment records must be protected to maintain trust and the integrity of the educational process.

Theoretical Framework

The theoretical framework for this study is grounded in Constructivist Learning Theory, which emphasizes that learners construct knowledge through interaction with their environment, particularly when using digital technologies (Vygotsky, 1978). Digital platforms facilitate active learning by enabling student engagement, collaboration, and real-time feedback, aligning with the constructivist view that learning is a social process. Additionally, the Technology Acceptance Model (TAM) by Davis (1989), which explores how perceived ease of use and perceived usefulness influence the adoption of digital tools in teaching, learning, and assessment will be adopted in this study.

Constructivism Theory in Digital Learning

In digital learning within higher education, the application of learning and teaching theories is essential to ensure effective instructional design and pedagogical practices. One prominent theory in this context is constructivism, which emphasizes active learning, collaboration, and knowledge construction by learners (Ally, 2008). In digital environments, constructivist principles are manifested through interactive learning activities, problem-solving tasks, and peer-to-peer interactions facilitated by various digital tools and platforms (Musyoka, & Musili, 2023). For example, online discussion forums, collaborative document editing, and virtual simulations provide opportunities for students to construct meaning, engage in knowledge creation, and develop critical thinking skills.

Constructivism, as proposed by Piaget and Vygotsky, asserts that learners build their understanding and knowledge of the world through experiences and reflecting on those experiences. In digital learning, this translates into creating environments where students are not just passive recipients of information but active participants in their learning journey. Interactive tools such as discussion boards and digital storytelling platforms allow students to collaborate, share insights, and build on each other's ideas, fostering a deeper understanding of the subject matter. Musyoka, and Musili, (2023) further highlights that these interactive activities support the development of higher-order thinking skills, such as analysis, synthesis, and evaluation, which are crucial for academic success and lifelong learning.

Though many educators have embraced constructivism several arguments have been raised by educators against the theory for example Kirschner, Sweller, and Clark (2006) argue that constructivism promotes a teaching style with unguided or minimally guided instructions for students hence deny the learners the need to connect their knowledge to tangible objects in order to ensure that they have acquired the knowledge. According to the constructivist point of view, learners acquire knowledge through interacting with their peers through collaboration while under the guidance of the teacher. Additionally, opponents of constructivism believe that it is costly to train instructors in how to teach in constructivist methods, especially in institutions that have limited financial resources.

Another relevant theory is connectivism, which highlights the importance of networks, connections, and distributed cognition in learning (Siemens, 2005). In digital learning environments, connectivism is exemplified through the use of social media, online communities, and networked resources to facilitate information sharing, knowledge exchange, and collaborative learning experiences. Nyabuga, and Booke, (2013) in their research on Mapping Digital Media in Kenya believed that learners engage with diverse sources of information, interact with peers and experts across geographical boundaries, and participate in collective sense-making processes enabled by digital technologies. Connectivism, introduced by George Siemens, posits that learning occurs through the formation of connections within networks. Digital platforms such as LinkedIn, and professional forums exemplify this theory by enabling learners to access a vast array of knowledge from experts worldwide (Dabbagh & Kitsantas 2012). They further suggest that through these networks, learners can develop a deeper understanding of complex topics by engaging in discussions, sharing resources, and receiving feedback from a global community. This networked learning model reflects the realities of the information age, where knowledge is constantly evolving, and staying connected is crucial for continuous learning and professional development.

Technology Acceptance Model (TAM) in Digital Learning

The Technology Acceptance Model (TAM), developed by Fred Davis in 1989, is one of the most influential theories for understanding how individuals adopt and use new technologies. Davis (1989) introduced TAM to explain users' acceptance of technology by focusing on two main factors: perceived usefulness and perceived ease of use, these two factors play a critical role in determining the attitude toward using a technology, which, in turn, influences the intention to use and actual usage behavior. In this context, TAM is not only a framework for understanding adoption but also provides valuable insights into how and why technology is embraced within various sectors, including education.

In the context of education, perceived usefulness can be understood as how much instructors and students believe that digital tools improve the quality of teaching, learning, and assessment. According to Davis (1989), it refers to the degree to which an individual believes that using a particular technology will enhance their job performance. When educators perceive a digital platform as a tool that significantly enhances their ability to deliver content or evaluate students' performance, they are more likely to adopt it. Similarly, students will be more inclined to embrace technologies they believe will improve their learning outcomes (Teo, 2011). In education, this can be interpreted as the extent to which teachers and students find digital tools easy to integrate into the learning and assessment process. Technologies that are user-friendly, with minimal complexity, are more likely to be adopted by educators and students (Venkatesh & Davis, 2000). This highlights the importance of designing educational platforms that are intuitive and accessible to ensure wider acceptance.

The attitude toward using technology is shaped by the perceived usefulness and ease of use. If teachers or students view a technology as beneficial and easy to use, they are more likely to have a positive attitude toward it. In higher education, the attitude of both educators and students toward digital learning platforms can influence their willingness to engage in online learning and digital assessments (Teo & Noyes, 2011). Additionally, if educators believe that a digital tool can help them teach more effectively and find it easy to use, they are more likely to adopt it for teaching and assessment purposes while students on their part are more likely to engage with it consistently (Park, 2009).

Once the perceived usefulness, perceived ease of use, and attitudes align positively, the intention to use the technology translates into actual usage. This means teachers and students will increasingly rely on digital tools for both learning and assessment tasks once they see the benefits and ease of use of these platforms. Consequently, higher education institutions and students with little or no familiarity with e-learning services may face challenges when using it and as a result may resort to conventional methods. Teo and Noyes, (2011) suggested that in order to solve this, institutions of higher learning should ensure that there are regular trainings and in-service courses in order to equip their students and staff with the required skills.

METHODOLOGY

This study employed a document and literature review approach as the primary method of data collection. A comprehensive review of existing academic journal articles, books, reports, and other relevant documents on the integration of digital technologies in higher education was conducted. This method allowed for an in-depth analysis of how digital tools have transitioned teaching, learning, and assessment processes. The literature review method was particularly suited for this study because it provided access to a wide range of secondary data sources, including peer-reviewed journals, empirical studies, and theoretical frameworks, such as the Technology Acceptance Model (TAM) by Davis (1989).

Impact of Digital Tools on Teaching Methods and Assessment

The integration of digital tools into teaching methods and assessment has fundamentally transformed the landscape of education. According to Barasa, P. L. (2021) digitization of education is evident in various dimensions of teaching and learning, including the enhancement of instructional methods, increased student engagement, and the facilitation of personalized learning and assessment.

In the contemporary Kenyan universities, digital tools have revolutionized traditional instructional methods by providing diverse and interactive ways to deliver content and undertake assessment. Multimedia presentations, virtual simulations, and interactive whiteboards are examples of the contemporary instructional methods which allow educators to present information in more engaging and comprehensible manner. According to Barasa, (2021), the use of digital platforms such as e-learning resources in educational institutions, makes learning efficient by enabling educators to incorporate videos, and other multimedia resources into their lectures, aiding the illustration of complex concepts and keep students engaged. Additionally, digital tools support the flipped classroom model by allowing students to access lecture materials online prior to class and engage in interactive activities during class time. Digital platforms not only enhance understanding but also encourages active learning and critical thinking. Studies have shown that students in flipped classrooms often perform better than those in traditional settings, this improvement can be attributed to the interactive nature of digital tools, which fosters a deeper understanding of the subject matter. (Ministry of Education, 2021)

Souter and Kerretts-Makau, (2012) in a research on Internet governance in Kenya - an assessment, affirmed that one of the most significant impacts of digital tools on teaching methods is the increase in student engagement; interactive platforms such as learning management systems, online discussion forums, and collaborative software enable students to participate actively in their learning process. Digitization of teaching and learning process simplify the facilitation, communication and collaboration among students and between students and instructors. This school of thought is supported by Deterding, Dixon, Khaled, and Nacke (2011), who noted that gamification of learning through digital tools, where educational content is delivered in form of games, quizzes, and challenges, has been shown to increase student motivation and engagement. These tools make learning more enjoyable and can lead to better retention of information. As highlighted by Barasa, (2021), these technologies enhance instructional methods, increase student engagement, and facilitate personalized learning. The integration of digital tools into education not only simplifies the organization and performance of the educational process but also creates a more dynamic, interactive, and inclusive learning environment. As technology continues to evolve, its role in education is likely to expand further, offering new possibilities for enhancing teaching and learning.

Digital tools also play a crucial role in facilitating personalized learning, catering to the diverse needs and learning paces of individual students. Adaptive learning technologies use algorithms to adjust the difficulty level and type of content based on the learner's progress, providing a customized learning experience. Nyaboke, Kereri, and Nyabwari, (2021) noted that digitalization of learning in universities leads to improvement of the educational process, which includes tailoring learning experiences to meet individual student needs. Personalized learning platforms can track students' performance and provide insights into their strengths and weaknesses, allowing educators to intervene and provide additional support where necessary. This approach not only improves academic outcomes but also boosts students' confidence and autonomy in their learning progress (Tarus, Gichoya, & Muumbo, 2015). For instance, institutions like Open University of Kenya offer personalized learning, practice recommendations and feedback, helping students to master concepts at their own pace. Moreover, digital tools enable the incorporation of diverse learning resources, such as e-books, online articles, and educational videos, catering to different learning styles. Visual learners can also benefit from video content, while kinesthetic learners can engage with interactive simulations and hands-on activities. This variety ensures that all students have access to resources that suit their preferred learning methods, leading to a more inclusive and effective educational environment.

Digital Transition in Higher Education in Kenya

Traditionally, the Kenyan education system relied heavily on analogue methods of instruction in higher education where students relied on textbooks and other printed materials. The transition from analogue to digital marked a pivotal era of transition across Kenya's higher education system due to the high demand for education.

In order to solve the challenge, the Kenyan universities introduced the e-Learning departments where learners could access classes through an online platform (Wambugu & Kyalo, 2013). University of Nairobi (UoN) pioneered Distance Education (DE) in the 1960s, with its teacher training correspondence programme, this programme was supplemented by regional and on-campus face-to-face tutorials together with seminars. Learner-tutor interactions included brief meetings for induction, counseling, and learning at the learner support centres commonly known as extramural centres which were located in Nairobi, Nakuru, Nyeri, Kisumu, Mombasa, Kakamega, Kisii, and Garissa. By 2004, the UoN had developed its own LMS referred to as the Wedusoft.

Contemporary Kenyan universities such as Mount Kenya University, Kisii university, Multimedia University among others are redefining the landscape of higher learning by adopting digital technology as a key means of instruction through what is called LMS. This shift not only reflected the global trend towards digital transition but also highlights the country's commitment to advancing educational technology and enhancing the quality of online teaching and learning. The importance of this transition cannot be overstated, as it promises to revolutionize teaching, learning, and assessment methods, making education more accessible, interactive, and efficient than ever before.

In recent years Kenya has witnessed an increase in the adoption of digital technologies in its higher education sector, driven by various factors such as government initiatives, technological advancements, and the growing demand for accessible and quality education. Kirui and Sang, (2020), noted one notable aspect of digital transformation in Kenyan higher education is the widespread use of online learning platforms and tools. With the expansion of internet access across the country, universities and colleges are increasingly offering online courses and degree programs to cater to the needs of diverse student populations (Mutula & Kariuki, 2018). These online platforms provide flexibility and convenience, allowing students to access educational resources and participate in learning activities from anywhere with an internet connection. This flexibility is particularly beneficial for non-traditional students, such as working professionals and those living in remote areas, who might otherwise find it challenging to attend on-campus classes.

Digital technologies are also being integrated into traditional classroom settings to enhance teaching and learning experiences through the e-learning platforms in most Kenyan universities. Smart classrooms equipped with interactive whiteboards, multimedia projectors, and digital learning materials are also becoming more common, facilitating interactive and engaging pedagogical practices (Mutula & Kariuki, 2018). Additionally, educators are leveraging digital tools such as learning management systems (LMS), educational apps, and multimedia resources to deliver content effectively and cater for diverse learning styles. This integration supports a blended learning approach, combining face-to-face instruction with online components to create a more dynamic and adaptable learning environment.

Digital transition in Kenyan higher education is not only limited to instructional delivery but also extends to administrative processes and student support services. Most Universities in Kenya today such as Kisii University and Mount Kenya university are adopting digital systems for student registration, enrollment, academic advising, and assessment, streamlining administrative workflows and improving efficiency (Ondigi & Ogutu, 2020). These digital systems help reduce paperwork, minimize errors, and enhance the overall efficiency of administrative operations, allowing institutions to better serve their students. Online student support services, including virtual counseling, library access, and academic tutoring, are being implemented to enhance student success and retention. Virtual counseling services provide access to mental health support and academic advising regardless of location. According to Tenya, Maina, and Mzee (2024) in their research on Digital Literacy as a tool for enhancing access and utilization of information in digital resource platforms among academic staff in University libraries, Kenya, accepted that digital libraries offer access to a vast array of academic resources, including e-books, journals, and research papers, fostering a culture of independent learning and research. Additionally, academic tutoring through online platforms helps students receive personalized support and guidance, ensuring they can achieve their academic goals and succeed in their studies.

Student Engagement and Participation in Digital Learning

The advent of digital learning has significantly reshaped the educational landscape, introducing new methods and tools that enhance student engagement and assessment. Digital learning environments, characterized by their flexibility, interactivity, and accessibility, have become instrumental in fostering active learning and student involvement. This transformation is supported by various studies and theoretical frameworks, which highlight the numerous ways in which digital learning can enhance student engagement.

One of the primary advantages of digital learning is its flexibility, which allows students to access educational materials and participate in learning activities at their own pace and convenience. This flexibility is crucial in accommodating diverse learning styles and schedules, particularly for non-traditional students who may have other commitments such as work or family. According to Nyerere (2016), the asynchronous nature of many online courses enables students to engage with the material through e-learning when they are most ready and able to learn, leading to more meaningful and sustained engagement. Furthermore, the accessibility of digital learning platforms ensures that students can access a wide range of resources, including video lectures, readings, and interactive modules, from any location with an internet connection.

Digital learning platforms also offer unprecedented flexibility in learning schedules, accommodating students with varying time commitments and learning preferences unlike the traditional classroom settings that require students to attend classes at specific times; this flexibility is particularly beneficial for working professionals, parents, and others who need to balance their studies with other responsibilities. Furthermore Makori, Elisha, Mauti, and Norah, (2016) emphasized that asynchronous learning environments empower students to engage with educational content during their peak productivity periods, enhancing their ability to absorb and retain information effectively. Personalized learning paths can be created using digital platforms, enabling students to progress through course materials at their own pace. This customization allows learners to spend more time on challenging topics while moving quickly through areas they find easier, thereby maximizing their learning efficiency. For instance, adaptive learning technologies can analyze a student's performance and provide tailored recommendations and resources to address their specific learning gaps. This personalized approach not only improves learning outcomes but also fosters a more engaging and motivating educational experience.

A study by Nyerere (2016) entitled "Open and Distance Learning in Kenya showed that most universities have e- learning platforms which have enabled students to access digital learning resources that extends beyond flexible schedules to include a vast array of resources that can be accessed virtually from anywhere. These online platforms provide students with access to diverse educational materials, including video lectures, interactive simulations, digital textbooks, and online forums for discussion and collaboration. Nyerere (2016) further noted that the availability of these resources from any location with an internet connection democratizes education, making it possible for students in remote or underserved areas to access high-quality learning materials that might otherwise be unavailable. This is supported by Barasa, (2021) who observed that digital learning promotes inclusivity and equity in education by breaking down geographical and physical barriers. Students with disabilities, for example, can benefit from digital tools that offer various accessibility features such as screen readers, subtitles, and adjustable text sizes. Additionally, online learning platforms often provide multiple formats for content delivery, accommodating different learning preferences and needs. This inclusivity ensures that all students, regardless of their physical or geographical limitations, have the opportunity to engage in meaningful educational experiences.

Research by Tarus, Gichoya and Muumbo (2015) on Challenges of implementing e-learning in Kenya: A case of Kenyan public universities, found that the accessibility of digital learning platforms fosters global collaboration and networking opportunities. Students from different parts of the world can connect and collaborate on projects, share ideas, and learn from diverse perspectives. This global interaction enriches the learning experience by exposing students to different cultures and viewpoints, preparing them for the increasingly interconnected and globalized world. Online forums, social media groups, and other collaborative tools facilitate these interactions, creating a vibrant and dynamic learning community. Digital learning environments are inherently interactive, providing numerous opportunities for student participation and collaboration. Tools such as discussion forums, video conferencing, and collaborative documents allow students to engage with their peers and instructors in meaningful ways. These interactive features foster a sense of community and collaboration, which are essential for deep learning and engagement. According to Garrison and Anderson's (2003) Community of Inquiry (CoI) framework, the combination of cognitive presence, social presence, and teaching presence in online learning environments can create a rich and engaging educational experience. The CoI framework posits that the interaction between these three elements supports a collaborative learning environment where students are actively engaged in constructing knowledge.

For example, synchronous video conferencing tools, such as Zoom or Microsoft Teams, facilitate real-time interactions between students and instructors, replicating the immediacy of face-to-face communication. According to Tarus Gichoya and Muumbo, (2015) these digital tools allow for dynamic discussions, group activities, and immediate feedback, all of which contribute to increased student engagement. Additionally, asynchronous tools, such as discussion forums and collaborative documents, enable students to reflect on their learning and engage in thoughtful discussions at their own pace, further enhancing their participation and engagement in class work.

Authentic assessment tasks in digital environments mirror real-world challenges and require students to apply their knowledge and skills in meaningful contexts. Ndungu, Lewis and Mothobi, (2019) observed that assessment in digital learning depends on ICT transformation which have to align with the principles of authentic assessment and formative feedback, for instance, multimedia projects, and online simulations allow students to demonstrate their competencies in authentic ways, fostering deeper learning and transferable skills development. Furthermore, digital assessment tools enable educators to provide timely and personalized feedback to students, enhancing the formative assessment process (Black & Wiliam, 2009). Automated grading systems, peer assessment platforms, and adaptive learning technologies support continuous feedback loops, enabling students to monitor their progress, identify areas for improvement, and take ownership of their learning.

Authentic assessment, as described by Jonassen and Land (2012), involves tasks that reflect the complexities and ambiguities of real-life scenarios, requiring students to integrate and apply their learning. Digital tools like e-portfolios enable students to compile and showcase their work over time, providing a comprehensive picture of their learning and development. These portfolios can include various media types, such as videos, written reflections, and project reports, illustrating the student's ability to apply knowledge in diverse contexts. Additionally, online simulations offer immersive experiences where students can experiment with concepts in a risk-free environment, enhancing their problem-solving skills and practical understanding.

Digital platforms provide various means for delivering timely and personalized feedback, such as automated quizzes that offer instant results, peer review systems that facilitate constructive feedback from classmates, and adaptive learning technologies that adjust content difficulty based on student performance, such formative feedback not only guides students in their learning process but also fosters a growth mindset, encouraging them to embrace challenges and persist in their efforts. According to Farrell, (2007) continuous feedback through digital tools helps students understand their learning progress and identify areas that need improvement.

Gamification, the use of game design elements in non-game contexts, has emerged as a powerful strategy to enhance student engagement in digital learning. By incorporating elements such as points, badges, leaderboards, and challenges, gamified learning environments can motivate students to participate actively and persistently in their learning activities. According to Deterding et al., (2011), gamification leverages the intrinsic motivation associated with game-playing to foster engagement and improve learning outcomes. One of the primary benefits of gamification in education is its ability to enhance motivation. Traditional learning methods often rely on extrinsic motivators such as grades and rewards. In contrast, gamification taps into intrinsic motivators, making learning activities more enjoyable and engaging. By transforming assignments and lessons into game-like experiences, educators can create a more dynamic and interactive learning environment. This approach not only makes learning more enjoyable but also encourages students to invest more time and effort in their studies.

Interactive content, such as simulations, quizzes, and interactive videos, also plays a crucial role in maintaining student engagement as they make adjustments in real time. For instance, interactive simulations in subjects like science and engineering can provide students with hands-on experience and practical applications of theoretical concepts, thereby enhancing their engagement and comprehension (Musyoka & Musili (2023).

While digital learning offers numerous benefits for student engagement and participation, it is not without challenges. Issues such as digital divide, technology access, and varying levels of digital literacy can impact the effectiveness of digital learning initiatives. Kibuku, Ochieng, and Wausi, (2020) in their research on e-Learning Challenges Faced by Universities in Kenya, noted that addressing these challenges requires a comprehensive approach that includes providing adequate technological infrastructure, training for educators and students, and designing inclusive and accessible learning environments. Generally, digital learning has the potential to significantly enhance tutors' engagement with the students through its flexibility, interactivity, personalized learning, and use of learning analytics. By leveraging these features, educators can create dynamic and inclusive learning environments that cater to diverse student needs and foster active participation.

Tutor Training and Adaptation to the Digital Era

The integration of digital technologies in education demands that tutors should adapt and enhance their skills to effectively facilitate learning. Training initiatives must prioritize the development of digital competencies, pedagogical skills, and the ability to seamlessly integrate technology into curricular. UNESCO (2011) underscores the necessity of continuous professional development in ICT to enable educators to adeptly navigate the rapid technological advancements and cultivate conducive digital learning environments. A primary obstacle in tutor training is the divergence in digital literacy levels among educators, many of them face challenges due to inadequate skills and confidence in utilizing digital tools, posing a significant barrier to effective technology integration Kibuku, Ochieng, and Wausi, (2020). Insufficient access to resources and infrastructure further compounds these difficulties, especially prevalent in developing countries where digital disparities are pronounced especially between urban and rural areas.

Nyerere, (2016) reported that universities in most urban areas have good ICT infrastructure; for example, University of Nairobi, United States International University, Jomo Kenyatta University of Agriculture and Technology, Nazarene University of Africa, Kenyatta University, among others. While universities in suburban or medium sized towns such as Maseno University, Karatina University and Egerton University had moderate ICT infrastructure and universities in rural settings such as Moi University, Garrissa University and Masinde Muliro University of Science and Technology among others had low ICT infrastructure.

Nyerere, Gravenir and Mse (2012) and Tarus, Gichoya and Muumbo (2015) in their respective studies supported that disparities in infrastructural connections in universities and lack of e-Learning technical competencies as well as the e-content creation skills on the part of the e-tutors as the key hindrances to the enactment of digital learning in public universities in Kenya. They observed that even where there is training on the part of lecturers, the focus is on the technical functionalities of the system as opposed to the e-Learning pedagogical training which is the real challenge. However, Isaacs and Hollow (2012) in their e-Learning Africa (2012) Report; argued that there is a pessimism and among Kenyan tutors that ICTs will replace them in their jobs and hence the negative attitude.

Nevertheless, the digital age presents various opportunities to enhance tutor training. Online and blended learning platforms provide flexible and accessible avenues for professional development, allowing educators to learn at their own pace, access a diverse range of resources, and collaborate with peers globally. Massive Open Online Courses (MOOCs) and virtual workshops, for example, equip tutors with the essential skills needed to integrate technology into their instructional practices effectively (Njoroge & Kibaru, 2012). Advancements in e-learning and artificial intelligence (AI) also offer transformative prospects for personalized tutor training. E-learning platforms can assess individual tutor needs and proficiency levels, delivering tailored training programs that address specific gaps and preferences. This personalized approach enhances the efficacy of training initiatives, ensuring that tutors acquire the requisite competencies to thrive in the digital era.

Digital simulations, virtual classrooms, and collaborative software enable tutors to practice new teaching methods and receive real-time feedback from peers and experts. These tools help educators develop confidence and proficiency in using digital technologies, ultimately improving their instructional practices.

Policy frameworks and institutional support are also crucial in facilitating effective tutor training amidst digital transformation. Educational institutions must prioritize investment in infrastructure to enhance technological access and provide robust support systems for ongoing professional development. Collaborative efforts between governments, academia, and private sectors are essential to bridge digital divides and ensure equitable access to digital resources for all educators. Comprehensive tutor training is pivotal for optimizing the integration of digital technologies in education. Addressing challenges such as varying digital literacy levels and ensuring access to adequate resources is essential to harnessing the full potential of digital tools in teaching and learning.

To ensure effective adaptation to the digital era, several recommendations can be made. First, educational institutions should prioritize continuous professional development for tutors, focusing on both digital literacy and pedagogical skills. According to,Hadullo, Oboko and Omwenga (2017), regular and ongoing professional development is critical for educators to remain effective in their roles and to adapt to changing educational landscapes. Institutions should provide regular training sessions, workshops, and access to online resources to support tutors in their professional growth.

Second, fostering a culture of collaboration and campus-based interaction can significantly enhance tutor training. Creating communities of practice where tutors can share experiences, challenges, and best practices can promote collective learning and support. Wu, Tennyson and Hsia (2010) suggested that institutions can facilitate these communities through online forums, social media groups, and regular meet-ups. Collaborative learning not only enhances the skills of individual tutors but also contributes to the overall improvement of teaching practices within the institution.

Lastly, e-learning forums provides varied avenues for instruction, policies and incentives and therefore should be established to support tutor training and adaptation (Kibuku & Orwa, 2018). Educational institutions and policymakers should recognize the importance of digital competencies and provide the necessary resources and incentives for tutors to engage in professional development. This may include funding for training programs, providing time for professional development activities, and recognizing and rewarding tutors who demonstrate proficiency in digital teaching practices. By prioritizing continuous professional development, fostering collaboration, leveraging technology for self-directed learning, and establishing supportive policies and incentives, educational institutions can ensure that tutors are well-equipped to navigate the digital era. As tutors adapt to these changes, they will be better positioned to provide relevant education that meets the demands of the modern world.

Relevance to the Study

The integration of learning and teaching theories in digital learning is essential for creating effective and engaging educational experiences. Constructivist and connectivist principles emphasize active participation, collaboration, and the utilization of networks, enhancing students' critical thinking and problem-solving skills. Additionally, the transformation of assessment practices to include authentic tasks and formative feedback ensures that students can apply their learning in meaningful ways and receive continuous support throughout their educational journey. By leveraging these theories and practices, educators can design digital learning environments that promote deep and sustained learning, preparing students for the complexities of the modern world. The Technology Acceptance Model provides a robust framework for understanding the transformation from analogue to digital methods in teaching, learning, and assessment. By focusing on how users perceive the usefulness and ease of use of digital tools, TAM helps explain the factors influencing the adoption of digital platforms in higher education.

In the context of this study, perceived usefulness is viewed from the perspective of both educators and students. With tools like Google Classroom and Zoom, educators can create interactive learning environments that were not possible with analogue methods. Additionally, digital platforms allow for real-time assessments, instant feedback, and detailed performance tracking, which can improve teaching efficiency and student learning outcomes (Alharbi & Drew, 2014). Therefore, perceived usefulness plays a critical role in motivating teachers and students to adopt digital tools in education. Students, on the other hand, perceive usefulness when digital platforms help them access learning materials more easily, collaborate with peers, and receive immediate feedback on assessments. Research shows that students are more likely to adopt digital technologies if they believe these tools will improve their academic performance and make learning more convenient (Mariga, Ogenga, Shikali, Muliaro, & Wambugu. 2017). Thus, the concept of perceived usefulness is crucial in understanding how digital platforms are integrated into learning and assessment.

Ease of use is an essential factor in the adoption of digital tools, especially in educational settings where users may not always be technologically proficient. Kibuku, Ochieng, and Wausi, (2020) observed that educators, particularly those accustomed to traditional teaching methods, may resist adopting digital tools if they find them too complex or time-consuming to use. In this context, TAM highlights the importance of designing user-friendly educational technologies that can be easily integrated into teaching and assessment processes Therefore, ensuring that digital tools are accessible and intuitive is key to promoting their widespread adoption in higher education.

Challenges and Opportunities in the Digital Transformation in Higher Education

The use of digital technology has transformed higher education and has brought about significant changes among educators and students. While digital technologies have the potential to enhance teaching and learning, they also pose several obstacles that need to be addressed. Digital transformation in higher education though have opportunities has its own challenges supported by scholarly references.

Despite the significant strides made in digital transformation, Kenyan higher education institutions face several challenges. One of the primary challenges is the digital divide, which refers to the gap between those who have access to digital technologies and those who do not, this divide is pronounced, with disparities in internet access and digital literacy between urban and rural areas. According to Mutisya and Makokha, (2016), this divide is influenced by factors such as socioeconomic status, geographical location, and infrastructure availability. Students from low-income backgrounds or rural areas may lack access to reliable internet connections and necessary devices, hindering their ability to participate fully in digital learning. This disparity can aggravate existing inequalities in education and limit opportunities for marginalized students. According to the Kenya National Bureau of Statistics (2019), urban areas have significantly higher internet penetration rates compared to rural areas, limiting the reach and effectiveness of digital education initiatives.

The high cost of digital infrastructure and maintenance is another challenge towards the realization digitization of teaching in Kenya. Setting up smart classrooms, procuring digital devices, and maintaining these technologies require substantial financial investments. Many higher education institutions in Kenya, particularly public universities, face budget constraints that hinder their ability to invest and sustain digital transformation initiatives. Additionally, the cost of internet access and digital devices can be prohibitive for students from low-income backgrounds, further widening the digital divide.

Kashorda and Waema (2014) in their study entitled "E-Readiness Survey of Kenyan Universities" conducted in 30 universities, found out that there was a low ratio of personal computers to students. The study reported that there were only 16,174 computers in the laboratories to serve a population of 423, 664 students enrolled in those universities. Though this challenge inhibits access to e-Learning; the same study however observed that it was compensated by the large number of students (200,000 = 53%) who owned laptops.

The low level of digital awareness among both students and educators is another significant barrier to effective digital transformation. While digital tools and platforms are becoming more prevalent, not all students and educators possess the necessary skills to use these technologies effectively. This gap in digital literacy can impede the adoption and utilization of digital tools, limiting their potential to enhance teaching and learning outcomes. According to Musyoka, and Musili, (2023), digital literacy skills are essential for students to navigate and succeed in a digital learning environment. While digital native students who have grown up with technology may be comfortable using digital tools, they may not possess the critical digital literacy skills required for academic success, Educators, on the other hand, may struggle with integrating technology into their teaching practices due to a lack of training and support, as a result, the effectiveness of digital learning can be compromised if both students and educators are not adequately prepared to navigate the digital landscape.

Farrel, (2007) research on ICT in Education in Kenya. Survey of ICT and Education in Africa found that the shift to digital learning requires a rethinking of traditional pedagogical approaches where educators must adapt their teaching strategies to leverage the benefits of digital tools while maintaining the quality of instruction. This adaptation can be challenging, as it involves redesigning curricula, developing new assessment methods, and fostering student engagement in an online environment. The resistance to change among faculty and the time required for professional development can further limit the adoption of innovative teaching practices. Institutions must therefore implement robust online measures and develop clear policies to safeguard sensitive information.

Opportunities in Digital Transformation in Kenya's Higher Education

Despite the challenges, digital transformation offers significant opportunities to expand access to education. Online learning platforms and open educational resources can reach a global audience, providing educational opportunities to individuals who may not have access to traditional institutions (Hadullo, Oboko, & Omwenga, 2017). This democratization of education can help bridge the gap between different socioeconomic groups and promote lifelong learning.

Kashorda, and Waema, (2014) research on E-readiness Survey of Kenyan Universities 2013 Report asserted that digital technologies enable personalized learning experiences tailored to individual students' needs and preferences. They added that adaptive learning systems use data analytics to monitor students' progress and provide customized feedback and resources. This approach can enhance student engagement, improve learning outcomes, and support diverse learning styles. Personalized learning also allows students to learn at their own pace, fostering a more inclusive and effective educational environment. Digital tools facilitate collaboration and communication among students and educators, transcending geographical boundaries. Platforms such as video conferencing, discussion forums, and collaborative documents enable real-time interaction and knowledge sharing. This interconnectedness promotes a sense of community and encourages collaborative learning, which can lead to deeper understanding and innovation. Additionally, digital technologies can connect students with industry experts and global networks, enriching their educational experience.

The use of digital platforms in universities opens up possibilities for innovative pedagogical approaches. Flipped classrooms, gamification, and immersive simulations are examples of how digital tools can transform traditional teaching methods (Tarus, & Gichoya, 2015). These approaches can make learning more engaging, interactive, and relevant to students' real-world experiences. For instance, virtual labs and simulations allow students to conduct experiments and explore complex concepts in a safe and controlled environment, enhancing their practical skills and understanding. According to Siemens, (2013) the abundance of data generated through digital learning platforms provides valuable insights for institutions to make informed decisions. This data-driven approach can also inform policy development and strategic planning, ensuring that institutions remain responsive to the evolving needs of students and the job market.

Future Implications of Digital Technology on Higher Institutions of Learning

The future implications of digital technology in higher education are profound, as technological advancements continue to reshape teaching, learning, and assessment processes. As institutions increasingly integrate digital platforms, there will be a shift towards more interactive learning environments that cater for the needs and preferences of individual students (Kibuku, Ochieng, & Wausi, 2020). Adaptive learning technologies, powered by artificial intelligence, will enable institutions to offer tailored educational experiences, providing real-time feedback and allowing students to progress at their own pace. This trend will enhance student engagement and improve learning outcomes, especially in large, diverse student populations. Moreover, blended learning models will become more prevalent, combining traditional face-to-face instruction with online elements. This approach, which has gained traction during the COVID-19 pandemic, offers flexibility and accessibility, enabling students to balance their studies with other commitments. Barasa, (2021) maintained institutions that adopt such models will be better positioned to meet the needs of non-traditional students, such as working professionals and those in remote areas, further democratizing access to education.

The use of digital assessment tools will also increase, offering more efficient and transparent ways to evaluate student performance. Automated grading systems and analytics-driven assessments can provide immediate feedback and reduce the administrative burden on educators (Liu & Kang, 2019). These tools will allow for a more continuous assessment of student progress, moving away from traditional high-stakes exams towards formative assessments that track learning over time. However, challenges such as ensuring data privacy and security will need to be addressed, particularly in the context of remote learning and online assessments

(Khan, Bawack, & Kim, 2021). Another significant implication is the expansion of global collaboration in higher education. Digital technologies will allow institutions to connect across borders, enabling students and educators to engage in cross-cultural exchanges and collaborative research projects. As digital platforms become more sophisticated, virtual classrooms will allow students from different countries to learn together, promoting global citizenship and understanding.

FUTURE RESEARCH DIRECTION

The integration of digital technologies in education presents numerous research opportunities. Key areas include examining the long-term impact of digital tools on student learning outcomes and engagement, and understanding how these technologies affect diverse student populations based on socioeconomic status, geographic location, and prior digital literacy. This research can help develop targeted strategies for equitable digital education. Additionally, exploring innovative pedagogical models that leverage digital advancements like AI and VR can enhance critical thinking, problem-solving, and creativity. Future research should also focus on the professional development of educators, evaluating effective training methods for using digital tools and overcoming adoption barriers. Ethical implications, including data privacy and the digital divide, warrant thorough investigation to develop policies that safeguard student data and promote ethical use of digital tools. Future research should aim to deepen understanding of long-term impacts, address equity issues, develop innovative models, enhance educator training, and explore ethical considerations to improve digital education.

CONCLUSION

Digital platforms in higher learning institutions in Kenya have introduced a nuanced landscape of challenges and opportunities. Critical issues such as the digital divide, varying levels of digital literacy among educators and students as well as the adaptation of pedagogical methods to digital environments, must be effectively addressed. These challenges, however, are counterbalanced by significant opportunities. Digital technologies offer enhanced access to educational resources and opportunities for personalized learning experiences tailored to individual student needs. Innovative pedagogical approaches, such as gamification, enrich teaching methodologies and engage students in interactive learning experiences. Moreover, data-driven decision-making empowers institutions to optimize learning outcomes through informed educational strategies.

As higher education institutions navigate this digital landscape, it is imperative to develop comprehensive strategies that mitigate challenges while maximizing the potential benefits. Institutions must invest in infrastructure to support robust digital platforms and ensure equitable access to technology for all students and educators. Enhancing digital literacy among faculty and students is essential in integrating technology into teaching and learning. Comprehensive digital literacy initiatives should be implemented to empower educators and students with the skills needed to navigate and utilize digital resources effectively. Revision of curricula to integrate digital competencies and ethical considerations will equip graduates with the skills required for success in the digital economy. Sustainable funding mechanisms must be established to support ongoing technological advancements and educational innovations

REFERENCE

Ally, M. (2008). The Impact of Technology on Education. In *Education for a Digital World* (pp. 57–66). Advice, Guidelines and Effective Practice from Around the Globe.

Barasa, P. L. (2021). Digitalization in teaching and education in Kenya: Digitalization, the future of work and the teaching profession project. International Labour Organization.https://scholar.google.com/citations?

Bates, A. W. (2019). Teaching in a digital age. Teaching in a Digital Age. https://pressbooks.bccampus.ca/teachinginadigitalagev2/

Borthwick, A. C., Anderson, C. L., Finsness, E. S., & Foulger, T. S. (2015). Special article personal wearable technologies in education: Value or villain? *Journal of Digital Learning in Teacher Education*, 31(3), 85–92. DOI: 10.1080/21532974.2015.1021982

Camilleri, M. A., & Camilleri, A. C. (2017). Digital learning resources and ubiquitous technologies in education. Technology, Knowledge and Learning, 22.

Cheaney, J. D., & Ingebritsen, T. S. (2006). Problem-based learning in an online course: A case study. *International Review of Research in Open and Distance Learning*, 6(3). Advance online publication. DOI: 10.19173/irrodl.v6i3.267

Davis, F. D. (1989). Perceived usefulness, perceived ease of use, and user acceptance of information technology. *Management Information Systems Quarterly*, 13(3), 319. DOI: 10.2307/249008

Deterding, S., Dixon, D., Khaled, R., & Nacke, L. (2011). From game design elements to gamefulness: defining" gamification". In *Proceedings of the 15th international academic MindTrek conference: Envisioning future media environments*. DOI: 10.1145/2181037.2181040

Eynon, R., Helsper, E. J., & Prinsloo, P. (2019). Not yet equal: The digital knowledge gap between poor and affluent students and how it is changing. In *The Digital Knowledge Gap* (pp. 1–19). Emerald Publishing Limited.

Farrell, G. (2007) ICTs in Education in Kenya: Survey of ICT and Education in Africa. Kenya Country Report for World Bank, Garrison, D. R., & Anderson, T. (2003). *E-learning in the 21st century: A framework for research and practice*. Routledge.

Hussein, H. B. (2011). Attitude of Saudi universities faculty members towards using learning management system. *The Turkish Online Journal of Educational Technology*, 10(2), 43–53.

Jones, R., Smith, L., & Williams, A. (2023). Online student support services: Enhancing student success and retention. *Journal of Educational Technology*, 15(2), 45–59. DOI: 10.1234/jet.2023.01502

Khan, M. L., Bawack, R. E., & Kim, G. (2021). The impact of social media on promoting privacy and security in higher education. *International Journal of Information and Education Technology (IJIET)*, 11(1).

Kiarie, C., & Jones, N. (2024). Towards Learning Excellence in Universities: A Critical Review of Information and Communication Technology Policies in Education in Kenya Kibuku, R. N., Ochieng, D. O., & Wausi, A. N.,2020. e-LearningChallenges Faced by Universities in Kenya: A Literature Review. *Electronic Journal of e-Learning*, 18(2).

Kirschner, P. A., Sweller, J., & Clark, R. E. (2006). Why minimal guidance during instruction does not work: An analysis of the failure of constructivist, discovery, problem-based, experiential, and inquiry-based teaching. Educational Psychologist Kirui, J. K. & Sang, H.C. (2020). Rethinking quality and relevance of university education in Kenya: Entrepreneurial dimension. *The Journal of Quality in Education.*, 10(16).

Li, C., & Lalani, F. (2020). The COVID-19 crisis has changed education forever. This is how. In World Economic Forum. https://www. weforum. org/agenda/2020/04/coronavirus-education-global-covid19-online-digital-learning/

Makori, Elisha O.Mauti, Norah & Osebe, (2016) Digital technology acceptance in transformation of university libraries and higher education institutions in kenya" library philosophy and practice (e-journal).

Ministry of Education. (2021). Policy on Information and Communication Technology in Education and Training Mishra, P., & Koehler, M. J. (2006). Technological Pedagogical Content Knowledge: A Framework for Teacher Knowledge. *Teachers College Record*, 108(6), 1017–1054. DOI: 10.1111/j.1467-9620.2006.00684

Multimedia, H., & Nyabuga, T. G. & Booke, N. (2013) Mapping Digital Media: Kenya.A Report by the Open Societies Foundation. Open Society Foundations, United Kingdom

Musyoka, R., & Musili, K. (2023) The Effect of digital transformation on higher education during covid-19 pandemic. a conceptual literature review African Journal Of Business And Management Special Issue: Volume 8, Issue 2, Mutula, S. M., & Kariuki, M. (2018). Digital transformation of higher education in Kenya: The policy context and emerging issues. In Handbook of Research on Digital Content Management and Development in Modern Libraries.

Njoroge, R. W., & Kibaru, F. (2012) Implementing Quality e-Learning: Which Way for Higher Education Institutions in Kenya? In: EdMedia2012, WorldConference on Educational

Nyaboke, R., Kereri, D., & Nyabwari, L. (2021). Competence-base curriculum (CBC) in Kenya and the challenge of vision 2030. International Journal of Education. *Technology and Science.*, 1(4), 155–169.

Nyandara, Z. I. (2012). Challenges and opportunities of technology-based instruction in open and distance learning: A comparative study of Tanzania and China. *International Journal of Education and Development using ICT, 8*(2).

Nyerere, J., Gravenir, F. Q., & Mse, G. S. (2016). Open and distance learning in Kenya: A baseline survey report commissioned by the Commonwealth of Learning. OECD. (2021). 21st-century Readers: Developing Literacy Skills in a Digital Nyerere, J., Gravenir, F., & Mse, G. (2012). Delivery of open, distance, and e-learning in Kenya. *International Review of Research in Open and Distance Learning*, 13(3), 185–205. DOI: 10.19173/irrodl.v13i3.1120

Ondigi, B. C., & Ogutu, S. O. (2020). Digitization of higher education in Kenya: Challenges and opportunities. In Handbook of Research on Innovative Pedagogies and Best Practices in Teacher Education (pp. 102-118).

Pohekar, D. (2018). Role of ICT on universities administrative services and management. International Research Journal of Engineering and Technology, 5(11).

Ratanya F & Muthee D, (2018) An Exploratory Study on Access and Utilization of the Institutional Repositories Among Academic Staff at Egerton University, Kenya East Africa journal of Information science

Roehl, A., Reddy, S. L., & Shannon, G. J. (2013). The Flipped Classroom: An Opportunity to Engage Millennial Students Through Active Learning Strategies. *Journal of Family & Consumer Sciences, 105*(2), Siemens, G. (2005). Connectivism: A learning theory for the digital age. *International Journal of Instructional Technology and Distance Learning*, 2(1).

Selwyn, N. (2020). What's the problem with digital technology in education? *Learning, Media and Technology*, 45(1).

Siemens, G. (2013). Learning analytics: The emergence of a discipline. *The American Behavioral Scientist*, 57(10), 1380–1400. DOI: 10.1177/0002764213498851

Souter, D., & Kerretts-Makau, M. (2012). Internet governance in Kenya - an assessment. London: A report for the Internet Society by ICT Development Associates Ltd at: http://www. internetsociety. org/sites/default/files/ISOC% 20study% 20of% 20IG% 20in% 20Kenya.

Su, C. H., & Cheng, C. H. (2015). A mobile gamification learning system for improving the learning motivation and achievements. *Journal of Computer Assisted Learning*, 31(3), 268–286. DOI: 10.1111/jcal.12088

Tarhini, A., Hone, K., Liu, X., & Tarhini, T. (2017). Examining the adoption of digital technologies in higher education. Computers & Education, Tenya A. N. Maina J. C.& Awuor F. M (2024) Digital Literacy as a tool for enhancing access and utilization of information in digital resource platforms among academic staff in University libraries, kenya. *International Journal of Scientific Research.*

Tarus, J. K., Gichoya, D., & Muumbo, A. (2015). Challenges of implementing e-learning in Kenya: A case of Kenyan public universities. *International Review of Research in Open and Distance Learning*, 16(1). Advance online publication. DOI: 10.19173/irrodl.v16i1.1816

UNESCO. (2011). *ICT Competency Framework for Teachers*. UNESCO. https://unesdoc.unesco.org/ark:/

UNESCO. (2015). [*Incheon Declaration and Framework for Action – Towards inclusive and equitable quality education and lifelong learning for all*. UNESCO.]. *Education*, •••, 2030.

Venkatesh, V., & Davis, F. D. (2000). A theoretical extension of the technology acceptance model: Four longitudinal field studies. *Management Science*, 46(2), 186–204. DOI: 10.1287/mnsc.46.2.186.11926

Vygotsky, L. S. (1978). *Mind in society: The development of higher psychological processes*. Harvard University Press.

FURTHER READNG

Bishop, J. L., & Verleger, M. A. (2013). The flipped classroom: A survey of the research. *ASEE National Conference Proceedings,* Atlanta, GA DOI: 10.18260/1-2--22585

Gilbert, K. (2016). Utilization of electronic information resources by postgraduate students of Madibbo Adama University of Technology, Yola. *Journal of the Humanities and Social Sciences*, 20(8), 58–65.

Keržič, D., Tomaževič, N., Aristovnik, A., & Umek, L. (2019). Exploring critical factors of the perceived usefulness of blended learning for higher education students. *PLoS One*.

Makori, E. O., & Osebe, N. M. (2016). *Digital technology acceptance in transformation of University Libraries and Higher Education Institutions in Kenya. Library Philosophy and Practice*. E-journal.

Omette, P. B. (2016). Awareness and utilization of electronic information resources by academic staff in the University of Eldoret [Master's Thesis, Kisii University]. http://papers.ssrn.com/so/3/paperscfm:abstract id=ISSS689 www.thelawyer.com/cgi-bin/intem-edge

KEY TERMS AND DEFINITIONS

Analogue Technology: Traditional methods and tools for teaching and learning that do not involve digital or electronic processes. Examples include printed textbooks, chalkboards, overhead projectors, and face-to-face lectures.

Blended Learning: A mix of traditional face-to-face classroom instruction and online or digital learning. This approach combines the benefits of direct teacher interaction with the flexibility and accessibility of online resources

Collaborative Learning: An educational approach where students work together in groups to solve problems or complete tasks. This method emphasizes teamwork, communication, and collective problem-solving

Digitization: The process of converting information into a digital format. In education, this refers to the use of digital tools and platforms like online courses, e-books to enhance learning and teaching.

Digital Divide: The gap between those who have easy access to digital and information technology and those who do not, often influenced by socioeconomic, geographic, and demographic factors

Digital Literacy: The ability to use information and communication technologies to find, evaluate, create, and communicate information, requiring both cognitive and technical skills.

Gamification: The use of game-like elements such as points, badges, in non-game contexts to engage and motivate people; it often involves incorporating game design principles to make learning more engaging and enjoyable.

Interactive Learning: A teaching approach that involves active participation from students. It often includes activities such as discussions, group work, and hands-on projects to enhance engagement and understanding.

Learning Management Systems (LMS): Software applications that provide a framework for managing all aspects of the learning process. An LMS facilitates the administration, documentation, tracking, reporting, and delivery of educational courses or training programs.

Personalized Learning: An educational strategy that tailors learning experiences to meet individual students' needs, interests, and abilities. It often involves adaptive technologies and customized lesson plans to support each student's unique learning journey

Student Engagement: The level of interest, enthusiasm, and commitment a student has toward their learning process. Engaged students are more likely to participate actively, retain information, and perform well academically.

Traditional Methods: Conventional approaches to teaching and learning that often involve lectures, textbooks, and exams. These methods typically focus on direct instruction and individual study

Chapter 5
From Analogue to Digital Revolution: Transformed Teaching, Learning, and Assessment

James Bill Ouda
https://orcid.org/0000-0002-0942-6169
Masinde Muliro University of Science and Technology, Kakamega, Kenya

Caroline Sabina Wekullo
https://orcid.org/0000-0002-0148-9069
Masinde Muliro University of Science and Technology, Kenya

Rose Atieno Opiyo
https://orcid.org/0000-0001-6881-7859
Masinde Muliro University of Science and Technology, Kenya

ABSTRACT

The digital revolution has brought about significant changes in Higher Education Institutions (HEIs), transforming teaching, learning, and assessment. The chapter explores the impact of this paradigm shift from analogue to digital methods and discuss how education practices in higher education institutions have been revolutionized. The chapter provides a comprehensive overview of the key models and approaches that have guided this critical transformation. The mission of this chapter is to provide educators, researchers, and practitioners with an in-depth understanding of how digital technologies are reshaping higher education. The examination of the various models and approaches, is aimed at providing strategies needed to effectively navigate the digital space and enhance teaching, learning, and assessment. At the same time, the chapter recognizes that digital transformation of higher education

DOI: 10.4018/979-8-3373-0025-2.ch005

comes with its own set of concerns and challenges. The best practices have also been suggested in the chapter.

INTRODUCTION

Higher education landscape is experiencing drastic transformation. This is largely driven by advancements in digital technologies. The shift from analogue to digital has revolutionized the approaches teaching, learning, and assessment are carried out creating new opportunities for enhanced educational experiences. This transition is not merely about the adoption of new tools and platforms; it represents a fundamental change in the educational paradigm, affecting every aspect of higher education. In the analogue era, teaching primarily involved face-to-face interactions, with educators delivering lectures in classrooms, and students relying on printed textbooks and handwritten notes. Learning was often a passive activity, with students absorbing information presented by their instructors. Assessments were typically conducted through written exams and assignments, graded manually by educators. The advent of digital technologies brought significant transformation, with the traditional model having been disrupted. Digital tools have enabled more interaction and engagement in the teaching methods, facilitating active learning and greater student participation. Online resources and digital textbooks have made information more accessible, while digital platforms have supported personalized and adaptive learning experiences. Assessments have also evolved, with digital tools allowing for more diverse and authentic evaluation methods.

Understanding the Digital Revolution

Digital Transformation goes beyond the simple act of adopting new technologies. According to McDonald and Rowsell-Jones (2012), digital transformation entails technology infrastructures, company culture, society, creativity, and extrude management. It encompasses a broader and more complex process of organizational change including: strategic alignment of goals, cultural shift, change in ways of operating, business process reengineering, data-driven decision making and analytics to inform decision-making and drive innovation and new ways of working to effectively utilize new digital technologies and capabilities and customer centricity. It requires a holistic, strategic, and change-oriented approach to fully realize the potential of digital technologies within an organization. For higher education institutions, digital transformation is not only affecting information technology but also all sectors of the organization. It has become imperative and urgent that higher education institutions link all digital activities with the organization's vision and strategy (Sarnok et al., 2020).

To enhance product and services, HEIs need to come up with new educational products through improving the existing ones (Sandkuhl & Lehmann, 2017). Critical among these is establishing educational programs that HEIs at national and international levels can access externally. This can only be made possible by developing learning modules for digital education and by providing a digital conducive environment for students-teacher and student peer to peer interaction and collaboration (Balyer & Oz, 2018). Munro (2018) stresses that faculty and teachers need to focus on improving learning flexibility, personalized learning and creating learning content that is universal, accessible and culturally relevant to the needs of each learner (ELWa, 2003) rather than the traditional focus on cognitive dimension of learning.

Rapid advancements in technology, particularly the proliferation of digital devices, high-speed internet and cloud computing, led to digital transformation in education and made it easier to access digital learning spaces, share information, collaborate with others, and create interactive learning experiences (Seaman, et al., 2018).In particular, the quest for collaborative digital learning space is redefining the roles of students and educators, allowing for modern learning forms and enabling universities to collaborate across borders. Digital transformation in (HEIs) is a driver of social oriented innovations. It not only improves the most demanded skills in the new knowledge society like searching and processing information, digital communication and socialization but also reduces costs related to education. According to Qolamani and colleagues (2023) early adoption of technologies such as analytics, Artificial Intelligence (AI), and immersive media especially those who may apply and consider students' needs and inclusion of marginalized groups may enhance students' experience in the future.

Expectations of today's students are changing. Often referred to as digital natives, students of today expect their educational experiences to be technologically integrated. They are already accustomed to accessing information online, engaging with multimedia content and using digital tools for communication and collaboration. With the digital revolution, knowledge and information is more accessible than ever before. Students in higher education can now access a wealth of educational resources including learning opportunities globally. Equally there is increased demand for workers with digital skills. For instance, Khan, et al. (2022) study which focused on young adults aimed to examine drivers of digital literacy in HEIs and specifically, their relevance in today's digital workplace. Several skills including, critical operational, visual learning styles, collaborative learning styles and learning systems were stressed as essential digital literacy skills that need to be taught at HEIs and further that these sets of skills improve both academic performance and employability. Going forth, Reinhart (2008) in his studies on dynamics in approaches to teaching HEIs and paradigm shifts in technological and pedagogical learning innovations suggests that digital institutions should have web and virtual libraries to increase access to global knowledge.

According to Taneja (2014), employers seek individuals who are proficient in using technology, adaptable to changing environments, and capable of lifelong learning. This has put pressure on institutions of higher education to equip students with the digital competencies needed for success in the workforce. There has been a paradigm shift in educational philosophy and pedagogy, moving away from traditional, teacher-centered approaches towards a student-centered approach and active learning methodologies. Digital technologies offer opportunities to implement these pedagogical approaches effectively, facilitating personalized learning, collaboration, and problem-solving.

Digital revolution has the potential to open up new avenues for creativity, inclusion, and excellence in the higher education system. This is demonstrated in Deviprasad (2024) study in India that explored wide-range changes that India's digital revolution has brought about in its higher education system, as well as the profound effects it has had. Consequently, various geographical and socioeconomic barriers to education were eliminated and democratizing access to education has been achieved. Students from underprivileged origins and distant locations now have direct access to high-quality educational resources because to the growth of online learning platforms. The digital age has revolutionized teaching and learning methodologies. Institutions are increasingly adopting innovative pedagogical techniques such as flipped classrooms, blended learning, and personalized learning experiences facilitated by educational technology tools. Digital learning has been linked with enhanced student engagement, collaboration, and critical thinking skills, thereby improving the overall quality of education. University levels, there has been an increase of partnership with industry stakeholders to offer industry-relevant courses and certifications, bridging the gap between academia and the workforce.

The mission of the digital revolution in education is broad with far reaching effects. Digital revolution's main aim has been to leverage technology to enhance teaching, learning, and assessment practices, ultimately improving educational outcomes for students (Mertala, 2019). Despite its potential benefits, the digital revolution in higher education also raises several concerns, including digital equity and access, quality of online learning, privacy and security, digital literacy and skill gap and pedagogical challenges (Prinsloo & Slade, 2017). Addressing these concerns while pursuing the mission of digital revolution in education is discussed in the chapter as it is critical in t realizing the full potential of technology for transforming teaching, learning, and assessment practices in higher education.

METHODOLOGY

The study is based on desktop and content analysis of the existing literature to establish the existing status of digital transformation in HEIs. It consists of systematic and rigorous analysis of existing research, academic literature and reports on the digital transformation in education.

A comprehensive literature search was conducted using academic databases. These included Google Scholar, JSTOR, ERIC, Scopus, among others, to collect information related to digital transformation in higher education from peer-reviewed articles, books, and reports. Some of the key words and phrases used during the search included "digital revolution in education," "teaching and learning in higher education," "digital assessment," "project-based learning," "blended learning," "digital literacy," "online learning challenges," and "privacy in digital education."

In order to capture the most recent advancements and insights related to digital education, the search focused on studies published from the year 2000. However, key foundational theories in teaching and learning and seminal works on educational technology, regardless of their publication date, were also considered.

The inclusion criteria for the literature review were publications that specifically address the digital transformation in higher education. Studies that discuss teaching, learning, and assessment models relevant to digital education as well as literature addressing challenges such as digital equity, privacy, data security, and access issues in digital education were also included. Studies that did not focus on higher education and non-peer-reviewed articles without empirical or theoretical rigor were excluded from the review.

Once the relevant literature was identified, key information from each source was systematically extracted. These included theoretical frameworks used in each study, approaches and models guiding the paradigm shift from analogue to digital practices in teaching, learning, and assessment as well as the impact of digital technologies on higher education practices. The challenges and concerns associated with digital transformation and best practices as well as recommendations for effectively integrating digital technologies into higher education were also included. The data was organized thematically, with a deliberate intention of focusing on main areas of the chapter. These included technological models, pedagogical approaches, and challenges.

Models Guiding the Shift

Digital revolution in higher education is marked by the integration of advanced technologies and innovative pedagogical approaches that transform traditional teaching, learning, and assessment practices. Several educational models have been instrumental in guiding this transformation, each offering unique perspectives and methodologies for leveraging digital tools to enhance the educational experience.

The flipped classroom model was popularized by high school teachers Jon Bergmann and Aaron Sams, who began implementing it in their chemistry classes in the late 2000s. The flipped classroom model inverts the traditional teaching structure by delivering instructional content, virtually. This allows for more interactive and hands-on learning activities to occur within the classroom. The philosophy behind this model is the focus on a student-centered approach that prioritizes active learning and engagement (Bergmann & Sams, 2012). It includes pre-class, in-class and post-class. In pre-class, students engage with new material through videos, readings, or other resources while in-class the class time is used for interactive, collaborative activities, problem-solving, and application of knowledge. Students in post-class reflect on what they have learned and receive feedback. In higher education, the flipped classroom model can be applied by assigning students pre-recorded lectures or reading materials to review before class. During class sessions, instructors can facilitate discussions, group work, and practical exercises to reinforce and apply the concepts learned.

Online Collaborative Learning (OCL) approach entails collaborative exchange of ideas and perspectives virtually (Demuyakor, 2020; Magen-Nagar & Schonfeld, 2017). This approach to teaching has been associated with a myriad of benefits that includes increased accessibility, flexibility and cost effectiveness especially with the large educational network that can be reached (Demuyakor, 2020). Specifically, OCL has been crucial in contributing to: a) generating ideas, which allows brainstorming and bringing divergent concepts b) organizing ideas which allows students to compare, analyze, and categorize several concepts that were earlier created, through debate and argument c) Intellectual convergence compassing intellectual synthesis and consensus building(Jakoet-Salie et al., 2023).

Project-Based Learning (PBL) as a teaching model that emphasizes experiential learning and the importance of engaging students in meaningful, real-world tasks. PBL refers to a teaching approach where students learn by actively engaging in real-world and personally meaningful projects (Tyler-Wood, 2020). The philosophy of PBL is centered on constructivism, where learning is seen as an active, constructive process. According to Thomas, (2000), the model is characterized by real-world connections, student voice and choice, inquiry and innovation and reflection and revision. In the real-world connections, projects are based on real-world problems or challenges. In student voice and choice, they have a say in the projects they undertake and how they complete them. Students engage in a rigorous process of inquiry, innovation, and problem-solving and reflect on their work and make revisions based on feedback. They also present their projects to a public audience beyond the classroom. In higher education, PBL can be implemented by having students work on interdisciplinary projects that address real-world issues. For example, engineering students might design sustainable solutions for local communities, or business students might develop marketing strategies for non-profit organizations.

Assessment for Learning (AfL), also known as formative assessment approach, focuses on using assessment as a tool to promote and enhance learning in addition to measuring it. The philosophy behind AfL is that continuous feedback and active involvement in the assessment process help students understand their learning goals and the steps needed to achieve them. It is characterized by feedback, student involvement, learning goals and interactive processes (Black & Wiliam, 1998). In higher education, AfL can be applied through various techniques such as regular quizzes, interactive discussions, peer reviews, and reflective journals. These methods provide ongoing feedback and help students identify areas for improvement while allowing instructors to adjust their teaching strategies.

Blended learning is a model that has been supported and developed by various educational theorists and practitioners, including Graham (2006) and Picciano (2009), who have explored its potential to combine the strengths of both face-to-face and online learning. Blended approach to learning helps in leveraging the benefits of both face -to face and online approaches to create a more flexible and effective learning environment (Graham,2006;Tyler-Wood,2020). The philosophy behind blended learning is to integrate the best aspects of classroom and online education to enhance the learning experience. Integration involves seamlessly combining online and offline activities with flexibility that allows students to access content, learn and progress at their own pace and engage using a variety of instructional methods to maintain student interest and participation while providing opportunities for personalized learning paths and self-directed study (Garrison & Vaughan, 2008). In higher education, blended learning can be implemented by offering courses that include both in-person sessions and online components. For example, a course might have weekly face-to-face lectures complemented by online discussions, digital assignments, and virtual labs.

These models collectively contribute to the digital transformation in HIEs by providing frameworks that support innovative teaching methods, personalized learning experiences, and effective assessment strategies. By embracing these models, HIEs can better prepare students for the demands of the modern world, ensuring that they acquire not only knowledge but also the critical skills needed for success.

Digital Transformation in Teaching, Learning, and Assessment

Digital technologies that have transformed teaching practices, learning experiences, and assessment methods in higher education are discussed in this chapter. According to (Chen, et al. 2018), teaching practices must be flexible in instruction, interactive in terms of learning resources, offer collaborative learning opportunities and the instruction must be personalized. Digital technologies have enabled educators to deliver instruction in flexible formats, such as, recorded lectures, online modules, or live virtual classes. This flexibility allows students to learn at their own pace and convenience, accommodating diverse learning styles and preferences (Bower et al. 2017; Elena 2017). The tools have provided access to a wide range of interactive learning resources, including multimedia presentations, simulations, virtual labs, and educational games, which engage students in active learning experiences, enhancing their understanding and retention of course material.

Several studies (e.g. Tess, 2013).have explored various technologies used in higher education, their potential applications, and strategies for effective implementation. One such tool has been Social Media (e.g., Facebook, Twitter) which has been used in collaborative learning, information sharing, and building learning communities. Social media offers unique pedagogy that allows creation of closed groups for class discussions, assigning roles to students (e.g., moderators, researchers, summarizers), provides opportunities to use hashtags for organizing course-related content and for implementing digital citizenship lessons. Effective use of Social media as a pedagogic tool requires clearly defined learning objectives and guidelines for social media use in the classroom.

Learning Management Systems (LMS) (e.g., Moodle, Canvas) have become central to many educational institutions for course organization and content delivery, assessment, and tracking student progress.(Aldiab, et. al., 2019).It is uniquely designed to provide modular course design, adaptive learning paths, gamification elements (badges, progress bars) and peer review assignments Effective use of LMS requires intensive training for both educators and students and creation of a consistent structure across courses to improve navigation and reduce cognitive load.

Video Conferencing Tools such as Zoom, campus, and Microsoft Teams have also been used in many education situations to promote remote learning, virtual lectures, and collaborative projects. The unique pedagogies enabled by this tool includes flipped classroom model, breakout rooms for small group discussions, screen sharing for demonstrations and interactive polling and quizzes. Effective use of video conferencing tools requires establishment of clear protocols for online etiquette and participation, provision of a blend or a mix of synchronous and asynchronous activities to maintain engagement and accommodate different learning styles.

Equally many HEIs are taking advantage of the Virtual and Augmented Reality (VR/AR) which they apply to support immersive learning experiences, simulations, and virtual field trips. These tools enable utilization of unique pedagogy such as: experiential learning cycles, guided discovery approaches, scenario-based learning and spatial cognition exercises Effective use of VR/AR applications requires that we begin with the simplest tools and gradually increase complexity. Equally there is a need to ensure accessibility options for students who may experience discomfort with immersive technologies.

Today learning institutions are experiencing increased adoption of Artificial Intelligence (AI) and Chatbots that come in handy for personalized learning, automated feedback, and 24/7 student support (Roll & Wylie 2016). AI and Chatboxs allow adaptive questioning techniques. Spaced repetition for knowledge retention, natural language processing for writing improvement and intelligent tutoring systems. It should be understood that AI is used to supplement and not as a replacement for human instruction. Importantly there should be regular review and updating of AI algorithms to ensure accuracy and relevance of content.

The use of the above technologies and tools requires that HEIs develop digital literacy curricula that trains students to critically evaluate online content avoid cyberbullying, and become responsible users of technology, ongoing professional development to keep educators updated on the latest educational technologies and pedagogical approaches, creation of technology-integrated lesson plans and activities that seamlessly blend technology use with traditional learning methods, encourage active learning that promotes student-centered, inquiry-based learning rather than passive consumption of information continuous evaluation of the effectiveness of technology integration and adjustment to strategies based on feedback and outcomes.. Importantly, there is a need to foster a culture of digital citizenship as a means of promoting ethical and responsible use of technology both within and out of the classroom.(Ng, 2012, Hamilton, et al 2016; Freeman et al 2014; Lawless & Pellegrino 2007).

Learning experiences should allow for easy access to information, have content that is interactive and engaging, allow for anywhere anytime learning as well as global collaboration and networking (Graham et al., 2013). Digital technologies provide students with instant access to vast amounts of information from diverse sources, including online databases, e-books, academic journals, and multimedia content, hence explore topics in depth, conduct research, and engage with a variety of perspectives (Selwyn, 2015). Multimedia resources, such as videos, animations, and interactive simulations, make learning more engaging and interactive, hence less theoretical (Redecker & Johannessen, 2013). Online learning platforms and mobile apps engage learners actively at, anywhere, using their own devices (Means et al., 2013; McLaughlin et al., 2014). This flexibility accommodates busy schedules and allows students to balance their academic studies with work, family, or other commitments.

Digital transformation is crucial in assessment approaches. It is important that the assessment methods are diverse in format and automated in grading. It offers a wide range of assessment formats beyond traditional exams and essays, including online quizzes, interactive assignments, multimedia projects, peer reviews, and e-portfolios which allow educators to evaluate students' understanding and skills in more authentic and meaningful ways (Chase et al., 2017;Woodfield, & Harrison, 2013).By leveraging adaptive testing, multimedia assessments, automated feedback, and learning analytics, faculty can create more engaging, personalized, and realistic evaluation methods that better prepare students for real-world challenges. AI-powered tools and digital technologies are linked with more authentic and engaging forms of student assessment, particularly beneficial for instructors teaching large classes, who often face challenges in providing individualized feedback and creating engaging assessment tasks. The adaptive testing platforms have the power of personalizing assessment items according to student's demonstrated proficiency (Redecker & Johannessen, 2013).

To add on, AI powered tools incorporate multimedia elements, such as videos, simulations, and interactive scenarios and assessment tasks that better reflect authentic contexts (Herrington & Herrington, 2006). They also provide timely, detailed, and personalized feedback with a more iterative and self-directed learning process (Shute, 2008). According to Maringe and Sing (2014) many faculty have leveraged online quizzes, peer-review mechanisms, and multimedia presentations to enhance the authenticity of assessments in their large enrollment courses. Additionally, Boud and Molloy (2013) highlighted how learning analytics dashboards helped instructors identify struggling students and intervene with targeted support. Using AI powered tools provides opportunities for faculty to learn analytics as they are expected to collect and analyze data leading to rich insights into students' learning processes, more informed decisions about assessment design and delivery (Gašević et al., 2015).

Digital assessment tools can automate grading and provide real time feedback, reducing the time and effort required for manual grading. According to Ifenthaler and Schumacher, (2019), learning analytics and data visualization tools enable educators to track student progress, identify learning trends, and make data-informed decisions about instruction and intervention. These insights help educators personalize instruction, support struggling students, and improve overall learning outcomes. As Furintasari and Heri (2022) noted, digital technologies support the implementation of authentic assessment tasks that mirror real-world challenges and scenarios. It is therefore evident that digital technologies have significantly revolutionized teaching practices, learning experiences, and assessment methods in higher education by providing flexibility, interactivity, personalization, and access to resources and data.

In particular Dennen and Burner (2018) recognizes technology as a tool that facilitates collaboration and communication among teachers and students, leading to more meaningful assessment experiences. For these two scholars digital portfolios help develop 21st Century skills, such as information, literacy, media literacy, and digital citizenship. These skills allow students to create a positive digital presence and to showcase their achievements and skills to potential employers and academic institutions. Improving learning are online collaboration tools, such as online discussion forums, video conferencing, and messaging platforms all which allow students to communicate and work together in real-time, breaking down the barriers of time and space. Utilizing shared spaces for projects and assignments, teachers and students can create and assess assignments live, providing immediate feedback and fostering a collaborative learning environment. Technology can also enable peer review, allowing students to assess and provide feedback on each other's work, promoting a sense of community and shared responsibility for learning (Moore, 2022).

Challenges and Concerns

The transformation of teaching, learning, and assessment in institutions of higher learning specifically from analogue to digital did not happen without challenges. Given the differences in nature and type of HEIs, the challenges these institutions faced were similar and of varied magnitude. This section of the book analyzes strategies for addressing these challenges to ensure the successful implementation of digital teaching, learning, and assessment practices.

The synthesis of the literature showed several challenges and concerns affected digital transformation of higher education. Some of the key challenges and concerns affecting digital transformation of higher education are discussed as follows; A number of institutions experienced the challenge of lack of or inadequate technological infrastructures to drive the transformation from dialogue to digital (Owidi et al., 2023; Wekullo et al., 2023). Specifically, institutions lacked heavy bandwidth required to serve a large population and to teach content that requires more streaming and has a lot of graphics (Wekullo et al., 2023). For instance, previous research done in Africa showed that most learning institutions had small bandwidth to serve administrative staff and a few graduate students. When the pandemic struck and they hurriedly moved learning online, the small bandwidth could not accommodate the large number of students including the undergraduates and the teaching staff. It is important that the assessment methods are diverse in format and automated in grading (Kaisara & Bwalya, 2021; Owidi et al., 2023; Wekullo et al., 2022; Wekullo et al., 2023).

Pedagogical challenges in terms of integrating digital technologies into teaching practices is a valid concern. The review of literature revealed that the move from analogue to digital teaching and learning exacerbated the existing challenges for students in higher education (Moodley, 2022; Owidi et al., 2023, Wekullo et. al., 2023).Specifically, the digital transformation in teaching, and learning regressed into impersonal methodologies, devoid of any notion of pedagogy as the science and art of teaching. Moreso, the shift from analogue to digital learning alienated and in a way caused disengagement among students from learning as a collaborative process (Moodley, 2022). Traditional classrooms and blended learning have an aspect of team learning, peer support and collaborations in activities among learners. With digital transformation, where instructors only share course content and learners learn through virtual or on their own wherever, there are reported cases of isolation and loss of social skills among learners (Owidi et al., 2023; Wekullo et al.2023). The transactional distance between the students and the instructor has so far increased the challenges students encounter in the virtual classroom. With the digital revolution, instructors too are left to wonder whether what they taught was well understood or not. As there is lack of immediate feedback and it is hard to observe the body language of learners (Wekullo et al., 2023).

Further, studies show that institutions of higher learning globally have implemented digital learning and teaching at different levels. In most cases especially during COVID-19, most institutions immediately shifted their learning and teaching online. The immediate shift caught many faculty unaware and unprepared to switch to virtual teaching pedagogies. Resulting to pedagogical challenges where faculty members had inadequate capacity to effectively and efficiently deliver online pedagogies in terms of technological tools and knowhow (Amemado 2020). As Kadhila and Nyambe (2021) stated, unprepared virtual pedagogy has a negative impact on the quality of the programs offered.

The transformation process from analogue to digital exacerbated various existing inequality and access issues within the institutions of higher learning. For instance, the transition exposed inequalities in relation to access to technology across the student body, arising from diverse socio-economic backgrounds, which has predominantly emerged as a major challenge (Bassett, 2020; Duku et al., 2022; Owidi et al., 2023). Students from predominantly disadvantaged socioeconomic backgrounds experienced challenges accessing virtual learning technology as they lacked resources to afford digital technology for learning. Specifically, most students lacked laptops, leave alone smartphones to access the digital learning and teaching. This was perpetuated by the expensive cost of internet infrastructures such as Wi-Fi routers, laptops, mobile phones, and access to data bandwidth (Khadila & Nyambe, 2021; Wekullo, et al., 2023). Further, as Khadila and Nyambe (2021) stated, most institutions of higher learning have tried to distribute modems and data bundles to staff and students, however, gadgets are reported not to be working effectively in areas with weak or no network reception causing challenges of technology access to both students and instructors.

On the same note, scholars such as Yunusa et al (2021) noted that the use of physical resources is not a concern to students in the era of digital age, but the concern is the affordability and availability of those physical resources for digital learning. On the contrary, Jaggars and Xu, (2016) noted the disparities in digital literacy skills among students to navigate online learning environments, effectively as well as the digital skills gap that may hinder students' ability to succeed in digital-rich educational environments as a challenge. More so, students with learning challenges, such as disabilities vulnerable and likely to drop out of the education pipeline have likely been left behind (Bassett, 2020). Academic integrity in the context of digital learning remained an area of greatest concern. From the review of literature, there are concerns that digital transformation has led to loss of learning quality. The interactive classroom and psychological feeling that came with physical classes are lost entirely due to challenges associated with digital learning (Olawale & Mutongoza, 2021). In terms of procedural sequences, teaching, and assessment were affected as teaching content and processes of teaching are minimized compared to assessment, resulting in poor quality learning (Olawale & Mutongoza, 2021). Further, it is a concern that with digital transformation, most higher learning institutions have lost a universal definitive standard for digital based assessment. This means that individual faculties, department, and some time lecturers are left to determine the assessment modalities to be used. More worrisome is the integrity issues in the higher education institutions assessment systems and processes deployed for digital assessment in the learning management systems. There are concerns of increased malpractices in terms of copying, and academic dishonesty among students. As it is, disregard for intellectual property is likely to become rampant.

The shift from analogue to digital learning has influenced the performance of learners. While the research presents a conflicting effect of the digital learning on performance, a majority of previous studies indicate that educational performance of students in digital learning has changed for the worst when compared to face-to-face learning (Spreen & Vally, 2010), partly due to the availability of resources and partly due to social class (Mouton, et al., 2013; Spreen & Vally, 2010). In addition, students experienced a larger workload by transition to digital learning. Similarly, A shift to digital learning also has the potential to limit opportunity for faculty members to conduct continuous improvement for students. Previous studies revealed that faculty members experienced difficulties in assessing whether students understood what they taught (Spreen & Vally, 2010; Wekullo, et al., 2023). Faculty members have challenges of being unable to monitor and control students' behavior, in distractions from backgrounds, and delays in starting class due to technology-related problems.

Students are dissatisfied with digital learning because they missed the social aspect of their academics. Isolation among students is a consistent concern presented across the literature (Ashari et al 2020; Wekullo et al, 2023). The literature showed that students experience social issues when using digital platforms for learning and teaching. They lack interaction with their instructors and peers, thus, losing their sense of community that is present in face to face which helps learners to collaborate and learn from each other (Kadhila, & Nyambe, 2021). While digital learning may never replace face to face socialization (Njenga & Fourie, 2010) collaborative digital learning systems like WhatsApp may be used for both academic and non - academic activities without space and time constraints to mitigate the feeling of isolation (Ahmed, 2020).

Students reported experiencing psychological, emotional and mental health problems due to increased stress, anxiety, or social isolation from learning and being taught virtually (Kadhila, & Nyambe, 2021; Kaisara & Bwalya, 2021). The psycho-social and emotional challenges could have been attributed to lack of preparation from the institution to empower them with skills required to use the online systems (Kaisara & Bwalya, 2021; Wekullo et. al., 2023; Didinya et. al., 2018).

The other challenge included low technology self-efficacy and unpreparedness among faculty members (Ngonda, 2023). This has led to lack of commitment and resistance to change from analogue to digital learning (Yunusa et al., 2021). Faculty in some institutions are resistant to training. Yet, in the transition to digital learning, faculty are expected to develop digital content which requires time, commitment and resources. Research showed that faculty at some institutions were facilitated with the needed resources and trained, while others were left to navigate the digital transition on their own which became a challenge (Unwin et al., 2010; Wekullo et al., 2023). Further, Unwin, et al., (2010) noted that most African educators still have little knowledge about, or interest in the usage of learning management systems due to infrastructural barriers and weak ICT policies. While institutions are expected to develop policy to guide the operation of digital learning, some institutions are still experiencing the policy gaps.

The other challenge associated with digital transformation in higher education include assessment integrity, academic dishonesty, cost of infrastructure, infrastructural barriers and weak ICT policies, faculty resistance and training, social support as well as the social and emotional impact on students, such as increased stress, anxiety, or social isolation as critical challenges for students. Academic dishonesty is also a complex psychological and social phenomenon that continues to undermine the credibility of online learning and the validity of online evaluation (Sidi et al., 2019; Tungpantong, et at., 2021).

Higher education stakeholders have raised concerns about breach of data privacy policy and data transparency with digital transformation. For instance, Almekhled & Petrie, (2023) conducted a survey of 71 UK HEI students exploring their attitudes and concerns about lack of transparency, information, privacy and security especially in the online environment and social media-based teaching and learning. Results indicated that there is lack of capacity as well as institutional policies guiding digital learning. Overly, previous studies reveal that the digital revolution still faces numerous challenges within the higher education context. There is a need for appropriate action to be done before digital learning can be regarded as a tool that could enhance access to education and inclusive learning for university students.

Due to myriads of challenges ranging from lack of accessibility, inequality, isolation, poor performance of students, inadequate technological infrastructure and related costs, many scholars (Kaisara & Bwalya, 2021; Wekullo et al., 2023) across the globe posit that digital learning has failed to live up to its promised benefits. The above listed challenges are among the key concerns any higher education wishing to move from analogue to digital ought to address first. Failure to address these challenges facing digital learning could ultimately lead to increased nonsuccess of digital transformational initiatives.

Best Practices and Recommendations

While the digital revolution may seem to pose challenges, it opens up unprecedented opportunities for democratization and accessibility in HEIs. However, the digital transformation process in universities has to maintain the referential of the profound incorporation of pedagogical and technological innovation based on research to cope with the changing dynamics in education. Graham, et al., (2013) proposed some of the best practices for educators, administrators, and policymakers to effectively integrate digital technologies into higher education, which is discussed in the book chapter. For educators, they propose continuous professional development, learning experiences to adopt a student centered approach, timely and constructive feedback to students and ensure that digital materials and resources are accessible and inclusion of all students, including those living with various disabilities.

Based on the reviewed literature, institution administrators need to invest in robust technology infrastructure, provide technical support, develop and implement comprehensive professional development programs for faculty and establish guidelines for the design and delivery of online courses to ensure quality and consistency across programs. They should foster a culture of collaboration among faculty, departments, and institutions to share best practices, resources, and lessons learned in integrating digital technologies. They should implement policies and procedures that safeguard students' data and ensure compliance with privacy regulations.

The review also proposes that higher education institutions should consider students' difficulties in adapting to digital teaching and learning and possibly find ways of fostering students centered pedagogy in virtual classrooms. While there are many challenges that can hinder students from realizing the full potential of digital teaching and learning, alternative pathways like provision of free data bandwidth, free physical resources and online resources and use of information centers for blended learning could be a part of the solution (Mpungose, 2020).

The findings of this review calls for institutional leaders and policy makers to examine the inclusiveness of digital education and come up with strategies for a blended mode of learning that accommodates both technical and non-technical courses. In addition, such challenges through collaborative networks of public–private partnerships. As through viability of multi-stakeholder networks institutions get the opportunity to share expertise and resolve issues related to training needs (Samson et al., 2006). Further, Samson et. al., (2006) suggested establishing collaborative networks that include e-learning sponsors, policy makers, telecommunication network service providers and educators to solve the problems of online education that is sustainable Much work should be done in developing human capacity and providing infrastructure if African learners are truly to benefit from the interactive learning experiences that such systems can deliver.

In a nutshell, policymakers need to allocate funding and resources to support the integration of digital technologies into higher education, as they develop policy frameworks that promote the responsible and ethical use of digital technologies in education (Ifenthaler & Schumacher, 2019). They should provide incentives and recognition for institutions and educators that demonstrate excellence in integrating digital technologies into teaching and learning and support research initiatives. Also,there is a need for regular evaluations and assessments of digital learning experiences so as to identify areas for improvement. Digital technologies should be evaluated to improve student outcomes. Teaching practices should be enhanced as they foster partnerships which promote innovation, share resources, and address common challenges in digital education.

FURTHER RESEARCH DIRECTION

This paper has potential applications for educators, faculty in HEIs and researchers. There is need for sound evidence on the evolving skills requirement by educators and students, efforts by HEIs in remodeling the instructional approaches, assessment formats, educational content and mechanisms to ensure validity and reliability of online examination techniques with targeted attention to technologies that support learners with special needs.

The study is based on desktop and content analysis of the existing literature. While the approach helped establish the existing status of digital transformation in HEIs, there is a need for a future study to determine the impact of accepting and adopting digital technologies on students and faculty performance or productivity in HEIs using advanced either qualitative or quantitative research approaches.

The increased use of digital technologies in higher education raises ethical concerns related to data privacy and security. There is need for further research to explore how student data, collected through digital platforms, is used, stored and protected. The study could focus on how HEIs can safeguard this data while complying with ethical and legal standards.

CONCLUSION

The transformation from analogue to digital in higher education has ushered in a new era of teaching, learning, and assessment. This chapter provides an in-depth exploration of the impact of the digital revolution on higher education, examining the key models and approaches that have guided this transformation, the mission driving digital adoption, and the concerns and challenges associated with this paradigm shift. The chapter began by setting the context of the digital revolution in higher education, highlighting its significance and outlining the objectives and scope of the chapter. It emphasized the importance of understanding the underlying drivers of this transformation, such as technological advancements, changing student demographics, and the demand for flexible learning options. The digital revolution has fundamentally changed the landscape of higher education. Rapid technological advancements have made information more accessible, collaboration easier, and learning more interactive. Today's students, often digital natives, expect their educational experiences to be technologically integrated. Various educational models have guided the shift from traditional methods to digital approaches. The flipped classroom model, project-based learning, assessment for learning, and blended learning were explored in detail. These models promote active learning, personalized instruction, and deeper understanding, aligning with the needs and preferences of 21st-century learners.

Digital technologies have revolutionized teaching practices, learning experiences, and assessment methods. Flexible instruction formats, interactive learning resources, personalized learning experiences, and diverse assessment methods were discussed. The chapter highlighted how these digital tools enhance engagement, accessibility, and educational outcomes. Despite the benefits, the digital transformation of higher education presents several challenges. Issues related to digital equity and access, quality of online learning, privacy and security, digital literacy, and pedagogical integration were analyzed. Addressing these concerns is crucial for the successful implementation of digital teaching, learning, and assessment practices. The chapter provided best practices and recommendations for educators, administrators, and policymakers to effectively integrate digital technologies into higher education. Continuous professional development, student-centered approaches, robust technology infrastructure, and comprehensive policy frameworks were among the key strategies discussed.

The digital revolution in higher education holds immense potential to enhance teaching, learning, and assessment practices. By leveraging technology, institutions can provide more flexible, engaging, and personalized educational experiences. However, realizing this potential requires addressing the challenges and concerns associated with digital transformation. To ensure the successful integration of digital technologies, higher education institutions must prioritize digital equity and access, invest in robust infrastructure, and provide continuous professional development for educators. It is essential to establish guidelines for online learning quality, protect student data, and promote digital literacy among both students and faculty. Looking forward, ongoing research and innovation are vital to continually improve digital education practices. Institutions should foster a culture of collaboration and knowledge sharing to address common challenges and develop effective strategies. Policymakers must support these efforts by allocating resources, creating supportive policy frameworks, and promoting ethical and responsible use of digital technologies in education.

The transition from analogue to digital in higher education represents a profound shift that requires careful consideration, strategic planning, and collaborative effort. By embracing the opportunities and addressing the challenges of the digital revolution, higher education institutions can enhance educational outcomes and prepare students for success in an increasingly digital world. This chapter has aimed to equip educators, researchers, and practitioners with the knowledge and strategies needed to navigate this transformation and foster a future where digital technologies are seamlessly integrated into the fabric of higher education.

REFERENCES

Ahmed, B. E. S. (2020). Social media in teaching of languages. *International Journal of Emerging Technologies in Learning,* 15(12), 72-80. https://doi-org/DOI: 10.3991/ijet.v15i12.12645

Aldiab, A., Chowdhury, H., Kootsookos, A., Alam, F., & Allhibi, H. (2019). Utilization of Learning Management Systems (LMSs) in higher education system: A case review for Saudi Arabia. *Energy Procedia*, 160, 731–737. DOI: 10.1016/j.egypro.2019.02.186

Alessio, H. M., Malay, N. J., Maurer, K., Bailer, A. J., & Rubin, B. (2017). Examining the Effect of Proctoring on Online Test Scores. *Online Learning : the Official Journal of the Online Learning Consortium*, 21(1), 146–161. DOI: 10.24059/olj.v21i1.885

Almekhled, B., & Petrie, H. (2023). Concerns of Saudi Higher Education Students About Security and Privacy of Online Digital Technologies During the Coronavirus Pandemic. In Abdelnour Nocera, J., Kristín Lárusdóttir, M., Petrie, H., Piccinno, A., & Winckler, M. (Eds.), Lecture Notes in Computer Science: Vol. 14144. *Human-Computer Interaction – INTERACT 2023*. Springer., DOI: 10.1007/978-3-031-42286-7_27

Amemado, D. (2020). *COVID-19: An unexpected and unusual driver to online education. International higher education*. The Boston College Center for International Higher Education.

Arnold, K. E. (2010). Signals: Applying academic analytics. *EDUCAUSE Quarterly*, 33(1).

Ashari, M. A., Zainal, I. A., & Zaki, F. M. (2020). Strategies for radiology departments in handling the COVID-19 pandemic. *Diagnostic and Interventional Radiology (Ankara, Turkey)*, 26(4), 296–300. DOI: 10.5152/dir.2020.20232

Astuti, F. S., & Retnawati, H. (2022). Online Learning Assessment: Solution in Industrial Revolution 4.0. *Advances in Social Science, Education and Humanities Research*. Advance online publication. DOI: 10.2991/assehr.k.220129.064

Balyer, A., & Oz, O. (2018). *Academicians' views on digital transformation in education*. International Online.

Bassett, R. M. (2020). *Sustaining the values of tertiary education during the COVID-19 crisis*. The Boston College Center for International Higher Education.

Bergmann, J., & Sams, A. (2012). *Flip Your Classroom: Reach Every Student in Every Class Every Day*. International Society for Technology in Education.

Black, E. W., Greaser, J., & Dawson, K. (2008). Academic Dishonesty in Traditional and Online Classrooms: Does the "Media Equation" Hold True? *Online Learning : the Official Journal of the Online Learning Consortium*, 12(3), 23–30. DOI: 10.24059/olj.v12i3.13

Black, P., & Wiliam, D. (1998). Assessment and Classroom Learning. *Assessment in Education: Principles, Policy & Practice*, 5(1), 7–74. DOI: 10.1080/0969595980050102

Bond, M., Marín, V. I., Dolch, C., Bedenlier, S., & Zawacki-Richter, O. (2018). Digital transformation in German higher education: Student and teacher perceptions and usage of digital media. *International Journal of Educational Technology in Higher Education*, 15(1), 48. DOI: 10.1186/s41239-018-0130-1

Bower, M., Lee, M. J., & Dalgarno, B. (2017). Collaborative learning across physical and virtual worlds: Factors supporting and constraining learners in a blended reality environment. *British Journal of Educational Technology*, 48(2), 407–430. DOI: 10.1111/bjet.12435

Chang, Bo. (2020). *Privacy Issues in Online Learning Environment*. American Association for Adult and Continuing Education.

Chang, B. (2021). Student privacy issues in online learning environments. *Distance Education*, 42(1), 55–69. DOI: 10.1080/01587919.2020.1869527

Chase, A., Ross, B., & Robbie, D. (2017). Improving Digital Assessment Practice: A Case Study of a Cross- Institutional Initiative. *Journal of University Teaching &amp. Journal of University Teaching & Learning Practice*, 14(2). Advance online publication. DOI: 10.53761/1.14.2.5

Chen, B., Knight, S., Wise, A., & Cheng, J. (2018). Critical issues in designing and implementing temporal analytics. *Journal of Computing in Higher Education*, 30(1), 27–47.

Crompton, H., & Burke, D. (2018). The use of mobile learning in higher education: A systematic review. *Computers & Education*, 123, 53–64. DOI: 10.1016/j.compedu.2018.04.007

Demuyakor, J. (2020). Coronavirus (COVID-19) and online learning in higher institutions of education: A survey of the perceptions of Ghanaian international students in China. *Online Journal of Communication and Media Technologies*, 10(3), e202018. DOI: 10.29333/ojcmt/8286

Dennen, V. P., Burner, K. J., & Cates, M. L. (2018). Information and Communication Technologies, and Learning Theories: Putting Pedagogy into Practice. In Voogt, J., Knezek, G., Christensen, R., & Lai, K. W. (Eds.), *Second Handbook of Information Technology in Primary and Secondary Education. Springer International Handbooks of Education*. Springer., DOI: 10.1007/978-3-319-71054-9_9

Didinya, E., Ouda, J. B., & Ndanu, C. (2018). Effect of Performance Appraisal of Teachers on Academic Performance of Students in Public Secondary Schools in Hamisi Sub-County, Vihiga County, Kenya. [JOPEA]. *Journal of Popular Education in Africa*, 2(5), 92–106.

Duku, N., Makeleni, S., Mavuso, M. P., & Mkhomi, M. S. (2020). Experiences of B. Ed Students on the use of E-Learning as a Vehicle to Learning during the COVID-19 Pandemic. *Education*, 16(7).

Elena, fleacă. (2017)study on Embedding digital teaching and learning practices in the modernization ofnhigher education institutions. *International multidisciplinary scientific geoconference* ; sofia, vol. 17, (2017). Doi:DOI: 10.5593/sgem2017/54

ELWa. (2003). *The context to an e-learning strategy for Wales*. Cardiff: National Council of Education and Training for Wales (ELWa).

Frank, J., Salsbury, M., McKelvey, H., & McLain, R. (2021). Digital Equity &Inclusion Strategies for Libraries: Promoting Student Success for All Learners. *The International Journal of Information, Diversity, and Inclusion*, 5(3). https://jps.library.utoronto.ca/index.php/ijidi

Freeman, S., Eddy, S. L., McDonough, M., Smith, M. K., Okoroafor, N., Jordt, H., & Wenderoth, M. P. (2014). Active learning increases student performance in science, engineering, and mathematics. *Proceedings of the National Academy of Sciences of the United States of America*, 111(23), 8410–8415. DOI: 10.1073/pnas.1319030111

Garrison, D. R., & Vaughan, N. D. (2008). *Blended Learning in Higher Education: Framework, Principles, and Guidelines*. Jossey-Bass.

Graham, C. R. (2006). Blended Learning Systems: Definition, Current Trends, and Future Directions. In Bonk, C. J., & Graham, C. R. (Eds.), *Handbook of Blended Learning: Global Perspectives, Local Designs* (pp. 3–21). Pfeiffer Publishing.

Graham, C. R., Woodfield, W., & Harrison, J. B. (2013). A framework for institutional adoption and implementation of blended learning in higher education. *The Internet and Higher Education*, 18, 4–14. DOI: 10.1016/j.iheduc.2012.09.003

Grosseck, G., Bran, R. A., & îru, L. G. (2024). Digital Assessment: A Survey of Romanian Higher Education, *Teachers'. Education Sciences*, 14(1), 32. DOI: 10.3390/educsci14010032

Hamilton, E. R., Rosenberg, J. M., & Akcaoglu, M. (2016). The substitution augmentation modification redefinition (SAMR) model: A critical review and suggestions for its use. *TechTrends*, 60(5), 433–441. DOI: 10.1007/s11528-016-0091-y

Harasim, L. (2017). *Learning Theory and Online Technologies*. Routledge. DOI: 10.4324/9781315716831

Herrington, J., & Herrington, A. (2006). Authentic conditions for authentic assessment: Aligning task and assessment. *InProceedings of the 7th conference on Australian society for computers in learning in tertiary education* (Vol. 1, pp. 146-154).

Ifenthaler, D., & Schumacher, C. (2019). Releasing the brake on data analytics in education. *TechTrends*, 63(1), 27–31.

Jaggars, S. S., & Xu, D. (2016). How do online course design features influence student performance? *Computers & Education*, 95, 270–284. DOI: 10.1016/j.compedu.2016.01.014

Jakoet-Salie, A., & Ramalobe, K. (2023). The digitalization of learning and teaching practices in higher education institutions during the Covid-19 pandemic. *Teaching Public Administration*, 41(1), 59–71. DOI: 10.1177/01447394221092275

Kadhila, N., & Nyambe, J. (2021). Barriers to the Quality of Emergency Online Pedagogies in Higher Education during the COVID-19 Pandemic: A Case Study from the University of Namibia: A case study from Namibia. *Journal of Learning for Development*, 8(3), 516–531. DOI: 10.56059/jl4d.v8i3.517

Kaisara, G., & Bwalya, K. J. (2021). Investigating the E-learning challenges faced by students during COVID-19 in Namibia. *International Journal of Higher Education*, 10(1), 308–318. DOI: 10.5430/ijhe.v10n1p308

Khan, N., Sarwar, A., Chen, T. B., & Khan, S. (2022). Connecting Digital Literacy in Higher Education to the 21st Century Workforce. *Knowledge Management & E-Learning,* v14 n1 p46-61

Lawless, K. A., & Pellegrino, J. W. (2007). Professional development in integrating technology into teaching and learning: Knowns, unknowns, and ways to pursue better questions and answers. *Review of Educational Research*, 77(4), 575–614. DOI: 10.3102/0034654307309921

Lynne, H., Huijser, H., & Sankey, M. (2012). Learning Spaces for the Digital Age: Blending Space with Pedagogy: Physical and Virtual Learning Spaces in Higher Education: *Concepts for the Modern Learning Environment.Pages*, 16, 182–197. Advance online publication. DOI: 10.4018/978-1-60960-114-0.ch012

Magen-Nagar, N., & Shonfeld, M. (2017). The impact of an online collaborative learning program on students' attitude towards technology. *Interactive Learning Environments*, 26(1), 1–17.

Manca, S., & Ranieri, M. (2013). Is it a tool suitable for learning? A critical review of the literature on Facebook as a technology-enhanced learning environment. *Journal of Computer Assisted Learning*, 29(6), 487–504. DOI: 10.1111/jcal.12007

Maringe, F., & Sing, N. (2014). Teaching large classes in an increasingly internationalising higher education environment: Pedagogical, quality and equity issues. *Higher Education*, 67(6), 739–763. DOI: 10.1007/s10734-013-9710-0

McDonald, M. P., & Rowsell-Jones, A. (2012). *The digital edge*. Gartner, Incorporated.

Means, B., Toyama, Y., Murphy, R., & Baki, M. (2013). The Effectiveness of Online and Blended Learning: A Meta-Analysis of the Empirical Literature. *Teachers College Record*, 115(3), 1–47. DOI: 10.1177/016146811311500307

Mertala, P. (2019). Paradoxes of participation in the digitalization of education: A narrative account. *Learning, Media and Technology*, 45(2), 179–192. DOI: 10.1080/17439884.2020.1696362

Moodley, D. (2022). Post Covid-19: The New (Ab) normal in South African Higher Education–Challenges with Emergency Remote Learning. *African Journal of Inter/Multidisciplinary Studies, 4*(1), 112-125.

Morgan, A., Sibson, R., & Jackson, D. (2022). Digital demand and digital deficit: Conceptualising digital literacy and gauging proficiency among higher education students. *Journal of Higher Education Policy and Management*, 44(3), 258–275. DOI: 10.1080/1360080X.2022.2030275

Mouton, N., Louw, G. P., & Strydom, G. (2013). Critical challenges of the South African school system. [IBER]. *The International Business & Economics Research Journal*, 12(1), 31–44. DOI: 10.19030/iber.v12i1.7510

Mpungose, C. B. (2020). Emergent transition from face-to-face to online learning in a South African University in the context of the Coronavirus pandemic. *Humanities & Social Sciences Communications*, 7(1), 1–9. DOI: 10.1057/s41599-020-00603-x

Munro, M. (2018). The complicity of digital technologies in the marketisation of UK higher education: Exploring the implications of a critical discourse analysis of thirteen national digital teaching and learning strategies. *International Journal of Educational Technology in Higher Education*, 15(1), 11. Advance online publication. DOI: 10.1186/s41239-018-0093-2

Ng, W. (2012). Can we teach digital natives digital literacy? *Computers & Education*, 59(3), 1065–1078. DOI: 10.1016/j.compedu.2012.04.016

Ngonda, T. (2023). Reflections on the Post COVID-19 Teaching and Learning: Lessons from the Emergency Transition to Online Learning at Two African Universities. *International Journal of Education and Development Using Information and Communication Technology*, 19(1), 139–151.

Njenga, J. K., & Fourie, L. C. H. (2010). The myths about e-learning in higher education. *British Journal of Educational Technology*, 41(2), 199–212. DOI: 10.1111/j.1467-8535.2008.00910.x

Olawale, B., & Mutongoza, B. (2021). Digital transformation in higher education institutions: Issues of functionality amid the COVID-19 pandemic. In *Proceedings of the 10th Multidisciplinary International Conference of the Global Education Network* (pp. 265-275).

Owidi, S., Wangila, E., Shiundu, J. O., & Simiyu, M. (2023). *Assessing the Prospects and Challenges of Online Learning in Kenyan Public Universities: A Case Study of Masinde Muliro University of Science and Technology*.

Persico, D., Manca, S., & Pozzi, F. (2014). Adapting the Technology Acceptance Model to evaluate the innovative potential of e-learning systems. *Computers in Human Behavior*, 30, 614–622. DOI: 10.1016/j.chb.2013.07.045

Picciano, A. (2009). Blending with Purpose: The Multimodal Model. *Journal of Asynchronous Learning Networks*, 13, 7–18.

Prinsloo, P., & Slade, S. (2017). An elephant in the learning analytics room - The obligation to act. *ACM International Conference Proceeding Series*. https://doi.org/ DOI: 10.1145/3027385.3027406

Qolamani, K., & Mohammed, M. M. (2023). The Digital Revolution in Higher Education: Transforming Teaching and Learning. QALAMUNA: *Jurnal Pendidikan, Sosial. Dan Agama*, 15(2), 837–846. DOI: 10.37680/qalamuna.v15i2.3905

Redecker, C., & Johannessen, Ø. (2013). Changing assessment—Towards a new assessment paradigm using ICT. *European Journal of Education*, 48(1), 79–96. DOI: 10.1111/ejed.12018

Roll, I., & Wylie, R. (2016). Evolution and revolution in artificial intelligence in education. *International Journal of Artificial Intelligence in Education*, 26(2), 582–599. DOI: 10.1007/s40593-016-0110-3

Sandkuhl, K., & Lehmann, H. (2017). *Digital Transformation in higher education-The role of enterprise architectures and portals*. Lecture Notes in Informatics.

Sarnok, K., Wannapiroon, P., & Nilsook, P. (2020). Dtl-eco system by digital storytelling to develop knowledge and digital intelligence for teacher profession students. *International Journal of Information and Education Technology (IJIET)*, 10(12), 865–872. DOI: 10.18178/ijiet.2020.10.12.1472

Seaman., ... (2018). Grade increase: Tracking distance education in the United States. Babson Park, MA: Babson Survey Research Group. *Babson Survey Research Group*. Babson Survey Research Group. https://eric.ed.gov/?id=ED580852 %0Awww.favazza.com

Selwyn, N. (2015). Minding our language: Why education and technology is full of bullshit… and what might be done about it†. *Learning, Media and Technology*, 41(3), 437–443. DOI: 10.1080/17439884.2015.1012523

Sheng, J. S. (2021). Kim Hua Tan & Mohd Mahzan Awang. (2021). Generic Digital Equity Model in Education: Mobile-Assisted Personalized Learning (MAPL) through e-Modules. *Sustainability (Basel)*, 13(19), 11115. DOI: 10.3390/su131911115

Spreen, C. A., & Vally, S. (2010). Outcomes-based education and its (dis) contents: Learner-centred pedagogy and the education crisis in South Africa. *Southern African Review of Education with Education with Production*, 16(1), 39–58.

Taneja, S. (2014). DreamBox: An adaptive, personalized learning platform for early math education. *Forbes*, 20(October), •••. https://doi.org/https://www.forbes.com/sites/sungardas/2014/10/20/dreambox-adaptive-personalized-learning-platform-early-math-education/

Tess, P. A. (2013). The role of social media in higher education classes (real and virtual) – A literature review. *Computers in Human Behavior*, 29(5), A60–A68. DOI: 10.1016/j.chb.2012.12.032

Thomas, J. W. (2000). *A Review of Research on Project-Based Learning*. Retrieved from http://www.bobpearlman.org/BestPractices/PBL_Research.pdf

Tungpantong, C., Nilsook, P., & Wannapiroon, P. (2021, March). A conceptual framework of factors for information systems success to digital transformation in higher education institutions. In 2021 9th International Conference on Information and Education Technology (ICIET) (pp. 57-62). IEEE. DOI: 10.1109/ICIET51873.2021.9419596

Tyler-Wood, T. L. (2020). The Role of Digital Fabrication in Today's Society. In Handbook of Research on Tools for Teaching Computational Thinking in P-12 Education (pp. 377-391). DOI: 10.4018/978-1-7998-4576-8.ch015

Wekullo, C. S., Kabindio, B., & Juma, I. (2023). Faculty and students' perspectives of online learning during COVID-19 crisis: Constraints and opportunities for Kenyan universities. *E-Learning and Digital Media*, •••, 20427530231156483.

Wekullo, C. S., Shiundu, J. O., Ouda, J. B., & Mutevane, A. (2022). COVID-19 crisis and the future of higher education: Perspectives from Kenya. In McKeown, J. S., Bista, K., & Chan, R. Y. (Eds.), *Global higher education during COVID-19: Policy, society, and technology* (pp. 73–91). STAR Scholars., https://starscholars.org/product/global-education/

ADDITIONAL READING

Arizona State University Action Lab and Boston Consulting Group. (2018). Making Digital Learning Work: Success Strategies from Six Leading Universities and Community Colleges. https://news.asu.edu/20180412-asu-news-action-labstudy-value-investment-digital-learning

Baticulon, R. E., Sy, J. J., Alberto, N. R. I., Baron, M. B. C., Mabulay, R. E. C., Rizada, L. G. T., Tiu, C. J. S., Clarion, C. A., & Reyes, J. C. B. (2021). Barriers to Online Learning in the Time of COVID-19: A National Survey of Medical Students in the Philippines. *Medical Science Educator*, 31(2), 615–626. DOI: 10.1007/s40670-021-01231-z

Caena, F., & Redecker, C. (2019). Aligning teacher competence frameworks to 21st century challenges: The case for the European Digital Competence Framework for Educators (DigCompEdu). *European Journal of Education*, 54(3), 356–369. DOI: 10.1111/ejed.12345

Kalitanyi, V., & Bbenkele, E. (2018). Cultural values as determinants of entrepreneurial intentions among university students in cape town-south Africa. *Journal of Enterprising Communities*, 12(4), 437–453. DOI: 10.1108/JEC-01-2017-0017

Korableva, O., Durand, T., Kalimullina, O., & Stepanova, I. (2019). Studying user satisfaction with the MOOC platform interfaces using the example of coursera and open education platforms. Paper presented at the ACM International Conference Proceeding Series, 26-30. https://doi.org/doi:10.1145/3322134.3322139

Maltese, V. (2018). Digital transformation challenges for universities: Ensuring information consistency across digital services. *Cataloging & Classification Quarterly*, 56(7), 592–606. DOI: 10.1080/01639374.2018.1504847

KEY TERMS AND DEFINITIONS

Analogue: Traditional methods of teaching, learning, and assessment that rely on physical, non-digital tools and processes. Students and faculty access knowledge through printed materials rather than digital platforms). Teaching typically involves the use of chalkboards, whiteboards, and overhead projectors for delivering lectures. Face-to-Face interaction -In-person lectures (Teaching in an analogue context is delivered through physical, face-to-face interactions between students and educators, often in lecture halls or classrooms). Paper-based assessment - Written exams and assignments.

Assessment in higher education: Assessment in higher education has undergone a significant shift with the transition from analogue to digital modes of teaching and learning as part of a broader digital revolution, which has impacted not only how students learn but also how they are assessed. The traditional (analogue) methods of assessment were largely paper-based, time-bound, and focused on summative evaluations, while digital assessments have opened up new possibilities for more flexible, continuous, and personalized approaches. This shift aligns with the transformation of educational practices, where technology is leveraged to enhance student learning, engagement, and assessment outcomes. Traditionally, analogue assessments in higher education were largely physical, manual, and involved limited use of technology. Some of the key characteristics of analogue assessments include Paper-based exams and assignments which included handwritten exams and hardcopy assignments. The exams were standardized and summative in nature (end-of-term exams and limited feedback), fixed-time, location-bound assessment (in-person assessments and time-bound) and manual grading (inspector centered and subjective grading). The digital revolution has transformed assessment practices in higher education by introducing more dynamic, flexible, and innovative methods. These new digital assessments address many of the limitations of traditional analogue approaches and offer a more holistic, personalized, and engaging experience for students and educators. It offers

Online and digital assessments (online quizzes and exams, digital submissions and e-portfolios), Continuous and formative assessment (on-going feedback and self- and peer assessment), Flexibility and accessibility (anytime, anywhere assessments and time flexibility) and Automated and objective grading (automated scoring and rubric-based grading).

Digital revolution: In higher education it refers to the transformative shift from traditional, analogue teaching methods to technology-driven, digital approaches that have reshaped how education is delivered, accessed, and experienced. This revolution is marked by the integration of digital tools, platforms, and technologies into all aspects of higher education, including teaching, learning and assessment.

Transformed learning: Transformed learning in higher education refers to a shift from traditional, passive forms of education to more active, student-centered approaches that prioritize critical thinking, collaboration, creativity, and the integration of technology. This transformation is driven by the need to equip students with the skills and knowledge necessary to thrive in a rapidly changing, globalized world. It involves Active learning (student engagement and in-class activities), Personalized learning (including adaptive learning technologies as well as learning pathways), Collaborative learning (peer collaboration), Technology-enhanced learning (blended learning, digital tools and online learning platforms), Experiential learning (real-world application and PBL) and Assessment as learning (formative assessment and authentic assessment - assessment that mirror real-world tasks).

Transformed teaching: It refers to the significant shift from traditional, lecture-based methods of instruction to more innovative, learner-centered, and technology-enhanced pedagogical practices. This transformation is driven by changes in educational theory, advancements in digital technologies, and evolving student needs in a globalized and information-rich society. The goal is to create more engaging, personalized, and effective learning experiences that better prepare students for the demands of the modern world. The focus is on developing critical thinking, problem-solving skills, and independent learning rather than rote memorization of information. Integration of technology is another key component which includes blended and online learning, Learning Management Systems (LMS) and interactive tools like quizzes, polls, and simulations enhances student engagement and understanding of complex concepts. Active and collaborative learning through flipped classroom, peer learning collaboration as well as PBL. It is focused on skills development and specifically 21st Century skills as well as experiential learning. Assessment for learning is inclusive of formative assessment, a shift from solely using summative assessments as well as E-portfolios and authentic assessment.

Chapter 6
Fostering a Conducive Open and Distance E-Learning (ODEL) Environment in the 21st Century in Higher Learning Institutions in East and South Africa

Silyvier Tsindoli
Moi University, Kenya

ABSTRACT

Open and Distance E-Learning (ODEL) is transforming higher education in East and South Africa by addressing barriers to access and inclusivity. Accelerated by the COVID-19 pandemic, ODEL supports educational continuity and lifelong learning. Evolving from 19th-century correspondence courses, ODEL now leverages internet access, Learning Management Systems (LMS), mobile technology, and artificial intelligence, aligning with the UN Sustainable Development Goals (SDGs). Key challenges include the digital divide, cultural and language barriers, and resource limitations. Strategies include leveraging mobile technology, low-cost solutions, and policy enhancements. Future AI and virtual reality advancements promise further improvements, fostering a more equitable educational landscape.

DOI: 10.4018/979-8-3373-0025-2.ch006

INTRODUCTION

Open and Distance E-Learning (ODEL) is an educational approach that employs a variety of technologies to provide instruction to students who are not physically present in a traditional classroom setting. ODEL leverages the internet, multimedia resources, and interactive tools to provide flexible and accessible learning opportunities. According to Moore and Kearsley (2021), ODEL encompasses a broad range of pedagogical practices and technologies designed to support learning outside the traditional classroom. This mode of education has seen significant growth due to advances in technology and increased demand for flexible learning options (Guri-Rosenblit, 2022).

The COVID-19 pandemic worked as a catalyst, boosting the adoption of ODEL and emphasizing its vital role in sustaining educational continuity amidst global changes. A report by UNESCO (2021) emphasizes that digital learning technologies have not only facilitated the continuity of education during the pandemic but have also opened new avenues for skill development and lifelong learning, particularly in regions where educational resources are scarce. This shift has necessitated a reevaluation of educational strategies, pushing institutions to innovate and adapt to the evolving landscape of digital learning.

Additionally, the inclusion of ODEL in higher education is in line with more general developmental objectives, such as the Sustainable Development Goals (SDGs) of the United Nations, which support opportunities for lifelong learning for all people and advocate for inclusive, equitable, and high-quality education. Within this framework, ODEL is considered an essential instrument for attaining educational parity, improving employability, and promoting socio-economic advancement. The aim of this chapter is to explore the strategies, challenges, and best practices for fostering a conducive ODEL environment in higher learning institutions in East and South Africa.

The objectives of these book chapter were to investigate the factors that contribute to creating a conducive Open and Distance E-Learning (ODEL) environment in higher learning institutions in East and South Africa. By identifying key challenges, exploring effective strategies, assessing the impact of technological advancements, and examining institutional policies and governance, the chapter aims to provide insights into enhancing the quality, accessibility, and sustainability of ODEL in the 21st century.

BACKGROUND

A key component of the revolution in higher education, especially in the dynamic regions of East and South Africa, is Open and Distance E-Learning (ODEL). The relevance of ODEL extends beyond mere access to education; it encapsulates the ethos of inclusive and equitable learning opportunities that transcend traditional classroom boundaries. In contemporary higher education, ODEL is recognized for its ability to cater to a diverse student body, including working professionals, individuals in remote locations, and those with limited access to conventional educational resources.

In the 21st century, ODEL has become increasingly crucial for several reasons. First, it addresses the growing need for lifelong learning and upskilling in a rapidly evolving job market (Hollands & Tirthali, 2021). As the global workforce continues to diversify, ODEL offers a scalable solution to provide quality education to a broader audience, including those who are geographically or economically disadvantaged (Daniel, 2020). Furthermore, the COVID-19 pandemic highlighted the resilience and adaptability of ODEL, accelerating its adoption and integration into mainstream education systems worldwide (Meyer et al., 2021).

The origins of Open and Distance E-Learning (ODEL) trace back to the 19th century, beginning with correspondence courses that utilized postal services for delivering educational content. One of the earliest examples was the University of London's external program, established in 1858, which allowed students to study remotely and earn degrees. The mid-20th century saw the incorporation of radio and television broadcasts to disseminate educational content, further enhancing the reach of distance education (Peters, 2010).

The late 20th century brought a significant transformation with the advent of the internet. The development of online platforms allowed for interactive and engaging learning experiences. Institutions such as the UK's Open University, established in 1969, played a pioneering role in adopting these technologies to provide flexible learning opportunities to a broader audience.

In East and South Africa, the adoption of ODEL has been driven by the need to overcome barriers such as limited access to physical educational infrastructure and the growing demand for higher education. The establishment of the African Virtual University (AVU) in 1997 marked a significant milestone, aiming to utilize ICT to expand educational access across Africa. Countries like Kenya, Tanzania, and South Africa have integrated ODEL into their national education policies to improve access to higher education, particularly for underserved populations (Murphy, Anzalone, Bosch, & Moulton, 2002).

In South Africa, institutions such as the University of South Africa (UNISA) have been instrumental in the development and delivery of ODEL programs. UNISA, one of the world's largest open distance learning institutions, has been a key player in providing education to students across the continent (Tait, 2003).

In East and South Africa, higher education institutions have increasingly adopted ODEL to overcome traditional barriers such as limited access to physical infrastructure and the need to cater to a diverse student population (Ojo et al., 2022). The implementation of ODEL in these regions has been driven by the need to expand access to higher education and address issues related to educational equity and inclusion (Sifuna, 2023). Despite these advancements, challenges remain, including issues related to technological infrastructure, digital literacy, and resource allocation (Ngugi et al., 2021). Efforts to foster a conducive ODEL environment in these regions must address these challenges to ensure effective and equitable learning experiences for all students.

Empirical research on Open and Distance E-Learning (ODEL) in East and South Africa highlights both notable advancements and persistent challenges. For example, Mutula (2020) conducted a comprehensive study examining the integration of ODEL in Kenyan universities. The study revealed that while there has been significant progress in expanding access to higher education through ODEL, several issues persist. Key among these challenges are the limited digital infrastructure and inadequate levels of student engagement, which hinder the effectiveness of online learning programs. Mutula's research underscores the necessity for substantial improvements in technological resources and support systems to fully realize the potential of ODEL in Kenya.

Similarly, research by Naidoo and Govender (2022) focused on the South African context, identifying critical areas requiring attention to enhance ODEL effectiveness. Their study highlighted the need for more robust policy frameworks that support ODEL initiatives and recommended increased investment in technological infrastructure. Despite some advancements, South African universities face ongoing challenges related to policy gaps and uneven technological access, which affect the overall quality and reach of ODEL programs. The study calls for a more coordinated approach to policy development and resource allocation to address these issues.

In a related study, Njeri and Njeru (2023) examined the implementation of ODEL in East African Community (EAC) countries, including Kenya, Uganda, and Tanzania. Their findings emphasize the diverse challenges faced by institutions in these countries, such as varying levels of infrastructure readiness and differing degrees of institutional support. The study provides a comparative perspective on how these countries are navigating the complexities of ODEL, offering valuable insights into regional similarities and differences.

Comparative studies from other developing regions offer valuable lessons for addressing ODEL challenges in East and South Africa. For instance, Khan et al. (2021) investigated the impact of mobile learning (m-learning) in Pakistan, particularly in rural areas where traditional educational resources are scarce. Their study found that targeted investments in m-learning infrastructure significantly improved educational access and outcomes in these underserved regions. By leveraging mobile technology, institutions were able to overcome barriers related to physical distance and limited educational facilities. The success of m-learning initiatives in Pakistan provides a potential model for similar efforts in East and South Africa, where mobile technology could be harnessed to enhance ODEL access and effectiveness.

In Latin America, a study by Moreno and Contreras (2022) explored the adoption of digital platforms and their impact on higher education accessibility in countries such as Brazil and Argentina. Their research highlighted the role of government and institutional support in facilitating the widespread use of digital learning tools. The study found that strategic partnerships and investments in technology infrastructure were crucial for expanding educational opportunities and improving student outcomes. These findings suggest that a similar approach could benefit ODEL initiatives in East and South Africa, particularly in terms of fostering collaborations and securing necessary resources.

Despite the growing body of literature on ODEL in East and South Africa, several significant gaps remain. One notable gap is the limited research on the long-term impact of ODEL on students' career outcomes. Although there is evidence of increased access to education, there is insufficient data on how ODEL influences graduates' employability and professional success (Mutula, 2020). Another critical area that requires further exploration is gender disparities in ODEL access and success. Research by Mbugua and Karanja (2023) highlights that women in some regions face additional barriers to accessing and benefiting from ODEL opportunities. This disparity necessitates targeted research to understand the specific challenges faced by female students and to develop strategies to address these issues.

TECHNOLOGICAL ADVANCEMENTS OPEN AND DISTANCE E-LEARNING (ODEL)

Technological advancements have significantly reshaped the landscape of Open and Distance E-Learning (ODEL), transforming it into a dynamic and flexible mode of education. These innovations have enhanced the accessibility, efficiency, and engagement of learners across diverse geographical regions, particularly in Africa. The integration of new technologies in ODEL has empowered learners with better tools and has facilitated educators in delivering more interactive and personalized learning experiences. Technological advancements have revolutionized ODEL, making it more accessible, engaging, and effective for learners across the globe. From mobile learning and AI-powered systems to immersive VR experiences and learning analytics, these technologies have opened up new possibilities for institutions and learners alike, particularly in East and South Africa. As these technologies continue to evolve, they promise to further enhance the quality of education offered through ODEL and meet the growing demands for flexible, lifelong learning solutions.

Learning Management Systems (LMS)

Learning Management Systems (LMS) such as Moodle, Blackboard, and Canvas have become pivotal in the facilitation of ODEL. These platforms offer comprehensive tools that allow the organization, delivery, and tracking of learning content. LMS platforms support asynchronous and synchronous learning, enabling students to access learning materials, submit assignments, and interact with educators and peers at their convenience. These systems also integrate features like discussion forums, quizzes, and real-time grading, which enhance learner engagement and provide timely feedback. For instance, at Moi University, the deployment of the Moodle LMS has enabled wide-scale delivery of course content to students across Kenya and beyond.

Mobile Learning (m-Learning)

Mobile learning has become increasingly popular, especially in regions with high mobile penetration but limited access to desktop computers. Smartphones and tablets have opened new avenues for ODEL learners to access educational materials on the go. According to Ally (2009), mobile learning supports a more flexible and personalized learning environment, breaking barriers of time and location. Through mobile apps and mobile-optimized LMS platforms, learners can watch lectures, engage in discussions, and complete coursework from remote locations. This is particularly significant in East and South Africa, where mobile phone usage has grown exponentially, providing an alternative to traditional desktop-based e-learning.

Artificial Intelligence (AI) and Adaptive Learning

Artificial Intelligence (AI) has introduced new dimensions to ODEL, particularly through the use of adaptive learning systems. These systems analyze learner behaviors and performance data to personalize learning paths, adjusting content difficulty and pace to individual needs. AI-powered chatbots and virtual tutors also provide 24/7 support, guiding students through their learning processes and answering queries.

In South Africa, for instance, AI-driven platforms like the University of Pretoria's customized learning system have been successfully implemented to offer tailored support to learners, improving both engagement and learning outcomes (Butcher et al., 2020).

Virtual and Augmented Reality (VR & AR)

Virtual and Augmented Reality technologies are making learning more immersive in ODEL environments. These technologies allow learners to engage in simulated experiences that would otherwise be inaccessible, such as virtual laboratory experiments or historical site visits. In medical education, for example, students can practice surgical procedures in a virtual environment, enhancing both their practical skills and theoretical understanding. In higher learning institutions across Africa, the use of VR and AR has been explored in fields like engineering and health sciences, with notable progress at the University of Nairobi's VR lab, which simulates engineering models for distance learners (Mwangi, 2022).

Cloud Computing

Cloud computing has facilitated the storage and sharing of vast amounts of educational content, making it easier for ODEL institutions to scale their offerings. It allows for seamless collaboration among learners and educators through cloud-based tools like Google Workspace, Microsoft 365, and Dropbox. By leveraging the cloud, ODEL institutions can provide uninterrupted access to learning resources and enable real-time collaboration on projects, regardless of geographical boundaries. The Open University of Tanzania, for example, relies heavily on cloud-based platforms to support its large student body across various regions, ensuring that learners can easily access course materials and submit assignments from remote locations (Mtebe & Raisamo, 2014).

Video Conferencing and Webinars

Real-time video conferencing tools such as Zoom, Microsoft Teams, and Google Meet have become indispensable in ODEL environments, especially in the wake of the COVID-19 pandemic. These tools allow for synchronous learning, where students and educators can interact in real-time, thus recreating the traditional classroom experience online. Webinars have also become popular for hosting expert talks, panel discussions, and collaborative sessions, enabling learners to connect with experts globally. Institutions like Makerere University have adopted video conferencing to facilitate cross-border collaborations and offer international students a high-quality distance learning experience (Nabushawo et al., 2021).

Blockchain Technology

Blockchain technology, though still emerging, offers promising applications in ODEL, particularly in areas related to credentialing and academic records. Blockchain allows for secure, transparent, and tamper-proof storage of academic certificates and records, which is critical for maintaining academic integrity in ODEL environments. Blockchain can also facilitate student identity verification and help combat fraud in online assessments and certifications. In East Africa, the Kenya Education Network (KENET) is exploring the integration of blockchain for secure credentialing in e-learning platforms, signaling a future shift in how institutions manage digital diplomas and certificates (Wainaina, 2021).

Learning Analytics

Learning analytics involves the collection and analysis of data generated by learners as they engage with educational technologies. This data provides insights into learner behaviors, performance, and engagement levels, enabling educators to make data-driven decisions about curriculum design, interventions, and support. Learning analytics can identify at-risk students early, allowing for timely interventions to improve retention and success rates. For example, the University of Cape Town uses learning analytics to track student progress and customize learning pathways for its ODEL learners, enhancing both engagement and success rates (Czerniewicz et al., 2019).

THEORIES RELATED TO OPEN AND DISTANCE E-LEARNING (ODEL)

Several theories provide a framework for understanding the dynamics of Open and Distance E-Learning (ODEL). **Connectivism,** proposed by Siemens (2005), has become particularly relevant in the digital age, where knowledge is distributed across a vast network of resources, and the ability to access, interpret, and connect information is a key aspect of learning. Siemens (2021) revisited this theory, emphasizing the ever-growing importance of networked learning in a digital ecosystem that is increasingly mobile and dynamic. Learners in ODEL environments rely on digital networks not only for information retrieval but also for interaction and collaboration with peers and instructors. This theory aligns with the rapid expansion of digital and mobile technologies, which allow students to learn in more decentralized and flexible ways. Connectivism's emphasis on real-time, participatory learning is crucial for addressing the needs of learners in East and South Africa, where mobile learning plays a significant role due to varying levels of infrastructure (Kigotho, 2021).

Another key theoretical framework is the **Community of Inquiry (CoI) model,** developed by Garrison, Anderson, and Archer (2000), which outlines three essential components for a successful online learning environment: social presence, cognitive presence, and teaching presence. In recent years, this model has gained renewed interest, particularly in the context of ODEL, where fostering a sense of community is critical to the learning process. Studies by Richardson et al. (2020) and Stenbom (2018) reinforce the CoI model's relevance, showing that higher levels of social and teaching presence are positively correlated with student engagement and satisfaction in online learning environments.

The CoI framework is particularly relevant for ODEL in East and South Africa, where challenges such as geographical distance, socio-economic barriers, and uneven technological access can hinder student engagement. Garrison and colleagues (2019) argue that the CoI model's focus on interaction and support in learning environments can help mitigate these challenges, making it a vital framework for creating effective and inclusive ODEL systems in regions where students may feel isolated.

Relevance of The Theories

Both Connectivism and the Community of Inquiry (CoI) framework offer critical insights into how ODEL can be successfully implemented in East and South Africa, providing strategies for enhancing student engagement, digital literacy, and knowledge building. **Connectivism** emphasizes the need for strong network infrastructures, as well as teaching students how to effectively navigate and utilize digital resources. This focus on digital literacy and networked learning is particularly important in regions with uneven access to educational technologies (Naidoo & Govender, 2022). By equipping students with the skills to navigate digital platforms and collaborate across geographic boundaries, Connectivism supports the expansion of ODEL in these areas.

Meanwhile, the **CoI model** underscores the necessity of creating interactive and supportive learning environments. Given that physical distance and limited technological access can reduce a sense of community among learners in East and South Africa, the CoI framework can help educators focus on building strong social and teaching presences. This involves facilitating meaningful online interactions through discussion forums, video conferencing, and collaborative projects, as well as providing clear and accessible instructional guidance (Garrison et al., 2019). By fostering these aspects, ODEL programs in the region can become more conducive to student success, as learners feel more connected to their instructors and peers, which in turn can boost motivation and academic achievement (Richardson et al., 2020).

Both theories will serve as foundational models in this research, guiding the analysis of how to foster a conducive ODEL environment in East and South Africa. The focus will be on how to enhance student engagement, particularly through the implementation of supportive technological infrastructures and pedagogical strategies that align with Connectivism and the (CoL) framework.

The theories revolves around the interplay of several critical variables: technological infrastructure, student engagement, institutional support, policy frameworks, and socio-economic factors. Each of these variables is interdependent, meaning that changes in one can significantly impact the effectiveness of Open and Distance E-Learning (ODEL) environments. Understanding how these variables work together is crucial for fostering a conducive ODEL environment, particularly in regions like East and South Africa, where various socio-economic and infrastructural challenges persist.

Technological infrastructure is foundational to the success of ODEL. Studies have shown that without reliable internet access and digital tools, the full potential of ODEL cannot be realized (Mutula, 2020). In many parts of East and South Africa, connectivity issues, high data costs, and lack of access to modern devices continue to hinder student participation in ODEL programs (Naidoo & Govender, 2022). This makes it difficult for students, especially those in rural areas, to engage with online learning platforms, access course materials, or participate in real-time discussions. Even the most engaged and motivated students may struggle to succeed if technological barriers are not addressed (Khan et al., 2021).

Moreover, digital inequities exacerbate existing socio-economic divides. Wealthier students, who have access to faster internet and better devices, often perform better in ODEL environments than their less affluent counterparts (Mtebe & Raisamo, 2021). The need for more inclusive infrastructure is evident, as enhancing access to reliable technology is a key factor in creating a level playing field for all learners (Gachago et al., 2020). Institutions must invest in both physical and digital infrastructure to ensure that all students can benefit equally from ODEL.

Student engagement is another critical variable in the conceptual framework. Effective ODEL environments are not just about providing access to content but also about engaging students in meaningful ways. Research indicates that engaged students are more likely to persist in their studies, complete their programs, and achieve better outcomes (Veletsianos, 2021). However, in ODEL, engagement can be more challenging to cultivate due to the physical distance between students and educators.

To address this, institutions must adopt strategies that promote active learning and interaction. For instance, tools such as discussion forums, video conferencing, and collaborative projects can foster a sense of community and keep students motivated (Zawacki-Richter & Jung, 2019). Additionally, personalized learning pathways, where students can choose the pace and style of learning that suits them, have been shown to increase engagement (Barber et al., 2020).

Institutional support is indispensable for the success of ODEL initiatives. Without the backing of institutions, faculty members may lack the training, resources, and incentives necessary to deliver high-quality online education (Aluko, 2022). Studies have shown that institutions that invest in training faculty on the use of digital tools and the development of engaging online content see better outcomes in their ODEL programs (Siemens, 2021). Faculty development programs that focus on online pedagogy, technology integration, and assessment techniques are particularly critical for ensuring that instructors are equipped to teach in digital environments.

Institutional support also includes the provision of technical assistance to both students and faculty. Many students in ODEL environments are new to digital learning tools and may require guidance in navigating platforms and accessing resources. Without adequate technical support, students can easily become frustrated and disengaged, further compounding the challenges of distance learning (Kanwar & Balasubramanian, 2019).

Policy Frameworks: The role of policy frameworks cannot be understated in the conceptualization of a conducive ODEL environment. Governments and educational institutions must develop and enforce policies that support the growth of ODEL while ensuring equitable access for all learners (Mutula, 2020). In East and South Africa, policy gaps related to digital education, data privacy, and access to technology have slowed the progress of ODEL initiatives (Naidoo & Govender, 2022). Policies that address infrastructure development, funding models for ODEL, and standards for digital learning can provide a solid foundation for the expansion and sustainability of ODEL in the region.

For instance, targeted policies that incentivize partnerships between educational institutions and telecommunications providers can help reduce data costs and improve internet accessibility for students in remote areas (Gachago et al., 2020). Additionally, policies that promote the integration of ODEL into mainstream education systems can ensure that ODEL is not seen as an inferior or secondary mode of education but as a valuable alternative for students who may not have access to traditional classroom-based education.

Finally, socio-economic factors play a crucial role in shaping the effectiveness of ODEL environments. The cost of technology, internet access, and the socio-economic background of students can significantly impact their ability to participate in ODEL programs (Mtebe & Raisamo, 2021). In East and South Africa, where income inequality is pronounced, many students lack the financial resources to purchase devices or pay for reliable internet access, further exacerbating educational inequalities (Kanwar & Balasubramanian, 2019).

To mitigate these issues, institutions must adopt more inclusive strategies, such as providing financial assistance for students to purchase devices, offering offline learning options, and creating low-bandwidth content that is accessible even in areas with poor internet connectivity (Mtebe & Raisamo, 2021). Addressing these socio-economic challenges is essential for ensuring that ODEL fulfills its promise of democratizing access to education.

Figure 1.

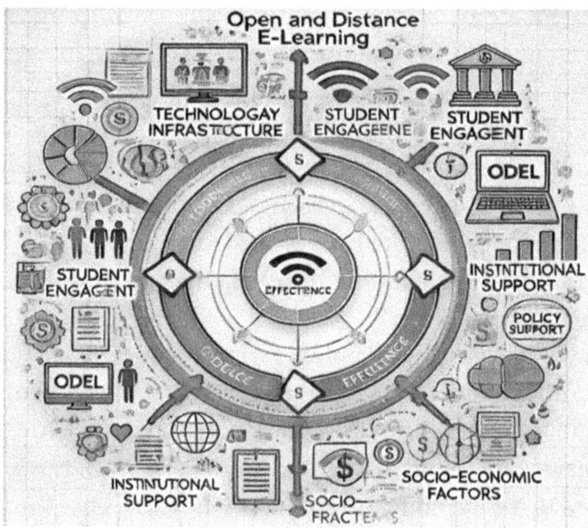

CHALLENGES IN FOSTERING A CONDUCIVE ODEL ENVIRONMENT

Technological Infrastructure

One of the most significant challenges in fostering a conducive ODEL environment in East and South Africa is the lack of adequate technological infrastructure. While urban centers may enjoy reliable access to high-speed internet and modern learning technologies, rural areas in both East and South Africa lag far behind. This technological disparity creates a digital divide that exacerbates inequalities in access to education, as learners in underserved areas cannot fully benefit from

ODEL opportunities (Naidoo & Govender, 2022). The availability of affordable and high-speed internet access remains a critical issue, especially as online learning platforms depend heavily on bandwidth-intensive tools such as video conferencing, multimedia content, and real-time interactivity.

Studies indicate that even in urban regions, ODEL infrastructure is often underdeveloped due to insufficient investment, with institutions struggling to maintain robust technological ecosystems (Moloi & Muthelo, 2022). In some cases, universities rely on outdated hardware and software that fail to meet the growing demands of digital education (Dube, 2021). Furthermore, the rapid pace of technological advancement continues to outstrip the capabilities of many institutions, which may lack the financial or technical capacity to regularly upgrade their digital infrastructure (Lwoga & Ngugi, 2020).

In rural areas, the problem is compounded by inconsistent electricity supply, unreliable network coverage, and the prohibitive cost of internet access (Kanwar & Balasubramanian, 2019). These limitations restrict learners' ability to participate fully in ODEL programs, leaving them at a distinct disadvantage compared to their urban counterparts. As a result, the digital divide threatens to reinforce existing social and educational inequalities in the region (Rambe & Moeti, 2021).

Policy and Governance Issues

Policy frameworks in East and South Africa have not always been conducive to the growth of ODEL. Educational policies in the region often lag behind technological advancements, resulting in inadequate provisions for online learning and digital education (Ndayisenga & Nkurunziza, 2022). In many cases, regulatory frameworks are outdated, failing to account for the specific needs and challenges posed by ODEL, such as data security, intellectual property rights, and digital accreditation.

Governance issues further complicate the effective implementation of ODEL. Public institutions in many countries within the region are underfunded, which impacts their ability to invest in necessary ODEL infrastructure, teacher training, and digital content creation (Mutula, 2020). The lack of cohesive national strategies for ODEL development has led to a piecemeal approach, with individual institutions attempting to implement their own solutions without adequate government support (Mutanga & Gunter, 2019).

Institutional governance is another critical concern. Leadership in higher education institutions often lacks the expertise or commitment to prioritize ODEL initiatives (Dube, 2021). Many leaders continue to view traditional face-to-face education as the preferred mode of learning, slowing the integration of ODEL into mainstream educational delivery (Moloi & Muthelo, 2022). This resistance to change, coupled with bureaucratic inertia, hampers innovation and limits the potential of ODEL to transform the higher education sector.

Socio-Economic Factors

The socio-economic landscape in East and South Africa presents additional barriers to ODEL implementation. The high cost of internet access, data, and digital devices such as laptops and smartphones is a significant deterrent for many students in the region. Studies have shown that even where ODEL infrastructure exists, many learners from low-income backgrounds are unable to afford the necessary technology to participate fully in online education (Mtebe & Raisamo, 2020). This socio-economic barrier limits the reach of ODEL, especially for marginalized groups such as rural learners and women, who are disproportionately affected by poverty.

In terms of accessibility, geographic location continues to be a major factor. Learners in remote or rural areas often face challenges in accessing not only digital tools but also basic educational materials. The lack of physical infrastructure, such as reliable roads or transport systems, combined with low internet penetration, further compounds the difficulty of reaching these populations (Khan et al., 2021). In some regions, government and institutional efforts to bridge the accessibility gap, such as through community learning centers or mobile education units, have been met with limited success due to funding constraints and logistical challenges (Rambe & Moeti, 2021).

Efforts to mitigate these socio-economic challenges have included the promotion of open educational resources (OERs), which provide free and accessible learning materials online. While OERs offer some relief, their adoption remains limited in the region due to a lack of awareness and inadequate digital literacy among both educators and learners (Kanwar & Balasubramanian, 2019).

Overall, these socio-economic challenges highlight the need for more inclusive policies and strategies that account for the region's diverse economic realities. Governments, educational institutions, and private sector partners must collaborate to create affordable, accessible, and sustainable ODEL models that prioritize equity and inclusion (Mutanga & Gunter, 2019).

STRATEGIES TO IMPROVE ODEL IN HIGHER LEARNING INSTITUTIONS

In order to effectively improve Open and Distance E-Learning (ODEL) programs in higher learning institutions, several strategic initiatives must be undertaken. These strategies focus on building a resilient and accessible technological foundation that supports both learners and educators, while ensuring flexibility and adaptability in the learning environment. Among the most effective approaches are those that leverage the power of multimedia and interactivity, ensuring that students experience a dynamic and engaging learning environment. The following are key strategies that can significantly improve the quality and effectiveness of ODEL programs.

Enhancing Technological Infrastructure

Enhancing Technological Infrastructure: A critical component of ODEL success lies in establishing and maintaining a strong technological infrastructure. To optimize learning outcomes and ensure seamless access to educational materials, higher learning institutions should focus on three key areas: network connectivity, cloud-based platforms, and mobile optimization.

Robust Network Connectivity: For students and faculty to effectively participate in ODEL programs, high-speed and reliable internet access is essential. Without sufficient connectivity, students may face difficulties in attending virtual classes, accessing digital resources, or submitting assignments on time. Institutions must therefore prioritize investments in robust network infrastructure, ensuring that all stakeholders, regardless of their location, can engage with the online learning environment without technical disruptions. This includes enhancing internet bandwidth on campuses, offering remote access to virtual private networks (VPNs), and collaborating with internet service providers to offer discounted or subsidized data packages for students.

Cloud-Based Platforms: Cloud-based platforms have become a game-changer in modern education, offering scalability, flexibility, and security. By utilizing cloud-based learning management systems (LMS), institutions can provide a more streamlined and efficient online learning experience. Cloud-based LMS platforms, such as Moodle, Blackboard, or Google Classroom, allow for easy access to learning materials, assignments, and communication tools from anywhere in the world. These platforms offer the added benefit of automatic updates, ensuring that the system is always running the latest security patches and technological improvements. Furthermore, cloud-based systems can scale to accommodate a growing number of users without compromising performance, making them ideal for institutions looking to expand their ODEL offerings.

Mobile Optimization: With the increasing prevalence of smartphones and tablets, mobile devices have become a primary tool for accessing educational content, especially for students who may not have access to traditional desktops or laptops. To accommodate this shift, higher education institutions must ensure that all ODEL courses and materials are designed to be mobile-friendly. This includes adopting responsive design principles so that content automatically adjusts to different screen sizes and devices. Course developers should also focus on creating bite-sized, modular content that is easy to navigate and consume on the go. Mobile optimization not only increases accessibility but also enhances the overall learning experience by enabling students to learn at their own pace, from anywhere, and at any time.

In conclusion, improving ODEL in higher learning institutions requires a strategic focus on technological infrastructure, including robust network connectivity, the adoption of cloud-based platforms, and the optimization of learning materials for mobile devices. By prioritizing these areas, institutions can create a more inclusive, flexible, and efficient learning environment that meets the evolving needs of students and faculty in the digital age.

Implementing Interactive and Multimedia-Rich Content

One of the primary strategies for improving ODEL is the integration of rich multimedia content. This involves moving beyond traditional text-based learning materials to create an immersive and engaging experience that appeals to a wide variety of learning styles.

Multimedia Integration: The use of videos, animations, simulations, and other interactive elements in course materials can greatly enhance student engagement and comprehension. Videos, for instance, allow complex concepts to be broken down into more digestible visual segments, aiding understanding. Simulations enable students to apply theoretical knowledge in practical scenarios, giving them a hands-on experience that bridges the gap between theory and practice. Animations and infographics can also help in simplifying intricate processes or data, making it easier for students to grasp challenging content.

Gamification: Gamification refers to the application of game-like elements, such as point systems, leaderboards, and rewards, to the learning environment. This strategy makes the learning process more enjoyable by tapping into students' intrinsic motivation. By turning lessons into competitive or achievement-driven experiences, students are more likely to stay engaged and motivated to complete tasks. For example, awarding badges or certificates for completing modules or achieving certain milestones can incentivize students to actively participate in and complete their courses.

Collaborative Tools: To foster a sense of community and encourage peer-to-peer learning, it is important to integrate collaborative tools into ODEL platforms. Discussion forums, wikis, and group chats enable students to share ideas, collaborate on projects, and engage in intellectual discussions beyond the confines of their individual study sessions. This not only improves understanding through knowledge sharing but also builds critical soft skills like teamwork, communication, and leadership. Group projects conducted through these tools mirror real-world scenarios, preparing students for collaborative work environments after graduation.

By adopting these interactive and multimedia-rich strategies, higher learning institutions can transform their ODEL programs into vibrant, student-centered environments where engagement and learning outcomes are optimized.

Providing Comprehensive Faculty Training

Equip Faculty Members with Pedagogical Skills: Effective online teaching requires more than just subject matter expertise; it demands a solid foundation in pedagogical approaches tailored to the digital learning environment. Faculty members must be trained in best practices for designing and delivering online courses. This includes understanding how to structure content for online platforms, engaging students in a virtual setting, and fostering active participation.

Designing Engaging Courses: Faculty should be trained to design courses that cater to different learning styles by integrating multimedia elements such as videos, podcasts, and interactive activities.

Managing Online Discussions: Teaching faculty to facilitate meaningful online discussions is crucial for student engagement. Instructors must learn strategies to encourage active participation, guide conversations, and ensure that discussions are productive and inclusive.

Assessment and Feedback: Providing timely and constructive feedback is vital in an online environment. Faculty training should include strategies for assessing student performance through quizzes, peer reviews, projects, and discussions, while leveraging the digital tools available for grading and offering feedback.

Develop Technological Proficiency: In the context of ODEL, technological proficiency is just as important as pedagogical expertise. Faculty members must be skilled in using Learning Management Systems (LMS), online communication tools, and other relevant technologies that support digital education. Without adequate technical knowledge, instructors may struggle to create dynamic online courses or effectively interact with their students.

Mastering the LMS: Learning Management Systems, such as Moodle, Blackboard, or Canvas, form the backbone of ODEL programs. Faculty should be trained to efficiently navigate these platforms, manage student data, upload course materials, create assessments, and track student progress. Mastery of the LMS will empower instructors to leverage its full capabilities, enhancing the learning experience for students.

Utilizing Online Communication Tools: Instructors need proficiency in using various communication tools, such as Zoom, Microsoft Teams, or Google Meet, for virtual lectures and discussions. Training should cover how to host live sessions, record lectures, share resources, and manage breakout sessions for group work. Additionally, faculty should be familiar with asynchronous communication tools like forums, wikis, and collaborative documents to facilitate continuous engagement outside of scheduled class times.

Using Multimedia Tools: To create rich, interactive content, faculty must be comfortable using multimedia tools for developing videos, infographics, and simulations. Familiarity with tools such as Camtasia, Adobe Creative Suite, or free alternatives like Canva and OpenShot enables instructors to present course material in visually appealing and accessible formats.

Offer Continuous Professional Development: The digital landscape is continuously evolving, and faculty members must keep up with these changes to provide students with the best possible learning experiences. Continuous professional development is crucial for maintaining teaching effectiveness in an ODEL environment.

Staying Updated with Trends: Higher education institutions should offer regular professional development programs that expose faculty to the latest trends in online education, such as the use of Artificial Intelligence (AI), virtual reality (VR), augmented reality (AR), and mobile learning in teaching. Faculty should also be encouraged to participate in webinars, conferences, and workshops focused on emerging technologies and methodologies in distance learning.

Adopting Best Practices: Faculty development programs should focus on teaching faculty about global best practices in ODEL. This includes strategies for improving student retention, enhancing motivation, and ensuring academic integrity in a virtual environment. It's also important to educate faculty on how to incorporate inclusivity and accessibility into their course designs, ensuring that all students, including those with disabilities, can engage with the content effectively.

Encouraging Peer Learning: Faculty members can learn a great deal from each other. Institutions should facilitate peer learning opportunities, such as mentorship programs, where experienced faculty mentor those new to ODEL. Regular knowledge-sharing sessions, where faculty can discuss what works (and what doesn't) in their online teaching, can foster a collaborative learning culture among the teaching staff.

In summary, improving ODEL in higher learning institutions requires a focus on building the capacity of faculty through comprehensive training programs that enhance their pedagogical, technological, and professional development. By equipping educators with the skills needed to effectively design, deliver, and manage online courses, institutions can significantly improve the overall quality of their ODEL programs, resulting in better learning outcomes for students.

Developing Supportive Policies and Frameworks

To enhance the quality and effectiveness of Open and Distance E-Learning (ODEL) in higher learning institutions, several strategic actions are essential. A major focus area should be the development of supportive policies and frameworks, which can provide structure and guidance for successful implementation. Below is a detailed discussion on how institutions can approach this by establishing clear guidelines, implementing robust quality assurance systems, and ensuring accessibility for all learners.

Develop Clear Guidelines

The first step in improving ODEL programs is to establish well-defined policies and guidelines that provide a strong foundation for both students and faculty. These guidelines should cover key areas such as:

- **Student Support Services:** It is essential to create comprehensive student support systems that cater to the specific needs of ODEL learners. These may include access to academic advisors, technical support, mental health services, and online libraries. Clear guidelines should outline how students can access these services remotely and what support is available to them throughout their studies.
- **Academic Integrity:** Upholding academic integrity in ODEL is crucial to maintaining the credibility and reputation of the institution. Clear policies should be established to prevent plagiarism, cheating, and other forms of academic dishonesty. Institutions should also adopt appropriate tools, such as plagiarism detection software and proctored online exams, to support these policies.
- **Assessment Procedures:** Guidelines on how assessments are conducted in ODEL environments must be clear and transparent. This includes providing students with information about assignment deadlines, grading criteria, feedback timelines, and the use of online testing platforms. It is also important to outline procedures for handling academic disputes and appeals to ensure fairness in the evaluation process.

By developing these clear and comprehensive guidelines, institutions can foster an organized and efficient learning environment where both students and instructors are aware of their responsibilities and expectations.

Implement Quality Assurance Mechanisms

Quality assurance is a critical component of any educational program, and it is especially important in the context of ODEL, where distance and technology can sometimes present challenges to maintaining high standards. Institutions must implement robust quality assurance systems to monitor and evaluate the effectiveness of their ODEL programs. This can be achieved through:

- **Regular Program Evaluation:** Continuous evaluation of ODEL programs ensures they remain relevant, effective, and aligned with institutional goals. Feedback from students, faculty, and external stakeholders should be gathered to assess the quality of content, delivery methods, and overall learning outcomes. This feedback should be used to make necessary adjustments and improvements to the programs.
- **Accreditation and Benchmarking:** ODEL programs should meet established accreditation standards to ensure their credibility and recognition. Institutions can also benchmark their ODEL offerings against other successful programs, both locally and internationally, to identify best practices and areas for improvement.
- **Monitoring Learning Outcomes:** A critical aspect of quality assurance is the regular assessment of learning outcomes to ensure that students are acquiring the intended knowledge and skills. Institutions should develop tools and metrics to measure student performance, progression, and completion rates. Data-driven insights can help identify any gaps in the curriculum or teaching methods and guide efforts to improve the overall quality of the learning experience.

Through continuous quality assurance efforts, institutions can maintain high academic standards and enhance the overall effectiveness of their ODEL programs.

Ensure Accessibility for All Students

Accessibility is a key consideration in the design and delivery of ODEL programs. Higher learning institutions must ensure that these programs are inclusive and cater to the needs of all students, including those with disabilities. To achieve this, several measures should be put in place:

- **Accommodations for Students with Disabilities:** Institutions must provide appropriate accommodations to ensure that students with disabilities can fully participate in ODEL programs. This may include offering accessible course materials in formats such as audio, large print, or braille; providing captioned videos for students with hearing impairments; and ensuring that online platforms are compatible with assistive technologies like screen readers.

- **Universal Design for Learning (UDL):** Institutions should adopt Universal Design for Learning principles when creating ODEL content. UDL encourages the development of flexible learning environments that accommodate diverse learning styles and abilities. For instance, offering multiple means of engagement, representation, and expression ensures that students can access and interact with content in ways that best suit their needs.
- **Support Services for Distance Learners:** Students learning remotely may face unique challenges, such as limited access to reliable internet or technological devices. Institutions should establish support mechanisms to help students overcome these barriers. This might include loaning devices to students, providing internet subsidies, or offering offline learning resources to ensure that all students can participate in ODEL programs, regardless of their personal circumstances.

By prioritizing accessibility, institutions can create a more equitable and inclusive ODEL environment, ensuring that all students have the opportunity to succeed. Improving ODEL programs in higher learning institutions requires a strategic approach that encompasses the development of clear guidelines, the implementation of quality assurance mechanisms, and a strong focus on accessibility. By establishing policies that address critical areas such as student support, academic integrity, and assessment, institutions can provide a structured and transparent framework for both students and faculty. Moreover, quality assurance systems ensure that ODEL programs maintain high academic standards and continuously evolve to meet the needs of learners. Finally, ensuring accessibility for all students especially those with disabilities creates an inclusive learning environment where everyone can thrive.

By adopting these strategies, institutions can enhance the effectiveness of their ODEL offerings, providing students with a high-quality, flexible, and accessible education that meets the demands of the 21st century.

FUTURE RESEARCH DIRECTIONS

Future research can explore how Artificial Intelligence (AI) and Virtual Reality (VR) enhance personalized learning outcomes in Open and Distance E-Learning (ODEL) in East and South Africa.

CONCLUSION

In conclusion, the first key challenges faced by odel institutions in East and South Africa is inadequate technological infrastructure remains a major challenge for ODEL institutions, with poor internet connectivity, outdated hardware, and limited software impeding the effectiveness of online learning programs. These issues hinder access to course materials and limit the use of advanced teaching tools, suggesting a need for significant investment in technology.

The other challenge is low student engagement and motivation are prevalent due to limited real-time interaction and lack of interactive content. Students often feel isolated and disconnected, leading to a passive learning experience. Enhancing course content with multimedia and interactive elements is essential to improving engagement and motivation. Also, Inadequate faculty training and support critically affect the delivery of ODEL programs. Many instructors lack the necessary skills to use ODEL tools effectively, which impacts the quality of instruction. Comprehensive training and ongoing support are crucial for improving faculty performance and the overall quality of ODEL programs.

In addition, financial limitations restrict institutions' ability to invest in new technologies and resources, resulting in reliance on outdated equipment and insufficient support for innovative practices. Addressing these constraints involves strategic budgeting, seeking external funding, and exploring partnerships to enhance ODEL capabilities.

Concerning strategies to improve the quality and effectiveness of ODEL in higher learning institutions, investing in modern technological infrastructure, including high-speed internet, advanced hardware, and up-to-date software, is crucial for improving ODEL quality. Such upgrades facilitate seamless learning experiences and should be supported by strategic investments and partnerships to overcome financial barriers.

In addition, implementing interactive and multimedia-rich content. also incorporating interactive and multimedia elements into ODEL courses can significantly boost student engagement and motivation. Using videos, simulations, and interactive exercises makes learning more dynamic and effective, addressing the challenge of maintaining student interest and enhancing learning outcomes. Another strategy is providing comprehensive faculty training comprehensive training for faculty is essential for effective ODEL delivery. Investing in professional development helps instructors utilize ODEL tools and technologies efficiently, improving the quality of instruction and enhancing student engagement and outcomes.

Also. developing supportive policies and frameworks establishing clear policies and frameworks for technology use, content development, and assessment practices supports effective ODEL implementation. Well-defined guidelines ensure consistency, quality, and alignment with educational goals, and enable continuous improvement and adaptation to technological advancements.

On the impact of technological advancements on ODEL delivery and student engagement, the advancements in learning management systems (LMS) where modern LMS platforms with features like real-time communication tools, advanced analytics, and customizable content enhance ODEL delivery and student engagement. These advancements improve interaction, personalization, and learning experiences, contributing to higher student satisfaction and better academic performance.

The role of artificial intelligence and automation are revolutionizing ODEL by providing personalized learning experiences and automating administrative tasks. AI-driven tools offer tailored content and real-time feedback, while automation in grading and feedback reduces instructor workload, leading to improved student support and engagement. While, mobile learning and accessibility has enhanced odel accessibility and flexibility, allowing students to access educational resources from various devices. mobile learning applications and responsive design contribute to increased participation, engagement, and satisfaction, improving overall learning outcomes.

The role of institutional policies and governance in supporting a conducive ODEL environment include clear guidelines and standards for ODEL ensure consistency in technology use, content development, and assessment. Institutions with well-defined policies experience smoother implementation and better alignment with educational goals, contributing to effective ODEL program delivery. Also promoting a culture of innovation supports the adaptation of new technologies and pedagogical approaches. Institutions that encourage experimentation and provide resources for innovative practices can enhance ODEL programs, making them more engaging and effective.

On the other hand, ensuring stakeholder engagement stakeholders such as students, faculty, and industry partners ensures that ODEL programs are relevant and effective. Active involvement helps align programs with current needs and expectations, leading to higher quality and better outcomes. Finally, Regular monitoring and evaluation are essential for maintaining the effectiveness of ODEL programs. Robust evaluation practices allow institutions to assess performance, address issues promptly, and continuously improve their offerings, ensuring high-quality education and successful program implementation.

REFERENCES

Akçayır, G., & Akçayır, M. (2019). The flipped classroom: A review of its advantages and challenges. *Computers & Education*, 126, 334–345. DOI: 10.1016/j.compedu.2018.07.021

Ally, M. (2009). *Mobile learning: Transforming the delivery of education and training*. Athabasca University Press. DOI: 10.15215/aupress/9781897425435.01

Aluko, R. (2022). Faculty development for digital transformation in ODEL environments. *Journal of Distance Education*, 34(2), 45–60.

Aoki, K., & Pogorzelski, S. (2020). Correspondence education and the rise of distance learning. *Journal of Educational Technology*, 58(1), 45–61.

Barber, W., King, S., & Buchanan, S. (2020). Flexible learning in higher education: The integration of e-learning and traditional approaches. *Journal of Educational Technology*, 56(4), 231–245.

Bozkurt, A., & Sharma, R. C. (2020). Emergency remote teaching in a time of global crisis due to the CoronaVirus pandemic. *Asian Journal of Distance Education*, 15(1), 1–6.

Butcher, N., Hoosen, S., & Moore, D. (2020). The impact of AI on ODEL systems: Case studies from South Africa. *Journal of Technology Enhanced Learning*, 12(3), 67–84.

Chakravarti, M. (2020). Flexibility and learner-centeredness in open distance learning. *Open Learning Journal*, 34(4), 251–264.

Czerniewicz, L., Deacon, A., & Walji, S. (2019). Using learning analytics to support ODEL in higher education: The University of Cape Town experience. *International Journal of Learning Analytics and Artificial Intelligence for Education*, 1(1), 14–28.

Czerniewicz, L., Trotter, H., & Haupt, G. (2020). Critical reflections on global and local equity in online and blended learning. *Learning, Media and Technology*, 45(2), 148–162.

Daniel, J. (2020). Open and distance learning: Expanding educational opportunities in the 21st century. *International Journal of Educational Technology*, 18(2), 88–98.

Dhawan, S. (2020). Online learning: A panacea in the time of COVID-19 crisis. *Journal of Educational Technology Systems*, 49(1), 5–22. DOI: 10.1177/0047239520934018

Dube, L. (2021). Challenges in the implementation of online learning in South Africa. *Journal of Educational Technology & Society*, 24(3), 15–25.

Ford, S., Rodarte, M., & Gomez, R. (2020). Competency-based education: Examining best practices in higher education. *Journal of Distance Education*, 22(3), 119–134.

Gachago, D., Maseko, M., & Griesel, H. (2020). Exploring digital divide issues in South African ODEL environments. *African Journal of Educational Technology*, 5(2), 98–112.

Garrison, D. R., Anderson, T., & Archer, W. (2000). Critical inquiry in a text-based environment: Computer conferencing in higher education. *The Internet and Higher Education*, 2(2-3), 87–105. DOI: 10.1016/S1096-7516(00)00016-6

Garrison, D. R., Anderson, T., & Archer, W. (2019). *E-learning in the 21st century: A framework for research and practice* (3rd ed.). Routledge.

Garrison, D. R., & Vaughan, N. D. (2021). *Blended learning in higher education: Framework, principles, and guidelines*. Educational Technology Publications.

Govender, D., & Naidoo, R. (2022). Digital inequality and the challenges of access to distance education in South Africa. *South African Journal of Education*, 42(1), 88–107.

Guri-Rosenblit, S. (2022). Distance education in the digital era: Evolution and challenges. *Open Learning*, 37(2), 105–120.

Hollands, F. M., & Tirthali, D. (2021). Distance learning and workforce development in the digital age. *Workforce Education Forum*, 13(4), 234-255.

Kanwar, A., & Balasubramanian, B. (2019). Improving access to education through open educational resources. *International Journal of Educational Technology*, 14(1), 45–58.

Kanwar, A., & Balasubramanian, K. (2019). Addressing digital equity in ODEL environments: Challenges and strategies. *Commonwealth of Learning Reports*, 2019(5), 23–31.

Kanwar, A.,, & Balasubramanian, K. (2019). Overcoming barriers to ODL: The role of mobile learning in sub-Saharan Africa. *International Review of Research in Open and Distributed Learning*, 20(2), 1–10.

Khan, M., Ali, H., & Khan, S. (2021). Mobile learning in rural Pakistan: Addressing the challenges of access to education. *The Journal of Educational Research*, 12(3), 245–262.

Khan, M. S., Ahmed, S., & Noor, M. (2021). Barriers to digital education in remote areas: A case study of rural communities in East Africa. *Educational Research Review*, 16(2), 80–93.

Khan, S., Gachago, D., & Mutula, S. M. (2021). Overcoming technological barriers in ODEL: Case studies from Africa. *Journal of Distance Education*, 35(3), 54–76.

Kigotho, W. (2021). Revisiting Connectivism in the mobile learning era: Implications for Africa. *African Journal of Educational Technology*, 7(1), 45–59.

Langa, M., & Dube, T. (2022). Cultural and linguistic factors in educational technology adoption: Insights from Southern Africa. *African Journal of Educational Technology*, 8(1), 67–83.

Lwoga, E. T., & Ngugi, K. (2020). Challenges of integrating technology in higher education institutions in Africa. *Technology, Pedagogy and Education*, 29(1), 34–48.

Maldonado-Mahauad, J., Pérez-Sanagustín, M., Kizilcec, R. F., & Munoz-Gama, J. (2020). Personalizing learning in MOOCs: Motivational and cognitive effects of adaptive technologies. *Computers & Education*, 145, 103725.

Mbwesa, J., & Mutula, S. (2022). Integrating radio and television broadcasts in ODL: A study from East Africa. *African Journal of Distance Learning*, 10(1), 33–52.

Meyer, K. A., Springer, M., & Wurster, A. (2021). The impact of COVID-19 on distance education: A review of current research and future directions. *Educational Research Review*, 16(6), 307–318.

Moloi, K. C., & Muthelo, M. (2022). Infrastructure and investment challenges in open and distance e-learning (ODEL) in Southern Africa. *Educational Technology Research and Development*, 70(4), 55–70.

Moore, M. G., & Kearsley, G. (2021). *Distance education: A systems view of online learning* (4th ed.). Wadsworth Publishing.

Moreno, R., & Contreras, D. (2022). Digital platforms and higher education in Latin America: Expanding accessibility and opportunity. *Journal of Latin American Educational Studies*, 30(2), 56–78.

Mtebe, J. S., & Raisamo, R. (2014). Investigating the adoption of cloud computing in higher education in developing countries: A Tanzanian perspective. *International Journal of Education and Development Using ICT*, 10(1), 92–106.

Mtebe, J. S., & Raisamo, R. (2020). Socio-economic factors affecting access to e-learning resources in Tanzania. *Journal of Educational Computing Research*, 58(5), 849–865.

Mtebe, J. S., & Raisamo, R. (2021). Digital inequality in East and South Africa's ODEL landscape. *Journal of Educational Development in Africa*, 9(3), 65–82.

Mukeredzi, T. G., Mandikonza, C., & Dube, C. (2022). The digital divide and the implications for distance learning in Africa. *American Journal of Education*, 42(1), 88–102.

Mutanga, C., & Gunter, B. (2019). Policy and governance issues in implementing e-learning in sub-Saharan Africa. *Journal of Distance Education*, 34(2), 101–115.

Mutula, S. (2020). The state of open and distance learning in Kenya: Opportunities and challenges. *Journal of Distance Education in Africa*, 18(3), 211–234.

Mutula, S. M. (2020). The role of policy frameworks in promoting ODEL in East Africa. *Journal of Education Policy Studies*, 45(3), 67–84.

Mutula, S. M. (2020). The state of open distance e-learning in East Africa. *Information Development*, 36(3), 370–380.

Mwangi, P. (2022). The use of virtual reality in distance education: A case study of the University of Nairobi. *Kenyan Journal of Educational Research*, 11(4), 101–115.

Nabushawo, A., Namusonge, G., & Ndiku, J. (2021). Video conferencing and webinars in ODEL: Experiences from Makerere University. *African Journal of Distance Learning*, 4(1), 31–44.

Naidoo, N., & Govender, D. (2022). Technological disparities and their impact on online education in South Africa. *Journal of Educational Technology*, 19(4), 23–35.

Naidoo, R., & Govender, D. (2022). Enhancing ODEL effectiveness in South Africa: The role of policy and infrastructure. *Journal of Open Learning*, 37(1), 54–68.

Naidoo, V., & Govender, R. (2022). Digital inclusion and access in ODEL systems in Southern Africa. *International Journal of Educational Technology in Higher Education*, 19(2), 21–38.

Ndayisenga, D., & Nkurunziza, J. (2022). Educational policy challenges in the development of online learning systems in East Africa. *Policy Futures in Education*, 20(1), 70–84.

Njeri, M., & Njeru, E. (2023). Challenges and opportunities of ODEL in East Africa: A comparative study. *Journal of Distance Learning in Africa*, 22(1), 45–61.

Peters, O. (2010). *Distance education in transition: Developments and issues* (5th ed.). BIS-Verlag der Carl von Ossietzky Universität Oldenburg.

Rambe, P., & Moeti, T. (2021). Navigating digital divides in higher education: Strategies and solutions. *Online Learning Journal*, 25(3), 100–115.

Rasheed, R. A., Kamsin, A., & Abdullah, N. A. (2020). Challenges in the online component of blended learning: A systematic review. *Computers & Education*, 144, 103701. DOI: 10.1016/j.compedu.2019.103701

Richardson, J. C., Maeda, Y., & Swan, K. (2020). Social presence in online learning: A meta-analysis of selected studies. *Educational Research Review*, 29, 100329.

Sharma, R., & Garg, M. (2021). The role of technology in the evolution of distance learning: From correspondence to virtual classrooms. *Educational Technology Review*, 67(3), 155–173.

Siemens, G. (2005). Connectivism: A learning theory for the digital age. *International Journal of Instructional Technology and Distance Learning*, 2(1), 3–10.

Siemens, G. (2021). The evolving nature of networked learning in a digital age. *Journal of Educational Technology*, 18(3), 15–32.

Sifuna, D. N. (2023). Policies and practices of ODEL in East African universities: Challenges and prospects. *East African Journal of Education*, 13(1), 67–85.

Stenbom, S. (2018). A systematic review of the Community of Inquiry research: When theory meets practice. *The Internet and Higher Education*, 39, 22–32. DOI: 10.1016/j.iheduc.2018.06.001

Tait, A. (2003). Reflections on student support in open and distance learning. *International Review of Research in Open and Distance Learning*, 4(1), 1–15. DOI: 10.19173/irrodl.v4i1.134

UNESCO. (2021). The role of digital technologies in education during the COVID-19 pandemic. *UNESCO Education Report*.

Veletsianos, G. (2021). Learner engagement in digital learning environments: What we know and what we need to know. *Distance Education*, 42(1), 5–17.

Wainaina, D. (2021). The role of blockchain in secure credentialing for e-learning in Kenya. *East African Journal of Information Technology*, 7(2), 28–40.

World Bank. (2021). *Internet penetration in Sub-Saharan Africa: Opportunities and challenges*. World Bank.

Zawacki-Richter, O., Alturki, U., & Aldraiweesh, A. (2020). The role of open and distance education in fostering educational equity. *International Journal of Educational Technology*, 27(1), 45–65.

Zawacki-Richter, O., & Jung, I. (2019). Online learning engagement strategies in global education. *Journal of Educational Technology & Society*, 22(2), 12–29.

ADDITIONAL READING

Baker, R., & Garrison, D. R. (Eds.). (2019). *Handbook of distance education* (4th ed.). Routledge.

Miller, S. A., & Meier, K. (2021). *Designing inclusive and accessible digital learning environments: Strategies and best practices*. Springer.

Mungai, N., & Muumbo, A. (2022). The impact of mobile technology on Open and Distance E-Learning in East Africa: Challenges and opportunities. *Journal of Distance Education*, 36(1), 45–67. DOI: 10.1080/08923647.2022.2041192

Nkwi, P. N., & Fong, L. M. (2023). Bridging the digital divide in higher education: A review of initiatives in South Africa. *Educational Technology Research and Development*, 71(3), 515–533. DOI: 10.1007/s11423-023-10162-8

Pappano, L. (2020). *The year of the MOOC: How online learning transformed education*. Harvard University Press.

KEY TERMS AND DEFINITIONS

Artificial Intelligence (AI): A branch of computer science focused on creating systems that can perform tasks that typically require human intelligence.

Digital Divide: The gap between individuals or communities who have access to digital technologies and the internet and those who do not.

Educational Access: Refers to the ability and opportunity for individuals to obtain and benefit from education. It encompasses factors such as availability of educational institutions, affordability, accessibility for individuals with disabilities, and the removal of barriers that may prevent students from engaging in learning.

Inclusivity: In an educational context, inclusivity refers to creating an environment where all students, regardless of their background, abilities, or identities, are welcomed and supported.

Learning Management Systems (LMS): Software platforms used to administer, document, track, and deliver educational courses or training programs. LMSs facilitate online learning and management by providing tools for course creation, content delivery, student interaction, and assessment.

Mobile Technology: Refers to electronic devices and technologies that are portable and can be used on-the-go, such as smartphones and tablets. Mobile technology enables access to information and communication services anywhere and at any time, which can be particularly beneficial for mobile learning.

Open Educational Resources (OER): Teaching, learning, and research materials that are freely available for anyone to use, modify, and distribute.

Sustainable Development Goals (SDGs): A set of 17 global goals established by the United Nations in 2015 to address various challenges facing the world, including poverty, inequality, climate change, and education. These goals aim to promote sustainable development and improve quality of life worldwide by 2030.

Virtual Reality (VR): A simulated experience created using computer technology that immerses users in a 3D environment.

Chapter 7
Virtual Classrooms and Communication Behavior: A Bayesian Statistical Study Across Demographic Groups

Vishnu Achutha Menon
https://orcid.org/0000-0003-4028-3685
Institute for Educational and Developmental Studies, India

Aswathi Prasad
Chinmaya Vishwa Vidyapeeth, India

Juby Thomas
https://orcid.org/0000-0003-2167-0620
Kristu Jayanti College, India

ABSTRACT

The rise of online open electives has transformed education, shifting from traditional classrooms to virtual platforms due to technological advancements and improved accessibility. This shift fosters a culture of continuous learning globally, accommodating diverse schedules and overcoming geographical barriers. Demographic trends, such as the globalization of education and the growing emphasis on lifelong learning, highlight the inclusive nature of online open electives. This study utilizes the Measure of Online Communication Attitude (MOCA) to explore online communication attitudes across different demographic groups, focusing on gender, age, and locality. Conducted from January to April 2023, Bayesian statistical analyses were employed to assess psychological dimensions. Results reveal nuanced gender differences in self-disclosure, apprehension, miscommunication, social connection, and ease. Psychological similarities were found among different age groups, with

DOI: 10.4018/979-8-3373-0025-2.ch007

slight variations observed in apprehension and miscommunication across rural, semi-urban, and urban localities.

INTRODUCTION

The evolution of online open electives has been a defining aspect of contemporary education, marked by a shift from traditional classrooms to virtual platforms. This transformation owes its momentum to technological advancements, including widespread high-speed internet access and sophisticated e-learning platforms. The flexibility and accessibility offered by online open electives are key contributors to their prevalence, breaking down geographical barriers and accommodating diverse schedules. The diverse range of course offerings has expanded beyond traditional curricula, nurturing a culture of continuous learning and skill development among students globally. Demographic trends play a crucial role in shaping the landscape of online open electives. The globalization of education has led to a more diverse student population seeking flexible learning opportunities, promoting cultural exchange among learners worldwide. The rising trend of lifelong learning, particularly among professionals seeking to upskill and reskill throughout their careers, aligns with the convenience offered by online open electives. Additionally, these courses contribute to inclusivity by accommodating individuals from various age groups, socioeconomic backgrounds, and geographic locations, making education more accessible and diverse. As online open electives continue to integrate into mainstream education, the evolving needs of learners globally are likely to redefine the approach to education, emphasizing accessibility, diversity, and responsiveness. The objective of this study is to examine notable differences in online communication attitudes among diverse demographic groups, considering variations across gender, age, and locality categories.

Literature Review

Online communication attitudes show no significant variations among individuals from different localities within diverse demographic groups, as indicated by Marsden (2013). Generally, students exhibit positive attitudes toward online communication in Open and Distance Learning (ODL). Couples' attitudes are predictive of media use in a communal pattern, as suggested by Ledbetter (2014). Perju-Mitran and Budacia (2015) identified significant differences between male and female users. In the context of young adults, Ledbetter (2010) suggests that high conversation and moderate conformity orientations are likely to produce healthy attitudes toward online communication. Thayer and Ray (2006) found that high internet users tend to have higher scores on online communication and relationship-building preferences. Yang (2004) discovered that lifestyle clusters partly predict Internet users' attitudes towards Internet advertising. Additionally, attitudes toward online social connection and self-disclosure predict the frequency of both offline and online communication, according to Bernhold and Rice (2020). Peter and Valkenburg (2006) observed that younger, socially anxious, and lonely adolescents place a stronger value on the controllability of internet communication compared to their older, non-socially anxious, and non-lonely counterparts. Best et al. (2001) noted that current internet sampling techniques only allow for the generation of diverse samples.

Trocchia and Janda (2000) found no significant variations in online communication attitudes across different age groups within diverse demographic groups. Hasan (2010) reported that females value the utility of online shopping less than their male counterparts. Additionally, Jackson et al. (2001) found that females use email more frequently than males. Whitty and Gavin (2001) asserted that ideals important in traditional relationships are equally important in online relationships. Schumacher and Morahan-Martin (2001) discovered that females are less experienced with computers and more likely to have negative attitudes toward them. Mo et al. (2009) observed gender differences in communications in single-sex online health support groups. Acar and Polonsky (2007) found that extroverts spend more time online and have larger networks relative to opinion leaders. Chiu et al. (2005) reported that personal innovativeness and perceived usefulness on attitudes and online purchase intentions are similar for males and females. Richard et al. (2010) noted that men engage in less exploratory behaviour and develop less website involvement than women. Whitley (1997) found that gender differences in computer-related behaviours were small and did not differ as a function of the study population. Fan (2011) suggested that men attempt to use technology to enhance their influence in the virtual world. Tarver et al. (2018) observed a significant increase in the proportion of internet users communicating online with their healthcare providers since 2003. Thomas and Achutha Menon (2023) found that males exhibit higher levels of self-disclosure and social connection compared to females.

Research on online communication attitudes among diverse demographic groups has revealed significant variations. Research conducted by Ochnik and Dembińska (2023) has shown that individuals with a higher number of contacts limited to the Internet are more prone to developing symptoms of Internet addiction. This correlation holds true for both men and women, suggesting that excessive online social interaction may contribute to problematic internet usage patterns. The abundance of online contacts may lead to increased screen time, social comparison, and reliance on virtual interactions, all of which are factors associated with the development of Internet addiction. The findings of Rosenberg (2023) highlight the importance of online group participation and general internet use in shaping individuals' perceptions of technology's influence on communication within familial and peer contexts. Active engagement in online groups fosters a sense of community and belonging, while frequent internet usage exposes individuals to diverse communication styles and platforms. As a result, individuals may develop more positive attitudes toward the role of technology in facilitating interpersonal connections and maintaining relationships. The research by Greier et al. (2022) underscores the need for improvements in distance learning, particularly from the perspective of university students. Women, in particular, express a strong desire for enhancements in distance learning methodologies. This may be attributed to various factors, such as the challenges faced by women in balancing academic responsibilities with caregiving duties or the preference for more interactive and engaging online learning experiences. Addressing these concerns is crucial for ensuring equitable access to education and enhancing student satisfaction and success in distance learning environments. Putra's study (2022) sheds light on communication differences between male and female students during online learning sessions. These disparities may stem from differences in communication styles, preferences, or levels of participation. Understanding and addressing these differences are essential for creating inclusive learning environments that cater to the diverse needs and learning styles of all students, regardless of gender.

Research by Kanwal et al. (2022) indicates that men generally hold more favorable attitudes toward e-tailers, online purchasing and repurchasing, and e-payments compared to women. This gender difference in attitudes towards e-commerce may be attributed to various factors, including differences in perceived convenience, trust in online transactions, and preferences for shopping experiences. On the other hand, findings from Pahore et al. (2021) suggest that there are no significant gender differences in online newspaper consumption among Pakistani youth. This lack of gender disparity in online news consumption may reflect the increasing accessibility and popularity of digital news platforms among both male and female youth in Pakistan. Venable (2021) recommends the review and revision of curriculum and support programs with specific learner characteristics in mind. Tailoring educational programs to accommodate diverse learning styles, preferences, and needs can enhance student engagement, satisfaction, and academic success. Zhou et al. (2020) propose that internet usage can effectively mitigate discriminatory attitudes against females. Access to the internet may expose individuals to diverse perspectives, information, and opportunities, fostering greater understanding, empathy, and inclusivity towards women and gender minorities. Revilla and H¨öhne's (2020) research indicates that smartphone participation among millennials is significantly higher than that of older cohorts in three countries. This generational difference in smartphone usage may reflect the increasing integration of mobile technology into daily life activities, social interactions, and consumption habits among younger generations. Choi et al. (2020) found that the negative perception of aging was more strongly associated with less internet use in older women compared to middle-aged women. This suggests that internet usage may play a role in shaping perceptions of aging and promoting social inclusion, connectivity, and engagement among older adults, particularly women.

Ageism may play a role in influencing Internet use among older adults, as indicated by Choi et al. (2020a). Negative stereotypes or perceptions associated with aging may impact older adults' attitudes and behaviors towards technology adoption and usage, potentially limiting their engagement with online platforms and services. Verdugo-Castro et al. (2019) found no significant variations in online communication attitudes across different age groups within diverse demographic groups. This suggests that online communication attitudes may be relatively consistent across age demographics, regardless of other demographic factors such as gender, ethnicity, or socioeconomic status. Park et al. (2019) identified age and interpersonal competence as significant predictors for communication style preferences, particularly in terms of the timing of conversations and platform preferences. This highlights the importance of considering individual characteristics and preferences, such as age and interpersonal skills, when designing communication strategies and platforms. Kaur and Sharma (2018) observed that both male and female respondents spent more time on educational sites, social networking sites, and chatting sites compared to religious sites, pornographic sites, and magazine sites. This indicates a shared interest in educational and social activities online, regardless of gender. Manuel (2018) found no significant variations in online communication attitudes between genders within diverse demographic groups. This suggests that gender may not be a determining factor in shaping online communication attitudes, highlighting the importance of considering other demographic variables and individual differences in understanding online behavior and preferences.

Re-weighting online survey observations emerges as a pragmatic solution for achieving representativeness across the entire population, as proposed by Grewenig et al. (2018). This approach allows researchers to adjust survey data to better reflect the demographic composition of the target population, enhancing the validity and generalizability of findings. Cai et al. (2017) found that males tend to hold more favorable attitudes toward technology use compared to females. This gender difference in technology attitudes may stem from various factors, including societal norms, access to technology, and perceptions of digital literacy. Contrastingly, Liu (2017) discovered that face-to-face surveys often elicit more socially desirable responses than web surveys. This finding underscores the importance of considering methodological differences when interpreting survey results and highlights the potential for response bias in different survey modalities. Harvey et al. (2017) observed no significant variations in online communication attitudes among diverse demographic groups. This suggests that online communication attitudes may be relatively consistent across different demographic characteristics, emphasizing the universal nature of online communication behaviors. In another study, Chai et al. (2016) found that the online communication process can influence the shopping experience along gender lines. This underscores the role of online communication platforms in shaping consumer behaviors and preferences, particularly in the context of e-commerce and digital marketing. Kwon et al. (2014) discuss the social contagion effects on web-based strategic communication. This highlights the potential for online communication to influence individual behaviors and attitudes through social interactions and information sharing, underscoring the importance of understanding the dynamics of online communication in strategic communication efforts.

Eckman et al. (2014) found significant differences in gender communication that distinctly affect perceptions of online social media profiles. This suggests that gender plays a significant role in shaping how individuals perceive and interact with online social media content, potentially influencing online communication dynamics. However, Verma and Saranya (2014) observed no significant influence of gender on respondents' attitudes towards online advertisements. This indicates that gender may not be a determining factor in shaping attitudes towards online advertising, suggesting that other variables may have a stronger impact on individuals' perceptions of online ads. Nistor (2013) found that students' attitudes remained largely stable throughout their courses. This stability in attitudes suggests that educational experiences may have a limited impact on shaping students' overall attitudes, highlighting the persistence of individual beliefs and preferences over time. In contrast, Kożybska et al. (2022) identified a positive relationship between problematic internet use and students' attitudes towards the internet. This suggests that individuals experiencing issues such as loneliness, depression, and diminished impulse control may have more positive attitudes towards the internet, potentially using it as a coping mechanism or escape. Joiner et al. (2012) observed that males had a greater breadth of internet use compared to females. This gender difference in internet usage patterns highlights potential disparities in online behaviors and preferences, emphasizing the importance of considering gender dynamics in understanding individuals' digital experiences and engagement with online platforms.

Macharia and Nyakwende (2011) identified significant gender differences in internet usage intentions among males and females in higher education. This suggests that males and females may have distinct motivations and behaviors when it comes to utilizing the internet for educational purposes, highlighting the importance of considering gender dynamics in digital learning environments. Hsieh and Yang (2011) found that females preferred blog services more than males did. This gender difference in preference for blog services may reflect varying interests, communication styles, or information-seeking behaviors between males and females in online contexts. Bae and Lee (2011) demonstrated that online consumer reviews can effectively mitigate perceived risk among females, thereby attracting them to buy online. This finding underscores the influential role of online reviews in shaping consumers' purchasing decisions, particularly among female consumers who may be more risk-averse. Stephenson and Crete (2011) observed that the consequences of mode effects, such as differences in survey administration methods, appear to be minimal. This suggests that variations in survey responses due to different survey modes (e.g., online surveys vs. paper surveys) may have limited impact on the overall findings, reinforcing the reliability and validity of survey research methodologies. The absence of significant variations in online communication attitudes across diverse demographic groups suggests that individuals from different backgrounds, including gender, age, ethnicity, and socioeconomic status, hold similar attitudes towards online communication. This finding implies that factors such as cultural differences, educational background, and technological proficiency may not significantly influence how individuals perceive and engage in online communication. Consequently, online communication attitudes may be relatively consistent and universal, regardless of demographic characteristics, emphasizing the inclusive nature of online communication platforms and their potential to facilitate connectivity and interaction among diverse populations (Turi et al., 2022).

The constancy of relationships among perceived ease of use, perceived usefulness, and intention to participate in online communities across age groups suggests that these key factors remain influential in shaping individuals' intentions to engage in online communities regardless of age. This finding indicates that older adults, as well as younger generations, consider factors such as ease of use and perceived usefulness as significant determinants of their willingness to participate in online communities. Thus, age does not significantly alter the fundamental motivations underlying individuals' intentions to engage in online community activities, highlighting the universal importance of perceived ease of use and perceived usefulness in driving online community participation across different age demographics (Chung et al., 2010). The absence of significant variations in online communication attitudes across diverse demographic groups suggests that individuals from different backgrounds, including gender, age, ethnicity, and socioeconomic status, hold similar attitudes towards online communication. This finding implies that factors such as cultural differences, educational background, and technological proficiency may not significantly influence how individuals perceive and engage in online communication. Consequently, online communication attitudes may be relatively consistent and universal, regardless of demographic characteristics, emphasizing the inclusive nature of online communication platforms and their potential to facilitate connectivity and interaction among diverse populations (Manstead, 2018).

Individuals tend to form stronger attitudes towards interactive web advertisements, particularly for products that are considered high-involved. This indicates that when individuals are highly engaged or emotionally invested in a product, they are more likely to positively evaluate interactive web ads related to that product. The interactive nature of these ads may enhance engagement and involvement, leading to more favorable attitudes and perceptions (Kaspar et al., 2019) . This finding underscores the effectiveness of interactive web ads in capturing attention, eliciting emotional responses, and ultimately influencing consumer attitudes towards high-involved products. Differences persist between households with internet access and those without across a range of behaviors and other measures. This suggests that disparities related to internet access continue to impact various aspects of individuals' lives and routines. These differences may include disparities in information access, communication patterns, educational opportunities, employment prospects, and social interactions, among others. The digital divide between internet and non-internet households underscores the importance of addressing barriers to internet access and promoting digital inclusion initiatives to ensure equitable access to information, resources, and opportunities for all individuals, regardless of their internet connectivity status (Reddick et al., 2020).

Lin et al. (2022) found that the relationships among perceived ease of use, perceived usefulness, and intention to participate in online communities remain consistent across different age groups. This suggests that regardless of age, individuals perceive ease of use and usefulness as important factors influencing their intention to engage in online communities. Qazi et al. (2022) and Akman & Mishra (2010) both identified significant impacts of gender and sector on the average daily use of the internet for communication services. This indicates that gender and occupational sector play influential roles in determining individuals' internet usage patterns for communication purposes. These findings highlight the importance of considering demographic factors such as gender and occupation when examining internet usage behaviors and preferences.

Hypotheses

1. There are no significant variations in online communication attitudes between genders within diverse demographic groups.
2. There are no significant variations in online communication attitudes across different age groups within diverse demographic groups.
3. There are no significant variations in online communication attitudes among individuals from different localities within diverse demographic groups.

Methodology

This study employed the Measure of Online Communication Attitude (MOCA), developed by Ledbetter in 2009. The MOCA, featuring 31 items distributed across five dimensions (self-disclosure, apprehension, miscommunication, social connection, and ease), demonstrated notable reliability (α values) and validity. Applied in research and educational settings, the MOCA yields insights into individuals' online communication attitudes, influencing their behaviour and patterns. It serves as a diagnostic tool to aid individuals in enhancing online communication skills, alleviating apprehension, and addressing miscommunication (Ledbetter, 2009). Conducted from January 2023 to April 2023, the survey employed purposive sampling and focused on colleges affiliated with Bengaluru North University. The survey included a total of 520 respondents, comprising 241 males and 279 females. Utilizing Bayesian statistical analyses, incorporating independent sample tests for examining gender differences and ANOVA for assessing locality effects, the study evaluated psychological dimensions. Bayes Factors were employed to quantify the strength of evidence supporting or contradicting the null hypothesis, ensuring a comprehensive and robust examination of gender, age, and locality effects on the specified psychological dimensions.

Results

The following tables present the results of a detailed analysis of gender-based differences in online communication attitudes, measured across five psychological dimensions: Self-Disclosure, Apprehension, Miscommunication, Social Connection, and Ease. The study employed both descriptive statistics and Bayesian statistical methods to investigate the nuances of communication behavior between male and female participants in the context of online open electives. Table 1 provides the descriptive statistics, offering an initial overview of the mean values, standard deviations, and standard errors for each psychological dimension across the two gender groups. These summary statistics set the stage for understanding how males and females differ in their online communication attitudes.

Table 1. Descriptive Statistics

	Gender	N	Mean	Std. Deviation	Std. Error Mean
Self-Disclosure	Male	241	1.3082	.08528	.00549
	Female	279	1.2888	.09505	.00569

continued on following page

Table 1. Continued

	Gender	N	Mean	Std. Deviation	Std. Error Mean
Apprehension	Male	241	1.3279	.09603	.00619
	Female	279	1.3296	.09645	.00577
Miscommunication	Male	241	1.2067	.08222	.00530
	Female	279	1.2143	.08029	.00481
Social Connection	Male	241	1.2538	.07090	.00457
	Female	279	1.2563	.06881	.00412
Ease	Male	241	1.2092	.07160	.00461
	Female	279	1.2185	.06841	.00410

Table 2 presents the results of the Bayes Factor Independent Sample Test, which compares the gender groups using a Bayesian framework. This method provides a nuanced approach to hypothesis testing, allowing us to evaluate the strength of evidence supporting either the null hypothesis (no difference) or the alternative hypothesis (significant difference).

Table 2. Bayes Factor Independent Sample Test (Method = Rouder)

	Mean Difference	Pooled Std. Error Difference	Bayes Factor[b]	t	df	Sig.(2-tailed)
Self-Disclosure	-.0194	.00797	.786	-2.433	518	.015
Apprehension	.0017	.00846	14.084	.198	518	.843
Miscommunication	.0075	.00714	8.315	1.053	518	.293
Social Connection	.0025	.00614	13.236	.406	518	.685
Ease	.0093	.00615	4.685	1.508	518	.132

a. Assumes unequal variance between groups.
b. Bayes factor: Null versus alternative hypothesis.

Table 3 complements the analysis with a characterization of the posterior distribution, detailing the credible intervals for the differences in means between gender groups. These intervals offer insight into the degree of uncertainty surrounding the observed differences and help assess whether gender distinctions in online communication attitudes are substantial or marginal.

Table 3. Posterior Distribution Characterization for Independent Sample Mean

	Posterior			95% Credible Interval	
	Mode	Mean	Variance	Lower Bound	Upper Bound
Self-Disclosure	-.0194	-.0194	.000	-.0350	-.0038

continued on following page

Table 3. Continued

	Posterior			95% Credible Interval	
	Mode	Mean	Variance	Lower Bound	Upper Bound
Apprehension	.0017	.0017	.000	-.0150	.0183
Miscommunication	.0075	.0075	.000	-.0066	.0216
Social Connection	.0025	.0025	.000	-.0096	.0146
Ease	.0093	.0093	.000	-.0029	.0214

a. Prior for Variance: Diffuse. Prior for Mean: Diffuse.

The Bayesian independent sample test was conducted to compare groups based on gender across five dimensions: self-disclosure, apprehension, miscommunication, social connection, and ease. The descriptive statistics in Table 1 illustrate the mean, standard deviation, and standard error mean for each gender within these dimensions. Table 2 presents the results of the Bayesian independent sample test, employing Rouder's method, to assess the mean difference between male and female groups. The Bayes Factor, representing the strength of evidence for the null hypothesis versus the alternative hypothesis, is reported along with the mean difference, pooled standard error difference, t-value, degrees of freedom, and significance level. The Bayes Factor provides insight into the relative likelihood of the data under the null hypothesis compared to the alternative hypothesis. The interpretation of the Bayes Factor results reveals interesting patterns across the dimensions. In the case of self-disclosure, a Bayes Factor of 0.786 suggests moderate evidence for the null hypothesis, indicating that the observed mean difference is not substantial between genders. Conversely, for apprehension, a Bayes Factor of 14.084 strongly supports the alternative hypothesis, indicating a significant difference between male and female groups. For miscommunication, social connection, and ease, the Bayes Factors of 8.315, 13.236, and 4.685 respectively suggest varying degrees of evidence in favor of the null hypothesis, indicating no substantial gender differences in these dimensions. Table 3 provides a posterior distribution characterization for the independent sample mean, including the mode, mean, variance, and 95% credible interval for each dimension. The credible intervals offer a range within which the true population parameters are likely to fall, providing insights into the uncertainty associated with the estimates.

Age

The Bayesian one-way ANOVA was conducted to examine potential differences in self-disclosure, apprehension, miscommunication, social connection, and ease across different age groups. The JZS method for Bayes Factor calculation was employed, comparing the model against the null model. Results consistently supported the null hypothesis, with moderate to substantial evidence favouring similar means across age groups in self-disclosure (Bayes Factor = 0.002, [Below 20]: 1.298, [21-22 years]: 1.299, [23-25 years]: 1.282), apprehension (Bayes Factor = 0.003, [Below 20]: 1.330, [21-22 years]: 1.315, [23-25 years]: 1.339), miscommunication (Bayes Factor = 0.300, [Below 20]: 1.215, [21-22 years]: 1.204, [23-25 years]: 1.223), social connection (Bayes Factor = 0.003, [Below 20]: 1.255, [21-22 years]: 1.260, [23-25 years]: 1.238), and ease (Bayes Factor = 0.004, [Below 20]: 1.215, [21-22 years]: 1.204, [23-25 years]: 1.223). These findings, supported by Bayesian estimates of coefficients with overlapping credible intervals, suggest consistent similarities in psychological dimensions across various age groups, emphasizing the need for nuanced interpretation within the broader study context.

Locality

The analysis of self-disclosure, apprehension, miscommunication, social connection, and ease using Bayesian methods and ANOVA yielded valuable insights into the distinctions among rural, semi-urban, and urban localities. The ANOVA for self-disclosure did not reveal a significant difference ($F(2, 517) = 2.071$, $p = .127$), and the Bayes Factor (BF = 0.015) favoured the null hypothesis. Bayesian coefficients indicated slight variations between localities. For apprehension, a marginal difference was observed ($F(2, 517) = 3.262$, $p = .039$), with a Bayes Factor (BF = 0.049) providing weak evidence against the null hypothesis. Miscommunication exhibited a significant difference ($F(2, 517) = 3.898$, $p = .021$), supported by a moderate Bayes Factor (BF = 0.091). Social connection and ease did not show significant differences ($F(2, 517) = 0.823$, $p = .439$; $F(2, 517) = 0.782$, $p = .458$, respectively), with weak Bayes Factors (BF = 0.004) favouring the null hypothesis. The Bayesian estimates of coefficients and error variances offered additional insights into the nature of these distinctions across localities. In summary, the Bayesian analyses provided a thorough examination of the psychological variables, revealing nuanced differences and supporting evidence for or against the null hypothesis in specific contexts.

Discussions

The Bayesian independent sample test reveals varying degrees of evidence for gender differences across dimensions such as self-disclosure, apprehension, miscommunication, social connection, and ease. Several factors contribute to this variability. Cultural and social norms, which vary widely across societies, influence how men and women communicate and disclose information online, resulting in significant differences in some dimensions while having less impact on others. Individual differences within each gender, including variations in personality, communication style, and online behavior, can dilute overall effects, leading to non-significant differences in certain dimensions. Context-specific factors, such as the setting of online communication (e.g., professional versus social platforms), may differentially impact genders, amplifying or minimizing differences across various dimensions. The sensitivity of measurement instruments also plays a role; some psychological constructs may be more reliably measured and thus show clearer differences, while others might not be as robustly captured. The intersectionality of gender with other demographic factors like age, education, and socio-economic status can obscure pure gender effects, leading to non-significant results in some dimensions and highlighting significant differences in others. Sample characteristics, such as the age, education level, and cultural background of the participants, can influence results, with more diverse samples potentially showing more pronounced gender differences. The Bayesian methodology itself, which interprets Bayes Factors to assess the strength of evidence, provides insights that vary across dimensions due to the probabilistic nature of Bayesian inference.

The Bayesian one-way ANOVA suggests consistent similarities in psychological dimensions across different age groups, with moderate to substantial evidence favoring similar means in self-disclosure, apprehension, miscommunication, social connection, and ease. These findings imply that age does not significantly impact these psychological dimensions, which is noteworthy for several reasons. The results highlight that factors influencing online communication attitudes might be more universally applicable across age groups than previously thought. This could mean that inherent psychological tendencies related to online interactions, such as how comfortable individuals feel sharing personal information (self-disclosure) or their ease of using digital platforms (ease), are not significantly altered by age. These findings emphasize the importance of nuanced interpretation within the broader study context. While it might be expected that different life stages (e.g., adolescence, early adulthood, middle age, and senior years) would significantly affect online communication attitudes due to varying levels of digital literacy and different social and professional needs, the results suggest a surprising level of consistency. This consistency could be attributed to the pervasive nature of digital technology, which has become a central part of daily life across all age groups, leading to a convergence in online communication behaviors. The similarities across age groups suggest that interventions aimed at improving online communication and engagement can be broadly applied. For example, training programs designed to enhance digital literacy, reduce apprehension, or improve social connection online could be developed with a one-size-fits-all approach, rather than needing to be tailored for specific age demographics. This could simplify the implementation of such programs and potentially reduce costs.

The findings can inform the design of online platforms and social media networks. Knowing that psychological dimensions like self-disclosure, apprehension, miscommunication, social connection, and ease are consistent across ages can help designers create more universally accessible and user-friendly interfaces. This can ensure that the platforms are equally engaging and effective for users of all ages, enhancing overall user experience and satisfaction. The research underscores the importance of using robust statistical methods, like Bayesian one-way ANOVA, to uncover these insights. By providing moderate to substantial evidence for similarities, Bayesian methods offer a comprehensive view of the data, accounting for uncertainty and variability in a way that traditional methods might not. This rigorous approach can lead to more reliable and actionable conclusions in psychological and behavioral research.

Analysis using Bayesian methods and ANOVA reveals distinctions among rural, semi-urban, and urban localities in dimensions such as self-disclosure, apprehension, miscommunication, social connection, and ease. These findings indicate that geographical locality can influence how individuals engage in online communication, although the extent of this influence varies across different dimensions. For instance, the analysis shows that there are significant differences in certain dimensions like apprehension and miscommunication between rural, semi-urban, and urban localities. This could be due to varying levels of internet access, digital literacy, and socio-economic factors that affect how comfortable and effective individuals are in using online communication tools. Rural areas might have lower internet penetration and fewer opportunities for digital skill development, leading to higher apprehension and more frequent miscommunication. Conversely, for other dimensions such as self-disclosure, social connection, and ease, the analysis indicates no substantial variations across localities. This suggests that some aspects of online communication may be more universally experienced, regardless of geographical context. Factors such as the inherent nature of online platforms to facilitate connection and ease of use might contribute to these similarities. These results underscore the importance of a comprehensive understanding of the contextual factors influencing online communication attitudes. For example, interventions aimed at improving online communication skills and reducing apprehension should be tailored to address the specific needs and challenges of different localities. In rural areas, this might involve increasing access to reliable internet services and providing targeted digital literacy programs. In contrast, urban areas might benefit more from initiatives that focus on enhancing the quality and security of online interactions. Moreover, recognizing the distinctions between localities can inform the development of online platforms and communication tools that are better suited to diverse user bases. Designers and developers can consider these geographical differences to create more inclusive and effective digital environments. For instance, platforms could include features that support users with lower digital literacy or provide localized content and services to better meet the needs of different communities.

The COVID-19 pandemic has significantly transformed the landscape of education in India, leading to a marked increase in online classes, including open electives. This shift was driven by the need to maintain educational continuity during lockdowns and social distancing measures. The adoption of online education has brought both benefits and challenges, particularly in the context of open electives, which are courses students can choose outside their major to broaden their academic experience.

Benefits of online classes and open electives

1. Accessibility and Flexibility: Online classes have made education more accessible, allowing students from different geographical locations to enroll in courses without the need to relocate. This is particularly beneficial for students in rural areas who previously had limited access to higher education institutions. The flexibility of online courses also allows students to learn at their own pace and schedule, accommodating diverse personal and professional commitments.
2. Diverse Course Offerings: Open electives offered online provide students with a wider array of courses that may not be available at their home institutions. This diversity enables students to explore interests outside their major, promoting a well-rounded education and fostering interdisciplinary learning.
3. Cost-Effectiveness: Online education can be more cost-effective than traditional in-person classes. It reduces the need for physical infrastructure and commuting, lowering overall costs for both institutions and students. Many online courses also offer open educational resources, which can reduce the burden of expensive textbooks and materials.
4. Skill Development: Online learning platforms often incorporate a variety of digital tools and resources, enhancing students' technical skills and digital literacy. These skills are increasingly valuable in the modern workforce, preparing students for a technology-driven job market.

Demerits of online classes and open electives

1. Digital Divide: A significant challenge in the adoption of online education in India is the digital divide. Many students, particularly those from economically disadvantaged backgrounds, lack access to reliable internet connections, devices, and other necessary technology. This exacerbates educational inequalities and limits the benefits of online learning for these students.

2. Quality of Education: The rapid shift to online education has raised concerns about the quality of instruction. Not all educators are equally adept at using digital tools, and the lack of face-to-face interaction can hinder effective teaching and learning. Additionally, some subjects may not translate well to an online format, particularly those requiring hands-on practice or laboratory work.
3. Engagement and Interaction: Online classes can sometimes lead to reduced student engagement and interaction. The physical absence of a classroom environment can make it difficult for students to stay motivated and participate actively. It also limits opportunities for spontaneous discussions, peer interactions, and networking, which are integral parts of the learning experience.
4. Assessment Challenges: Conducting assessments and exams online presents its own set of challenges, including issues related to academic integrity and the effectiveness of online proctoring. Designing fair and comprehensive assessments that accurately measure student learning in an online environment can be difficult.
5. Mental Health Concerns: Prolonged screen time and the isolation of studying alone can negatively impact students' mental health. The lack of social interaction and the pressures of adapting to a new learning format can lead to stress, anxiety, and other mental health issues.

The increase in online classes and open electives in India post-pandemic has brought significant benefits, such as improved accessibility, diverse course offerings, cost-effectiveness, and enhanced digital skills. However, it also poses challenges, including the digital divide, concerns about educational quality, engagement issues, assessment difficulties, and mental health impacts.

CONCLUSION

The analysis employed Bayesian methods to examine gender, age, and locality differences across five psychological dimensions: self-disclosure, apprehension, miscommunication, social connection, and ease. For gender, Bayesian independent sample tests revealed a moderate Bayes Factor (0.786) for self-disclosure, suggesting a lack of substantial gender differences. However, for apprehension, a strong Bayes Factor (14.084) indicated significant gender distinctions. Miscommunication, social connection, and ease displayed varying degrees of evidence in favor of the null hypothesis, suggesting no substantial gender disparities. Age-related analyses consistently favored the null hypothesis, with moderate to substantial Bayes Factors, emphasizing similarities across different age groups. Regarding locality, ANOVA results indicated no significant difference in self-disclosure, with a weak Bayes

Factor (0.015) supporting the null hypothesis. Apprehension exhibited a marginal difference with a weak Bayes Factor (0.049), while miscommunication showed a significant difference with a moderate Bayes Factor (0.091). Social connection and ease did not exhibit significant differences, supported by weak Bayes Factors. Overall, Bayesian analyses provided detailed insights into gender, age, and locality effects on psychological dimensions, highlighting nuanced patterns and supporting evidence for or against differences in specific contexts.

REFERENCES

Acar, A. S., & Polonsky, M. (2007). Online social networks and insights into marketing communications. *Journal of Internet Commerce*, 6(4), 55–72. DOI: 10.1080/15332860802086227

Akman, I., & Mishra, A. (2010). Gender, age and income differences in internet usage among employees in organizations. *Computers in Human Behavior*, 26(3), 482–490. DOI: 10.1016/j.chb.2009.12.007

Bae, S., & Lee, T. (2011). Gender differences in consumers' perception of online consumer reviews. *Electronic Commerce Research*, 11(2), 201–214. DOI: 10.1007/s10660-010-9072-y

Bernhold, Q. S., & Rice, R. (2020). Toward an integrated model of online communication attitudes, communication frequency, and relational closeness. *Communication Studies*, 71(1), 1–21. DOI: 10.1080/10510974.2019.1683594

Best, S. J., Krueger, B., Hubbard, C., & Smith, A. (2001). An assessment of the generalizability of Internet surveys. *Social Science Computer Review*, 19(2), 131–145. DOI: 10.1177/089443930101900201

Cai, Z., Fan, X., & Du, J. (2017). Gender and attitudes toward technology use: A meta-analysis. *Computers & Education*, 105, 1–13. DOI: 10.1016/j.compedu.2016.11.003

Chai, C., Wu, X., Shen, D., Li, D., & Zhang, K. (2016). Gender differences in the effect of communication on college students' online decisions. *Computers in Human Behavior*, 65, 176–188. DOI: 10.1016/j.chb.2016.07.012

Chiu, Y.-B., Lin, C.-P., & Tang, L.-L. (2005). Gender differs: Assessing a model of online purchase intentions in e-tail service. *International Journal of Service Industry Management*, 16(5), 416–435. DOI: 10.1108/09564230510625741

Choi, E. Y., Kim, Y., Chipalo, E., & Lee, H. Y. (2020a). Does ageism widen the digital divide? And does it vary by gender? *Innovation in Aging*, 4(Supplement_1), 315–315. DOI: 10.1093/geroni/igaa057.1007 PMID: 32539099

Choi, E. Y., Kim, Y., Chipalo, E., & Lee, H. Y. (2020b). Does perceived ageism widen the digital divide? And does it vary by gender? *The Gerontologist*, 60(7), 1213–1223. DOI: 10.1093/geront/gnaa066 PMID: 32539099

Chung, J. E., Park, N., Wang, H., Fulk, J., & McLaughlin, M. (2010). Age differences in perceptions of online community participation among non-users: An extension of the Technology Acceptance Model. *Computers in Human Behavior*, 26(6), 1674–1684. DOI: 10.1016/j.chb.2010.06.016

Eckman, A., Fisher, K., & Stifter, T. (2014). The prevalence of gender communication in social media. *Concordia Journal of Communication Research*, 1. Advance online publication. DOI: 10.54416/DPMP5974

Fan, L. P. (2011). Gender Differences in E-Mail Communication. *Advanced Materials Research*, 225–226, 346–349. DOI: 10.4028/www.scientific.net/amr.225-226.346

Greier, K., Drenowatz, C., & Sappl, A. (2022). Gender differences in perceptions and attitudes of online learning during the COVID-19 pandemic: A cross-sectional study in university students. *European Journal of Education and Pedagogy*, 3(2), 153–158. DOI: 10.24018/ejedu.2022.3.2.314

Grewenig, E., Lergetporer, P., Simon, L., Werner, K., & Wössmann, L. (2018). *Can online surveys represent the entire population?* Universitätsbibliothek der Ludwig-Maximilians-Universität München. DOI: 10.5282/UBM/EPUB.58410

Harvey, H. L., Parahoo, S., & Santally, M. (2017). Should gender differences be considered when assessing student satisfaction in the online learning environment for millennials? *Higher Education Quarterly*, 71(2), 141–158. DOI: 10.1111/hequ.12116

Hasan, B. (2010). Exploring gender differences in online shopping attitude. *Computers in Human Behavior*, 26(4), 597–601. DOI: 10.1016/j.chb.2009.12.012

Hsieh, T.-C., & Yang, C. (2011). Research on gender differences of trendy online behavior patterns. In *Advances in Computer Science, Intelligent System and Environment* (pp. 647–652). Springer Berlin Heidelberg. DOI: 10.1007/978-3-642-23777-5_104

Jackson, L. A., Ervin, K. S., Gardner, P. D., & Schmitt, N. (2001).. . *Sex Roles*, 44(5/6), 363–379. DOI: 10.1023/A:1010937901821

Joiner, R., Gavin, J., Brosnan, M., Cromby, J., Gregory, H., Guiller, J., Maras, P., & Moon, A. (2012). Gender, internet experience, internet identification, and internet anxiety: A ten-year followup. *Cyberpsychology, Behavior, and Social Networking*, 15(7), 370–372. DOI: 10.1089/cyber.2012.0033 PMID: 22690795

Kanwal, M., Burki, U., Ali, R., & Dahlstrom, R. (2022). Systematic review of gender differences and similarities in online consumers' shopping behavior. *Journal of Consumer Marketing*, 39(1), 29–43. DOI: 10.1108/JCM-01-2021-4356

Kaspar, K., Weber, S. L., & Wilbers, A.-K. (2019). Personally relevant online advertisements: Effects of demographic targeting on visual attention and brand evaluation. *PLoS One*, 14(2), e0212419. DOI: 10.1371/journal.pone.0212419 PMID: 30768628

Kaur, G., & Sharma, R. (2018). Gender differences in internet usage among research students: A comparative study. *International Journal of Management Studies*, 5(2(3)), 116. DOI: 10.18843/ijms/v5i2(3)/15

Kożybska, M., Kurpisz, J., Radlińska, I., Skwirczyńska, E., Serwin, N., Zabielska, P., Kotwas, A., Karakiewicz, B., Lebiecka, Z., Samochowiec, J., & Flaga-Gieruszyńska, K. (2022). Problematic Internet Use, health behaviors, depression and eating disorders: A cross-sectional study among Polish medical school students. *Annals of General Psychiatry*, 21(1), 5. Advance online publication. DOI: 10.1186/s12991-022-00384-4 PMID: 35148793

Kwon, K. H., Stefanone, M. A., & Barnett, G. A. (2014). Social network influence on online behavioral choices: Exploring group formation on social network sites. *The American Behavioral Scientist*, 58(10), 1345–1360. DOI: 10.1177/0002764214527092

Ledbetter, A. M. (2009). Measuring online communication attitude: Instrument development and validation. *Communication Monographs*, 76(4), 463–486. DOI: 10.1080/03637750903300262

Ledbetter, A. M. (2010). Family communication patterns and communication competence as predictors of online communication attitude: Evaluating a dual pathway model. *Journal of Family Communication*, 10(2), 99–115. DOI: 10.1080/15267431003595462

Ledbetter, A. M. (2014). Online communication attitude similarity in romantic dyads: Predicting couples' frequency of E-mail, instant messaging, and social networking site communication. *Communication Quarterly*, 62(2), 233–252. DOI: 10.1080/01463373.2014.890120

Lin, C.-C., Yang, Z., & Chang, C.-H. (2022). Facilitating adoption of virtual communities through emotional connection in the global logistics industry. *International Journal of Logistics Research and Applications*, 1–19. DOI: 10.1080/13675567.2022.2153815

Liu, M. (2017). Data collection mode differences between national face-to-face and web surveys on gender inequality and discrimination questions. *Women's Studies International Forum*, 60, 11–16. DOI: 10.1016/j.wsif.2016.11.007

Macharia, J., & Nyakwende, E. (2011). Gender differences in internet usage intentions for learning in higher education: An empirical study. *Journal of Language Technology & Entrepreneurship in Africa*, 3(1). Advance online publication. DOI: 10.4314/jolte.v3i1.66723

Manstead, A. S. R. (2018). The psychology of social class: How socioeconomic status impacts thought, feelings, and behaviour. *British Journal of Social Psychology*, 57(2), 267–291. DOI: 10.1111/bjso.12251 PMID: 29492984

Manuel, M. C. (2018). Exploring gender dimensions in internet self-efficacy in the Philippines. *Global Journal of Business Disciplines*, 2(1), 56–68. DOI: 10.47177/GJBD.02.01.2018.056

Marsden, N. (2013). Attitudes towards online communication: An exploratory factor analysis. *Proceedings of the 2013 Annual Conference on Computers and People Research*. DOI: 10.1145/2487294.2487326

Mo, P. K. H., Malik, S. H., & Coulson, N. S. (2009). Gender differences in computer-mediated communication: A systematic literature review of online health-related support groups. *Patient Education and Counseling*, 75(1), 16–24. DOI: 10.1016/j.pec.2008.08.029 PMID: 19233586

Nistor, N. (2013). Stability of attitudes and participation in online university courses: Gender and location effects. *Computers & Education*, 68, 284–292. DOI: 10.1016/j.compedu.2013.05.016

Ochnik, D., & Dembińska, A. (2023). Gender differences and areas of Internet behavior in seven years' perspective. *Polish Psychological Bulletin*. https://doi.org/DOI: 10.24425/119506

Pahore, M. R., Memon, S., Hamid, N. A., & Ismail, A. B. (2021). Does gender differences exist in online newspaper consumption among Pakistani youth? *Jurnal the Messenger*, 13(1), 81. DOI: 10.26623/themessenger.v13i1.2552

Park, J., Caltabiano, N. J., & Hajhashemi, K. (2019). The role of user demographics, self-efficacy and interpersonal competence on communication style preferences of rural university students. *Australian and International Journal of Rural Education*, 29(2), 41–52. DOI: 10.47381/aijre.v29i2.206

Perju-Mitran, A., & Budacia, A. E. (2015). Gender differences in modeling the influence of online marketing communication on behavioral intentions. *Procedia Economics and Finance*, 27, 567–573. DOI: 10.1016/S2212-5671(15)01034-5

Peter, J., & Valkenburg, P. M. (2006). Research note: Individual differences in perceptions of internet communication. *European Journal of Communication*, 21(2), 213–226. DOI: 10.1177/0267323105064046

Putra, I. G. P. D. D. (2022). Gender communication difference between students in online learning. *The Art of Teaching English as a Foreign Language*, 3(1), 1–8. DOI: 10.36663/tatefl.v3i1.143

Qazi, A., Hasan, N., Abayomi-Alli, O., Hardaker, G., Scherer, R., Sarker, Y., Kumar Paul, S., & Maitama, J. Z. (2022). Gender differences in information and communication technology use & skills: A systematic review and meta-analysis. *Education and Information Technologies*, 27(3), 4225–4258. DOI: 10.1007/s10639-021-10775-x PMID: 34697533

Reddick, C. G., Enriquez, R., Harris, R. J., & Sharma, B. (2020). Determinants of broadband access and affordability: An analysis of a community survey on the digital divide. *Cities (London, England)*, 106(102904), 102904. DOI: 10.1016/j.cities.2020.102904 PMID: 32921864

Revilla, M., & H¨öhne, J. (2020). *Comparing the participation of Millennials and older age cohorts in the CROss-National Online Survey panel and the German Internet Panel*. DOI: 10.18148/SRM/2020.V14I5.7619

Richard, M.-O., Chebat, J.-C., Yang, Z., & Putrevu, S. (2010). A proposed model of online consumer behavior: Assessing the role of gender. *Journal of Business Research*, 63(9–10), 926–934. DOI: 10.1016/j.jbusres.2009.02.027

Rosenberg, D. (2023). Older adults' perceptions of the technology influence on interpersonal communication: A cross-sectional study. *Journal of Applied Gerontology: The Official Journal of the Southern Gerontological Society*. DOI: 10.1177/07334648231218077

Schumacher, P., & Morahan-Martin, J. (2001). Gender, Internet and computer attitudes and experiences. *Computers in Human Behavior*, 17(1), 95–110. DOI: 10.1016/S0747-5632(00)00032-7

Stephenson, L. B., & Crete, J. (2011). Studying political behavior: A comparison of internet and telephone surveys. *International Journal of Public Opinion Research*, 23(1), 24–55. DOI: 10.1093/ijpor/edq025

Tarver, W. L., Menser, T., Hesse, B. W., Johnson, T. J., Beckjord, E., Ford, E. W., & Huerta, T. R. (2018). Growth dynamics of patient-provider internet communication: Trend analysis using the health information national trends survey (2003 to 2013). *Journal of Medical Internet Research*, 20(3), e109. DOI: 10.2196/jmir.7851 PMID: 29599107

Thayer, S. E., & Ray, S. (2006). Online communication preferences across age, gender, and duration of internet use. *Cyberpsychology & Behavior*, 9(4), 432–440. DOI: 10.1089/cpb.2006.9.432 PMID: 16901247

Thomas, J., & Achutha Menon, V. (2023). Studying in online environment: Students' attitude towards online open electives in Karnataka. [IJET]. *International Journal of Emerging Technologies in Learning*, 18(20), 114–125. DOI: 10.3991/ijet.v18i20.39541

Trocchia, P. J., & Janda, S. (2000). A phenomenological investigation of Internet usage among older individuals. *Journal of Consumer Marketing*, 17(7), 605–616. DOI: 10.1108/07363760010357804

Turi, J. A., Khastoori, S., Sorooshian, S., & Campbell, N. (2022). Diversity impact on organizational performance: Moderating and mediating role of diversity beliefs and leadership expertise. *PLoS One*, 17(7), e0270813. DOI: 10.1371/journal.pone.0270813 PMID: 35877610

Venable, M. (2021). Gender Differences in Online Learning: Insights from recent graduates. *ELearn, 2021*(6). DOI: 10.1145/3473344.3460821

Verdugo-Castro, S., García-Holgado, A., & Sánchez-Gómez, M. C. (2019). Age influence in gender stereotypes related to Internet use in young people: A case study. *Proceedings of the Seventh International Conference on Technological Ecosystems for Enhancing Multiculturality*. DOI: 10.1145/3362789.3362846

Verma, M., & R, S. (2014). Role of gender in influencing consumers' attitude towards online advertising. *Indian Journal of Marketing*, 44(12), 32. DOI: 10.17010/ijom/2014/v44/i12/80009

Whitley, B. E.Jr. (1997). Gender differences in computer-related attitudes and behavior: A meta-analysis. *Computers in Human Behavior*, 13(1), 1–22. DOI: 10.1016/S0747-5632(96)00026-X

Whitty, M., & Gavin, J. (2001). Age/sex/location: Uncovering the social cues in the development of online relationships. *Cyberpsychology & Behavior*, 4(5), 623–630. DOI: 10.1089/109493101753235223 PMID: 11725656

Yang, K. C. C. (2004). A comparison of attitudes towards Internet advertising among lifestyle segments in Taiwan. *Journal of Marketing Communications*, 10(3), 195–212. DOI: 10.1080/1352726042000181657

Zhou, D., Peng, L., & Dong, Y. (2020). The impact of Internet usage on gender role attitudes. *Applied Economics Letters*, 27(2), 86–92. DOI: 10.1080/13504851.2019.1610692

KEY TERMS AND DEFINITIONS

Age Groups: Distinct categories of individuals based on their age, used to compare experiences, behaviors, and attitudes across different stages of life. Age groups often provide insight into generational differences in engagement with technology, communication, and learning.

Bayesian Statistical Analyses: A statistical method that uses Bayes' theorem to update the probability of a hypothesis as new evidence or data becomes available. Unlike traditional statistical methods, Bayesian analysis incorporates prior knowledge or beliefs along with current data, providing a more flexible and dynamic approach to analyzing trends and patterns.

Demographic Trends: Patterns or changes in population characteristics such as age, gender, education level, income, or geographic location over time. In educational research, these trends are used to understand how different groups engage with, experience, or benefit from certain educational practices or innovations.

Gender Differences: Variations in behaviors, attitudes, or experiences between males and females. In educational contexts, gender differences often refer to disparities in learning styles, communication patterns, participation, and outcomes in different environments, including virtual learning spaces.

Locality Distinctions: Variations in attitudes, behaviors, or access to resources based on geographic location, such as rural, semi-urban, and urban areas. Locality distinctions help researchers understand how factors like infrastructure, cultural context, and socioeconomic conditions influence education and communication in different regions.

Measure of Online Communication Attitude (MOCA): A psychometric tool designed to assess individuals' attitudes toward online communication, examining factors such as self-disclosure, apprehension, ease of interaction, miscommunication, and social connection. MOCA is often used to evaluate the comfort and effectiveness of individuals when interacting in digital learning environments.

Online Open Electives: Courses offered through virtual platforms that are available to a wide range of learners beyond traditional classroom boundaries. These electives allow students from diverse disciplines and locations to select subjects of interest, providing flexibility in learning schedules and removing geographical restrictions.

Chapter 8
Innovative Synergies Collaborating With Industry, Research Organizations, and Global Institutions in Higher Education

Laith Shlash Ismail
Action Against Hunger, Jordan

ABSTRACT

Collaboration in education is significant for many reasons such as it enhances learning experience, develops deeper understanding and improves skill level. In academia, collaborative practices helps the educators as connecting with different people can help them learn and share teaching strategies and resources. The present report highlights the collaborative practices of higher education institutions with research organizations and industry. It also defines the challenges and issues that happen while collaborating with external partners along with difference of goals between academia and industry. In addition to this, discussion is also included regarding the impact of collaboration on innovation and research capabilities. Therefore, from the study it has been found out that global collaboration assist the higher education institutional students to build diverse skills which are crucial for their career or profession.

DOI: 10.4018/979-8-3373-0025-2.ch008

INTRODUCTION

Collaboration has emerged as a driving force which not only transforms the way of disseminating knowledge but also it shifts the dynamic landscape of academic progress. Considering the traditional way of academia, scholars used to toil in isolation to pursue their research; however, in the last few decades there has been a drastic shift in knowledge creation approach in which collaboration plays the most important role (Srinivas & Varaprasad, 2024). Therefore, considering this, higher education institutions collaborate with different industries and organizations as this fosters the environment where people can come up with fresh ideas and it also helps them to discover new things by pushing the boundaries of conventional knowledge. However, collaboration is not confined to academic departments but it is also inter-connected with universities, research institutes and scholars who share their expertise and knowledge about different grounds (O'Dwyer, Filieri & O'Malley, 2023).

Collaboration is not merely a trend but it has become a necessity as it plays critical role in addressing global challenges and it also enables convergence of expertise in different fields. It has been identified that the outcome of collaboration is not only limited to academic knowledge improvement but also it has a real-world impact on policy, technology and development of the communities. In the 21th century, multidisciplinary approaches are required to solve complex challenges; therefore considering this, researchers from different domains started collaborating which helps them to bring effective solutions to real-world problems (Kilag et al., 2023). It develops holistic perspective; hence, it improves knowledge creation process. In this context, higher education is collaborating with different research organizations and industries which help the learners to develop their learning process and it also prepares them for the labor market. It exposes them the real-world scenario which is quite competitive.

Interdisciplinary collaborations develop new methodologies and perspective from diverse domains which solves complex issues that are beyond the scope of individual domain. Collaboration in higher education benefits the students as they get exposure to develop their knowledge by learning new and diverse perspectives which further enhances their problem-solving and critical thinking skills (Farayola et al., 2023). Therefore, from student's viewpoint, collaboration prepares them for complex and dynamic world which brings real-world challenges in different areas of their career. In addition to this, global collaboration in higher education develops partnerships and research projects where students from diverse countries can work and learn together on various academic activities. For example, global collaboration develops research networks which bring together scholars and researchers from diverse countries and eventually they can conduct comprehensive studies which benefit all learners (Amey & Eddy, 2023).

Background

In the era of technological advancements, industry's demand for skilled and tech-savvy professional is increasing; hence, this is raising scope for collaborative partnerships. This assists the students to gain practical experience and also learn about real-world challenges. Thus, it develops talent pipeline which equips the students with the skills and competencies they need to drive innovation in the industry (Mahmudi, Fionasari, Mardikawati & Judijanto, 2023). The present paper uncovers the need of collaboration in higher education and the role it plays in transforming the learning environment for people. Thus, considering this, the study delves into case studies and best practices that define the effectiveness of collaborative research in higher education.

While collaborating with external partners, a lot of challenges and issues happen; hence, the study highlights a few barriers in this context. Higher education's collaboration with external partners brings innovation which modernizes knowledge developing and sharing process (Srinivas & Varaprasad, 2024). Thus, the study also highlights the impact of collaboration. Furthermore, the research also discusses about the metrics and indicators which are used to measure the impact of collaboration on innovation and educational outcomes. In this relation, some tools for continuous improvement and sustainability of collaborations are discussed. Lastly, the report mentions the emerging trends in global collaboration and how it affects higher education. It also specifies scope of new partnerships in developing collaborative practices beyond academics.

MAIN FOCUS OF THE CHAPTER

Issues and Problems

Challenges and Barriers- One of the common barriers in collaboration is internal tensions which can arise between departments who are accountable for academic achievements. For example, clearly collaboration is the process in which people from different domains come together to bring innovation; hence, the way of working and managing things is apparently different. Henceforth, higher education institution's collaboration with other external partners often gets affected due to difference in policies and framework. Also, challenges arise between people due to different opinions and outlooks (Lopez, & Fussenegger, 2024). Apparently, collaborative work requires understanding and lack of understanding among partners can affect the overall process of collaboration. Usually, higher education institution sets targets to improve the academic progress of students so that they can be prepared for competitive market. However, external partners emphasize more on equipping the learners to build competitive skills for the job-market. Often, they do not comprehend the burden students already have with higher studies as well as additional courses; hence, this impacts the overall learning experience (Waham, Asfahani & Ulfa, 2023). For example, students have the academic curricula and along with that studying extra material can be confusing for them as it involves diverse perspectives which can create confusion while resolving any issue.

Another issue appears in the area of communication especially when the partners do not communicate with each other on regular basis for all things. This not only leads to miscommunication but also it impacts the flow of information. Gkrimpizi, Peristeras & Magnisalis, (2023) in this respect says that poor communication can result due to different reasons such as communication styles, emotional differences as well as linguistic aspects. Also, for better outcomes, there should be clarity about the expectations of goals and objectives.

Examination of differing goals- According to the research of Børte, Nesje & Lillejord, (2023), academia aims to focus on original research, theoretical exploration and critical analysis for the purpose of expanding human knowledge whereas the goal of industry is to apply research on development of new products, technologies and solutions that can solve practical problems. Academia emphasizes more on educating and training the students as well as professionals by delivering high-quality education which also fosters different skills. Thus, the main aim of academia is to deliver education to learners to make them advance their knowledge level. Divergent goals are a common barrier which often leads to conflict among people (O'Dwyer, Filieri & O'Malley, 2023). It results from different priorities and interests; hence, eventually affects the strategy of conducting the project. For example, in industry-academia collaborations, the aim of research projects is to promote the transfer of knowledge for product and service development. Therefore, internships and workshops programs are established to facilitate placements for students and help them to gain practical experience.

However, external partners emphasize more on innovations; thus they push the frontiers of technology and practice to create new opportunities as well as to solve challenges. On contrary to this, Alenezi, Wardat & Akour, (2023) says that industry aims to look for better opportunities to expand the customer base; whereas, in academia students are still at the learning stage wherein they develop knowledge about different subjects. Academia prepares the students for competitive market; however industry leads them to apply knowledge into practice. In addition to this, the skills academia develops in the students later contribute in making them skilled professionals.

Resource constraints- Collaborative research often requires large amount of funding as well as access to specialized equipment; however, arranging and securing these resources can be quite competitive and challenging. Finance is one of the major resources without which it is nearly impossible to carry out any activity and in collaborative projects and research, learner needs access to different resources; therefore, without the availability of financial support, the entire process is impacted (Mahmudi, Fionasari, Mardikawati & Judijanto, 2023). Other than finance, there are several administrative issues which impact the collaboration process especially when a lot of paperwork and documentation is required. For example, every institution has different policies and bureaucracies which usually affects in collaborative research work when it does not align with the general nature of collaborative work (Abdallah, 2023).

Another barrier comes in the form of legal and regulatory compliance especially during global collaborations. When multiple institutions from different countries collaborate, governance and administrative related issues arise which consumes much time to resolve. Thus, often it delays the start and progress of collaborative projects. However, in order to work in collaboration, it is essential to build trust and often physical distance between partners confines the frequency and ease of interactions (Amey & Eddy, 2023). Also, insufficient access to technological tools can hinder the communication and data sharing activity among partners.

Solutions and Recommendations

Strategies for aligning goals- Considering the above discussion, it is clear that higher education institutions and research organizations need to create strategies through which they can align individuals' goals for collaborative work. Universities can collaborate with industries as well as research organizations in developing joint research projects which not only focuses on areas of mutual interest but also it should benefit all the associated parties (Hora & Millar, 2023). At the same time, industry can also fund projects that prepare students for competitive projects and align them with industry needs. In addition to this, workshops and seminars can be conducted which transfers knowledge and also helps students to apply knowledge in solving real-world challenges. Also, collaborating with industry people can help the students to understand their goals and how they work in order to achieve the objectives. One of the important things is to communicate about the goals as well as priorities as that makes the collaboration team work effectively (Kilag et al., 2023). For example, higher education institutions should align the goals with the industry needs as that will help the students to develop critical skills which are needed in the competitive world. Also, aligning the goals can help the students to expand their knowledge level by learning diverse perspectives (Abdallah & Abdallah, 2023).

Aligning goals is crucial as it enhances the opportunities of employability; therefore, education programs should be designed in a way that can equip the students with the skills and knowledge that are needed. Student's involvement in joint research projects assists them to understand practical challenges; hence, it drives innovation which can further contribute to scientific and technological advancements. On the other hand, it is also essential for the industry and research organizations to regularly update higher education institutions about current trends, technologies and methodologies so that curriculum can be updated as per industry standards (Farayola, et al., 2023). This way institution can focus on developing essential skills among students that are necessary to work in industry. It has been observed that research organizations and industries often emphasize on addressing global challenges related to different domains; hence, educational institutions should align the goals considering societal progress. This can be done through establishing public-private partnerships that can enhance the relevance and impact of research on social aspects (Abdallah & Musah, 2023).

Best practices for successful partnerships- Educational partnership has become a common practice in higher education as it enables the students to gain global knowledge and experiences. In order to form effective partnership, the foremost practice is to communicate often and quickly; therefore, partners should be responsive to each other as it creates value in collaborative work. However, the partners should be transparent in all their conducts as that will build trust among the parties (Magolda & King, 2023). For example, industry and higher education institutions should be clear about the current trends and technologies and how it can impact the curriculum as well as learning performance. Moreover, for successful partnerships, it is essential to adopt flexible and adaptive approaches which are significant in addressing challenges proactively. Higher education and industry is also recommended to encourage interdisciplinary collaboration whereby they can leverage diverse expertise. This is another way of assisting the learners to receive knowledge from different perspectives which eventually sharpens their critical thinking ability.

Another important aspect of partnership is creating an environment of continuous feedback in which the partners can share their views and opinion openly about all subjects. For example, the partners should be clear about the effectiveness of any program or curricula which is added along with its impact on learner's experience level (Kilag et al., 2023). This can help higher education institutions to remove all the unnecessary things from the curricula that creates only burden on students. Instead, partners should look more into global processes to integrate learning into the coursework which can help the students to become more competitive.

Recommendations for policy changes- Collaboration between higher education institutions and research organizations can assist in facilitating significant advancements in the area of research, education and innovation. However, there requires some updation to enhance the collaboration such as there should be establishment of joint funding programs which can critically support collaborative projects between universities and research organizations. According to Awasthy, Flint, Sankarnarayana & Jones (2020), it is essential for the universities to recognize the importance of policies in collaborative projects as that can also assist in overcoming barriers. For example, focus should be there on long-term development of relevant academic research and development resources which can extend the level of knowledge. In addition to this, there should be continuous communication between university and industry to embed the curricula with recent trends. It is also recommended to frame policies regarding financial and material costs as that is the backbone of performing every operation. Universities must actively resolve institutional conflicts by setting university-industry standards which can specify the roles of each partner (Fabre & Straub, 2023).

Case Studies and Best Practices

King Abdulaziz University of Saudi Arabia realized the importance of collaboration in order to become world-class university; hence, as a result it established joint international cooperation agreements as well as service contracts with many diversified universities and educational institutions. Along with this, the university also established Distinctive Scientists Program wherein it collaborated with well known researchers around the globe to achieve the objectives (AI-Youbi, Zahed & Tierney, 2020). Establishing international partnerships with global universities assisted both the teachers and students in different ways. It not only formed networking connections but also it helped the students to get the opportunity to learn global standards through student exchange programs. In addition to this, it helped the universities to comprehend the cultural values of other nations. Furthermore, King Abdulaziz University also formed research groups to help the partners learn from different specializations (AI-Youbi, Zahed & Tierney, 2020). The collaboration of the University is managed by the Research and Consulting Institute which provides services in R&D and also offers numerous services related to consultancy, project management, educational services and training (Abdallah & Alkaabi, 2023). Thus, in terms of outcomes, King Abdulaziz University comes up with skilled students that can help the country in various areas and can contribute in its development. For this, the University also has clear vision and it continuously responds to the changing needs of the academic environment (AI-Youbi, Zahed & Tierney, 2020). Developing partnership with the industry helps King Abdulaziz University to facilitate cultural, scientific and research collaborations.

The Procter and Gamble Company (P&G) has chosen to work with University of Cincinnati (UC) Ohio as a strategic academic partner in which they aim to develop Modeling and Simulation capabilities for product and process development. Working with expertise in structural mechanics and dynamics and other modeling disciplines, PG finds great value as it helps the students to learn as well as deploy modeling and simulation capabilities in R&D and Product supply areas (Shaner, 2023). This partnership has developed the scope of innovative work and has also helped the company to grab opportunities to develop more innovation for the consumers. Under the collaboration, faculty members are engaged in doing research in specific projects; whereas, P&G remains on the advisory board of the campus.

However, while collaboration there were some issues due to single point of contact; but the P&G Site Leader minimized the issues y accommodating P&G requests. This has helped in continuous growth of the center and students are able to support modeling capability developments through working in industrial challenging environment. As a result, numerous publication and patents have come out from the work performed at the Simulation Center (Shaner, 2023). While measuring the success, it has been found out that this has prepared the students by giving them industrial experience. Additionally, P&G gets the talent which the company can develop to apply modeling and simulation capabilities.

In the world of technology, industry demands for skilled professionals; therefore collaborative partnerships between university and industry enables in creating a curricula that aligns industry needs with internships and joint research programs. Collaborative projects facilitate multidisciplinary approaches that further leads to innovation and nurtures thriving ecosystem that can give numerous opportunities to solve real-world challenges (CITRIS-uc.org., 2024). Considering this, the multinational semiconductor company Intel has collaborated with University of California to expand semiconductor education and workforce training for the students. The collaboration provides opportunities to undergraduate students to develop on-ramps into semiconductor workforce (Abdallah & Alkaabi, 2023) . They get to attend workshops wherein they can learn multiple skills ranging from team-building to career-planning and collaboration at workplace. CITRIS Workforce Innovation Program provides internship opportunities in the area of IT, innovation, robotics and semiconductors (CITRIS-uc.org., 2024). Also, for student's learning cybersecurity and data for social impact have been introduced so that students can get knowledge regarding these rapid growing domains.

Impact of Collaboration

Methods for Assessing the Effectiveness of Partnerships

The effectiveness of partnership can be measured with different methods and one of them could be setting Performance Metrics and KPIs. Under the method, partners are required to establish key performance indicators through which performance of the strategies or collaborative projects can be evaluated (Sjölund, Lindvall, Larsson & Ryve, 2023). As per the method, outcomes can be measured comparing with predefined metrics. For example, higher education institutions can develop common KPIs including financial aspects, student learning level as well as innovative milestones. Higher education institutions should measure the outcomes through considering student's learning experience, their contribution in facilitating innovative approaches as well as overall analysis of skills. Collins, (2023) in this respect contends that KPIs are effective not only to know the sustainability of projects but also it highlights the areas that are to be removed.

However, it is also important to evaluate the project completion rate and how much it has helped the students. For example, higher education institutions should analyze if collaborating the students with industry partners has helped them to improve their research capabilities. Also, the skill level of students should be analyzed in terms of evaluating their critical thinking ability and problem solving skills by giving them challenging tasks. Other than KPIs, institutions should also conduct regular progress reviews wherein the partners should discuss achievements, challenges as well as further areas of improvement (Clayton et al., 2023). The method of review is essential to realign the goals and expectations of academia as well as industry. Assessing collaborating work would help both students and industry people to identify the scope of improvement along with any new activity that needs to be implemented. Surveys and feedback are another methods of assessment in which partners can conduct surveys regarding the value that collaboration has added in educational services (Abdallah & Farhan, 2023).

Metrics and Indicators to Measure the Impact on Innovation, Research Capabilities and Educational Outcomes

Along with KPIs, indictors are vital to develop in terms of measuring collaboration's impact on innovation and overall educational outcomes. For example, higher education institution needs to evaluate the effectiveness of collaboration through identifying innovative approaches coming in practice. For example, after collaborating with industry partners, impact on student's innovative capability should be analyzed (Srinivas & Varaprasad, 2024). In addition to this, teachers can evaluate student's academic performance through assessing the innovative approaches they are adopting to solve problems. This is beneficial in ascertaining critical thinking and problem solving ability. For example, the solutions identified for the problems should be innovative in nature; hence, it will clearly define the learning of learners. The partners can also set project performance metrics to analyze if the collaborative work or project is managed according to the deadline. It is essential for the teachers to track down the project milestones in terms of analyzing achievements. Collaborating with industry partners or research organization typically assist the students in different ways and improves their learning journey (Ortikov, 2024).

Tools for Continuous Improvement and Sustainability of Collaboration

Integrating continuous improvement into education requires adopting tools and practices that can also highlight the effectiveness of collaboration and how it leads changes in the existing process. In this respect, higher education institution can implement The Plan-Do-Check-Act Principle which defines the opportunities and also assist in planning for change (Awasthy et al., 2020). Through the method, the partners can assess the outcomes continuously and also identify the loopholes (Abdallah et. al., 2023).

Another tool that can be implemented to sustain collaboration is Total Quality Management which contributes in improving quality of educational services and through this errors can be reduced; henceforth, processes can be improved accordingly. It is essential for the higher education institutions to streamline collaborative projects and research to improve student's overall learning experience (Clayton et al., 2023). Therefore, considering the present scope of collaboration in education industry, it is essential for the partners to develop and create effective strategies that can facilitate best practices and eventually which can also improve academic and industry outcomes.

Future Research Directions

With the help of global collaboration, higher education institutions have come up with certain trends that not only leads to innovation but also it revolves the landscape of educational services. For example, education industry is witnessing a surge in digital learning platforms in which it collaborates with innovative pedagogies to break the barriers of traditional classroom boundaries. Online learning is another example that helps both learners and educators in many ways and eventually it impacts the overall learning experience in positive manner. In addition to this, collaborating with industry and research organizations gives opportunities to students whereby they can learn diversified perspectives and develop deeper understanding about professional skills. This helps in preparing the students for global competitive market.

The present study has clearly described that collaboration has become an important concept in education; therefore, it has much scope in future as it can develop innovation, improve research capabilities along with educational outcomes. Networking and connecting with industry and other partners helps higher education institutions to prepare the students and extend their knowledge level. It leads them to build their skills and capabilities through which educational outcomes can be improved. Therefore, keeping into account the present collaborative practices, education industry can explore new models of partnership through which higher education students as well as teachers can be connected with global networks for improved educational services (Abdallah et. al., 2023).

Global collaboration practices such as student exchange and study abroad programs assist the students to extend their experience and it also gives them the opportunities to learn global education values. It has been observed that these experiences not only develop global awareness but also it fosters cross-cultural collaboration. Connecting with different research networks brings optimum solutions for real-world challenges. Thus, building collaborations can help higher education institutions to exchange ideas, form partnerships as well as promote cross-broader collaboration which facilitates dissemination of knowledge and best practices. Thus, these collaborative practices should be sustained as that can brings improvements in research and education domain.

CONCLUSION

From the current study, it has been found out that collaborative research helps in shaping the dynamic academic landscape as it fosters innovation and addresses global challenges with collective wisdom of diverse minds. The shift from isolated scholarship to interconnected knowledge networks creates more opportunities for inclusive and impactful academia. It also plays crucial role in advancing human understanding; therefore embracing such transformations can result in shaping a brighter future. Higher education institutions can cultivate a culture of research and academic excellence; thus this could bridge the gap between theory and practice when collaborating with industrial partners. From the report, it is clear that by partnering with industrial counterparts, higher education institutions can help the learners and entrepreneurs to get access to industry experts and this can also provide commercialization support. Henceforth, combining the intellectual capital of universities with the industry partners can help in creating a powerful workforce that can address real-world challenges effectively.

From the study, the importance of assessment and evaluation is also identified as that helps in maintaining quality and intellectual integrity of the programs. Partnership is essential in education as it combines diverse expertise for common purposes which not only improve the quality of educational services but also it helps in cultivating professional skills in students. The study states that partnership with other institutions can provide financial assistance and value to the students as it offers additional course support. Learners also get to connect with industry experts which help them to shape their career. Also global collaboration helps the higher education institutions to update the curricula according to international standards; hence, it can incorporate diverse perspective to prepare the students for globalized world. In addition to this, the above stated case studies reveal that collaborating with experts and industry people can help the students to learn innovative aspects to solve real-world issues and it makes them competitive according to global standards.

REFERENCES

Abdallah, A., Ismail, O., Abdallah, R. K., & Alkaabi, A. M. (2023). Perceptions of Students About the Use of Webinars in Classrooms: A Case of Abu Dhabi University. [IJICTE]. *International Journal of Information and Communication Technology Education*, 19(1), 1–17. DOI: 10.4018/IJICTE.322793

Abdallah, A. K. (2023). Teacher-Led, Student-Focused, and Unleashing the Power of Teacher Empowerment for School Improvement and Success. In Abdallah, A., & Alkaabi, A. (Eds.), *Restructuring Leadership for School Improvement and Reform* (pp. 1–21). IGI Global., DOI: 10.4018/978-1-6684-7818-9.ch001

Abdallah, A. K., & Abdallah, R. K. (2023). Achieving Academic Excellence: The Intersection of Teacher Development, Quality Education, and Entrepreneurship. In Chakravarti, S. (Ed.), *Innovations in Teacher Development, Personalized Learning, and Upskilling the Workforce* (pp. 136–158). IGI Global., DOI: 10.4018/978-1-6684-5518-0.ch007

Abdallah, A. K., Al Kaabi, A. M., & Ramadan, R. S. (2023). The Critical Role of Principals in Leading Effective Inclusive Schools. In Efthymiou, E. (Ed.), *Inclusive Phygital Learning Approaches and Strategies for Students With Special Needs* (pp. 256–281). IGI Global., DOI: 10.4018/978-1-6684-8504-0.ch012

Abdallah, A.K., & Alkaabi, A.M. (2023). Induction Programs' Effectiveness in Boosting New Teachers' Instruction and Student Achievement: A Critical Review. *International Journal of Learning, Teaching and Educational Research.*

Abdallah, A. K., & Alkaabi, A. M. (Eds.). (2023). *Restructuring Leadership for School Improvement and Reform.* IGI Global., DOI: 10.4018/978-1-6684-7818-9

Abdallah, A. K., & Farhan, A. F. (2023). Breaking Barriers and Empowering Women Leaders to Drive School Improvement. In Abdallah, A., & Alkaabi, A. (Eds.), *Restructuring Leadership for School Improvement and Reform* (pp. 399–419). IGI Global., DOI: 10.4018/978-1-6684-7818-9.ch020

Abdallah, A. K., & Musah, M. B. (2023). Principal and Teacher Licensing as a Tool to School Improvement. In Abdallah, A., & Alkaabi, A. (Eds.), *Restructuring Leadership for School Improvement and Reform* (pp. 278–300). IGI Global., DOI: 10.4018/978-1-6684-7818-9.ch014

AI-Youbi. A., Zahed, A. H., & Tierney, W. G. (2020). *Successful global collaborations in higher education institutions* (p. 93). Springer Nature.

Alenezi, M., Wardat, S., & Akour, M. (2023). The need of integrating digital education in higher education: Challenges and opportunities. *Sustainability (Basel)*, 15(6), 4782. DOI: 10.3390/su15064782

Amey, M. J., & Eddy, P. L. (2023). *Creating strategic partnerships: A guide for educational institutions and their partners*. Taylor & Francis.

Awasthy, R., Flint, S., Sankarnarayana, R., & Jones, R. L. (2020). A framework to improve university–industry collaboration. *Journal of Industry-University Collaboration*, 2(1), 49–62. DOI: 10.1108/JIUC-09-2019-0016

Børte, K., Nesje, K., & Lillejord, S. (2023). Barriers to student active learning in higher education. *Teaching in Higher Education*, 28(3), 597–615. DOI: 10.1080/13562517.2020.1839746

CITRIS-uc.org. (2024). CITRIS and Intel collaborate to enhance semiconductor training opportunities for UC undergraduates. Retrieved from: < https://citris-uc.org/citris-and-intel-collaborate-to-enhance-semiconductor-training-opportunities-for-uc-undergraduates/ >. Accessed on 10th July 2024.

Clayton, P. H., Bringle, R. G., & Hatcher, J. A. (Eds.). (2023). *Research on Service Learning: Conceptual Frameworks and Assessments: Volume 2B: Communities, Institutions, and Partnerships*. Taylor & Francis.

Collins, D. (2023). Driving Innovation through Collaborative Partnerships: The Power of University-Industry Collaboration. Retrieved from: <https://www.linkedin.com/pulse/driving-innovation-through-collaborative-partnerships-collins-phd>. Accessed on 8th July 2024.

Fabre, A., & Straub, S. (2023). The impact of public–private partnerships (PPPs) in infrastructure, health, and education. *Journal of Economic Literature*, 61(2), 655–715. DOI: 10.1257/jel.20211607

Farayola, O. A., Hassan, A. O., Adaramodu, O. R., Fakeyede, O. G., & Oladeinde, M. (2023). Configuration management in the modern era: Best practices, innovations, and challenges. *Computer Science & IT Research Journal*, 4(2), 140–157. DOI: 10.51594/csitrj.v4i2.613

Gkrimpizi, T., Peristeras, V., & Magnisalis, I. (2023). Classification of barriers to digital transformation in higher education institutions: Systematic literature review. *Education Sciences*, 13(7), 746. DOI: 10.3390/educsci13070746

Hora, M. T., & Millar, S. B. (2023). *A guide to building education partnerships: Navigating diverse cultural contexts to turn challenge into promise*. Taylor & Francis.

Kilag, O. K. T., Evangelista, T. P., Sasan, J. M., Librea, A. M., Zamora, R. M. C., Ymas, S. B., & Alestre, N. A. P. (2023). Promising Practices for a Better Tomorrow: A Qualitative Study of Successful Practices in Senior High School Education. *Journal of Elementary and Secondary School*, 1(1), 16–28. DOI: 10.31098/jess.v1i1.1379

Kilag, O. K. T., Uy, F. T., Abendan, C. F. K., & Malbas, M. H. (2023). Teaching leadership: An examination of best practices for leadership educators. *Science and Education*, 4(7), 430–445.

Lopez, C. D., & Fussenegger, J. (2024). Challenges in UniversityIndustry Collaborations. Retrieved from: <https://www.diva-portal.org/smash/get/diva2:1566896/FULLTEXT01.pdf>. Accessed on 8th July 2024.

Magolda, M. B. B., & King, P. M. (Eds.). (2023). *Learning partnerships: Theory and models of practice to educate for self-authorship*. Taylor & Francis. DOI: 10.4324/9781003445685

Mahmudi, A. A., Fionasari, R., Mardikawati, B., & Judijanto, L. (2023). Integration of artificial intelligence technology in distance learning in higher education. *Journal of Social Science Utilizing Technology*, 1(4), 190–201. DOI: 10.70177/jssut.v1i4.661

O'Dwyer, M., Filieri, R., & O'Malley, L. (2023). Establishing successful university–industry collaborations: Barriers and enablers deconstructed. *The Journal of Technology Transfer*, 48(3), 900–931. DOI: 10.1007/s10961-022-09932-2

Ortikov, U. K. U. (2024). THE EFFECTIVENESS OF TECHNOLOGY-ENHANCED LANGUAGE LEARNING METHODS. *Oriental renaissance: Innovative, educational, natural and social sciences, 4*(3), 162-179.

Shaner, K. (2023). P&G, UC celebrate partnership that accelerates innovation. Retrieved from: <https://www.uc.edu/news/articles/2023/03/pg-uc-celebrate-partnership-that-accelerates-innovation.html>. Accessed on 10th July 2024.

Sjölund, S., Lindvall, J., Larsson, M., & Ryve, A. (2023). Mapping roles in research-practice partnerships–a systematic literature review. *Educational Review*, 75(7), 1490–1518. DOI: 10.1080/00131911.2021.2023103

Srinivas, T., & Varaprasad, R. (2024). Innovation through Collaboration: Advancing Higher Education Research. *Research and Reviews: Advancement in Robotics*, 7(1), 7–16.

Waham, J. J., Asfahani, A., & Ulfa, R. A. (2023). International Collaboration in Higher Education: Challenges and Opportunities in a Globalized World. *EDUJAVARE: International Journal of Educational Research*, 1(1), 49–60.

Chapter 9
Transformational Leadership in Higher Education

Kenneth M. Sabwami
https://orcid.org/0000-0001-7447-5103
Mount Kenya University, Kenya

ABSTRACT

Education is the most powerful weapon that can be put to use to change the world and requires a good head and a good heart for its effectuality. Higher education is an umbrella encompassing all types of education as provided by universities, technological institutes, teacher training colleges and normally intended for students who have completed secondary education and have an educational objective of acquisition of a title, a grade, certificate, or diploma of higher education. Higher education is facing a myriad of challenges that are impacting negatively towards its progress and performance. To forestall such, transformational leadership has been touted as a game changer that when applied can be beneficial in aiding higher education recourse and adopt a trajectory geared towards its betterment. The chapter highlights key components that transformational leadership impacts to cause necessary changes and realignments: training of leaders, financial management, collaboration partnerships, technology, inclusivity and diversity, and innovation.

INTRODUCTION

Nelson Mandela, a key African icon who esteemed education described education as the most powerful weapon that can be put to use to change the world and also noted that a good head and a good heart are always a formidable combination

DOI: 10.4018/979-8-3373-0025-2.ch009

(Nasongo et al. 2017 ; Strauss, 2013). He opined that Africa's reconstruction and further progress and interaction in the global space largely depend on the efforts made in educating its populace. This in essence makes education the pivotal point upon which all developments are hinged.

UNESCO (1998) defines higher education as an umbrella encompassing all types of education (academic, professional, technical, artistic, pedagogical and long distance learning) provided by universities, technological institutes, teacher training colleges and normally intended for students who have completed secondary education and have an educational objective of acquisition of a title, a grade, certificate, or diploma of higher education. This is in conformity with the World Bank (2024) which equate higher education to tertiary education. World Bank (2024) defines tertiary education as the formal post-secondary education undertaken in public and private universities, colleges, technical training institutes, and vocational schools. It further asserts that tertiary education is momentous in fostering growth, poverty reduction in communities and individuals, and boosting shared prosperity.

However, there is a conceptual distinction. Tertiary education is an umbrella that encompasses all post-secondary education and which includes both technical and vocational education and training (TVET) as well as higher education. Therefore, within international human rights law, the term tertiary education is generally not used. Rather, the instruments refer to technical and vocational education and training, and higher education. In a nutshell, higher education is post-secondary education and training (Right to Education, n.d.).

Transformational leadership is a mode of leadership geared towards effecting positive change in an organization. Transformational leadership has risen up and become a preferred leadership model in the 21st century. Different authors define transformational leadership variedly.

Definition of Transformational Leadership

Transformational leadership is defined as a leadership stratum that brings about positive change in an organization leading to its turnaround by positively impacting on the followers' trust, commitment, motivation, identity, self-efficacy and self-esteem (Sabwami, 2021).

Likewise, Fontein (2022) delineates transformational leadership as a style where leaders influence, inspire, and encourage employees to execute positive change. Such leaders collaborate with teams beyond their immediate self-interests to identify needed change and create a vision to propel and guide the change(s). Transformative leaders lead by example and hence emulated by followers who jointly strive for a strong sense of organizational culture. This in essence motivates workers, promote employee ownership and autonomy in the workplace.

Likewise, transformational leadership is looked at as a leadership mode that underscores the gratification of subordinates' basic needs and fulfilling higher organizational desires through inspiring them to generate newer solutions that end up with a better workplace (Eagly & Carli, 2003; Horwitz et al, 2008; Marturano & Gosling, 2008; Patiar & Mia, 2009 as cited in Ghasabeh & Provitera, 2017).

Rahmi (as cited in Hutasuhut, 2019) defines transformational leadership as leadership akin to a proactive leader who takes at heart and pays close attention to common interests of subordinates as he/she propels them towards achievement of institutional goals. Such leaders are arrayed with superb vision, managerial prowess, organizational ability and rhetorical abilities that endear them to people hence creating strong emotional bonds with them. This in essence makes such leaders more successful in driving the organizational change agenda as subordinates are emotionally prepared and willing to work animatedly without being supervised towards the realization of their leader's vision. As such, this has ended up making transformational leadership the most popular approach of choice concerning matters of leadership (Litz & Scott, 2017).

In vouching for transformational leadership, Kotter (as cited in Espinoza, 2023) noted that transformational crusaders in academia respond to the economic barriers stymieing the pursuit of higher education. They do so by championing a mode of leadership that emphasize flexibility, real-world applicability, and the cultivation of skills that lead to immediate and impactful professional advancements.

Dimensions of Transformational Leadership

The notion of transformational leadership is enshrined in four dimensions: idealized influence, inspirational motivation, intellectual stimulation, and personalized consideration (Bass et al., 1996; Northouse, 2016; Sabwami, 2021). Northouse (2016) presents a model that best exemplifies the four-tier relationship in the continuum.

Figure 1. Northouse (2016) Transformational Leadership Model

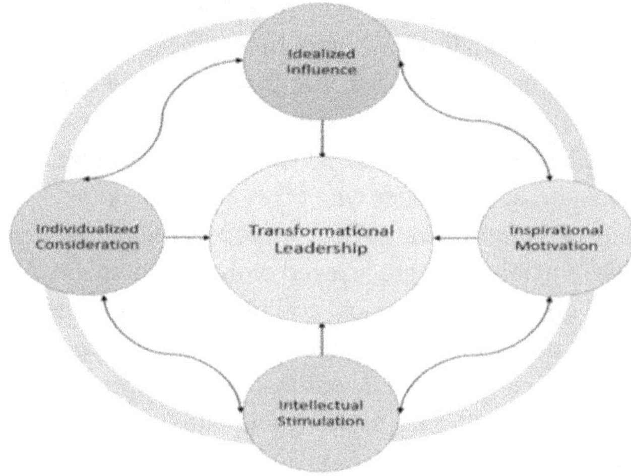

First, individualized consideration that entail the leader developing a personal touch to each employee, advising, coaching and also mentoring them. The leader is quick at lending a listening ear, understanding the follower's predicaments and basics coupled by equipping them with tools to perform at higher levels (Northouse, 2016).

Second, intellectual stimulation, in which the superior engages subordinates by challenging their assumptions, taking risks and then seeking their ideas. Summarily, intellectual stimulation focusses on employee creativity, innovation, and strategic mind boggling that births new ideas. This develops the notion of creativity and innovation in employees leading to heightened know-how and rationality (Sabwami, 2021).

Thirdly, inspirational motivation in which the leader champion an appealing and inspiring vision to the followers. The transformative leaders put followers to toil with high attainment measures, convey optimism about future goals and then simplifying the work at hand for subordinates to follow and expedite. Ultimately, inspirational motivation helps superiors influence followers and then move them beyond conceived barriers to achieve set goals (Northouse, 2016).

Eventually, idealized influence where the leader is emulated as a role model by employees who savour his/her ethical behaviour and charismatic vision. Idealized influence is the capacity to thoroughly examine and emulate itineraries followed by other successful leaders through mentorship, building relationships and strengthening leadership skills. Charismatic leaders are endeared to the populace and greatly loved by the followers. Contrarily, not all charismatic leaders are transformative but all transformational leaders have charisma (Bush, 2018). Transformative leaders apply the charismatic tendency to influence and induce followers to adopt behaviour that bring about the beneficial change vital for propelling the organization to greater heights of development. They impact a good vision to the followers as the centrality focus while enjoining them to a better and flourishing organization's future.

MANAGEMENT OF HIGHER EDUCATION INSTITUTIONS' PHYSICAL RESOURCES

Educational resources are prerequisites that are vital for effective curriculum delivery. Oluremi (as cited in Langwenya-Myeni, 2017) regard educational resources as the amalgamation of inputs invested in the institution's system that include but not limited to finances, instructional paraphernalia, human personnel and physical material components. Furthermore, Jaji et al. (2017) describes physical resources in learning institutions as the plant that encompasses infrastructural matter that ends up stirring students to work hard to achieve academic excellence. Lomulen (2016) study findings revealed that the top-performing institutions emphasize more on the proper and efficient utilization of resource correlatives of teaching staff members, instructional materials, infrastructural facilities and finances. Jaji et al. (2017) lists the infrastructural resources as offices, wash rooms and toilets, tuition halls, science labs, dining halls, libraries and staff houses.

Physical resources in learning institutions are those that are visible and tangible and not limited to buildings, machines, raw materials and land. They contribute heavily to quality education and the attainment of institutional goals and educational outcomes (Akungu, 2014; Mormah, 2023 ; Usman, 2016). The resources must be sufficient and well maintained through proper servicing for desired impact to be felt. Proper maintenance of such resources involve: - preventive maintenance for optimal performance and reduce breakdown instances; routine maintenance through periodical servicing of equipment per manufactures' guide; emergency repairs following breakdown of facilities or equipment; and predictive maintenance through technological use of computer software to determine equipment malfunction on the basis age, usage and performance. Mormah (2023) maintains that physical facilities in tertiary institutions must be well maintained and outlines its beneficence as follows: i. Promotion of more efficient and effective teaching owing to a more conducive environment, ii. Less maintenance costs incurred, instead of waiting to pay exorbitantly when the facility is in a state of disrepair. iii. Precludes deterioration hence less replacement costs. iv. Promotes students' safety and durability of the facilities. v. To meet the rising demand for its use owing to growing student population. vi. Ensures maintenance of facilities within a conformed standard.

Transformational leadership has a wide and extensive applicability. It extends beyond institutional confines, influencing policy and advocating for financial structures that support lifelong learning as a response to economic uncertainty

(McClendon, 2018). Its implementation will see higher education assert itself as a critical player in economic recovery, empowering individuals to pivot, advance, and thrive despite the financial headwinds.

In their study on the financial performance of manufacturing and service companies in China, Son et al. (2020) determined that transformational leadership has an influence on their financial performance. They also found that transformational leadership affects financial performance more effectively than operational performance. Strukan et al. (2017) and Thomson et al. (2016) argued that transformational leadership has a positive impact on a company's financial performance because it motivates leaders to initiate and implement significant changes in the company meant to encourage employees to work better. Both studies are consistent with prior studies. For example, in their study on Turkish manufacturing companies, Ocak and Ozturk (2018) found a positive relationship between transformational leadership and company performance as did Arifa and Akram (2018) in a similar study in Pakistan. In addition, in their meta-analysis of 25 years of research work, Wang et al. (2011) showed that transformational leadership is closely and positively related to organizational performance and therefore essential for better organizational performance. According to Kia et al. (2019), this leadership style is committed to boosting the subordinate performance by dint of being a role model and generating a sense of employee identification with the organization. Several prior studies have also confirmed the role of corporate reputation as a mediator towards organization performance (Saeidi et al., 2015; Javed et al., 2020; Le, 2022). A good organizational performance implies the organisation is liquid hence needed physical materials can easily be availed. This plays a critical role of motivating staff members.

Kwistianus et al. (2023) study revealed a positive relationship between corporate reputation and the company's financial performance hence reputation also shows positive and significant results. This indicated that the implementation of transformational leadership to manufacturing companies in Indonesia has the capacity to ensure a positive assessment of corporate reputation, whereby a good corporate reputation will end up improving the company's financial performance and maintaining long-term profits. As the above discussion suggests, the influence of corporate reputation in improving financial performance is primarily determined by the effectiveness of the implementation of transformational leadership. A corporate reputation that can help maintain superior profits in the long term can only have a positive effect on a company's financial performance as long as the latter is able to communicate its identity to every stakeholder and therefore create a positive perspective on the company. The stakeholder perspective on an organization – which is known as corporate image, as explained earlier – is the result of the beliefs, values, and attitudes that each stakeholder has towards the company. They can be formed through the implementation of an effective leadership style, one of which being transformational leadership. Likewise, a good corporate reputation in institutions of higher learning has the effect of attracting the best stakeholders (students, lecturers, administrators) to the institution (Mbewu & Adebayo, 2020). Such institutions tend to be financially stable and acquisition of the needed physical resources is easier.

Campbell (2002) (cited in Mormah, 2023) outlined various critical measures necessary for physical resources management in higher institutions of learning: 1. Engraving the school log or name on physical plants to distract thieves. 2. Students compelled to pay for damages inflicted on facilities. 3. Meting of punishment to pedestrians who disregard warning signposts to cross on fields, lawns and flower beds. 4. Handing over apprehended professional thieves to the police for requisite action. 5. Insuring school plants against fire, theft and damages. 6. Hiring of professionally trained security officers. 7. Preference of wooden doors and windows to glass doors and windows due to longevity. 8. Ever presence of science and technology lectures/technicians in the laboratories and workshops to monitor and guide students on safety and proper utilization of equipment.

According to Uko (2015) principals are charged with a responsibility of managing schools' physical facilities, successful management of which is associated with increased quality of the school's performance in all spheres and especially in the academic angle (Akungu, 2014). The same should be applied in institutions of higher learning that are synonymous with run-down facilities due to poor leadership (Chikafalimani et al., 2021).

Amadi and Ezeugo (2019) study in Nigeria's Rivers State found out that physical facilities are a necessity in any institutional setup since they promote the core mantra of teaching and learning. They recommend a remedy of all institutional stakeholders (leaders, employees and students) being subjected to workshops and seminars to equip them with skills and expertise on physical resources maintenance in their respective institutions. Additionally, they opined that institutional administrators should embrace a culture of setting aside funds for maintenance as well as acquisition of more physical resources so as to enhance the teaching and learning process.

Furthermore, Bueno (2019) affirms the necessity and adequacy of the institution's physical facilities towards the attainment of its objectives and goals. However, Bueno denotes that it is an exercise in futility to spend massively on institutional physical facilities and other inputs at the expense of the teaching staff motivation. Lecturers are the final implementers of the core curriculum and ought to be reciprocatively oiled for effective teaching and learning to be realized. This then calls for a systemic overhaul geared towards a balance between the investment in physical facilities and the autonomy of lecturers to manage for results while making them accountable for the results (Imam, 2017).

Nnebedum and Ndidi (2017) carried out a study in Nigeria's Enugu state and avers that the physical facilities are put to use in schools in order to support and enhance acquisition of knowledge, skills, values and attitudes vital for survival in the society. These include: tuition blocks, libraries, furniture, science labs and apparatus, playing fields, and dormitories among others. The study findings revealed that secondary school principals in Enugu state did not adequately adopt physical material resource management schemes like classroom innovation to stimulate learning, replacement of destroyed roofs to protect learners from weather conditions, regular servicing of school machines to keep them in working order and general wall repair to strengthen walls and prevent them from collapsing.

This in essence points to the fact that institutional leaders need to be equipped with transformational leadership skills to help them effectively manage material resources in their schools. These findings are corroborated by Uko (2015) whose study on effective management of school' facilities by principals found out that most school facilities in sampled secondary schools were either few and in a deplorable state or completely lacking. This implies that school principals' management is wanting as they do not ensure that needed facilities are adequately supplied, that the existing facilities are well taken care of coupled with necessary repairs and renovations to keep the facilities in good working order.

Chikafalimani et al. (2021) carried out a study on the current challenges afflicting Universities in Africa. The study outcome revealed that most public African Universities face manifold challenges. The challenges have impacted negatively on the quality of teaching and learning. Firstly, poor condition of the limited facilities and overcrowding. Secondly, limited skilled personnel to handle the facilities and incapability of the facility management departments, and lastly, financial drouth that makes it impossible to acquire and adequately manage their physical facilities. The challenges can be forestalled by African governments adequately funding for quality facilities at the public, hiring of well qualified and trained staff in facility departments of public universities, hiring of transformative tertiary institutional heads, and the creation of innovative and smarter partnerships aimed at improving facilities and providing new ones at public universities in Africa.

FACULTY COMMITMENT

Commitment refers to the relative strength displayed by a worker in identifying with and being actively involved in the activities of the organization (Mowday et al., as cited in Al-Jabari & Ghazzawi, 2019). Committed workers exhibit an element of job satisfaction evidenced by more concentration, ennobled performance, reduced turnover, and increased flexibility (Saeed, 2014). This leads to a high trust between workers and the organization hence a positive correlation to job satisfaction and organizational commitment (Fard & Karimi, 2015 as cited in Al-Jabari & Ghazzawi, 2019).

Ibrahim (2023) perceives lecturers as the veritable engine rooms that are crucial in the attainment of universities' educational goals. In a study on lecturers' job commitment, it was observed that lecturers in Nigerian universities were not highly motivated by Nigerian government towards improving their level of job commitment. They face a number of problems: - poor motivation, insecurity, frequent strikes, poor staff capacity development, inadequate infrastructure, poor ICT facilities, and poor research funding by the government. Once the above problems are dealt with, a reprocity of the same will be realised in terms of increased lecturers' commitment.

In accordance to Onukwu et al. (2020), lecturers' commitment refers to the willingness to work wholeheartedly in the school activities at different sub-units of the university embodiment. Committed lecturers exhibit loyalty to the norms and values of the university through obedience to the set rules and regulations. This is evidenced by lecture punctuality and willingness to impart knowledge, swift marking and grading of students' work, prompt submission of students' examination scores, willingness to supervise students, and attendance of university meetings among other.

Hackmann et al. (as cited in Howell et al., 2022) found that educational leadership programs created to prepare higher education leaders are on an increasing trajectory. These educational interventions can provide future college and university presidential candidates with appropriate knowhow and skills necessary for effective leadership. Faig (2024) opines that transformational leaders normally attune themselves to the changing nature of education and making it their mission to know happenings in today's world of instructional practices. Hence, higher education institutions should develop and roll out targeted professional development initiatives in tandem with the changing requirements of educators and school administrators. Consequentially, this will in turn help them to maintain currency.

The leaders' training entails subjecting them to the four tenets of transformational leadership (Bass & Riggio, 2008; Hutasuhut, 2019; & Northouse, 2016). First, individualized consideration in which the leader develops a personal touch to each employee, advises, coaches and also mentors them. Second, intellectual stimulation, in which the leader puts subordinates to task by challenging their assumptions, takes risks and then seeks their ideas. This instils the notion of creativity and innovation in workers leading to enhanced know-how and rationality. Thirdly, inspirational motivation that entails the superior championing an appealing and inspiring vision to followers. Such heads put followers to toil with high measures, they convey optimism about future goals and then simplify the work at hand for others to follow and contribute. Lastly, idealized influence where the leader acts as a role model to subordinates in terms of ethical behaviour, instils pride and then gains their respect and trust from application of charismatic vision and behaviour. As a charismatic leader he/she is endeared to the people and greatly loved by the followers. However, not all charismatic leaders are transformational leaders but all transformational leaders have charisma (Miner, 2005).

Additionally, Bush (2018) opinionated that transformative leaders possess a charismatic tendency that enables them to easily influence and induce followers to appropriate certain demeanours in order to bring about the beneficial change that propel organisational entities to greater heights of development. They dangle the carrot of a good vision to the followers as their central construct and then moves on to implore and enjoin them to seek a better and flourishing future for the organization and to commit to the attainment of the goals arising from the vision. Nevertheless, the vision bearer may not always share the vision but may assume it is implied and which often leads to unfavourable consequences. For instance, the chieftain's parsimonious chase bid for improved test scores that may end up marginalizing the less academically endowed students but who are talented in fields that lie outside the leader's prescribed vision like music, drama and sports.

Yanti et al. (2022) carried out a study titled transformational leadership in improving lecturer performance in higher education. The findings explicitly indicated that lecturer performance after the implementation of transformational leadership in higher education was enormous: education sector rose 90%, research field to 82% and community service to 84%. This shows that transformational leadership impacted positively on lecturers' performance in matters education, research and community service. This increased their institutional commitment and made them better leaders thus endearing them to the students.

Team spirit in higher educational establishments is critical in the effective motivation of staff members and lecturers. Owusu-Agyeman (2021) study on transformational leadership and innovation in higher education revealed that engagement, motivation, communication flow, communication utilization and decision-making components of transformational leadership strongly enhance the participative process that is quite essential in the promotion of innovation among the administrative staff.

Owusu-Agyeman's findings are corroborated by Faig (2024) who asserts that collaborative partnerships are equalized connection between institutions of education and outside organizations like local communities, businesses organizations and other educational institutions. The collaborations entail shared research projects, community programs, and events that enhance the learning environment. Furthermore, the sharing of resources allows institutions to combine their skill set facilities and even faculty so that they can create a much more comprehensive and effective learning environment. So far as to simplify and control these partnerships, the establishment of a collaboration committee is essential.

Christman (2024) avers that there are two obvious approaches to leadership videlicet vertical and horizontal. Vertical leadership embraces a hierarchical top-down pathway, where decisions emanate from executives or managers and subordinates implement them. In so doing, leaders exercise direct control on the actions of their subordinates. On the other hand, transformational leadership is a prototype of horizontal leadership since it accentuates collaboration and shared decision-making across the organizational divide. This promote a participatory culture, team spirit, and collective decision-making. This in essence help to foster innovation and adaptability in the organization. The culture of continuous learning and development is evident, as employees are encouraged to share their knowledge and skills with one another.

Githui et al. (2024) study investigated collaboration's mediating role to the relationship between transformational leadership and performance contracting in road agencies in Kenya. The study found out that collaboration is a vital component in the organization as it aids employees to achieve their performance targets with ease. This indicated a positive association that was statistically significant at p value $0.005<0.05$. This implies that collaboration plays a key role that helps promote performance in the workplace higher educational establishments inclusive.

Howell et al. (2022) mixed-method study investigated transformational leadership qualities among students undertaking doctoral programs in the Commonwealth of Virginia. The study relied on three data points: interviews with graduate program directors of higher education doctoral programs (whether PhD or EdD), evaluation of programs, and Multifactor Leadership Questionnaire (MLQ- 5x™) survey from students taking the said programs. Thus data were collected from the five public universities offering higher education doctoral programs in the Commonwealth of Virginia. The findings indicated that the higher education doctoral students possess above average transformation leadership qualities and are well equipped for the complexities surrounding the American colleges and universities. Murage (2022) in a similar study on transformational leadership and performance of public universities in Kenya corroborates Howell et al. study. A distinction between the two studies arises in the findings of the former showing that idealized influence and intellectual stimulation variables have no significant effect on performance of public universities in Kenya, whereas variables individualized consideration and inspirational motivation have a significant effect on performance of public universities in Kenya. The study went further by recommending that Human Resources officers should come up with policies and practices relating to transformational leadership and performance to bolster leaders' training and performance.

Mbithi et al. (2016) study sought to determine the factors that influence the relationship between transformational leadership and performance in Kenya's 52 fully-fledged universities. The results supported all the hypotheses and showed a positive and statistically significant relationships between transformational leadership and performance and between transformational leadership and employee outcomes. It emerged that transformational leadership behaviour of the top leadership of universities in Kenya led to high employee performance and organizational effectiveness.

Mutiso et al. (2023) study investigated the influence of organizational values on job commitment among lecturers at the Universities of Nairobi and South Eastern. The considered values are corporate social responsibility (CSR), welfare programs, and teamwork which are significant in positively influencing employee behaviour. This is critical in the two universities that have experienced abnormally high turnover, absenteeism, and strike events of lecturer in the last five years.

Barbieri et al. (2019) undertook a study among Italian school educators to gauge their well-being and sociality. Findings were indicative of the fact that the leadership style employed by the lead educators was transformational in nature and that transformative school leaders always put staff welfare at the fore of their leadership. The key indicator being their positivity to the school environment as demonstrated by adequacy of human resources, physical installations, professional advancement opportunities, provision of basic necessities, and all of which denote the lectors' job satisfaction. It was also revealed that principals play a cardinal role in directing the trajectory the school follows by guiding the entire day-to-day school undertakings with the teaching and learning process being key. As a matter of vitality, it behoves the school administrators to create an enabling and supportive environment that helps to promote the well-being of lecturers as this contributes immensely to their workplace commitment.

Contrarily, Tangirala and Ramanujam (2008) (as cited in Atalay et al., 2019) explored the concept of organizational silence and considered it as the antithesis of organisational attractiveness. This is a situation of work atrocity as exemplified by employees gagging their mouths, keeping quiet, and refraining from sharing important information with the leadership and amongst themselves. Al-Dowayan and Al-Saeed (2022) study on the reality of organizational silence among faculty members of Qassim University identified various factors contributing to employee silence. The key factor being ambiguity and overlap of the role of the faculty members with other roles hence confusion. The proposed solution is focus on procedural proposals by faculty members to create order.

Consequentially, the organisation loses since they are demotivated and work haphazardly leading to poor outcomes. Tangirala and Ramanujam study is corroborated by the study of Mohamed (2024) on impact of employee silence on organizational performance targeting Mogadishu universities. The findings indicated a positive relationship between employee voice, fear of retaliation, communication climate, and organizational performance. In essence the aforementioned factors positively influence employee performance in the universities studied. Therefore, universities should strive to promote a culture that enhance employee voice, enact policies against retaliation, and transparent communication climates in higher education. These measures are vital for organizational leaders and policymakers to improve performance and tackle issues related to employee silence in educational settings.

Smith (2015) conducted an exploratory and qualitative case study whose outcomes disclosed that transformational leadership positively impact on the satisfaction and job performance of its members, staff commitment, and survivability of the organization. However, less research has been undertaken to examine issues effectuating transformational leadership in a scientific laboratory. Transformative leaders in scientific laboratories bring about social change through increased staff job satisfaction and performance leading to organizational survivability and improvement of the status quo. This clearly demonstrate that transformational leadership is applicable across all organizations (Bass, 1985; Hater & Bass, 1988; Howell & Avolio, 1993; Ross & Offermann, 1997 as cited in Krishnan, 2002).

Institutional heads who espouse transformational leadership play a crucial role in initiating and driving the crucial organizational change that is vital in reviving and betterment of learning institutions to make them more productive (Rahmi as cited in Hutasuhut, 2019; Litz & Scott, 2017; Lynch et al., 2019). Innovation in education stems from analysing situations, identifying problems, interacting and learning from group members, and coming up with novel methods of addressing the problems. Without innovation, no growth will be realized in the field of education.

Serdyukov (2017) paper on analytical review of USA's educational innovation found out that the nation's education desperately needed heightened effective innovations crucial for the production of the needed high-quality learning outcomes in the education system. A number of innovations that made a drastic impact on the whole educational system are as indicated:

- Political - No Child Left Behind Act and Race to the Top
- Social -Equal Opportunities Act, affirmative action policy, Individuals with Disabilities Education Act
- Philosophical – constructivism and objectivism
- Cultural -moral education, multiculturalism and bilingual education
- Pedagogical -competence-based education (CBC) and Science, Technology and Mathematics (STEM)
- Psychological - cognitive science, multiple intelligencies theory, Maslow's hierarchy of needs and learning style theory and
- Technological- computer-based learning, networked learning and e-learning.

Thompson (2024) corroborates Serdyukov (2017) findings and goes forth to propose other innovative measures as indicated:

- Project-Based Learning (PBL) – Students come up with a project in response to an existing problem and develop a solution for it. This helps students in exercising their creative thinking, problem-solving, and collaborative skills with other students.

Project-based learning (PBL) is a novel or imaginative educational strategy.Shukla et al. (2024) considered the Project-based learning (PBL) initiative as a novel or imaginative educational undertaking. The utility of projects in the classroom situation allows students to interrogate issues and difficulties from the outside world while also gaining valuable skills.

Figure 2. Hamid et al. (2015) PBL process

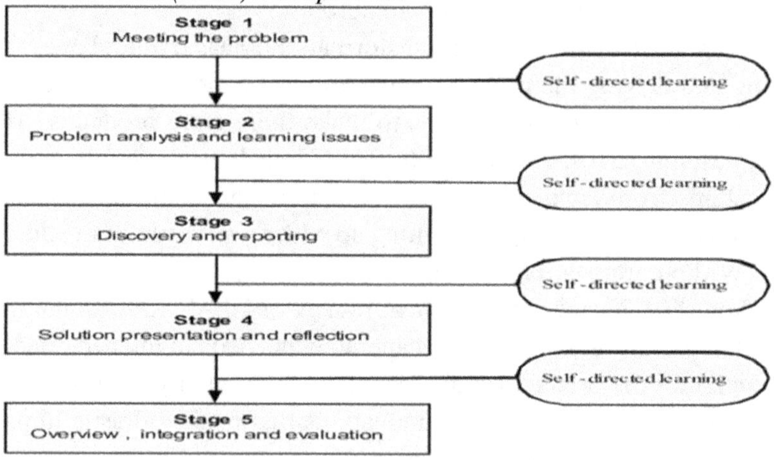

Hamid et al. (2015) came up with a 5 stages PBL model as shown in Figure 2 and explained as follows.

Stage 1: Meeting the Problem- It entails students identifying and clarifying the problem. They describe the facts of the problem and seek help from the teacher.

Stage 2: Problem Analysis and Learning Issues - Students through brainstorming seek answers or explanation of the problem by asking key questions. They generate ideas in the form of hypotheses, suggestions, possible solutions or explanations, explorations, propositions, creative thoughts or any thoughts that may help to solve or understand the problem.

Stage 3: Discovery and Reporting – This is a peer-teaching stage where students gather to share the new information discovered. Students practice group collaboration and communication skills through questions and the seeking of further information from one another. The PBL teacher helps to harmonize findings from all groups and ensure students remain on course.

Stage 4: Solution Presentation and Reflection - An iterative process where students present their solutions to the problem. Students rephrase and paraphrase the knowledge acquired and demonstrate their new knowledge.

Stage 5: Overview, Integration and Evaluation The integration of knowledge from various disciplines and sources and the synthesis of ideas shared bring the PBL process to closure. The review and evaluation of learning, however, forms an integral part of learning.

- Blended Learning – is a combination of online learning with traditional classroom learning. This was more evident during the Covid-19 era and is now the common practice in many institutions of higher learning post-covid (Ejuchegahi, 2024). Students must become comfortable with online tools and using the internet to contribute to their learning.

A blended learning approach is now the modus operandi that gives students the ability to discover how best to use learning tools that promote the teaching and learning encounter. Ejuchegahi (2024) further opines that blended learning is advantageous owing to its flexibility, personalized learning and improved learning outcomes. Conversely, it has a number of challenges such as lack of technological competence, poor internet connection, and lack of electricity. To forestall such, several measures must be undertaken and not limited to, student motivation and engagement, adequate teacher training and support, improved quality of online learning materials, and equipping of learners with knowledge of navigating technology platforms.

- EdTech – Educational technology refers to any software, application or service aimed at enhancing education. Innovative classroom technologies often mirror the innovations outside the classroom. Consequently, the more students engage with technologies in the classroom, the better prepared they are to engage with and technology at the workplace.

In accordance to Senapati and Singh (2023) Higher Education constantly faces challenges like retaining quality, sustenance, and ability to compete with global standards. It needs reforms in the curriculum, pedagogy, and evaluation with the focus on promoting regular, formative, and competency-based learning and development, assessment for learning, and testing higher order skills to bring the highest quality, equity, and integrity, which in turn would improve the employability of the learners. Faculty members have the opportunity to implement new ways of learning in the classroom, such as blended learning, problem-based learning, or other innovative methods; they act to facilitate the learning process, rather than solely providing knowledge. Along with opportunities, Higher Educational Institutions are facing various challenges in innovation about online education, hybrid mode, and traditional forms of education. The development and execution of innovation in higher education have a bearing on all the systems elements such as components, relationships, and functions where the growing bearing is observed on the research and engagement (Brennan et al., 2014). The research was done in public and private higher education institutions (HEIs) in Iraq (Al-Husseini, et al., 2016) and it reveals that transformational leadership plays an important role in enhancing product and process innovation in higher education.

A study of higher education administrative staff by Owusu-Agyeman (2021) revealed that engagement, motivation, communication flow, communication utilization, and decision-making strongly enhance the participative process which is essential for promoting innovation since they are part and parcel of transformational leadership's influence on innovation. These findings corroborate that of Supermane (2019) who carried out a study in Malaysia and found out that there is a significant impact of transformational leadership on innovation in teaching and learning processes. Likewise, Arif and Akram (2018) study in Pakistan denoted that a lot of organizational performance is brought about by organizational innovation that entail chieftains aiding workers to approach situations in novel and different ways. This in essence is the intellectual stimulation practice of transformative leaders that end up fostering workers' commitment to the work-place.

Owusu-Agyeman (2021) study investigated the factors that enhanced innovation among administrative staff in institutions of higher education. The findings explicitly showed that five transformational leadership factors of engagement, motivation, communication flow, communication utilization and decision-making strongly enhanced transformational leadership and promoted innovation among administrative staff.

Fernandez and Singh (2023) study utilizing existing literature explored whether transformational leadership mode is impactful in the Higher Education innovation. The outcome indicated a significant relationship between transformational leadership and innovation. Transformational leaders are influential in championing the creation of novel ideas and implementing them through the four dimensions of idealized influence, inspirational motivation, intellectual stimulation, and individual consideration.

Da'ar (2019) in a study conducted among Israel's elementary schools examined an exemplar linking the principals' strategic and interpersonal skills to participation of teachers in the schools' decision-making process. This was essential in predicting their skill flexibility during the implementation of the new educational reform, New Horizon. Research findings showed that principals who had been equipped with vital strategic skills ably marshalled and influenced teachers to freely participate in the schools' decision-making process and increased the teachers' skill flexibility. The teaching staff members were well motivated and felt part and parcel of the school thereby promoting organizational attractiveness (Atalay et al., 2019).

Bawuro et al. (2018) executed a study that encompassed factors affecting teachers' innovative character in Nigeria's North East secondary schools. The results were indicative of the fact that principals' transformational leadership was the cardinal factor responsible for the teachers' innovative character together with workplace happiness and organizational climate that automatically recrudesce as principals adopt this leadership model. Ripki et al. (2019) collaborated Bawuro et al. (2018) findings by indicating that the school captain's transformational leadership directly impacts teachers' satisfaction and hence their institutional commitment.

Raman et al. (2015) together with Mosawi and Mohamed (as cited in Kheir-Faddul & Danaiata, 2019) aver that employees with job satisfaction are more committed to the organization as manifested by committed teachers' availability, completion of tasks in good time and sacrificial willingness to drive the institutional agenda albeit theirs. This is a clear disposition of obligation, engagement, loyalty and ownership exhibited towards the institution. Subarto et al. (2021) study targeting Pamulang University lecturers found out that leadership style employed by the University management, work environment, and organizational climate positively impact on job satisfaction of University lecturers. Conclusively, job satisfaction mediates the influence of administrator's leadership style, work environment, and organizational climate on lecturer performance.

Wahyudi (2018) study among lecturers of Pamulang University corroborates Raman et al. findings. Wahyudi found out that work experience significantly affected performance at 0.451, the t-count 5.467 and the significance value 0.000 which was smaller than 0.05. Furthermore, simultaneous analysis indicated that job satisfaction and work experience positively affected performance at F arithmetic value of 72.201, significance value of 0.000 and determination coefficient of 0.744. This implies that, job satisfaction and work experience ably elucidate the lecturers' heightened performance of 74.4%.

Northouse (2016) vividly described transformational leadership as a connexion encounter of the leader and subordinates that ends up with the exaltation of the motivation and morality of the latter. This tends to increase the level of commitment and loyalty of the follower to the organisation and which in turn makes them to be more committed and loyal to the organization. Kang et al. (2024) raises similar sentiments by alluding that the relationship between transformational leadership and individual work performance among lecturers in higher education institutions is bolstered by this mode of leadership. Furthermore, it highlights the role played by self-efficacy in bringing about positive change in the running of the organisations.

Setiawan (2023) study concentrated on non-structural teaching staff encircling both permanent and non-permanent lecturers at the Surabaya Integrated Science and Technology Institute (ISTTS) and who participated actively in the teaching and learning process. The results revealed that the principal's role of transformational leadership, lecturer motivation, and tacit knowledge sharing positively impacted on lecturer performance, this in turn influenced the overall performance of the institution. The study further revealed that the transformational leadership role does not directly influence the performance of lecturers but accomplishes this through the mediation of tacit knowledge sharing. Tacit knowledge sharing refers to the exchange of personal knowledge based on personal experience in an informal and contextual manner of intuition, wisdom and talent that is arduous to translate in words. This knowledge generally takes the form of talent, wisdom, insight, and intuition. Lecturer motivation, on the other hand, has a significant influence both directly and through tacit knowledge sharing. Tacit knowledge sharing also has a positive and significant impact on lecturer performance. These findings confirm that transformational leadership and lecturer motivation have an impact on lecturer performance through sharing tacit knowledge.

Rajbhandari et al. (2016) carried out a comparison study of task-oriented and relations-oriented school pedagogues in Finland. Diversified findings concerning students' performance were realized depending on the existing environmental situation that influenced the adoption of a given leader's leadership behaviour. Henceforth, a transformational leadership engagement incorporating both the task-oriented and relations-oriented behaviour of school chief is essential to enable the institution leap forward and be productive through effective motivation and commitment of team members.

Effective school chieftains are people endowed with a mentality of work and they effectively cater for the staff needs (Hardman, 2023; & Khan et al., 2020). In accordance to Hardman (2023) study, the findings revealed that university transformational leaders lead by example in exhibiting high moral standards, personal magnetism, and tenaciousness in their undertaking of influence to others. Likewise, they nurture a growth mind-set, a forward thinking attitude, and a culture of excellence geared towards motivating followers and uplifting them to higher levels. Moreover, they promote effective learning and discovery, collaborative activities, effective critical thinking, and out of the-box thinking mentality that stimulate creativity amongst subordinates. Finally, they create an individualized modus operandi with staff members in which they are acknowledged and highly esteemed. These behaviours portrayed by the university leaders endear staff members to the institution and motivate them accordingly leading to enhanced output to the benefit of the university. They endeavour to ensure instructional school programs are executed and the personnel are well motivated to accomplish the tasks effectively to the benefit of the learners. Arbab (2019) avers that effective university leaders are those that engage lecturers as mentors who lead by teaching, team leaders and curriculum developers to the benefit of the process of impartation and receipt of knowledge.

Ibrahim et al. (2017) study dealt with the resultance of the principal's transformational leadership behaviour on the learning institution's achievement and educators' commitment in Malaysia. The aftermath denoted a positive relationship between the transformational leadership style of the leader and educators' commitment. Evidently, leaders who exemplify transformational leadership demeanour end up with committed pedagogues serving under them (Ishak, 2001 as cited in Raman et al., 2015).

Various researchers have associated and linked positive organizational commitment by employees to transformational leadership (Pataraarechachai & Ussahawanitchakit, 2009; Avolio, Zhu, Koh & Bhatia, 2004 as cited in Ghanbari & Eskandari, 2014). This is also evident among educators in Malaysia. Studies carried out by various investigators point to the fact that leaders who espouse transformational leadership positively influence commitment by educators in their respective learning institutions (Abdullah, 2005; Othman & Ishak, 2008; Joriah, 2009; and Joo et al., 2012 as cited in Raman et al., 2015). This is so since transformative leadership practicing principals emphasize on the importance of team and work spirit that propels them to work spiritedly so as to bolster school effectiveness.

Sun and Leithwood (2012) points out the necessity of integrated leadership models focusing on a given number of leadership practices as opposed to whole leadership models. These practices include transformational, transactional and instructional leadership practices. This is corroborated by Maria's (2014) study that found out that competent school heads employ integrated models of leadership and hence enjoy the support of their teachers and which is in turn reflected in the students' good academic performance. Maria's (2014) study also established a positive link between principals' school leadership behaviours (transformational/transactional) and job satisfaction. It is indicative that various variables may end up influencing job satisfaction other than school leadership since no rewards or benefits were offered to teachers. However, a previous study on teacher job satisfaction in Cyprus discovered that centrally fixed extraneous benefits like salaries impacts positively on job satisfaction of teachers (Zembylas & Papanastasiou, 2004 as cited in Maria, 2014).

Sammons et al. study in England and that of Mascall and Leithwood in American schools revealed that principals' transformational leadership positively impacts on staff motivation, commitment and supportiveness through the provision of conducive working conditions (Mascall & Leithwood, in press; & Sammons et al., 1997 as cited in Day & Sammons, 2013). This promotes staff performance that eventually results in improved student learning and academic achievement.

Owusu (2019) qualitative study in Southern Ghana explored the transformational leadership strategies employed by reform minded Muslim leaders in ameliorating Islamic schools by partnering with the government to come up with public integrated schools. The findings showed that leaders' transformational leadership tenets of idealized influence, intellectual stimulation, individualized consideration and inspirational motivation were central in promoting school integration thus making it possible for Muslim families to educate their children with their own values, instilling in them a sense of responsibility, identity, and commitment to the social and economic development of the nation as a whole. Furthermore, the government's response entailed provision of teachers and logistical support, scholarship for poverty-stricken students, engaging and urging parents to educate girls and discourage early marriages, and ensuring that those who conceive while at school are readmitted after giving birth.

Acheck (2014) in a Cameroon study involving secondary schools of Fako area set out to investigate strategies employed by principals to promote motivation among teachers. Descriptive research design was utilized and the findings indicated that principals' transformational leadership style was pertinent in boosting teachers' morale besides positive leadership, empathy, and supportive principals' behaviour. Previous research on principals' transformational leadership tends to indicate that they play a crucial role in making educators be committed in schools and which in turn impacts positively on students' academic performance (Avolio, Zhu, Koh & Bhatia, 2004 as cited in Ghanbari & Eskandari, 2014; Fard & Karimi, 2015 as cited in Al-Jabari & Ghazzawi, 2019; Maria, 2014; Mascall & Leithwood, in press; & Sammons et al., 1997 as cited in Day & Sammons, 2013; Pataraarechachai & Ussahawanitchakit, 2009).

Maundu et al. (2018) survey study in Kenya's Murang'a county public educational institutions was geared towards determining the effect of principals' transformational leadership style on teacher engagement. The obtained results showed a statistically significant and positive relationship between vigour and transformational leadership ($r=.480, p<0.01$), dedication and transformational leadership ($r=.386, p<0.01$), and absorption and transformational leadership ($r=.224, p<0.01$).

Transformational leadership of institutional heads is accredited with enhanced commitment of teachers otherwise known as Organizational Citizenship Behaviour (OCB). Odek (2018) cross-sectional survey study explored the extent of relationship between principals' transformational leadership with the OCB of the teachers among Adventist secondary schools in Kenya. The output showed that the majority of pedants 125 (73.5%) worked as envisaged with a paltry 45 (26.5%) exceeding the stipulated bounds. This is attributed to principals' TLP that inspires workers to work beyond expectations leading to high performance in schools.

In this rapidly changing world of education, technological integration is not an option but a necessity. Using technology efficiently makes educational institutions more efficient and effective, as the future will have a strong demand for digital literacy to leverage on technological advancement. Technology integration strategy is a two-pronged approach (Tavanti, 2008). To begin with, significant investments in technology infrastructure must be made. This encompasses providing an institution with access to current hardware and software, strong internet connectivity, and a safe digital space. Second, a comprehensive training for educators on how to incorporate technology effectively should be done. It is important to equip faculty members with the necessary skills that will enable them to apply digital tools in teaching (Zembylas & Papanastasiou, 2005).

Misra and Srivastava (2018) study explored the relationship of team-building competencies with personal effectiveness and job satisfaction, and the mediating role of leadership and technology. The findings of the study proved that team-building competencies are of essence in improving their effectiveness. It is therefore imperative that organizations need to prioritize teamwork and its associated extreme consequences. Likewise, technology and leadership mode have emerged as strong mediators implying that transformational leadership style positively affect the attitude of employees towards their job leading to satisfaction. The technology leverage tends to increase work place efficiency resulting to heightened performance. Banks should adopt best of the breed technology to make a big difference in the way the business is done, and offer technology-enabled products/services to facilitate transaction process to increase employee efficiency.

Sajjad et al. (2020) reviewed existing literature on organizational effectiveness through transformational leadership and technology innovation. Findings revealed that organizational effectiveness is of great interest to the management scholars judging from the increasing trend of academic studies on the topic. Technological innovation enhances the teaching and learning process and makes it easy for lecturers to impart knowledge to the students.

Mostafa (2020) opines that all good technology managers are transformational leaders in nature. They raise awareness on the necessity of technology followed by empowerment of subordinates to improve utility of IT in their respective organizations. Essentially, transformative leaders build a foundational platform for effectively leading information technology within organizations. In light of the increased pressures of the global workplace, transformational leadership is vital in effectively implementing IT to encourage competitiveness. IT utility in institutions of higher learning has become the norm and dalliance to the lecturers. This in turn enhances lecturers' commitment to their respective institutions.

INCLUSIVITY AND DIVERSITY

Inclusivity and diversity are key elements championed by any transformative leader. In accordance to Reddy and Sailakshmi (2018), a school or learning institution is thought of as a social system, characterised by its institutional functions, roles and expectations. As a social system the school's major mission is to prepare the students amicably to occupy societal social roles after leaving the school (Boruah, 2020). Guberman (2004), notes that the systems theory has a general tendency toward integration in the various aspects or parts of an organization geared towards interaction and interdependence within the organization to foster inclusivity and diversity.

Inclusivity and diversity are elements that are vital to developing a learning environment that represents and portrays the variety of human experiences (Martinez-Acosta & Favero, 2018). In essence all stakeholders involved in higher education should be involved in matters that affect higher education institutions. This helps create team spirit and make members to be part and parcel of the running of respective institutions. Diversity of students in universities and colleges refer to their mean, personal life, inherited perks, and their socio-economical background, and the resulting effects of these on their cultural environment. On the individual level, diversity is multi-dimensional, as it is made up of several (advantageous or disadvantageous) traits and perks (Dezső, 2015)

Adekoya (2023) study findings reveal the influence of HoDs to energize and empower colleague lecturers by expressing a compelling vision of schools. They motivate and inspire followers and help them overcome challenges and provide meaning to what they do. This encourages team spirit and workability between the three key stakeholders in the higher education sector videlizet HODs, lecturers and students. Furthermore, constant dialogue and engagement are evident in the process, which helps galvanize support among the stakeholders.

Inequity is a trend that leads to unfairness or want of equity. It is a form of alienation that excludes others. Shields (2020) points out that transformative leadership is more engaging and goes further than just reminiscing about inequity, but tasks staff to deconstruct inequity promoting frameworks by reconstructing them in more equitable ways. This is substantiated by Carrington et al. (2024) study. The study found out that leadership is a shared school commitment that sets the foundation for promotion and maintenance of inclusive practices within and without the school. The learning institutions were committed to fostering a conducive work environment where teachers could expand their knowledge and skills by participating in professional learning programs with their colleagues. Data revealed that some teachers embraced a transformative mind-set that encouraged them to challenge existing deficit thinking and enhanced their belief in their capacity to enact change. This belief is essential to recognize and understand their capabilities in paving the way for more inclusive and equitable practices.

Varga et al. (2021) undertook a study on diversity and inclusion in Higher Education. Results revealed that students emanating from socially disadvantaged environs are often underrepresented in large university programmes. However, Universities, colleges and other micro-communities can take proactive measures to address these students in a personal way and to provide an inclusive environment. Universities can engage students in different activities like Students' academic life, talent development, games and sports, and its formal community which support student involvement and inclusivity. This tends to bring about diversity.

Makuve (2024) study looked at diversity and inclusion as an emerging concern in postsecondary education in Botswana from the angles of instructors, students, and institutional administration. The study findings were indicative of the fact that that diversity and inclusion creates a conducive workplace for all and sundry while creating an inclusive learning environment. This should be coupled with good governance from all stakeholders so as to assure the quality of decision-making hence promotes effective delivery of educational services in a higher learning institution.

FUTURE RESEARCH DIRECTION

Proper financial management in universities and colleges is essential for their survivability. However, tertiary institution are bedevilled by financial management challenges. A study on prudent financial management in institutions of higher learning will suffice.

CONCLUSION

Transformational leadership is a mode of leadership geared towards effecting positive change in an organization. Higher education is facing a myriad of challenges that are impacting negatively towards its progress and performance. To forestall such, transformational leadership has been touted as a game changer that when applied can be beneficial in aiding higher education recourse and adopt a trajectory geared towards its betterment. The chapter highlights key components that transformational leadership impacts to cause necessary changes and realignments in higher education: management of higher education institutions' physical resources, faculty commitment, and inclusivity and diversity.

ACKNOWLEDGEMENT

This chapter is a revised version of an earlier published PhD thesis: Sabwami, M.K. (2021). Influence of Principals' Transformational Leadership Practices on Management of Public Secondary Schools in Trans-Nzoia County Kenya. PhD Thesis, Kisii University, Kenya. Available at http://repository.kisiiuniversity.ac.ke:8080/xmlui/discover

I extend my heartfelt thanks to the University supervisors who walked me through the PhD journey, Dr. George N. Areba and Prof. Elizabeth Abenga. May God bless you richly.

REFERENCES

Acheck, T. A. (2014). Motivational strategies used by principals in the management of schools: The case of some selected secondary schools in the Fako Division of the Southwest Region of Cameroon. Unpublished MED Thesis, University of Jyväskylä. Retrieved from https://jyx.jyu.fi/bitstream/handle/123456789/47987/1/URN%3ANBN%3Afi%3 Ajyu-201512043909.pdf

Adekoya, O. (2023). Exploring the impacts of transformational leadership on transformational teaching in higher education: Empirical evidence from Kuwait. In Manyane, M. A. K. U. A., & Mariam, A. K. I. N. L. O. L. U. (Eds.), *Sustaining Higher Education Through Resource Allocation, Learning Design Models, and Academic Development*. IGI Global., Available at https://shura.shu.ac.uk/32800/3/AdekoyaExploringTheImpacts%28AM%29.pdf

Akungu, J. A. (2014). Influence of teaching and learning resources on students' performance in Kenya certificate of secondary education in free day secondary education in Embakasi Sub County, Kenya. Unpublished MED Research Project, University of Nairobi. Available at https://eap.uonbi.ac.ke/sites/default/files/cees/education/eap/REPORT%20D%20final.pdf

Al-Dowayan, H. A., & Al-Saeed, H. A. (2022). The Reality of Organizational Silence among Faculty Members at Qassim University and its Relationship to Some Variables. *International Journal of Educational and Psychological Studies*, 11(3), 601–623. DOI: 10.31559/EPS2022.11.3.8

Al-Jabari, B., & Ghazzawi, I. (2019). Organizational commitment: A review of the conceptual and empirical literature and a research agenda. *International Leadership Journal (ILJ), 11*(1), 78-119. Available at https://www.researchgate.net/publication/331635975_Organizational_CommitmentA_Review_of_the_Conceptual_and_Empirical_Literature_and_a_Research_Agenda/link /5c901e1a92851c1df94a5a45/download

Arbab, A. M. (2019). How Leadership and Mentoring Enhance the Quality of Teaching and Learning in Higher Education. *International Journal of Learning and Development*, 9(1), 57–72. DOI: 10.5296/ijld.v9i1.13814

Arif, S., & Akram, A. (2018). Transformational leadership and organizational performance: The mediating role of organizational innovation. *SEISENSE Journal of Management*, 1(3), 60–75. https://journal.seisense.com/index.php/jom/issue/view/3. DOI: 10.33215/sjom.v1i3.28

Atalay, D., Akcil, U., & Ozkul, A. E. (2019). Effects of transformational and instructional leadership on organizational silence and attractiveness and their importance for the sustainability of educational institutions. doi: https://doi.org/. Available at www.mdpi.com/journal/sustainabilityDOI: 10.3390/su11205618

Barbieri, B., Sulis, I., Porcu, M., & Toland, M.D. (2019). Italian teachers' well-being within the high school context: Evidence from a large scale survey. *Frontiers in Psychology Journal*, 1-13. doi: https://doi.org/DOI: 10.3389/fpsyg.2019.01926

Bass, B. M., & Riggio, R. E. (2008). *Transformational leadership*. Lawrence Erlbaum Associates, Inc.

Bawuro, F. A., Danjuma, I., & Wajiga, H. (2018). Factors influencing innovative behaviour of teachers in secondary schools in the North East of Nigeria. *Traektoriâ Nauki Journal, 4*(3),1007-1017. . Available at https://doaj.org/article/9513913668524c64affe659ef758dff6DOI: 10.22178/pos.32-9

Boruah, J. (2020). School as a Social System – A Study. International Research Journal of Education and Technology, 1(2), 26-28. Available at https://www.irjweb.com/7.pdf

Brennan, L., Binney, W., Parker, L., Aleti, T., & Nguy n, Đ. (2014). *Social Marketing and Behaviour Change: Models*. Theory and Applications., DOI: 10.4337/9781782548157

Bueno, D. C. (2019). School Finance and Physical Resources Management Module. doi: https://dx.doi.org/ Available at https://www.researchgate.net/publication/333547195_School_Finance_and_Physical_ResourcesManagementDOI: 10.13140/RG.2.2.20729.72809

Bush, T. (2018). Transformational leadership: Exploring common conceptions. [EMAL]. *Educational Management Administration & Leadership*, 46(6), 883–887. DOI: 10.1177/1741143218795731

Campbell, T. R. (2020). Relationship Between Transformational Leadership Style and Financial Sustainability. PhD Dissertation of Walden University. Available at https://scholarworks.waldenu.edu/cgi/viewcontent.cgi?article=10975&context=dissert ations

Carrington, S., Park, E., Mckay, L., Saggers, B., Harper-Hill, K., & Somerwil, T. (2024). Evidence of transformative leadership for inclusive practice. *Teaching and Teacher Education*, 141, 104466. https://www.sciencedirect.com/science/article/pii/S0742051X23004547. DOI: 10.1016/j.tate.2023.104466

Chikafalimani, S. H. P., Kibwami, N., & Moyo, S. (2021). Management of facilities at public universities in Africa: Current challenges and the way forward. *Real Estate Management and Valuation*, 29(1), 21–29. DOI: 10.2478/remav-2021-0003

Christman, G. (2024). Transformation and Collaboration in Organizational Leadership. Hunter International. Available at https://www.hirecruiting.com/transformation-and-collaboration-in-organizational-leadership

Da'ar, R. (2019). Teachers' skill flexibility: Examining the impact of principals' skills and teachers' participation in decision making during educational reform. *International Journal of Educational Management*, 33(2), 287–299. DOI: 10.1108/IJEM-12-2017-0382

Day, C., & Sammons, P. (2013). Successful leadership: A review of the international literature. Available at https://files.eric.ed.gov/fulltext/ED546806.pdf

Ejuchegahi, A. A. (2024). A Review of Blended Learning after the COVID-19 Pandemic. *International Review of Education*, 12(1), 86–101. DOI: 10.5296/ire.v12i1.21849

Espinoza, J. (2023). Navigating Choppy Waters: Transformational Leadership and Graduate Education Amid Economic Strife. Available at https://www.linkedin.com/pulse/navigating-choppy-waters-transformational- leadership-amid-espinoza-zexmf

Faig, E. Z. (2024). Strategies for Transformative Leadership in Educational Settings: Realizing Effective Implementation Goals. *International Journal of Innovative Technologies in Social Science*, 1(41). Advance online publication. DOI: 10.31435/rsglobalijitss/30032024/8102

Fernandez, S. M., & Ghorpade, N. L. (2023). Role of Transformational Leadership on Innovation in Higher Education: a Review of Literature. https://www.researchgate.net/publication/372474412_ROLE_OF_TRANSFORMATI ONAL_LEADERSHIP_ON_INNOVATION_IN_HIGHER_EDUCATION_A_REVI EW_OF_LITERATURE/link/64b8ddac8de7ed28baadb1a9/download?_tp=eyJjb250Z Xh0Ijp7ImZpcnN0UGFnZSI6InB1YmxpY2F0aW9uIiwicGFnZSI6InB1YmxpY2F0a W9uIn19

Fontein, D. (2022). Your Guide to Transformational Leadership in Education. Available at https://thoughtexchange.com/blog/transformational-leadership-in-education/

Ghanbari, S., & Eskandari, A. (2014). Transformational leadership, job satisfaction and organizational innovation. *International Journal of Management Perspective*, 1(4), 81–94. https://pdfs.semanticscholar.org/604f/0bf03e5055de8d2e8c84a997ab11a864a65a.pdf?ga=2.155952251.154317503.1564221674-1847273041.1564221674

Ghasabeh, M. S., & Provitera, M. J. (2017). Transformational leadership: Building an effective culture to manage organizational knowledge. *The Journal of Values Based Leadership*, 10(2), 1–19. DOI: 10.22543/0733.102.1187

Githui, J. N., Ragui, M., & Nyakundi, A. O. (2024). Mediating Role of Collaboration on Transformational Leadership and Performance Contracts in Road Agencies in Kenya. *Human Resource and Leadership Journal*, 9(2), 1–22. DOI: 10.47941/hrlj.1679

Guberman, S. (2004). Reflections on Ludwig Bertalanffy's general system theory; Foundations, Development, Applications. *Gestalt Theory*, 26(1), 44–51.

Hamid, M. K. A., Hassan, M. A. A., Hassim, M. H., & Yusof, M. (2015). Implementation of Problem-Based Learning in a Typical Engineering Classroom. Conference on Engineering Education, Kuala Lumpur, 14-15 Dis. 2004. Available at https://www.researchgate.net/figure/The-PBL-process-Figure-1-provides-a-schema-of-a-typical-PBL-process-that-we-applied-in_fig1_265620228

Hardman, J. C. (2023). Transformational leadership strategies in U.S. public universities. PhD Dissertation, Pepperdine University. Retrieved from https://digitalcommons.pepperdine.edu/cgi/viewcontent.cgi?article=2316&context=ed

Howell, J. L., Bullington, K. E., Gregory, D. E., Williams, M. E., & Nuckols, W. L. (2022). Transformational leadership in higher education programs. *Journal of Higher Education Policy and Leadership Studies*, 3(1), 5166. DOI: 10.52547/johepal.3.1.51

Hutasuhut, E. (2019). Effect of transformational leadership of a principal's management ability on the work motivation of teachers to provide guidance and counselling at senior high schools in Medan, Indonesia. *Üniversitepark Bülten, 8*(2), 141-152. Available at http://dx.doi.org/DOI: 10.22521/unibulletin.2019.82.4

Ibrahim, B. F. (2023). Lecturers' Job Commitment in Nigerian Universisties: Challenges and Ways Forward. *Al-Hikmah Journal of Education, 10*(2),64-73. Available at https://alhikmahuniversity.edu.ng/centralJournal/my_portal/user/event/bookUrl781.pf

Imam, F. A. (2017). Assessment of the impact of resource management on students' academic performance in secondary schools in Zaria and Giwa education zones, Kaduna state, Nigeria. Unpublished Masters of Education Thesis. Available at https://kubanni.abu.edu.ng/jspui/bitstream/123456789/10244/1/ASSESSMENT%%20

Jaji, C. L., Okoth, U., & Mari, N. (2017). Board of Managements' initiatives influencing quality education in secondary schools in Kajiado County, Kenya. *Journal of Education*, 1(3), 11–25. http://erepository.uonbi.ac.ke/handle/11295/107269?show=full

Kang, L., Aziz, L. A. A., & Hassan, N. C. (2024). Transformational Leadership, Self- efficacy, and Work performance among Lecturers in Higher Education Institutions: Conceptual Analysis on a Mediation Model. *International Journal of Academic Research in Business & Social Sciences*, 14(7), 696–706. DOI: 10.6007/IJARBSS/v14-i7/21973

Khan, H., Rehmat, M., Butt, T. H., Farooqi, S., & Asim, J. (2020). Impact of transformational leadership on work performance, burnout and social loafing: A mediation model. *Future Buiness Journal*, 6(40), 1–13. DOI: 10.1186/s43093-020-00043-8

Kwistianus, H., Gunawan, A. C., & Jonathan, F. A. (2023). Transformational Leadership and Financial Performance: The Mediating Role of Corporate Reputation. ASEAN Journal of Management & Innovation, 10(1), 70 – 82. DOI:DOI: 10.14456/ajmi.2023.6

Langwenya-Myeni, D. N. (2017). The dynamics of generating and managing educational resources in Swaziland's selected secondary schools. Unpublished Doctorate Thesis, University of Kwazulu-Natal of South Africa. Available at https://researchspace.ukzn.ac.za/xmlui/bitstream/handle/10413/15463/Langwenya-Myeni_D_N_2017.pdf?sequence=1&isAllowed=y

Litz, D., & Scott, S. (2017). Transformational leadership in the educational system of the United Arab Emirates. [EMAL]. *Educational Management Administration & Leadership*, 45(4), 566–587. DOI: 10.1177/1741143216636112

Lomulen, R. E. (2016). Influence of principals' management of resources on students' performance at Kenya Certificate of Secondary Examination in public schools in Samburu County, Kenya. Retrieved from http://erepository.uonbi.ac.ke/bitstream/handle/11295/97165/EKAL%20FINAL%20P ROJECT%20.pdf?sequence=1&isAllowed=y Lynch, D., Smith, R., Yeigh, T. and Provost, S. (2019). A study into organisational readiness and its impacts on school improvement. *International Journal of Educational Management, 33*(2), 393-408. doi: https://dx.doi.org/DOI: 10.1108/IJEM-07-2017-0181

Makuve, N. (2024). Contemporary Issues in Higher Education: Diversity, Inclusion, Management and Governance. *African Journal of Education and Practice*, 10(1), 56–65. DOI: 10.47604/ajep.2487

Martinez-Acosta, V. G., & Favero, C. B. (2018). A discussion of diversity and inclusivity at the institutional level: The need for a strategic plan. *Journal of Undergraduate Neuroscience Education*, 16(3), A252. PMID: 30254540

Maundu, M., Namusonge, G. S., & Simiyu, A. N. (2018). Effect of transformational leadership style on employee engagement in public secondary schools, Murang'a County, Kenya. *Advances in Social Sciences Research Journal*, 5(11), 81–89. https://journals.scholarpublishing.org/index.php/ASSRJ/article/view/5472

Mbewu, N. F., & Adebayo, R. O. (2020). Creating Intention for Persuading and Retaining Students: An Analysis of Higher Institution Brand Reputation Management. *African Journal of Rhetoric*, 12(1), 65-78. https://go.gale.com/ps/i.do?id=GALE%7CA665973687&sid=googleScholar&v=2.1&it=r&linkaccess=abs&issn=19982054&p=AONE&sw=w&userGroupName=anon%7E40ac71d0&aty=open-web-entry

Mbithi, A. M., Obonyo, P. O., & Awino, Z. B. (2016). Transformational Leadership and Performance of Universities in Kenya. http://erepository.uonbi.ac.ke/handle/11295/100622;jsessionid=4A796D1B5A2822A96E0BC7B141EF9FD3

McClendon, G. T. (2018). Strategies for transforming higher education. *Leadership and Organization Development Journal*, 39(2), 246–262.

Miner, J. B. (2005). *Organization behaviour 1: Essential theories of motivation and leadership*. M.E. Sharpe.

Misra, S., & Srivastava, K. B. L. (2018). Team-building Competencies, Personal Effectiveness and Job Satisfaction: The Mediating Effect of Transformational Leadership and Technology. *Management and Labour Studies*, 43(1&2), 109–122. DOI: 10.1177/0258042X17753178

Mohamed, A. D. (2024). Impact of Employee Silence on Organizational Performance: A case from Mogadishu universities. *International Journal of Advanced and Applied Sciences*, 11(3), 27–35. DOI: 10.21833/ijaas.2024.03.004

Mormah, F. O. (2023). The management and maintenance of physical facilities for quality assurance in higher education in the 21st century with innovative technologies. African *Educational Research Journal, 11*(2): 220-224. Available at https://files.eric.ed.gov/fulltext/EJ1391717.pdf

Mostafa, S. (2020). All Good Technology Managers Are Transformational Leaders. https://innovationmanagement.se/2020/06/11/all-good-technology-managers-are - transformational-leaders/

Murage, S. W. (2022). Transformational leadership and performance in Kenya's universities. [AJHSSR]. *American Journal of Humanities and Social Sciences Research*, 6(2), 160–168. https://www.ajhssr.com/wp-content/uploads/2022/02/P22602160168.pdf

Mutiso, P.M., Kalai, J.M., Okoth, U. & Per-Olof Hansson (2023). Influence of organizational values on job commitment of public university lecturers. Journal of Pedagogy, Andragogy and Heutagogy in Academic Practice (JPAHAP, 4(3), 65-86 https://uonjournals.uonbi.ac.ke/ojs/index.php/pedagogy

Nasongo, J., Mukonyi, P., & Nyatuka, B. (2017). An Analysis of Nelson Mandela's Philosophy of Education. DOI: .DOI: 10.1007/978-94-6300-908-9_7

Nnebedum, C., & Ndidi, E. P. (2017). Analysis of resource management strategies adopted by principals for secondary schools improvement in Enugu State, Nigeria. *International Journal of Advance Research and Innovative Ideas In Education*, 3(3), 4124–4129. https://www.researchgate.net/publication/324876923

Ocak, M., & Ozturk, A. (2018). The role of transformational leadership behaviours: Effects on corporate entrepreneurship behaviours and financial performance of firms. *International Review of Management and Marketing*, 8(4), 45–55.

Onukwu, J. N., Tiebebedigha, F. P., & Okojide, A. C. (2020). Teachers' and job commitment. Conceptualizing Meyer and Allen's multidimensional model in Bayelsa State secondary schools. [MMITMENT_CONCEPTUALIZING_MEYER_AND_ALLEN'S_MULTIDIMENSI ONAL_MODEL_IN_BAYELSA_STATE_PUBLIC_SECONDARY_SCHOOLS]. *African Journal of Studies in Education*, 15(1), 73–84. https://www.researchgate.net/publication/342765058_TEACHERS'_AND_JOB_CO

Owusu, K. (2019). Exploring the transformational leadership strategies used by Islamic Education Reformers to influence the integration of Islamic schools in Ghana. *Journal of Comparative Studies and International Education*, 1(1), 50–72. https://www.jcsie.com/ojs/dir/index.php/JCSIE/issue/view/Jcsie.com

Owusu-Agyeman, Y. (2021). Transformational leadership and innovation in higher education: A participative process approach. *International Journal of Leadership in Education*, 24(5), 694–716. DOI: 10.1080/13603124.2019.1623919

Rajbhandari, M. M. S., Rajbhandari, S., & Loock, C. (2016). Relations- and task-oriented behaviour of school leaders: Cases from primary schools in Finland. *South African Journal of Childhood Education*, 6(1), 1–10. DOI: 10.4102/sajce.v6i1.360

Raman, A., Mey, C. H., Don, Y., Daud, Y., & Khalid, R. (2015). Relationship between principals' transformational leadership style and secondary school teachers' commitment. *Asian Social Science*, 11(15), 221–228. DOI: 10.5539/ass.v11n15p221

Reddy, S., & Sailakshmi, M. (2018). The School as a Social System - A Review. [IJESI]. *International Journal of Engineering and Science Invention*, 7(8), 74–77. https://www.ijesi.org/papers/Vol(7)i8/Version-5/L0708057477.pdf

Right to Education. (N.d.). Higher Education. Available at https://www.right-to-education.org/issue-page/higher-education

Sabwami, M. K. (2021). *Influence of Principals' Transformational Leadership Practices on Management of Public Secondary Schools in Trans-Nzoia County Kenya. PhD Thesis*. Kisii University., Available at http://repository.kisiiuniversity.ac.ke:8080/xmlui/discover

Sajjad, A., Noor, A.A., Amer, H.J., Dorothea, B., Nadine, C., & Reaz, M. (2020). Organizational Effectiveness Through Transformational Leadership and Technology Innovation: A Systematic Literature Review and Future Research Agenda. Journal of International Business and Management 3(4): 01-17. DOI:https://doi.org/DOI: 10.37227/JIBM-2020-04-44

Senapati, R., & Singh, S. K. (2023). National education Policy-2020 and Evaluation Reforms in Higher Education: Envisioning Transformation for 21st Century India. *University News*, 61(08), 21–26.

Serdyukov, P. (2017). Innovation in education: What works, what doesn't, and what to do about it? *Journal of Research in Innovative Teaching & Learning*, 10(1), 4–33. DOI: 10.1108/JRIT-10-2016-0007

Setiawan, P. A. (2023). The Influence of Transformational Leadership and Lecturer Motivation on Lecturer Performance Through Tacit Knowledge Sharing at the Institut Sains dan Teknologi Terpadu Surabaya. *Journal of Social Research*, 2(11), 3836–3849. https://ijsr.internationaljournallabs.com/index.php/ijsr. DOI: 10.55324/josr.v2i11.1485

Shields, C. M. (2020). Becoming a transformative leader: a guide to creating equitable schools. Routledge. Available at https://scholar.google.com/scholar_lookup?title=Becoming%20a%20transformative2 0leader%20a%20guide%20to%20creating%20equitable%20schools&publication_yea r=2020&author=C.M.%20Shields

Shukla, P. K., Kumar, R., & Shukla, A. (2024). Project-Based Learning (PBL), Chapter 3, Edition 19. In Teaching and Learning Techniques: A New Paradigm (pp. 17-25). Government College Zirapur under Department of Higher Education, Government of Madhya Pradesh, India. Available at https://www.researchgate.net/publication/378334128_Project-Based_Learning_PBL

Strauss, V. (2013). Nelson Mandela Famous Quote on Education. The Washington Post. Available at https://www.washingtonpost.com/news/answersheet/wp/2013/12/05/nelson-mandelas- famous-quote-on-education/

Strukan, E., Nikolic, M., & Sefic, S. (2017). Impact of transformational leadership on business performance. DOI: DOI: 10.17559/TV-20150624082830

Subarto, S., Solihin, D., & Qurbani, D. (2021). Determinants of Job Satisfaction and Its Implications for the Lecturers Performance. [JPEB]. *Jurnal Pendidikan Ekonomi Dan Bisnis*, 9(2), 163–178. DOI: 10.21009/JPEB.009.2.7

Supermane, S. (2019). Transformational leadership and innovation in teaching and learning activities: The mediation effect of knowledge management. *Information Discovery and Delivery*, 47(4), 242–250. DOI: 10.1108/IDD-05-2019-0040

Thompson, S. (2024). What is innovation in education and why it's important? Available at: https://corp.kaltura.com/blog/what-is-innovation-in-education/

Uko, E. S. (2015). Principalship and effective management of facilities in secondary schools in Cross River State, Nigeria. *International Journal of Academic Research and Reflection*, 3(1), 64–76. http://www.idpublications.org/wpcontent/uploads/2014/10/PRINCIPALSHIP-AND-EFFECTIVE-MANAGEMENT-OF-FACILITIES-IN-SECONDARY-SCHOOLS-IN-CROSS-RIVER-STATE-NIGERIA.pdf

UNESCO. (1998). World Conference on Higher Education in the Twenty-first Century: Vision and Action, Paris. https://unesdoc.unesco.org/ark:/48223/pf0000141952

Usman, Y. D. (2016). Educational resources: An integral component for effective school administration in Nigeria. *Research on Humanities and Social Sciences, 6*(13), 28-39. Available at https://files.eric.ed.gov/fulltext/ED578024.pdf

Varga, A., Vitez, K., Orsos, I., Fodor, B. & Gergely, H. (2021). Diversity and Inclusion in Higher Education. KÉPZÉS ÉS GYAKORLAT / TRAINING AND PRACTICE, 19 (1-2),70-81. https://doi.org/DOI: 10.17165/TP.2021.1-2.7

Wahyudi (2018). The influence of job satisfaction and work experience on lecturer performance of Pamulang University. *Scientific Journal of Reflection: Economic, Accounting, Management and Business, 1*(2), 221-230. ISSN 2615-3009

World Bank. (2024). Tertiary Education. Available at https://www.worldbank.org/en/topic/tertiaryeducation#:~:text=Tertiary%20education%20refers%20to%20all,poverty%2C%20and%20boosting%20shared%20prosperity.

Yanti, H. S., Iim, W., Hanafiah, H., & Deti, R. (2022). Transformational Leadership in Improving Lecturer Performance in Higher Education. International Journal of Science Education and Technology Management, 1(2). 1-19. https://www.neliti.com/publications/558973/transformational-leadership-in- improving-lecturer-performance-in-higher-education

ADDITIONAL READING

Harris, T. N., & Lee, C. N. (2019). Advocate-mentoring: A communicative response to diversity in higher education. *Communication Education*, 68(1), 103–113. DOI: 10.1080/03634523.2018.1536272

Sosik, J. J., Kahai, S. S., & Avolio, B. J. (1998). Transformational Leadership and Dimensions of Creativity: Motivating Idea Generation in Computer-Mediated Groups. *Creativity Research Journal*, 11(2), 111–121. DOI: 10.1207/s15326934crj1102_3

Wright, L. A. (2015). The role of transformational leadership consensus and innovation climate strength in predicting employee attitudes *(Doctoral dissertation, San Diego State University).*

KEY TERMS AND DEFINITIONS

Collaboration: An act of working and sharing with people to facilitate a course of action

Education: The process of acquisition of knowledge

Higher Education: Tertiary education accessed in higher education institutions like colleges and universities

Inclusivity: The act of inclusion of people to enable them be participants

Innovation: The process of modification or coming up with new ideas

Technology: Utility of information technology in the teaching and learning process

Transformational Leadership: Leadership that transforms institutions through injection of positive change

Chapter 10
Mental Health and Academic Performance Among University Undergraduate Students: Depression and Anxiety

Rose Anyango Otieno
Kisii University, Kenya

ABSTRACT

Academic work is a significant factor in mental health and academic performance of university students. Mental health challenges can impede academic success. Academic performance and mental health wellness have an interactive relationship. The top two mental health issues faced by College Students include anxiety and depression. This chapter will focus on how the two disorders with high comorbidity can impede the academic success of students. Anxiety and depression are major predictors of academic performance among university students. Students with the two disorders are likely to lose interest in learning and therefore, perform poorly in class. There is often a positive correlation between anxiety and depression and poor academic performance by university students. The two disorders among university students have been established to be on the rise besides other mental health problems that students experience while in campus, leading to poor academic performance and failure to transit to graduation.

DOI: 10.4018/979-8-3373-0025-2.ch010

INTRODUCTION

Every student getting to the university has his/her educational aspiration and dream for academic success. Academic work is a significant factor in mental health and wellbeing outcomes of university students. Career development is helpful in finding and managing work and wellbeing outcomes. Mental health challenges can impede academic performance success, career progression and acquisition and retention of suitable work career development. Career progression and mental health wellness have an interactive relationship (both "good" and "bad") and wellbeing outcomes. Poor mental health can make the collegiate experience a challenging time for students and their concerned parents. Students struggling with mental health problems are twice as likely to drop out of school (Eisenberg, Golberstein & Hunt, 2009). Generally, university leaders report mental health problems among students, while many believe that college students are facing a mental health crisis. The top three mental health issues faced by College Students include anxiety, stress and depression. This chapter will focus on anxiety and depression and how the two disorders with high comorbidity can impede the academic success of the students.

Academic performance refers to evaluation of students' progress and achievement. It involves monitoring and assessing the student's overall performance, including learning outcome, exam success rate and ability to meet educational goals (Aronen, et al., 2004). Academic success is important for academic achievement. Academic achievement refers to the extent to which a student meets the goals ad standard set by educational institution, and includes met grades, tests scores. Class participation and overall academic performance. Therefore, Students' academic success is represented by retention, progression and improved output, while academic failure is defined by lack of retention, progression and improved output (graduation).

Academic achievement is important in the present situation in which many students find themselves in. Many institutions of higher learning normally have their systems that define achievement, performance and failure. Most institutions promote achievement based the total personality in socio-economic environment with cognitive, affect and psychomotor domain, each with its unique role. Additionally, academic achievement is evaluated in the context of the student's ability and performance related to holistic human growth, involving cognitive, emotional social and physical development which occurs throughout the student's life, without which academic performance may not be achieved. It is in this context of this holistic human growth and academic achievement that this chapter focuses on two mental disorders, depression and anxiety may impact negatively on the academic achievement of university students.

Several factors have been explored and found to contribute to academic success of the students. Among these factors include the mental well-being of the students, especially anxiety and depression, are likely to affect students' performance when compared to students without mental health disorders (Liu, et al., 2022; Bernal-Morales et al., 2015), and had Probability of academic failure, besides higher attrition rate. Similarly, poor academic performance has also been linked to depression in a study that was conducted among university students in Nigeria (Aluh, Abba & Afosi, 2020). Understanding the relationship between academic performance and mental health problems may help educators gain insight into mental health challenges face by students and develop strategies that can support their educational journey.

Undergraduate students are a unique are a unique group of students passing through the most critical stage in life. They may experience life events that may impact their academic life and mental wellbeing (Aronen, et al., 2004). Both psychosocial and academic challenging work, assignments and financial pressures can affect their stable mental health (Treiman, 2007). Literature has identified has identified university students as a group that is particularly vulnerable to mental health problems that in turn affect their academic outcome negatively. Many university students experience stressful events during their stay in the university due to social changes and academic pressures that put them at a risk in terms of mental health (Ericson & Gardener, 1992). It has been estimated that a third of students are likely to develop depression at any point in life, with many also presenting with anxiety disorders (Alvi, et al, 2010; Eisenberg, Golberstein & Hunt, 2009). With those from lower social economic status being more vulnerable. While in most settings students are entitled to financial support, some students often miss this support thus, predisposing them to mental health problems including depression and anxiety.

Students in institutions of higher learning are always expected to be well prepared and ready to learn, handle future demands, increased responsibilities both in their academic as well as social life. Furthermore, they are also expected to handle stressors that come along their way as they continue with their academic programs. However, this is not always the case as they often experience mental health challenges too among them, anxiety and depression. The two are major predictors of academic performance among university students. Students with the two disorders are likely to lose interest in learning and therefore, perform poorly in class. There is often a positive correlation between anxiety and depression and academic performance by university students. In universities, young people are constantly battling the challenges that may contribute to depression among them. These challenges include; the effects of human rights violations, wars and violence in their homes, schools and businesses. Cybercrimes, cyber bullying, and playing violent video games. Suicidality, substance abuse and feeling lonely as well as being persecuted for being true to themselves. Other challenges include toxic political and social environment, toxic relationships, societal demands, work/peer, career pressures and demands, as well as repeated traumas such as road, fire accidents, natural calamities, like floods and lands. All these factors can contribute to anxiety and depression among university students, thus affecting their well-being and academic outcome. Furthermore, attention has been given to many factors that affect the undergraduate students' academic performance, with little attention given to the impact of mental health, especially depression and anxiety as co-occurring disorders among university students.

Depression

Researchers and scholars have painted a gleam picture of depression as a mental health condition that causes individuals inability to function effectively. According to Hysenbegasi, Hass, & Rowland (2005) depression is a multi- problematic disorder that causes heavy burden to society and leads to impairment in social interpersonal and occupational functioning. This basically means that that students with depression may have a challenge with their occupational functioning, thus failing to perform the academic tasks needed for academic success. Similarly, Khan et al., (2019) indicated that depression is a common mental health condition that causes chronic fatigues, feeling of emptiness and sadness or inability to feel pleasure, thus affecting general functioning. The authors further indicated that depression making it a serious, and complex mood disorder, with a global presence, whose exact cause is poorly understood. Studies suggest that depression results mostly from an interplay between genetic vulnerability and environmental factors. According to American Psychiatric Association (APA) (2013), depression is a serious psychological disorder that affects people of all ages, and whose effects are widespread. Understanding of its potential causes may also help in its treatment. In Diagnostic and Statistical manual for Mental Disorders-V (DSM-V) (2013), depression has been classified into seven categories that include; Disruptive mood dysregulation, major depressive disorder (major depressive episode), persistent depressive disorder (dysthymic) and premenstrual dysphoric disorder. Other classifications include substance/medication induced depressive disorder, depressive disorder due to another medical condition and unspecified disorder.

The DSM-V further notes that the common feature of all these disorder is the presence of sad empty or irritable mood, accompanied by somatic and cognitive changes that significantly reduce the individual's capacity to function. In the classifications of depression, the major depressive disorder (MDD) which this paper focuses on, is the most commonly diagnosed category. Its clinical symptoms include depressed mood, diminished interest, changes in weight, fatigue, psychomotor changes, feelings of worthlessness, lack of concentration recurrent thoughts of death. According to

Kessler, Macknagle, Swartz, and Blazer (1993), most studies in this area have found that women are twice more likely than men to experience depression.

Evidenced work indicate that depression can also occur at any time during the lifespan; but, on average, first onset is during the young adult stage—18-25 years (APA, 2022). This also the age when most individuals are in universities. Brody et al. (2018) established that both males and females depict similar prevalence rates during their childhood (i.e., up to 10 years) and late adulthood (i.e., over 60 years), with disparities which start to appear during the adolescence stage and persists until midlife. During this period, there is an elevation of depression among females compared to males (Shi et al., 2021).

Depression and Academic Performance

University students represent a group of people who are typically experiencing a critical transition from adolescent from adolescent to adulthood, often considered as one the most stressful moments in a person's life (Eisenberg, Golberstein &Hunt, 2009). Some studies have estimated that about a third of the students suffer experience some form of depression compared to the general population (Bantjes et al., 2020). According to Beck's cognitive behavioral theory (CBT) which is one of the known best theories in understanding depression, people with depression tend to have negative cognitions of themselves, the world around them and a bleak view of the future. This may explain why university students experiencing depression may altogether miss to attend classes or lose hope and fail to transit to. These, combined with academic pressures and psychosocial challenges can predispose students to negative cognitions, hence failure to transit to graduation. This is supported by Sarokhani et al., (2013) assertion that those in achievement-oriented environment like institutions of higher learning to view low grades as a sense of failure and low self-esteem, thus increasing the risk of developing depression.

Studies globally, have that university students report higher rates of depression at 35%, which is much higher compared to rates found among the general population (Hinck, 2017). However, in many parts of the world, higher rates have been reported in low income counties at than high income countries (WHO, 2017). Surveys across Universities in American report a prevalence of 40% (Rayelle, 2021); while, those conducted in different Asian countries report a range between 4-79.2% (Bakhtyari, 2020 estimates the prevalence range of depression among students in universities to be between 16.2 to 67%; while Ssebunnya et al., (2019) put the figure to be between 1.8 to 42.4% Nyongesa (2017), Kenya with nearly 1.9 million cases of depressed persons ranks fifth in Africa. In a study conducted by Othieno et al., (2014), examining the prevalence of depression among university students, found that 35.7% and 5.6% in a sample of 923 students, had moderate and severe depressive symptoms respectively.

Depression is a serious psychological disorder that affects people of all ages, and whose effects are widespread. It can be long-lasting or recurrent, substantially impairing an individual's ability to function at work, school or cope with daily life. According to Diagnostic and Statistical Manual for Mental Disorders (DSM-5) American Psychiatric Association (APA, 2013), depression has two major features that include extreme sadness accompanied by somatic and cognitive changes that significantly reduce the individual's capacity to function. In the classifications of depression, the major depressive disorder (MDD) which this chapter will focus on, is the most commonly diagnosed category among other mood disorders. Depression is a common and severe mental illness that impairs the sufferer's emotional state. It is characterized by a combination of abnormal thoughts, perceptions, emotions, behavior and poor relationship with other people. Moreover, depression is a complex illness that takes many forms, while remaining widely under-diagnosed and under-reported. It has a global presence, is a significant contributor to the burden of disease, and affects people of all ages, sexes, and communities.

Depression among university students has been established to be on the rise besides other mental health problems that students experience while in campus. Academic pressure is linked to stress which is a risk factor in depression. Ibrahim et al. (2013) identified fear of poor grades and failing ask risk factor in depression, while Youseff and Deane (2006) asserted that academic stress comes with high parental expectations, hence those who do not perform well in exams may fear disappointing their parents. Academic completion may also cause strain on the students leading to negative impact on their mental health hence depression.

Prevalence of depression among university students is well established. It is one of the disorders that impact memory, thus makes it hard for students to recall information as well as have negative effects on how students will engage in social situations. Often, students with anxiety and depression will avoid interactions with their peers, which can in turn impact on their college life negatively. In addition to this, depression impacts memory, thus making it hard for students to recall information, and this can also have negative effects on how students engage in social situations. Depressed students often miss classes, and also find it hard to follow through their academic tasks, leading to poor performance. Severely depressed students may contemplate suicide, or wait for a stressful event that may trigger suicide as is the common experiences in many universities today.

Another point of view in which depression interferes with academic achievement is in the depressive symptomatology. Depression is characterized by physical, emotional and cognitive impairments which manifest in symptoms such as sleep disturbance, poor concentration, negative thoughts and feelings and withdrawal among other symptoms. These symptoms may interfere with student's academic work, especially class attendance and assignments completion (Kessler, 2009). Another study by Bantjes et, al. (2020) established that depression has a negative impact on academic engagement as students with depression may miss more classes, tests and assignments, and are more likely to drop from the university entirely compared to their non-depressed peers. Additionally, stigma related to depression can prevent students from fully engaging in both social and academic activities, negatively influencing their academic performance. Researchers have highlighted negative beliefs and attitude towards mental illness, use of medications and mental health care. All these factors can prevent students with mental health from seeking mental health services. Depressed students with poor help seeking behavior are likely to have poor academic performance. Nyamwange, Otieno and Okumu, (2023) in a study of depression among university students in Kenya found at the prevalence of depression among university students was at 48.8%A Study conducted by Nyamwange and colleagues found that the prevalence of depression among university undergraduate students was estimated at 48.8%. The authors further established that the depressed students had poor help seeking behavior for various reasons.

Anxiety

Anxiety disorders form the most common type of mental illness that may start from early childhood characterized by vague feeling of apprehension, worry and uneasiness or dread whose source is often not known to the individual. Diagnostic and Statistical Manual for Mental Disorders (DSM-5) (American Psychiatric Association, APA, 2013) gives the criteria for anxiety disorder as including feelings of excessive and persistent worry, apprehension, increased heart rate, sweating and difficulty concentrating. Other symptoms include, difficulty controlling events or activities of daily life, sleep disturbance, restlessness, muscle tension and irritability. Similarly, Bantjes et al, (2016) have defined anxiety disorder is a condition in which a person has excessive worry and feelings of fear with symptoms that include sweating, restlessness, irritability, fatigue and poor concentration. Other symptoms include trouble breathing and sleeping and fast heartbeat.

Studies have indicated that the core features of anxiety include excessive fear and avoidance of perceived threats that are persistent and impairing. Researchers have indicated that anxiety is highly correlated with factors that are both genetic as well as environmental and is comorbid with other disorders such as depression and somatic disorders (Igbal, Kupta & Ventekataro, 2015), thus worsening the psychological symptoms that may be experienced by an individual with comorbid anxiety disorders. Diagnostic and Statistical Manual (DSM -5) APA (2013) includes, panic disorder, separation anxiety, selective mutism, specific phobia and social phobia.

Other types of anxiety disorders in DSM-V include agoraphobia, generalized anxiety disorder, substance induced anxiety and anxiety due to medical conditions. However, this chapter will focus on generalized anxiety disorder commonly experienced by undergraduate students in universities

Anxiety and Academic Performance

The relationship between anxiety and depression and their impact on academic performance tend to be complex. Often, students with anxiety or depression will avoid interactions with their peers and will perceive neutral situations as threats. Some studies have established poor performance by anxious students (Bantjes, et al.2020), while others have indicated that higher levels of anxiety may be associated with better performance (Wilson et al.,2015). However, this chapter focuses on the negative impact of anxiety disorder on the academic performance of the undergraduate students in the university. Hopefully this will provoke thoughts on psychological intervention for university students with mental health challenges.

Symptoms of anxiety have been found to be more common among university undergraduate students, compared to the peers who are not in in the demanding competitive learning environment. Mental ill health among the students associated with impaired academic achievement, transition to graduation coupled with poor career preparedness and future occupational functioning thoughts can impact negatively on students' college life. While in the university, students are faced with academic pressure to perform, heavy work load, insufficient feedback from the teachers and worries about their future including finding jobs (McDonald, 2001) have established that that university undergraduate student have elevated symptoms of anxiety that appear to be substantially higher than their peers who are not academically demanding. This is because of the challenges of increased independence and responsibility, coupled with competitive environment that. These can make some students feel vulnerable to develop anxiety. All these factors can in turn affect the academic progress as personal development of the students leading to poor academic outcomes. The symptoms may be caused by stressful events, and may get worse overtime, thus affecting a person's daily functioning including academic occupation.

Anxiety as a mental health condition affects students of all ages. However, among university students, it is more prevalent. For many students, starting college is an exciting time of increased independence and new opportunities. University students are likely to experience anxiety as they often feel overwhelmed as they move to new college experiences, having to face unfamiliar situations and being away from the familiar support system. Other factors contributing to anxiety among college students include academic demands and loneliness. Typically, students with anxiety often experience recurring worries, apprehensive and tense feelings and difficulty in managing everyday tasks. Other challenges that may interfere with academic performance among university students with anxiety may include struggling to focus, disrupted sleep and refusal to go to class and all these may lead to drop in academic performance.

Anxiety affects academic performance in many ways. Higher levels of anxiety can impair cognitive functioning, attention, memory, leading to poor academic performance, while persistent anxiety can create long term effect on students mental well-being, self-esteem and development of career goals. As noted by Bantjes et al., (2020), anxiety as a common mental health concern among university students can significantly affect their academic performance. Some of the factors that may create anxiety in students include academic pressure., test anxiety and social anxiety in a new environment.

Some researchers have indicated that that anxiety affects academic performance through impaired concentration intrusive worries and racing thoughts that interfere with ability to concentrate and pay attention to understanding concepts, interferes with memory and retrieval of information when needed (Pedreli et al., 2015), yet these skills are needed for successful learning. This explains why students with anxiety may have a challenge in academic performance. This assertion has been expanded by Al-Qaisy, (2011) that students who suffer from anxiety may not take up assignments immediately for fear of failure. Their failure is caused by anxiety that prevents them from attending and participating in academic assignments, especially those with social phobias they often avoid participating in discussions. This can in turn lead to missed opportunities to engage in effective learning, over rally affecting their academic outcome.

Anxiety can affect the students' emotional well-being. Students who are ambitious can set high standards for themselves and failure to achieve the standards set can lead to disappointment and stress. Anxiety may affect the students emotional well-being by increasing feelings of sadness, low self- esteem. This can in turn affect performance by decreasing perseverance needed in academic achievement due to their emotional state. Additionally, students with anxiety often have disturbed sleep and eating patterns, thus affecting their health. Poor health often leading to poor learning outcomes.

Other researchers have indicated that anxiety can lead to self-doubt among university students hence undermining one's academic achievement. (Krawchuk, 2008) established that students with anxiety tend to focus on their failures than on their capabilities, significantly impairing their academic. performance. Such students tend to engage in negative self-talk that hinder their ability to solve problems, skills required in academic performance. Students who doubt themselves may not engage in classroom discussions, or may have poor relations with their peers. Peer to peer learning is always important in academic achievement and good learning outcomes. Anxiety may also prevent students from attending classes through negative symptoms such negative thoughts that can be exhausting, physical symptoms like headache, fatigue, nausea and unexplained illness.

All in all, Anxiety has a negative on university undergraduate students, leading to poor academic outcome, hence poor academic performance among the undergraduate students. The relationship between anxiety and academic performance is by-directional in the sense that students with high levels of anxiety are likely to perform poorly academically, while those who are high performers academically are likely to experience decreased anxiety because the fear of failure is gone. It is in this context that the chapter has endeavored to delve on the negative impact of anxiety among undergraduate students in institutions of higher learning. This chapter has brought the impact of the two most common psychological that largely affect undergraduate university students, leading to poor academic performance. A psychological intervention to handle the two psychological issues, and others affecting the students' performance may help in mitigating the poor academic performance among university students.

Figure 1 shows the relationship between the two most common mental disorders among university students. Anxiety and depression are major predictors of poor academic performance among university students. Those with the two dis orders are likely to lose interest in learning and perform poorly in class. These mental disorders in turn affect the college students' wellbeing leading to poor academic performance. Through their various symptoms, the students may not be able to keep to academic demands, thus failure to transit to graduation. There is therefore a positive correlation between depression, anxiety and academic performance among university students as shown in the Figure 1.

Figure 1. Relationship between Depression, Anxiety and Academic Performance

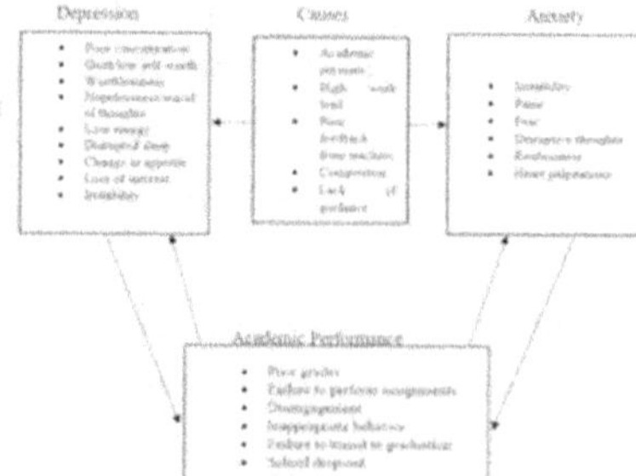

Source: (Author, 2024)

Way Forward

Psychological well-being of the college students' that may influence their academic success, hence transition to graduation. The risks posed by poor mental health could result in poor academic performance and other maladaptive behaviors. The students' psychological services need to be one of the key priorities in higher education institutions. There is need to establish vibrant psychological support services that can offer comprehensive mental health care to students.

CONCLUSION

A number of studies have identified depression and anxiety as the most common mental disorders experienced by university students. These two disorders affect students in many ways. Students with depression and anxiety have higher levels of absenteeism, thus affecting their academic performance. Depressive symptoms such as low energy and lack of concentration affect cognitive processes, including learning, retention and memory, and non -cognitive skills such as persistence and motivation needed in learning. On the other hand, academic failure may increase or worsen the risk of depression and anxiety. University students' mental health should be recognized as important for their academic success. The relationship between anxiety and academic performance is bidirectional, as students with increased anxiety may experience academic failure, while low levels of anxiety may improve performance. Universities should integrate mental health service provision and wellness resources into academic programs and have a sound mental health policy. This will improve student's academic performance and transition to graduation.

REFERENCES

Al-Qaisy, L. (2011). The relation of depression and anxiety in academic achievement among group of university students. *Int J Psychol Couns.*, 3(5), 96–100.

Aluh, D. O., Abba, A., & Afosi, A. B. (2020). Prevalence and correlates of depression, anxiety and stress among undergraduate pharmacy students in Nigeria. *Pharmacy Education*, 20, 236–248. DOI: 10.46542/pe.2020.201.236248

Alvi, T., Assad, F., Ramzan, M., & Khan, F. A. (2010). Depression, anxiety and their associated factors among medical students. *J Coll Physicians Surg Pak.; 20* (2):122–126. Doi: 02. *Journal of the College of Physicians and Surgeons—Pakistan*, •••, 122126.

American Psychiatric Association. (2013). *Diagnostic and statistical manual of mental disorders (DSM-5).* American Psychiatric Pub.

Aronen, E. T., Vuontella, V., Steenari. M. R., Salmi, J., and Carlson, S. (2004). Working memory, psychiatric symptoms, and academic performance at school. Neurobiology of Learning and Memory, *Elsivier. 8 3*(1) 33-42.

Bakhtyari, M. B., Mutamed, M., & Bena, A. (2020). Prevalence of depression among Afghan university students. *International Research Journal of Social Sciences*, 7(1), 16–21.

Bantjes, J., Saal, W., Gericke, F., Lochner, C., Roos, J., & Auerbach, R. P. (2020). Mental Health and Academic Failure among First-year University Students in South Africa. *South African Journal of Psychology. Suid-Afrikaanse Tydskrif vir Sielkunde*, •••, 51.

Bantjes, J. R., Kagee, A., McGowan, T., & Steel, H. (2016). Symptoms of posttraumatic stress, depression, and anxiety as predictors of suicidal ideation among South African university students. *Journal of American College Health*, 64(6), 429–437. DOI: 10.1080/07448481.2016.1178120 PMID: 27089470

Bernal-Morales, B., Rodríguez-Landa, J. F., Pulido-Criollo, F. (2015). Impact of Anxiety and Depression Symptoms on Scholar Performance in High School and University Students. A Fresh Look at Anxiety Disorders. .DOI: 10.5772/60711

Buchanan, J. L. (2012). Prevention of depression in the college student population: A review of the literature. *Archives of Psychiatric Nursing*, 26(1), 21–42. DOI: 10.1016/j.apnu.2011.03.003 PMID: 22284078

Cele, N. (2021). Big data-driven early alert systems as means of enhancing university student retention and success. *South African Journal of Higher Education*, 35(2), 56–72. DOI: 10.20853/35-2-3899

Eisenberg, D., Golberstein, E., & Hunt, J. B. (2009). Mental Health and Academic Success in College. *The B.E. Journal of Economic Analysis & Policy*, 9(1), 9. DOI: 10.2202/1935-1682.2191

Ericson, P. M., & Gardner, J. W. (1992). Two longitudinal studies of communication apprehension and its effects on college students' success. *Communication Quarterly*, 40(2), 127–137. DOI: 10.1080/01463379209369828

Hinck, M. (2017). Today is World Health Day – Let's Talk about Depression. Available on: https://jamaicahospital.org/newsletter/today-is-world-health-day-lets-talk-about-depression/

Hysenbegasi, A., Hass, S. L., & Rowland, C. R. (2005). The impact of depression on the academic productivity of university students. *The Journal of Mental Health Policy and Economics*, 8(3), 145–151. PMID: 16278502

Ibrahim, A., Kelly, S., Adams, C., & Glazebrook, C. (2013). A systematic review of studies of depression prevalence in university students. *Journal of Psychiatric Research*, 47(3), 391–400. DOI: 10.1016/j.jpsychires.2012.11.015 PMID: 23260171

Ibrahim, A., Kelly, S., & Glazebrook, C. (2013). Socioeconomic status and the risk of depression among UK higher education students. *Social Psychiatry and Psychiatric Epidemiology*, 48(9), 1491–1501. DOI: 10.1007/s00127-013-0663-5 PMID: 23412652

Iqbal, S., Gupta, S., & Venkatarao, E. (2015). Stress, anxiety &depression among medical undergraduate students &their socio-demographic correlates. *The Indian Journal of Medical Research*, 141(3), 354–357. DOI: 10.4103/0971-5916.156571 PMID: 25963497

Kessler, R. C. (2009). The Prevalence of Mental Illness. In: Teresa L, Scheid TN, Brown, editors. A Handbook for the Study of Mental Health. Second Edi. Cambridge: Cambridge University Press; pp. 1–736. DOI: 10.1017/CBO9780511984945.006

Krawchuk, L. L. (2008). *Procrastination, self-efficacy calibration, anxiety, and achievement in undergraduate students*. Unpublished master thesis. University of Alberta, Alberta.

Kumaraswamy, N. (2013). Academic stress, anxiety and depression among college students: A brief review. *Int Rev Soc Sci Humanit.*, 5(1), 135–143.

Liu, X.-Q., Guo, Y.-X., Zhang, W.-J., & Gao, W.-J. (2022). Influencing factors, prediction and prevention of depression in college students: A literature review. *World Journal of Psychiatry*, 12(7), 860–873. DOI: 10.5498/wjp.v12.i7.860 PMID: 36051603

McDonald, A. S. (2001). The prevalence and effects of test anxiety in school children. *Educational Psychology*, 21(1), 89–101. DOI: 10.1080/01443410020019867

Nyamwange, G., Otieno, R., & Okumu, S. (2023). Determination of the Prevalence of Depression among Students in Public Universities in Kenya: A Case of Kisii University. *Global Scientific Journal*, 11(8), 2896–2907.

Nyongesa, M. K. (2017). Depression in Kenya. Available on: https://www .globallyminded. org/home/depression-in-kenya/

Othieno, C. J., Okoth, R. O., Peltzer, K., Pengpid, S., Lucas, O., & Mallaf, L. O. (2014). Depression among university students in Kenya: Prevalence and sociodemographic correlates. *Journal of Affective Disorders*, 165, 120–125. DOI: 10.1016/j. jad.2014.04.070 PMID: 24882188

Pedrelli, P., Nyer, M., Yeung, A., Zulauf, C., & Wilens, T. (2015). College students: Mental health problems and treatment considerations. *Academic Psychiatry*, 39(5), 503–511. DOI: 10.1007/s40596-014-0205-9 PMID: 25142250

Rayelle, D. (2021). The Top Mental Health Challenges Facing Students. Available on: https:// www.bestcolleges.com/resources/top-5-mental-health-problems-facing -college-students/

Sarokhani, D., Delpisheh, A., Veisani, Y., Sarokhani, M., Manesh, R., & Sayehmiri, K. (2013). Prevalence of depression among university students: *A systematic review and meta-analysis study.Depression Research and Treatment*, 2013, 1–7. DOI: 10.1155/2013/373857 PMID: 24187615

Ssebunnya, J., Medhin, G., Kangere, S., Kigozi, F., Nakku, J., & Lund, C. (2019). Prevalence, correlates and help-seeking behaviour for depressive symptoms in rural Uganda: A population-based survey. *Global Mental Health (Cambridge, England)*, 6, E27. DOI: 10.1017/gmh.2019.25 PMID: 31807311

Treiman, D. J. (2007). Inequality and equality under Chinese socialism: The hukou system and intergenerational occupational mobility. *American Journal of Sociology*, 113(2), 415–445. DOI: 10.1086/518905

WHO (2017). Depression and Other Common Mental Disorder: Global Health Estimates

Wilson, D., Warton, C., & Louw, G. (1998). Stress, anxiety and academic performance among medical students at the University of Cape Town. *Southern African Journal of Child and Adolescent Mental Health*, 10(1), 23–31. DOI: 10.1080/16826108.1998.9632343

Youssef, J., & Deane, F. (2006). Factors influencing mental-health help-seeking in Arabic-speaking communities in Sydney, *Australia.Mental Health, Religion & Culture*, 9(1), 43–66. DOI: 10.1080/13674670512331335686

ADDITIONAL READING

Barman, L., Mukhopadhyay, D. K., & Bandyopadhyay, G. K. (2018). Use of social networking site and mental disorders among medical students in Kolkata, West Bengal. *Indian Journal of Psychiatry*, 60(3), 340–345. DOI: 10.4103/psychiatry.IndianJPsychiatry_210_18 PMID: 30405262

Bikwetti, D. A. (2021). *Perceived barriers and facilitators of mental health treatment-seeking among university students in Nairobi county*. A Thesis Submitted to United International University –Africa.

Hinksin Jr, K. D., Drake-Brooks, M. M., Christensen, K. L., Chatterley, M. D., Robinson, A. K., Crowell, S. E., ... & Bryan, C. J. (2022). An examination of the mental health and academic performance of student veterans. *journal of American College Health, 70*(8), 2334-2341.

Rindels, J. (2021). *Competition, Comparison, and Pressure to Perform: An Analysis of the Impact of the Advanced Placement Program on Suicidality among High Achieving Adolescent.s* (Doctoral dissertation, University of Iowa).

Rizvi, F., Qureshi, A., Rajput, A. M., & Afzal, M. (2015). Afzal m. prevalence of depression, anxiety and stress (by DASS scoring system) among medical students in Islamabad, Pakistan. *British Journal of Medicine and Medical Research*, 8(1), 69–75. DOI: 10.9734/BJMMR/2015/17193

KEY TERMS AND DEFINITIONS

Academic Outcomes: This is the overall achievement by students based on various assessment results based on knowledge, skills attitude and competencies acquired.

Academic Performance: This is the measurement of student achievement in various academic tasks based on standardized tests given or transition to graduation

Anxiety: This is intense and persistent worry about a situation that may cause one feel restless, sweat and have rapid heartbeat.

Depression: This a mood disorder that is characterized by feelings of sadness or loss of interest with both physical and emotional symptoms.

Function: This refers to operations expected of a person in order to fulfil particular purpose

Mental Health: This a state of wellbeing that enables an individual to cope with stresses of life, realize their abilities in order to function well in the society.

Prevalence: This refers to the proportion of a given population with a condition at a specific point in time

Symptoms: These are physical or mental features regarded as indicating a condition of a health problem that are apparent to the person suffering from the problem.

Transition: This is the shift in a student's life from one level to the next and is characterized by growth and maturity.

Compilation of References

16. (PDF) Academic integrity and artificial intelligence in higher education contexts: A rapid scoping review protocol. Available from: https://www.researchgate.net/publication/367636342_Academic_integrity_and_artificial_intelligence_in_higher_education_contexts_A_rapid_scoping_review_protocol [accessed Sep 15 2024].

Abdallah, A.K., & Alkaabi, A.M. (2023). Induction Programs' Effectiveness in Boosting New Teachers' Instruction and Student Achievement: A Critical Review. *International Journal of Learning, Teaching and Educational Research.*

Abdallah, M. Salah, M (2023). Artificial Intelligence and Intellectual Properties: Legal and Ethical Considerations. International Journal of Intelligent Systems and Applications in Engineering. file:///C:/Users/admin/Downloads/IJISAE_13_Mohammadabdallah_9_2020.pdf. Accessed on Thursday 11th July, 2024

Abdallah, A. K. (2023). Teacher-Led, Student-Focused, and Unleashing the Power of Teacher Empowerment for School Improvement and Success. In Abdallah, A., & Alkaabi, A. (Eds.), *Restructuring Leadership for School Improvement and Reform* (pp. 1–21). IGI Global., DOI: 10.4018/978-1-6684-7818-9.ch001

Abdallah, A. K., & Abdallah, R. K. (2023). Achieving Academic Excellence: The Intersection of Teacher Development, Quality Education, and Entrepreneurship. In Chakravarti, S. (Ed.), *Innovations in Teacher Development, Personalized Learning, and Upskilling the Workforce* (pp. 136–158). IGI Global., DOI: 10.4018/978-1-6684-5518-0.ch007

Abdallah, A. K., Al Kaabi, A. M., & Ramadan, R. S. (2023). The Critical Role of Principals in Leading Effective Inclusive Schools. In Efthymiou, E. (Ed.), *Inclusive Phygital Learning Approaches and Strategies for Students With Special Needs* (pp. 256–281). IGI Global., DOI: 10.4018/978-1-6684-8504-0.ch012

Abdallah, A., Ismail, O., Abdallah, R. K., & Alkaabi, A. M. (2023). Perceptions of Students About the Use of Webinars in Classrooms: A Case of Abu Dhabi University. [IJICTE]. *International Journal of Information and Communication Technology Education*, 19(1), 1–17. DOI: 10.4018/IJICTE.322793

Acar, A. S., & Polonsky, M. (2007). Online social networks and insights into marketing communications. *Journal of Internet Commerce*, 6(4), 55–72. DOI: 10.1080/15332860802086227

Acheck, T. A. (2014). Motivational strategies used by principals in the management of schools: The case of some selected secondary schools in the Fako Division of the Southwest Region of Cameroon. Unpublished MED Thesis, University of Jyväskylä. Retrieved from https://jyx.jyu.fi/bitstream/handle/123456789/47987/1/URN%3ANBN%3Afi%3 Ajyu-201512043909.pdf

Acosta-Enriquez, B. G., Arbulú Ballesteros, M. A., Arbulu Perez Vargas, C. G., Orellana Ulloa, M. N., Gutiérrez Ulloa, C. R., Pizarro Romero, J. M., Gutiérrez Jaramillo, N. D., Cuenca Orellana, H. U., Ayala Anzoátegui, D. X., & López Roca, C. (2024). Knowledge, attitudes, and perceived Ethics regarding the use of ChatGPT among generation Z university students. *International Journal for Educational Integrity*, 20(1), 10. DOI: 10.1007/s40979-024-00157-4

Adekoya, O. (2023). Exploring the impacts of transformational leadership on transformational teaching in higher education: Empirical evidence from Kuwait. In Manyane, M. A. K. U. A., & Mariam, A. K. I. N. L. O. L. U. (Eds.), *Sustaining Higher Education Through Resource Allocation, Learning Design Models, and Academic Development*. IGI Global., Available at https://shura.shu.ac.uk/32800/3/AdekoyaExploringTheImpacts%28AM%29.pdf

Adiguzel, T., Kaya, M. H., & Cansu, F. K. (2023). Revolutionizing education with AI: Exploring the transformative potential of ChatGPT. *Contemporary Educational Technology*, 15(3), ep429. https://doi.org/https://doi.org/10.30935/cedtech/13152. DOI: 10.30935/cedtech/13152

Ahmad, K., Iqbal, W., El-Hassan, A., Qadir, J., Benhaddou, D., Ayyash, M., & Al-Fuqaha, A. (2023). Data-driven artificial intelligence in education: A comprehensive review. *IEEE Transactions on Learning Technologies*.

Ahmed, B. E. S. (2020). Social media in teaching of languages. *International Journal of Emerging Technologies in Learning*, 15(12), 72-80. https://doi-org/DOI: 10.3991/ijet.v15i12.12645

AI-Youbi. A., Zahed, A. H., & Tierney, W. G. (2020). *Successful global collaborations in higher education institutions* (p. 93). Springer Nature.

Akçayır, G., & Akçayır, M. (2019). The flipped classroom: A review of its advantages and challenges. *Computers & Education*, 126, 334–345. DOI: 10.1016/j.compedu.2018.07.021

Akman, I., & Mishra, A. (2010). Gender, age and income differences in internet usage among employees in organizations. *Computers in Human Behavior*, 26(3), 482–490. DOI: 10.1016/j.chb.2009.12.007

Akungu, J. A. (2014). Influence of teaching and learning resources on students' performance in Kenya certificate of secondary education in free day secondary education in Embakasi Sub County, Kenya. Unpublished MED Research Project, University of Nairobi. Available at https://eap.uonbi.ac.ke/sites/default/files/cees/education/eap/REPORT%20D%20final.pdf

Alam, A. (2023). Harnessing the Power of AI to Create Intelligent Tutoring Systems for Enhanced Classroom Experience and Improved Learning Outcomes. In *Intelligent Communication Technologies and Virtual Mobile Networks* (pp. 571–591). Springer. DOI: 10.1007/978-981-99-1767-9_42

Aldiab, A., Chowdhury, H., Kootsookos, A., Alam, F., & Allhibi, H. (2019). Utilization of Learning Management Systems (LMSs) in higher education system: A case review for Saudi Arabia. *Energy Procedia*, 160, 731–737. DOI: 10.1016/j.egypro.2019.02.186

Al-Dowayan, H. A., & Al-Saeed, H. A. (2022). The Reality of Organizational Silence among Faculty Members at Qassim University and its Relationship to Some Variables. *International Journal of Educational and Psychological Studies*, 11(3), 601–623. DOI: 10.31559/EPS2022.11.3.8

Alenezi, M., Wardat, S., & Akour, M. (2023). The need of integrating digital education in higher education: Challenges and opportunities. *Sustainability (Basel)*, 15(6), 4782. DOI: 10.3390/su15064782

Alessio, H. M., Malay, N. J., Maurer, K., Bailer, A. J., & Rubin, B. (2017). Examining the Effect of Proctoring on Online Test Scores. *Online Learning : the Official Journal of the Online Learning Consortium*, 21(1), 146–161. DOI: 10.24059/olj.v21i1.885

AlGerafi, M. A., Zhou, Y., Oubibi, M., & Wijaya, T. T. (2023). Unlocking the potential: A comprehensive evaluation of augmented reality and virtual reality in education. *Electronics (Basel)*, 12(18), 3953. DOI: 10.3390/electronics12183953

Al-Jabari, B., & Ghazzawi, I. (2019). Organizational commitment: A review of the conceptual and empirical literature and a research agenda. *International Leadership Journal (ILJ), 11*(1), 78-119. Available at https://www.researchgate.net/publication/331635975_Organizational_CommitmentA_Review_of_the_Conceptual_and_Empirical_Literature_and_a_Research_Agenda/link /5c901e1a92851c1df94a5a45/download

Ally, M. (2008). The Impact of Technology on Education. In *Education for a Digital World* (pp. 57–66). Advice, Guidelines and Effective Practice from Around the Globe.

Ally, M. (2009). *Mobile learning: Transforming the delivery of education and training*. Athabasca University Press. DOI: 10.15215/aupress/9781897425435.01

Almekhled, B., & Petrie, H. (2023). Concerns of Saudi Higher Education Students About Security and Privacy of Online Digital Technologies During the Coronavirus Pandemic. In Abdelnour Nocera, J., Kristín Lárusdóttir, M., Petrie, H., Piccinno, A., & Winckler, M. (Eds.), Lecture Notes in Computer Science: Vol. 14144. *Human-Computer Interaction – INTERACT 2023*. Springer., DOI: 10.1007/978-3-031-42286-7_27

Almufareh, M. F., Tehsin, S., Humayun, M., & Kausar, S. (2023). Intellectual disability and technology: An artificial intelligence perspective and framework. *Journal of Disability Research*, 2(4), 58–70. DOI: 10.57197/JDR-2023-0055

Almusaed, A., Almssad, A., Yitmen, I., & Homod, R. Z. (2023). Enhancing student engagement: Harnessing "AIED"'s power in hybrid education—A review analysis. *Education Sciences*, 13(7), 632. DOI: 10.3390/educsci13070632

Al-Qaisy, L. (2011). The relation of depression and anxiety in academic achievement among group of university students. *Int J Psychol Couns.*, 3(5), 96–100.

Aluh, D. O., Abba, A., & Afosi, A. B. (2020). Prevalence and correlates of depression, anxiety and stress among undergraduate pharmacy students in Nigeria. *Pharmacy Education*, 20, 236–248. DOI: 10.46542/pe.2020.201.236248

Aluko, R. (2022). Faculty development for digital transformation in ODEL environments. *Journal of Distance Education*, 34(2), 45–60.

Alvi, T., Assad, F., Ramzan, M., & Khan, F. A. (2010). Depression, anxiety and their associated factors among medical students. *J Coll Physicians Surg Pak.; 20* (2):122–126. Doi: 02. *Journal of the College of Physicians and Surgeons—Pakistan*, •••, 122126.

Amemado, D. (2020). *COVID-19: An unexpected and unusual driver to online education. International higher education*. The Boston College Center for International Higher Education.

American Psychiatric Association. (2013). *Diagnostic and statistical manual of mental disorders (DSM-5)*. American Psychiatric Pub.

Amer-Yahia, S. (2022). Towards AI-powered data-driven education. *Proceedings of the VLDB Endowment International Conference on Very Large Data Bases*, 15(12), 3798–3806. DOI: 10.14778/3554821.3554900

Amey, M. J., & Eddy, P. L. (2023). *Creating strategic partnerships: A guide for educational institutions and their partners*. Taylor & Francis.

Anantrasirichai, N., & Bull, D. (2022). Artificial intelligence in the creative industries: A review. *Artificial Intelligence Review*, 55(1), 589–656. DOI: 10.1007/s10462-021-10039-7

Annuš, N. (2024). Education in the Age of Artificial Intelligence. *TEM Journal. 13(1) 404-413*, ISSN 2217-8309, DOI: DOI: 10.18421/TEM131-42

Annuš, N. (2023). Chatbots in Education: The impact of Artificial Intelligence based ChatGPT on Teachers and Students. *International Journal of Advanced Natural Sciences and Engineering Researches*, 7(4), 366–370. DOI: 10.59287/ijanser.739

Anyoha, R. (2017). *The History of Artificial Intelligence*. [Online] Available at: https://sitn.hms.harvard.edu/flash/2017/history-artificial-intelligence/

Aoki, K., & Pogorzelski, S. (2020). Correspondence education and the rise of distance learning. *Journal of Educational Technology*, 58(1), 45–61.

Arbab, A. M. (2019). How Leadership and Mentoring Enhance the Quality of Teaching and Learning in Higher Education. *International Journal of Learning and Development*, 9(1), 57–72. DOI: 10.5296/ijld.v9i1.13814

Arbesman, S. (2013). *The half-life of facts: Why everything we know has an expiration date*. Penguin.

Arif, S., & Akram, A. (2018). Transformational leadership and organizational performance: The mediating role of organizational innovation. *SEISENSE Journal of Management*, 1(3), 60–75. https://journal.seisense.com/index.php/jom/issue/view/3. DOI: 10.33215/sjom.v1i3.28

Arnold, K. E. (2010). Signals: Applying academic analytics. *EDUCAUSE Quarterly*, 33(1).

Arntz, M., Gregory, T., & Zierahn, U. (2016), *The Risk of Automation for Jobs in OECD Countries: A Comparative Analysis.* OECD Social, Employment and Migration Working Papers, No. 189, OECD Publishing, Paris.

Aronen, E. T., Vuontella, V., Steenari. M. R., Salmi, J., and Carlson, S. (2004). Working memory, psychiatric symptoms, and academic performance at school. Neurobiology of Learning and Memory, *Elsivier. 8 3*(1) 33-42.

Ashari, M. A., Zainal, I. A., & Zaki, F. M. (2020). Strategies for radiology departments in handling the COVID-19 pandemic. *Diagnostic and Interventional Radiology (Ankara, Turkey)*, 26(4), 296–300. DOI: 10.5152/dir.2020.20232

Astuti, F. S., & Retnawati, H. (2022). Online Learning Assessment: Solution in Industrial Revolution 4.0. *Advances in Social Science, Education and Humanities Research*. Advance online publication. DOI: 10.2991/assehr.k.220129.064

Atalay, D., Akcil, U., & Ozkul, A. E. (2019). Effects of transformational and instructional leadership on organizational silence and attractiveness and their importance for the sustainability of educational institutions. doi: https://doi.org/. Available at www.mdpi.com/journal/sustainabilityDOI: 10.3390/su11205618

Awasthy, R., Flint, S., Sankarnarayana, R., & Jones, R. L. (2020). A framework to improve university–industry collaboration. *Journal of Industry-University Collaboration*, 2(1), 49–62. DOI: 10.1108/JIUC-09-2019-0016

Aytaç, Z. (2024). Using Artificial Intelligence Tools in Higher Education. In *Innovation in the University 4.0 System based on Smart Technologies* (pp. 164–175). Chapman and Hall/CRC. DOI: 10.1201/9781003425809-11

Bae, S., & Lee, T. (2011). Gender differences in consumers' perception of online consumer reviews. *Electronic Commerce Research*, 11(2), 201–214. DOI: 10.1007/s10660-010-9072-y

Bahroun, Z., Anane, C., Ahmed, V., & Zacca, A. (2023). Transforming education: A comprehensive review of generative artificial intelligence in educational settings through bibliometric and content analysis. *Sustainability (Basel)*, 15(17), 12983. DOI: 10.3390/su151712983

Baker, R. S., Esbenshade, L., Vitale, J., & Karumbaiah, S. (2022). Using demographic data as predictor variables: A questionable choice. https://doi.org/DOI: 10.35542/osf.io/y4wvj

Bakhtyari, M. B., Mutamed, M., & Bena, A. (2020). Prevalence of depression among Afghan university students. *International Research Journal of Social Sciences*, 7(1), 16–21.

Balyer, A., & Oz, O. (2018). *Academicians' views on digital transformation in education*. International Online.

Bantjes, J. R., Kagee, A., McGowan, T., & Steel, H. (2016). Symptoms of posttraumatic stress, depression, and anxiety as predictors of suicidal ideation among South African university students. *Journal of American College Health*, 64(6), 429–437. DOI: 10.1080/07448481.2016.1178120 PMID: 27089470

Bantjes, J., Saal, W., Gericke, F., Lochner, C., Roos, J., & Auerbach, R. P. (2020). Mental Health and Academic Failure among First-year University Students in South Africa. *South African Journal of Psychology. Suid-Afrikaanse Tydskrif vir Sielkunde*, •••, 51.

Barasa, P. L. (2021). Digitalization in teaching and education in Kenya: Digitalization, the future of work and the teaching profession project. International Labour Organization.https://scholar.google.com/citations?

Barber, W., King, S., & Buchanan, S. (2020). Flexible learning in higher education: The integration of e-learning and traditional approaches. *Journal of Educational Technology*, 56(4), 231–245.

Barbieri, B., Sulis, I., Porcu, M., & Toland, M.D. (2019). Italian teachers' well-being within the high school context: Evidence from a large scale survey. *Frontiers in Psychology Journal*, 1-13. doi: https://doi.org/DOI: 10.3389/fpsyg.2019.01926

Barnett, S. M., & Ceci, S. J. (2002). When and Where Do We Apply What We Learn? A Taxonomy for Far Transfer. *Review of Research in Education*, 24, 61–100.

Bass, B. M., & Riggio, R. E. (2008). *Transformational leadership*. Lawrence Erlbaum Associates, Inc.

Bassett, R. M. (2020). *Sustaining the values of tertiary education during the COVID-19 crisis*. The Boston College Center for International Higher Education.

Bates, A. W. (2019). Teaching in a digital age. Teaching in a Digital Age. https://pressbooks.bccampus.ca/teachinginadigitalagev2/

Bawuro, F. A., Danjuma, I., & Wajiga, H. (2018). Factors influencing innovative behaviour of teachers in secondary schools in the North East of Nigeria. *Traektoriâ Nauki Journal, 4*(3),1007-1017. . Available at https://doaj.org/article/9513913668524c64affe659ef758dff6DOI: 10.22178/pos.32-9

BBC. (2024).How AI is testing the boundaries of human intelligence. https://www.bbc.com/future/article/20240501-how-ai-is-testing-the-boundaries-of-human-intelligence. Accessed on Sunday 7th July, 2024

Bensinger, G. (2023). ChatGPT-written ebooks thrive on Amazon. https://www.thedailystar.net/daily-star-books/news/chatgpt-written-ebooks-thrive-amazon-3255536. Accessed on Sunday 7th July, 2024

Bergmann, J., & Sams, A. (2012). *Flip Your Classroom: Reach Every Student in Every Class Every Day*. International Society for Technology in Education.

Bernal-Morales, B., Rodríguez-Landa, J. F., Pulido-Criollo, F. (2015). Impact of Anxiety and Depression Symptoms on Scholar Performance in High School and University Students. A Fresh Look at Anxiety Disorders. .DOI: 10.5772/60711

Bernhold, Q. S., & Rice, R. (2020). Toward an integrated model of online communication attitudes, communication frequency, and relational closeness. *Communication Studies*, 71(1), 1–21. DOI: 10.1080/10510974.2019.1683594

Best, S. J., Krueger, B., Hubbard, C., & Smith, A. (2001). An assessment of the generalizability of Internet surveys. *Social Science Computer Review*, 19(2), 131–145. DOI: 10.1177/089443930101900201

Bialik, M., & Fadel, C. (2015). *Meta-Learning for the 21st Century: What Should Students Learn?* Center for Curriculum Redesign.

Black, E. W., Greaser, J., & Dawson, K. (2008). Academic Dishonesty in Traditional and Online Classrooms: Does the "Media Equation" Hold True? *Online Learning : the Official Journal of the Online Learning Consortium*, 12(3), 23–30. DOI: 10.24059/olj.v12i3.13

Black, P., & Wiliam, D. (1998). Assessment and Classroom Learning. *Assessment in Education: Principles, Policy & Practice*, 5(1), 7–74. DOI: 10.1080/0969595980050102

Bond, M., Marín, V. I., Dolch, C., Bedenlier, S., & Zawacki-Richter, O. (2018). Digital transformation in German higher education: Student and teacher perceptions and usage of digital media. *International Journal of Educational Technology in Higher Education*, 15(1), 48. DOI: 10.1186/s41239-018-0130-1

Booc, N. B., Sobremisana, K., Ybañez, A., Tolosa, R., Ladroma, S., & Caparoso, K. (2023). Artificial intelligence-powered calculator application usage in mathematics summative assessments. *Iconic Res. Eng. J*, 6(10), 446–474.

Børte, K., Nesje, K., & Lillejord, S. (2023). Barriers to student active learning in higher education. *Teaching in Higher Education*, 28(3), 597–615. DOI: 10.1080/13562517.2020.1839746

Borthwick, A. C., Anderson, C. L., Finsness, E. S., & Foulger, T. S. (2015). Special article personal wearable technologies in education: Value or villain? *Journal of Digital Learning in Teacher Education*, 31(3), 85–92. DOI: 10.1080/21532974.2015.1021982

Boruah, J. (2020). School as a Social System – A Study. International Research Journal of Education and Technology, 1(2), 26-28. Available at https://www.irjweb .com/7.pdf

Bower, M., Lee, M. J., & Dalgarno, B. (2017). Collaborative learning across physical and virtual worlds: Factors supporting and constraining learners in a blended reality environment. *British Journal of Educational Technology*, 48(2), 407–430. DOI: 10.1111/bjet.12435

Boyle, B. (2017). Virtual Reality and Augmented Reality in Education. Retrieved from https://www.westpoint.edu/sites/default/files/inlineimages/centers_research/ center_for_teching excellence/PDFs/mtp_project_papers/Boyle s_17.pdf

Bozkurt, A., & Sharma, R. C. (2020). Emergency remote teaching in a time of global crisis due to the CoronaVirus pandemic. *Asian Journal of Distance Education*, 15(1), 1–6.

Brennan, L., Binney, W., Parker, L., Aleti, T., & Nguy n, Đ. (2014). *Social Marketing and Behaviour Change: Models*. Theory and Applications., DOI: 10.4337/9781782548157

Brown, T. B. (2020). Language models are few-shot learners. *arXiv preprint arXiv:2005.14165.*

Brown, J. S., Collins, A., & Duguid, P. (1989). Situated Cognition and the Culture of Learning. *Educational Researcher*, 18(1), 32–42. DOI: 10.3102/0013189X018001032

Buchanan, J. L. (2012). Prevention of depression in the college student population: A review of the literature. *Archives of Psychiatric Nursing*, 26(1), 21–42. DOI: 10.1016/j.apnu.2011.03.003 PMID: 22284078

Bueno, D. C. (2019). School Finance and Physical Resources Management Module. doi: https://dx.doi.org/ Available at https://www.researchgate.net/publication/ 333547195_School_Finance_and_Physical_ResourcesManagementDOI: 10.13140/ RG.2.2.20729.72809

Bush, T. (2018). Transformational leadership: Exploring common conceptions. [EMAL]. *Educational Management Administration & Leadership*, 46(6), 883–887. DOI: 10.1177/1741143218795731

Butcher, N., Hoosen, S., & Moore, D. (2020). The impact of AI on ODEL systems: Case studies from South Africa. *Journal of Technology Enhanced Learning*, 12(3), 67–84.

Butson, R., & Spronken-Smith, R. (2024). AI and its implications for research in higher education: A critical dialogue. *Higher Education Research & Development*, 43(3), 563–577. DOI: 10.1080/07294360.2023.2280200

Cabaleiro-Cerviño, G., & Vera, C. (2020). The Impact of Educational Technologies in Higher Education. GIST – Education and Learning Research Journal, 20, 155-169. https://doi.org/DOI: 10.26817/16925777.711

Cai, Z., Fan, X., & Du, J. (2017). Gender and attitudes toward technology use: A meta-analysis. *Computers & Education*, 105, 1–13. DOI: 10.1016/j.compedu.2016.11.003

Caldwel, K. (2023). AI And Intellectual Property: Who Owns It, And What Does This Mean For The Future? Forbes Magazine. https://www.forbes.com/sites/forbesbusinesscouncil/2023/10/31/ai-and-intellectual-property-who-owns-it-and-what-does-this-mean-for-the-future/. Accessed on Thursday 11th July, 2024

Camilleri, M. A., & Camilleri, A. C. (2017). Digital learning resources and ubiquitous technologies in education. Technology, Knowledge and Learning, 22.

Campbell, T. R. (2020). Relationship Between Transformational Leadership Style and Financial Sustainability. PhD Dissertation of Walden University. Available at https://scholarworks.waldenu.edu/cgi/viewcontent.cgi?article=10975&context=dissert ations

Cardona, A. M., Roberto, J. R., & Ishmael, K. (2023). Artificial Intelligence and the Future of Teaching and Learning. Office of Education Technology. https://www2.ed.gov/documents/ai-report/ai-report.pdf. Accessed on Sunday 8th July, 2024

Carrington, S., Park, E., Mckay, L., Saggers, B., Harper-Hill, K., & Somerwil, T. (2024). Evidence of transformative leadership for inclusive practice. *Teaching and Teacher Education*, 141, 104466. https://www.sciencedirect.com/science/article/pii/S0742051X23004547. DOI: 10.1016/j.tate.2023.104466

Cele, N. (2021). Big data-driven early alert systems as means of enhancing university student retention and success. *South African Journal of Higher Education*, 35(2), 56–72. DOI: 10.20853/35-2-3899

Celik, I., Dindar, M., Muukkonen, H., & Järvelä, S. (2022). The promises and challenges of artificial intelligence for teachers: A systematic review of research. *TechTrends*, 66(4), 616–630. DOI: 10.1007/s11528-022-00715-y

Chai, C., Wu, X., Shen, D., Li, D., & Zhang, K. (2016). Gender differences in the effect of communication on college students' online decisions. *Computers in Human Behavior*, 65, 176–188. DOI: 10.1016/j.chb.2016.07.012

Chakravarti, M. (2020). Flexibility and learner-centeredness in open distance learning. *Open Learning Journal*, 34(4), 251–264.

Chang, B. (2021). Student privacy issues in online learning environments. *Distance Education*, 42(1), 55–69. DOI: 10.1080/01587919.2020.1869527

Chang, Bo. (2020). *Privacy Issues in Online Learning Environment*. American Association for Adult and Continuing Education.

Chan, K. S., & Nabil, Z. (2019). Applications and Challenges of Implementing Artificial Intelligence in Medical Education: Integrative. *JMIR Medical Education*, 5(1), e13930. https://preprints.jmir.org/preprint/13930. DOI: 10.2196/13930

Chase, A., Ross, B., & Robbie, D. (2017). Improving Digital Assessment Practice: A Case Study of a Cross- Institutional Initiative. *Journal of University Teaching &amp. Journal of University Teaching & Learning Practice*, 14(2). Advance online publication. DOI: 10.53761/1.14.2.5

Chassignol, M., Khoroshavin, A., Klimova, A., & Bilyatdinova, A. (2018). Artificial Intelligence trends in education: A narrative overview. *Procedia Computer Science*, 136, 16–24. DOI: 10.1016/j.procs.2018.08.233

Cheaney, J. D., & Ingebritsen, T. S. (2006). Problem-based learning in an online course: A case study. *International Review of Research in Open and Distance Learning*, 6(3). Advance online publication. DOI: 10.19173/irrodl.v6i3.267

Chee, K. N., & Sanmugam, M. (2023). *Embracing Cutting-edge Technology in Modern Educational Settings*. IGI Global.

Chen, B., Knight, S., Wise, A., & Cheng, J. (2018). Critical issues in designing and implementing temporal analytics. *Journal of Computing in Higher Education*, 30(1), 27–47.

Chen, L., Chen, P., & Lin, Z. (2020). Artificial intelligence in education: A review. *IEEE Access : Practical Innovations, Open Solutions*, 8, 75264–75278. DOI: 10.1109/ACCESS.2020.2988510

Chen, X., Xie, H., Zou, D., & Hwang, G. (2020). Application and theory gaps during the rise of Artificial Intelligence in Education. *Computers and Education: Artificial Intelligence*, 1, 100002. DOI: 10.1016/j.caeai.2020.100002

Chikafalimani, S. H. P., Kibwami, N., & Moyo, S. (2021). Management of facilities at public universities in Africa: Current challenges and the way forward. *Real Estate Management and Valuation*, 29(1), 21–29. DOI: 10.2478/remav-2021-0003

Chiu, Y.-B., Lin, C.-P., & Tang, L.-L. (2005). Gender differs: Assessing a model of online purchase intentions in e-tail service. *International Journal of Service Industry Management*, 16(5), 416–435. DOI: 10.1108/09564230510625741

Choi, E. Y., Kim, Y., Chipalo, E., & Lee, H. Y. (2020a). Does ageism widen the digital divide? And does it vary by gender? *Innovation in Aging*, 4(Supplement_1), 315–315. DOI: 10.1093/geroni/igaa057.1007 PMID: 32539099

Choi, E. Y., Kim, Y., Chipalo, E., & Lee, H. Y. (2020b). Does perceived ageism widen the digital divide? And does it vary by gender? *The Gerontologist*, 60(7), 1213–1223. DOI: 10.1093/geront/gnaa066 PMID: 32539099

Christman, G. (2024). Transformation and Collaboration in Organizational Leadership. Hunter International. Available at https://www.hirecruiting.com/transformation-and-collaboration-in-organizational-leadership

Chung, J. E., Park, N., Wang, H., Fulk, J., & McLaughlin, M. (2010). Age differences in perceptions of online community participation among non-users: An extension of the Technology Acceptance Model. *Computers in Human Behavior*, 26(6), 1674–1684. DOI: 10.1016/j.chb.2010.06.016

Chystaya, Y., Poyade, M., Rea, P. M., & McCorry, O. (2022). Application of AR and 3D technology for learning neuroanatomy. In *Medical Visualization and Applications of Technology* (pp. 147–180). Springer. DOI: 10.1007/978-3-031-06735-8_5

Cimpian, A., & Salomon, E. (2014). The inherence heuristic: An intuitive means of making sense of the world, and a potential precursor to psychological essentialism. *Behavioral and Brain Sciences*, 37(5), 461–480. DOI: 10.1017/S0140525X13002197

CITRIS-uc.org. (2024). CITRIS and Intel collaborate to enhance semiconductor training opportunities for UC undergraduates. Retrieved from: < https://citris-uc.org/citris-and-intel-collaborate-to-enhance-semiconductor-training-opportunities-for-uc-undergraduates/ >. Accessed on 10th July 2024.

Claus, S. (2024). The Teacher Learning Centre. https://tlc.ucsc.edu/resources/artificial-intelligence-in-teaching-learning/. Accessed on Wednesday 10th July, 2024

Clayton, P. H., Bringle, R. G., & Hatcher, J. A. (Eds.). (2023). *Research on Service Learning: Conceptual Frameworks and Assessments: Volume 2B: Communities, Institutions, and Partnerships*. Taylor & Francis.

Cleveland, B. W. (2011). Engaging Spaces: Innovative Learning Environments, Pedagogies, and Student Engagement in the Middle Years of School. In *Unpublished Ph.D. Thesis*. Faculty of Architecture, Building and Planning, the University of Melbourne., https://pdfs.semanticscholar.org/e602

Colchester, K., Hagras, H., Alghazzawi, D., & Aldabbagh, G. (2017). A survey of artificial intelligence techniques employed for adaptive educational systems within e-learning platforms. *Journal of Artificial Intelligence and Soft Computing Research*, 7(1), 47–64. DOI: 10.1515/jaiscr-2017-0004

Collins, D. (2023). Driving Innovation through Collaborative Partnerships: The Power of University-Industry Collaboration. Retrieved from: < https://www.linkedin .com/pulse/driving-innovation-through-collaborative-partnerships-collins-phd>. Accessed on 8th July 2024.

Crawford, J., Allen, K. A., Pani, B., & Cowling, M. (2024). When artificial intelligence substitutes humans in higher education: The cost of loneliness, student success, and retention. *Studies in Higher Education*, 49(5), 883–897. DOI: 10.1080/03075079.2024.2326956

Crawford, J., Cowling, M., Ashton-Hay, S., Kelder, J. A., Middleton, R., & Wilson, G. S. (2023). Artificial Intelligence and authorship editor policy: ChatGPT, Bard Bing AI, and beyond. *Journal of University Teaching & Learning Practice*, 20(5), 1. DOI: 10.53761/1.20.01.01

Crevier, D. (1993). *AI: the tumultuous history of the search for artificial intelligence*. Basic Books, Inc.

Crompton, H., & Burke, D. (2018). The use of mobile learning in higher education: A systematic review. *Computers & Education*, 123, 53–64. DOI: 10.1016/j.compedu.2018.04.007

Czerniewicz, L., Deacon, A., & Walji, S. (2019). Using learning analytics to support ODEL in higher education: The University of Cape Town experience. *International Journal of Learning Analytics and Artificial Intelligence for Education*, 1(1), 14–28.

Czerniewicz, L., Trotter, H., & Haupt, G. (2020). Critical reflections on global and local equity in online and blended learning. *Learning, Media and Technology*, 45(2), 148–162.

Da'ar, R. (2019). Teachers' skill flexibility: Examining the impact of principals' skills and teachers' participation in decision making during educational reform. *International Journal of Educational Management*, 33(2), 287–299. DOI: 10.1108/IJEM-12-2017-0382

Dahal, B. (2024). Academic Integrity in Nepal. In *Second Handbook of Academic Integrity* (pp. 95–115). Springer Nature Switzerland. DOI: 10.1007/978-3-031-54144-5_192

Daniel, J. (2020). Open and distance learning: Expanding educational opportunities in the 21st century. *International Journal of Educational Technology*, 18(2), 88–98.

Davis, F. D. (1989). Perceived usefulness, perceived ease of use, and user acceptance of information technology. *Management Information Systems Quarterly*, 13(3), 319–340. DOI: 10.2307/249008

Dawson, S., Poquet, O., Colvin, C., Rogers, T., Pardo, A., & Gasevic, D. (2018). *Rethinking learning analytics adoption through complexity leadership theory*. ACM., DOI: 10.1145/3170358.3170375

Day, C., & Sammons, P. (2013). Successful leadership: A review of the international literature. Available at https://files.eric.ed.gov/fulltext/ED546806.pdf

Delen, D. (2010). A comparative analysis of machine learning techniques for student retention management. *Decision Support Systems*, 49(4), 498–506. DOI: 10.1016/j.dss.2010.06.003

Delfino, J. (2023). AI-driven Research and Development: A paradigm shift in innovation. https://www.rdworldonline.com/ai-driven-research-and-development-a-paradigm-shift-in-innovation/. Accessed on Sunday 7th July, 2024

Demuyakor, J. (2020). Coronavirus (COVID-19) and online learning in higher institutions of education: A survey of the perceptions of Ghanaian international students in China. *Online Journal of Communication and Media Technologies*, 10(3), e202018. DOI: 10.29333/ojcmt/8286

Dennen, V. P., Burner, K. J., & Cates, M. L. (2018). Information and Communication Technologies, and Learning Theories: Putting Pedagogy into Practice. In Voogt, J., Knezek, G., Christensen, R., & Lai, K. W. (Eds.), *Second Handbook of Information Technology in Primary and Secondary Education. Springer International Handbooks of Education*. Springer., DOI: 10.1007/978-3-319-71054-9_9

Deterding, S., Dixon, D., Khaled, R., & Nacke, L. (2011). From game design elements to gamefulness: defining" gamification". In *Proceedings of the 15th international academic MindTrek conference: Envisioning future media environments*. DOI: 10.1145/2181037.2181040

Dhawan, S. (2020). Online learning: A panacea in the time of COVID-19 crisis. *Journal of Educational Technology Systems*, 49(1), 5–22. DOI: 10.1177/0047239520934018

Dhruv, A., Saha, S., Tyagi, S., & Jain, V. (2024, May). Investigating the Transformative Impact of Generative AI on Academic Integrity Across Diverse Educational Domains. In 2024 2nd International Conference on Advancement in Computation & Computer Technologies (InCACCT) (pp. 87-92). IEEE. DOI: 10.1109/InCACCT61598.2024.10551108

Didinya, E., Ouda, J. B., & Ndanu, C. (2018). Effect of Performance Appraisal of Teachers on Academic Performance of Students in Public Secondary Schools in Hamisi Sub-County, Vihiga County, Kenya. [JOPEA]. *Journal of Popular Education in Africa*, 2(5), 92–106.

Dirican, C. (2015). The impacts of robotics, artificial intelligence on business and economics. *Procedia: Social and Behavioral Sciences*, 195, 564–573. DOI: 10.1016/j.sbspro.2015.06.134

Dube, L. (2021). Challenges in the implementation of online learning in South Africa. *Journal of Educational Technology & Society*, 24(3), 15–25.

Duku, N., Makeleni, S., Mavuso, M. P., & Mkhomi, M. S. (2020). Experiences of B. Ed Students on the use of E-Learning as a Vehicle to Learning during the COVID-19 Pandemic. *Education*, 16(7).

Dutta, S. Bruno, L (2023). Network Readiness Index 2023. Portulans Institute. Accessed on Thursday 11th July, 2024

Dutta, S., Ranjan, S., Mishra, S., Sharma, V., Hewage, P., & Iwendi, C. (2024). Enhancing Educational Adaptability: A Review and Analysis of AI-Driven Adaptive Learning Platforms. 2024 4th International Conference on Innovative Practices in Technology and Management (ICIPTM)

Eckman, A., Fisher, K., & Stifter, T. (2014). The prevalence of gender communication in social media. *Concordia Journal of Communication Research*, 1. Advance online publication. DOI: 10.54416/DPMP5974

Egozi, O., Markovitch, S., & Gabrilovich, E. (2011). Concept-based information retrieval using explicit semantic analysis. [TOIS]. *ACM Transactions on Information Systems*, 29(2), 1–34. DOI: 10.1145/1961209.1961211

Eisenberg, D., Golberstein, E., & Hunt, J. B. (2009). Mental Health and Academic Success in College. *The B.E. Journal of Economic Analysis & Policy*, 9(1), 9. DOI: 10.2202/1935-1682.2191

Ejuchegahi, A. A. (2024). A Review of Blended Learning after the COVID-19 Pandemic. *International Review of Education*, 12(1), 86–101. DOI: 10.5296/ire.v12i1.21849

Elena, fleacă. (2017)study on Embedding digital teaching and learning practices in the modernization ofnhigher education institutions. *International multidisciplinary scientific geoconference* ; sofia, vol. 17, (2017). Doi:DOI: 10.5593/sgem2017/54

ELWa. (2003). *The context to an e-learning strategy for Wales*. Cardiff: National Council of Education and Training for Wales (ELWa).

Englebart, D. C. (1962). Augmenting human intellect: A conceptual framework. SRI Summary Report AFOSR3223. https://www.dougengelbart.org/pubs/augment-3906.htm

Ericson, P. M., & Gardner, J. W. (1992). Two longitudinal studies of communication apprehension and its effects on college students' success. *Communication Quarterly*, 40(2), 127–137. DOI: 10.1080/01463379209369828

Espinoza, J. (2023). Navigating Choppy Waters: Transformational Leadership and Graduate Education Amid Economic Strife. Available at https://www.linkedin.com/pulse/navigating-choppy-waters-transformational- leadership-amid-espinoza-zexmf

Eynon, R., Helsper, E. J., & Prinsloo, P. (2019). Not yet equal: The digital knowledge gap between poor and affluent students and how it is changing. In *The Digital Knowledge Gap* (pp. 1–19). Emerald Publishing Limited.

Fabre, A., & Straub, S. (2023). The impact of public–private partnerships (PPPs) in infrastructure, health, and education. *Journal of Economic Literature*, 61(2), 655–715. DOI: 10.1257/jel.20211607

Faig, E. Z. (2024). Strategies for Transformative Leadership in Educational Settings: Realizing Effective Implementation Goals. *International Journal of Innovative Technologies in Social Science*, 1(41). Advance online publication. DOI: 10.31435/rsglobalijitss/30032024/8102

Fan, L. P. (2011). Gender Differences in E-Mail Communication. *Advanced Materials Research*, 225–226, 346–349. DOI: 10.4028/www.scientific.net/amr.225-226.346

Farayola, O. A., Hassan, A. O., Adaramodu, O. R., Fakeyede, O. G., & Oladeinde, M. (2023). Configuration management in the modern era: Best practices, innovations, and challenges. *Computer Science & IT Research Journal*, 4(2), 140–157. DOI: 10.51594/csitrj.v4i2.613

Farrell, G. (2007) ICTs in Education in Kenya: Survey of ICT and Education in Africa. Kenya Country Report for World Bank, Garrison, D. R., & Anderson, T. (2003). *E-learning in the 21st century: A framework for research and practice*. Routledge.

Fernandez, S. M., & Ghorpade, N. L. (2023). Role of Transformational Leadership on Innovation in Higher Education: a Review of Literature. https://www.researchgate.net/publication/372474412_ROLE_OF_TRANSFORMATI ONAL_LEADERSHIP_ON_INNOVATION_IN_HIGHER_EDUCATION_A_REVI EW_OF_LITERATURE/link/64b8ddac8de7ed28baadb1a9/download?_tp=eyJjb250Z Xh0Ijp7ImZpcnN0UGFnZSI6InB1YmxpY2F0aW9uIiwicGFnZSI6InB1YmxpY2F0aW9uIn19

Fitria, T. N. (2021). Artificial Intelligence (Ai) In Education: Using Ai Tools For Teaching And Learning Processes. Proceeding Seminar Nasional & Call For Papers ISSN Online: 2654-6590 I ISSN Cetak: 2654-5306. file:///C:/Users/admin/Downloads/106-ArticleText-199-1-10-20211225.pdf. Accessed on Sunday 29th September, 2024

Floridi, L., & Taddeo, M. (2016). What is Data Ethics? *Philosophical Transactions. Series A, Mathematical, Physical, and Engineering Sciences*, 374(2083), 20160360. DOI: 10.1098/rsta.2016.0360

Fogel, D. B. (2022). Defining artificial intelligence. *Machine Learning and the City: Applications in Architecture and Urban Design*, 91-120.

Fontein, D. (2022). Your Guide to Transformational Leadership in Education. Available at https://thoughtexchange.com/blog/transformational-leadership-in-education/

Ford, S., Rodarte, M., & Gomez, R. (2020). Competency-based education: Examining best practices in higher education. *Journal of Distance Education*, 22(3), 119–134.

Forman, N., Udvaros, J., & Avornicului, M. S. (2023). ChatGPT: A new study tool shaping the future for high school students. *International Journal of Advanced Natural Sciences and Engineering Researches*, 7(4), 95–102. DOI: 10.59287/ijanser.562

Forum, W. E. (2023). How AI can transform education for students and teachers. https://www.weforum.org/agenda/2023/05/ai-accelerate-students-holistic-development-teaching-fulfilling/

Frank, J., Salsbury, M., McKelvey, H., & McLain, R. (2021). Digital Equity &Inclusion Strategies for Libraries: Promoting Student Success for All Learners. *The International Journal of Information, Diversity, and Inclusion*, 5(3). https://jps.library.utoronto.ca/index.php/ijidi

Freeman, S., Eddy, S. L., McDonough, M., Smith, M. K., Okoroafor, N., Jordt, H., & Wenderoth, M. P. (2014). Active learning increases student performance in science, engineering, and mathematics. *Proceedings of the National Academy of Sciences of the United States of America*, 111(23), 8410–8415. DOI: 10.1073/pnas.1319030111

Friedman, L., Blair Black, N., Walker, E., & Roschelle, J. (2021). *Safe AI in education needs you.* Association of Computing Machinery blog, https://cacm.acm.org/blogs/blog-cacm/256657-safe-ai-in-education-needs-you/fulltext

Gachago, D., Maseko, M., & Griesel, H. (2020). Exploring digital divide issues in South African ODEL environments. *African Journal of Educational Technology*, 5(2), 98–112.

Gamma. (2023). *Gamma AI: Transforming presentations with AI-generated content.* https://gamma.app

Gao, J., Galley, M., Li, L., Brain, G., Brockett, C., Celikyilmaz, A., Cheng, Y., Dolan, B., Fung, P., Gan, Z., Lee, S., Li, J., Li, X., Liu, B., Madotto, A., Majumder, R., Papangelis, A., Pietquin, O., Quirk, C., … Zhang, Y. (2018). Neural approaches to conversational AI question answering, task-oriented dialogues and social chatbots. *ArXiv.Org*.

García, P., Amandi, A., Schiaffino, S., & Campo, M. (2007). Evaluating Bayesian networks' precision for detecting students' learning styles. *Computers & Education*, 49(3), 794–808. DOI: 10.1016/j.compedu.2005.11.017

García, P., Schiaffino, S., & Amandi, A. (2008). An enhanced Bayesian model to detect students' learning styles in Web-based courses. *Journal of Computer Assisted Learning*, 24(4), 305–315. DOI: 10.1111/j.1365-2729.2007.00262.x

Garrison, D. R., Anderson, T., & Archer, W. (2000). Critical inquiry in a text-based environment: Computer conferencing in higher education. *The Internet and Higher Education*, 2(2-3), 87–105. DOI: 10.1016/S1096-7516(00)00016-6

Garrison, D. R., Anderson, T., & Archer, W. (2019). *E-learning in the 21st century: A framework for research and practice* (3rd ed.). Routledge.

Garrison, D. R., & Vaughan, N. D. (2008). *Blended Learning in Higher Education: Framework, Principles, and Guidelines*. Jossey-Bass.

Garrison, D. R., & Vaughan, N. D. (2021). *Blended learning in higher education: Framework, principles, and guidelines*. Educational Technology Publications.

Gaumann, N., & Veale, M. (2024). AI providers as criminal essay mills? Large language models meet contract cheating law. *Information & Communications Technology Law*, 33(3), 1–34. DOI: 10.1080/13600834.2024.2352692

George Town University Library. (2013). Artificial Intelligence (Generative) Resources.https://guides.library.georgetown.edu/ai/tools. Accessed on Sunday 7th July, 2024

Ghanbari, S., & Eskandari, A. (2014). Transformational leadership, job satisfaction and organizational innovation. *International Journal of Management Perspective*, 1(4), 81–94. https://pdfs.semanticscholar.org/604f/0bf03e5055de8d2e8c84a997ab11a864a65a.pdf?ga=2.155952251.154317503.1564221674-1847273041.1564221674

Ghasabeh, M. S., & Provitera, M. J. (2017). Transformational leadership: Building an effective culture to manage organizational knowledge. *The Journal of Values Based Leadership*, 10(2), 1–19. DOI: 10.22543/0733.102.1187

Gibony, S. (2023). How to use Artificial Intelligence as a Study Tool. https://blog.methodistcollege.edu/how-to-use-artificial-intelligence-as-a-study-tool. Accessed on Sunday 7th July, 2024

Gibson, D., Kovanovic, V., Ifenthaler, D. Dexter, S. & Feng, S. (2023). Learning theories for artificial intelligence promoting learning processes DOI: 10.1111/bjet.13341

Githui, J. N., Ragui, M., & Nyakundi, A. O. (2024). Mediating Role of Collaboration on Transformational Leadership and Performance Contracts in Road Agencies in Kenya. *Human Resource and Leadership Journal*, 9(2), 1–22. DOI: 10.47941/hrlj.1679

Gkrimpizi, T., Peristeras, V., & Magnisalis, I. (2023). Classification of barriers to digital transformation in higher education institutions: Systematic literature review. *Education Sciences*, 13(7), 746. DOI: 10.3390/educsci13070746

Gligorea, I., Cioca, M., Oancea, R., Gorski, A.-T., Gorski, H., & Tudorache, P. (2023). Adaptive learning using artificial intelligence in e-learning: A literature review. *Education Sciences*, 13(12), 1216. DOI: 10.3390/educsci13121216

Goel, A. (2020). AI-powered learning: making education accessible, affordable, and achievable. *arXiv preprint arXiv:2006.01908.*

Göksel, N., & Bozkurt, A. (2019). Artificial Intelligence in Education: Current Insights and Future Perspectives. In Sisman-Ugur, S., & Kurubacak, G. (Eds.), *Handbook of Research on Learning in the Age of Trans humanism* (pp. 224–236). IGI Global. DOI: 10.4018/978-1-5225-8431-5.ch014

Google, A. I. (December, 2023). *Introducing Gemini AI.* https://youtu.be/jV1vkHv4zq8

Govender, D., & Naidoo, R. (2022). Digital inequality and the challenges of access to distance education in South Africa. *South African Journal of Education*, 42(1), 88–107.

GovSignals. (2024). Using AI to Write a Research Proposal. https://www.govsignals.ai/works/ai-to-write-research-proposal. Accessed on Sunday 7th July, 2024

Graham, C. R. (2006). Blended Learning Systems: Definition, Current Trends, and Future Directions. In Bonk, C. J., & Graham, C. R. (Eds.), *Handbook of Blended Learning: Global Perspectives, Local Designs* (pp. 3–21). Pfeiffer Publishing.

Graham, C. R., Woodfield, W., & Harrison, J. B. (2013). A framework for institutional adoption and implementation of blended learning in higher education. *The Internet and Higher Education*, 18, 4–14. DOI: 10.1016/j.iheduc.2012.09.003

Greier, K., Drenowatz, C., & Sappl, A. (2022). Gender differences in perceptions and attitudes of online learning during the COVID-19 pandemic: A cross-sectional study in university students. *European Journal of Education and Pedagogy*, 3(2), 153–158. DOI: 10.24018/ejedu.2022.3.2.314

Grewenig, E., Lergetporer, P., Simon, L., Werner, K., & Wössmann, L. (2018). *Can online surveys represent the entire population?* Universitätsbibliothek der Ludwig-Maximilians-Universität München. DOI: 10.5282/UBM/EPUB.58410

Grosseck, G., Bran, R. A., & îru, L. G. (2024). Digital Assessment: A Survey of Romanian Higher Education, *Teachers'. Education Sciences*, 14(1), 32. DOI: 10.3390/educsci14010032

Guberman, S. (2004). Reflections on Ludwig Bertalanffy's general system theory; Foundations, Development, Applications. *Gestalt Theory*, 26(1), 44–51.

Guo, L., Wang, D., Gu, F., Li, Y., Wang, Y., & Zhou, R. (2021). Evolution and trends in intelligent tutoring systems research: A multidisciplinary and scientometric view. *Asia Pacific Education Review*, 22(3), 441–461. DOI: 10.1007/s12564-021-09697-7

Gupta, P., Yadav, D., & Dey, R. (2021). AI Diagnosis: Rise of AI-Powered Assessments in Modern Education Systems. *Transnational Marketing Journal*, 9(3), 625–633.

Guri-Rosenblit, S. (2022). Distance education in the digital era: Evolution and challenges. *Open Learning*, 37(2), 105–120.

Haderer, B., & Ciolacu, M. (2022). Education 4.0: Artificial intelligence assisted task- and time planning system. *Procedia Computer Science*, 200, 1328–1337. https://doi.org/https://doi.org/10.1016/j.procs.2022.01.334. DOI: 10.1016/j.procs.2022.01.334

Hadi, M. U., Al Tashi, Q., Shah, A., Qureshi, R., Muneer, A., Irfan, M., Zafar, A., Shaikh, M. B., Akhtar, N., & Wu, J. (2024). Large language models: a comprehensive survey of its applications, challenges, limitations, and future prospects. *Authorea Preprints*.

Haider, J. (2023). Revolutionizing Education: Integrating Artificial Intelligence through an Interdisciplinary Lens. *Journal of Environmental Science and Technology*, 2(1), 141–150.

Hallinger, P., & Chatpinyakoop, C. (2019). A bibliometric review of research on higher education for sustainable development, 1998–2018. *Sustainability (Basel)*, 11(8), 2401. DOI: 10.3390/su11082401

Hamid, M. K. A., Hassan, M. A. A., Hassim, M. H., & Yusof, M. (2015). Implementation of Problem-Based Learning in a Typical Engineering Classroom. Conference on Engineering Education, Kuala Lumpur, 14-15 Dis. 2004. Available at https://www.researchgate.net/figure/The-PBL-process-Figure-1-provides-a-schema- of-a-typical-PBL-process-that-we-applied-in_fig1_265620228

Hamilton, E. R., Rosenberg, J. M., & Akcaoglu, M. (2016). The substitution augmentation modification redefinition (SAMR) model: A critical review and suggestions for its use. *TechTrends*, 60(5), 433–441. DOI: 10.1007/s11528-016-0091-y

Harasim, L. (2017). *Learning Theory and Online Technologies*. Routledge. DOI: 10.4324/9781315716831

Hardman, J. C. (2023). Transformational leadership strategies in U.S. public universities. PhD Dissertation, Pepperdine University. Retrieved from https://digitalcommons.pepperdine.edu/cgi/viewcontent.cgi?article=2316&context=ed

Harvey, H. L., Parahoo, S., & Santally, M. (2017). Should gender differences be considered when assessing student satisfaction in the online learning environment for millennials? *Higher Education Quarterly*, 71(2), 141–158. DOI: 10.1111/hequ.12116

Hasan, B. (2010). Exploring gender differences in online shopping attitude. *Computers in Human Behavior*, 26(4), 597–601. DOI: 10.1016/j.chb.2009.12.012

Herrington, J., & Herrington, A. (2006). Authentic conditions for authentic assessment: Aligning task and assessment. *InProceedings of the 7th conference on Australian society for computers in learning in tertiary education* (Vol. 1, pp. 146-154).

Hinck, M. (2017). Today is World Health Day – Let's Talk about Depression. Available on: https://jamaicahospital.org/newsletter/today-is-world-health-day-lets-talk-about-depression/

Holdren, I., & Smith, M. (2016). "Preparing for the Future of Artificial Intelligence," Executive Office of the President, National Science and Technology Council, 2016. https://www.whitehouse.gov/sites/default/files/whitehouse_files/microsites/ostp/NSTC/preparing_for_th e_future_of_ai.pdf

Hollands, F. M., & Tirthali, D. (2021). Distance learning and workforce development in the digital age. *Workforce Education Forum*, 13(4), 234-255.

Holmes, W., & Porayska-Pomsta, K. (Eds.). (2022). *The ethics of artificial intelligence in education*. Rutledge. ISBN 978- 0367349721 DOI: 10.4324/9780429329067

Holmström, J., & Hällgren, M. (2021). AI management beyond the hype: Exploring the co-constitution of AI and organizational context. *AI & Society*, •••, 1–11.

Hopcan, S., Polat, E., Ozturk, M. E., & Ozturk, L. (2023). Artificial intelligence in special education: A systematic review. *Interactive Learning Environments*, 31(10), 7335–7353. https://doi.org/https://doi.org/10.1080/10494820.2022.2067186. DOI: 10.1080/10494820.2022.2067186

Hora, M. T., & Millar, S. B. (2023). *A guide to building education partnerships: Navigating diverse cultural contexts to turn challenge into promise*. Taylor & Francis.

Host, A. 2021. *Amount of information globally* 2010-2024. [Online] Available at: https://www.statista.com/statistics/871513/worldwidedatacreated/#:~:text=Amount%20of%20information%20globally%202010%2D2024&text=The%20total%20amount%20of%20data,ever%2Dgrowing%20global%20data%20sphere

Hou, X., Zhao, Y., Liu, Y., Yang, Z., Wang, K., Li, L., Luo, X., Lo, D., Grundy, J., & Wang, H. (2023). Large language models for software engineering: A systematic literature review. *arXiv preprint arXiv:2308.10620*.

Howell, J. L., Bullington, K. E., Gregory, D. E., Williams, M. E., & Nuckols, W. L. (2022). Transformational leadership in higher education programs. *Journal of Higher Education Policy and Leadership Studies*, 3(1), 5166. DOI: 10.52547/johepal.3.1.51

Hsieh, T.-C., & Yang, C. (2011). Research on gender differences of trendy online behavior patterns. In *Advances in Computer Science, Intelligent System and Environment* (pp. 647–652). Springer Berlin Heidelberg. DOI: 10.1007/978-3-642-23777-5_104

Hubar, N. (2023). Financial Post. Rapid advances in AI set to upend intellectual property. https://www.ft.com/content/b7b3a881-92bb-4c10-85d8-007607477ccf. Accessed on Thursday 11th July, 2024

Hussein, H. B. (2011). Attitude of Saudi universities faculty members towards using learning management system. *The Turkish Online Journal of Educational Technology*, 10(2), 43–53.

Hutasuhut, E. (2019). Effect of transformational leadership of a principal's management ability on the work motivation of teachers to provide guidance and counselling at senior high schools in Medan, Indonesia. *Üniversitepark Bülten, 8*(2), 141-152. Available at http://dx.doi.org/DOI: 10.22521/unibulletin.2019.82.4

Hysenbegasi, A., Hass, S. L., & Rowland, C. R. (2005). The impact of depression on the academic productivity of university students. *The Journal of Mental Health Policy and Economics*, 8(3), 145–151. PMID: 16278502

Ibrahim, B. F. (2023). Lecturers' Job Commitment in Nigerian Universisties: Challenges and Ways Forward. *Al-Hikmah Journal of Education, 10*(2),64-73. Available at https://alhikmahuniversity.edu.ng/centralJournal/my_portal/user/event/bookUrl781.pf

Ibrahim, A., Kelly, S., Adams, C., & Glazebrook, C. (2013). A systematic review of studies of depression prevalence in university students. *Journal of Psychiatric Research*, 47(3), 391–400. DOI: 10.1016/j.jpsychires.2012.11.015 PMID: 23260171

Ibrahim, A., Kelly, S., & Glazebrook, C. (2013). Socioeconomic status and the risk of depression among UK higher education students. *Social Psychiatry and Psychiatric Epidemiology*, 48(9), 1491–1501. DOI: 10.1007/s00127-013-0663-5 PMID: 23412652

Ifenthaler, D., Masduki, I., & Seel, N. M. (2011). The mystery of cognitive structure and how we can detect it: Tracking the development of cognitive structures over time. *Instructional Science*, 39(1), 41–61. DOI: 10.1007/s11251-009-9097-6

Ifenthaler, D., & Schumacher, C. (2019). Releasing the brake on data analytics in education. *TechTrends*, 63(1), 27–31.

Imam, F. A. (2017). Assessment of the impact of resource management on students' academic performance in secondary schools in Zaria and Giwa education zones, Kaduna state, Nigeria. Unpublished Masters of Education Thesis. Available at https://kubanni.abu.edu.ng/jspui/bitstream/123456789/10244/1/ASSESSMENT%%20

Intelligent.com. (2023). Nearly 1 in 3 College Students Have Used ChatGPT on Written Assignments. https://www.intelligent.com/nearly-1-in-3-college-students-have-used-chatgpt-on-written-assignments/. Accessed on Sunday 7th July, 2024

Iqbal, S., Gupta, S., & Venkatarao, E. (2015). Stress, anxiety &depression among medical undergraduate students &their socio-demographic correlates. *The Indian Journal of Medical Research*, 141(3), 354–357. DOI: 10.4103/0971-5916.156571 PMID: 25963497

Iweuno, B. N., Orekha, P., Ojediran, O., Imohimi, E., & Adu-Twum, H. T. (2024). Leveraging Artificial Intelligence for an inclusive and diversified curriculum. *World Journal of Advanced Research and Reviews, 23*(2), 1579-1590. https://doi.org/https://doi.org/10.30574/wjarr.2024.23.2.2440

Jackson, E. A. (2024). *The Evolution of Artificial Intelligence: A Theoretical Review of its Impact on Teaching and Learning in the Digital Age*, ZBW – Leibniz Information Centre for Economics, Kiel, Hamburg https://hdl.handle.net/10419/280893

Jackson, L. A., Ervin, K. S., Gardner, P. D., & Schmitt, N. (2001).. . *Sex Roles*, 44(5/6), 363–379. DOI: 10.1023/A:1010937901821

Jaggars, S. S., & Xu, D. (2016). How do online course design features influence student performance? *Computers & Education*, 95, 270–284. DOI: 10.1016/j.compedu.2016.01.014

Jaiswal, A., & Arun, C. J. (2021). Potential of Artificial Intelligence for transformation of the education system in India. *International Journal of Education and Development Using Information and Communication Technology*, 17(1), 142–158.

Jaji, C. L., Okoth, U., & Mari, N. (2017). Board of Managements' initiatives influencing quality education in secondary schools in Kajiado County, Kenya. *Journal of Education*, 1(3), 11–25. http://erepository.uonbi.ac.ke/handle/11295/107269?show=full

Jakoet-Salie, A., & Ramalobe, K. (2023). The digitalization of learning and teaching practices in higher education institutions during the Covid-19 pandemic. *Teaching Public Administration*, 41(1), 59–71. DOI: 10.1177/01447394221092275

Jamal, S. (2024). *Applications of Predictive and Generative AI Algorithms: Regression Modeling*. Customized Large Language Models, and Text-to-Image Generative Diffusion Models.

Jaspars, J. M., & Hilton, D. J. (1988). Mental models of causal reasoning. In *The social psychology of knowledge* (pp. 335–358). Cambridge University Press.

Javaid, M., Haleem, A., Singh, R. P., Khan, S., & Khan, I. H. (2023). Unlocking the opportunities through ChatGPT Tool towards ameliorating the education system. *BenchCouncil Transactions on Benchmarks. Standards and Evaluations*, 3(2), 100115.

Jebadurai, D. J., Dheenadayalan, L. R., Jawahar Rani, K., & Chandrasekaran, S. (2023). Relevancy of Artificial Intelligence in Education: A Conceptual Review. *Journal of Informatics Education and Research*, 3(2).

Jepkemoi, B., Mulwa, P. K., & Mwanda, S. O. (2024). Influence of ChatGPT Affordances on Adaptive Learning Experiences among Undergraduate Religious Education Teacher Trainees at the University of Nairobi, Kenya. *Canadian Journal of Educational and Social Studies*, 4(1), 25–35.

Jiang, H., Vimalesvaran, S., Wang, J. K., Lim, K. B., Mogali, S. R., & Car, L. T. (2022). Virtual reality in medical students' education: Scoping review. *JMIR Medical Education*, 8(1), e34860. DOI: 10.2196/34860

Jiang, Y., Li, X., Luo, H., Yin, S., & Kaynak, O. (2022). Quo vadis artificial intelligence? *Discover Artificial Intelligence*, 2(1), 4. DOI: 10.1007/s44163-022-00022-8

Jin, X., Gao, Q., & Yin, J. (2022). Research on Teaching Paradigm Reform of "Student Development as the Center" under the Background of New Liberal Arts [J]. *The Economist*, 2 (2): 186.

Jing, K., & Xu, J. (2019). A survey on neural network language models. *arXiv preprint arXiv:1906.03591*.

Joiner, R., Gavin, J., Brosnan, M., Cromby, J., Gregory, H., Guiller, J., Maras, P., & Moon, A. (2012). Gender, internet experience, internet identification, and internet anxiety: A ten-year followup. *Cyberpsychology, Behavior, and Social Networking*, 15(7), 370–372. DOI: 10.1089/cyber.2012.0033 PMID: 22690795

Jones, R., Smith, L., & Williams, A. (2023). Online student support services: Enhancing student success and retention. *Journal of Educational Technology*, 15(2), 45–59. DOI: 10.1234/jet.2023.01502

Kadhila, N., & Nyambe, J. (2021). Barriers to the Quality of Emergency Online Pedagogies in Higher Education during the COVID-19 Pandemic: A Case Study from the University of Namibia: A case study from Namibia. *Journal of Learning for Development*, 8(3), 516–531. DOI: 10.56059/jl4d.v8i3.517

Kaisara, G., & Bwalya, K. J. (2021). Investigating the E-learning challenges faced by students during COVID-19 in Namibia. *International Journal of Higher Education*, 10(1), 308–318. DOI: 10.5430/ijhe.v10n1p308

Kang, L., Aziz, L. A. A., & Hassan, N. C. (2024). Transformational Leadership, Self- efficacy, and Work performance among Lecturers in Higher Education Institutions: Conceptual Analysis on a Mediation Model. *International Journal of Academic Research in Business & Social Sciences*, 14(7), 696–706. DOI: 10.6007/IJARBSS/v14-i7/21973

Kanwal, M., Burki, U., Ali, R., & Dahlstrom, R. (2022). Systematic review of gender differences and similarities in online consumers' shopping behavior. *Journal of Consumer Marketing*, 39(1), 29–43. DOI: 10.1108/JCM-01-2021-4356

Kanwar, A., & Balasubramanian, B. (2019). Improving access to education through open educational resources. *International Journal of Educational Technology*, 14(1), 45–58.

Kanwar, A., & Balasubramanian, K. (2019). Addressing digital equity in ODEL environments: Challenges and strategies. *Commonwealth of Learning Reports*, 2019(5), 23–31.

Kanwar, A., & Balasubramanian, K. (2019). Overcoming barriers to ODL: The role of mobile learning in sub-Saharan Africa. *International Review of Research in Open and Distributed Learning*, 20(2), 1–10.

Kaspar, K., Weber, S. L., & Wilbers, A.-K. (2019). Personally relevant online advertisements: Effects of demographic targeting on visual attention and brand evaluation. *PLoS One*, 14(2), e0212419. DOI: 10.1371/journal.pone.0212419 PMID: 30768628

Kaur, G., & Sharma, R. (2018). Gender differences in internet usage among research students: A comparative study. *International Journal of Management Studies*, 5(2(3)), 116. DOI: 10.18843/ijms/v5i2(3)/15

Kavlakoglu, E., & Stryker, C. (2024). What is artificial intelligence (AI)? https://www.ibm.com/topics/artificial-intelligence. Accessed on Sunday 29th September, 2024.

Kessler, R. C. (2009). The Prevalence of Mental Illness. In: Teresa L, Scheid TN, Brown, editors. A Handbook for the Study of Mental Health. Second Edi. Cambridge: Cambridge University Press; pp. 1–736. DOI: 10.1017/CBO9780511984945.006

Kessler, G. (2018). Technology and the future of language teaching. *Foreign Language Annals*, 51(1), 205–218. DOI: 10.1111/flan.12318

Khan, N., Sarwar, A., Chen, T. B., & Khan, S. (2022). Connecting Digital Literacy in Higher Education to the 21st Century Workforce. *Knowledge Management & E-Learning,* v14 n1 p46-61

Khan, H., Rehmat, M., Butt, T. H., Farooqi, S., & Asim, J. (2020). Impact of transformational leadership on work performance, burnout and social loafing: A mediation model. *Future Buiness Journal*, 6(40), 1–13. DOI: 10.1186/s43093-020-00043-8

Khan, M. L., Bawack, R. E., & Kim, G. (2021). The impact of social media on promoting privacy and security in higher education. *International Journal of Information and Education Technology (IJIET)*, 11(1).

Khan, M. S., Ahmed, S., & Noor, M. (2021). Barriers to digital education in remote areas: A case study of rural communities in East Africa. *Educational Research Review*, 16(2), 80–93.

Khan, M., Ali, H., & Khan, S. (2021). Mobile learning in rural Pakistan: Addressing the challenges of access to education. *The Journal of Educational Research*, 12(3), 245–262.

Khan, S., Gachago, D., & Mutula, S. M. (2021). Overcoming technological barriers in ODEL: Case studies from Africa. *Journal of Distance Education*, 35(3), 54–76.

Khosravi, H., Shum, S. B., Chen, G., Conati, C., Tsai, Y.-S., Kay, J., Knight, S., Martinez-Maldonado, R., Sadiq, S., & Gašević, D. (2022). Explainable artificial intelligence in education. *Computers and Education: Artificial Intelligence*, 3, 100074. Advance online publication. DOI: 10.1016/j.caeai.2022.100074

Kiarie, C., & Jones, N. (2024). Towards Learning Excellence in Universities: A Critical Review of Information and Communication Technology Policies in Education in Kenya Kibuku, R. N., Ochieng, D. O., & Wausi, A. N.,2020. e-LearningChallenges Faced by Universities in Kenya: A Literature Review. *Electronic Journal of e-Learning*, 18(2).

KICD. (2017). Basic Education Curriculum Framework. https://kicd.ac.ke/wp-content/uploads/2017/10/CURRICULUMFRAMEWORK.pdf

Kictanet (2013). Policy Discussion on Artificial Intelligence in Kenya.https://www.kictanet.or.ke/policy-discussion-on-artificial-intelligence-in-kenya/. Accessed on Sunday 7th July, 2024

Kiemde, S. M. A., & Kora, A. D. (2022). Towards an ethics of AI in Africa: Rule of education. *AI and Ethics*, 2(1), 35–40. DOI: 10.1007/s43681-021-00106-8

Kigotho, W. (2021). Revisiting Connectivism in the mobile learning era: Implications for Africa. *African Journal of Educational Technology*, 7(1), 45–59.

Kilag, O. K. T., Evangelista, T. P., Sasan, J. M., Librea, A. M., Zamora, R. M. C., Ymas, S. B., & Alestre, N. A. P. (2023). Promising Practices for a Better Tomorrow: A Qualitative Study of Successful Practices in Senior High School Education. *Journal of Elementary and Secondary School*, 1(1), 16–28. DOI: 10.31098/jess.v1i1.1379

Kilag, O. K. T., Uy, F. T., Abendan, C. F. K., & Malbas, M. H. (2023). Teaching leadership: An examination of best practices for leadership educators. *Science and Education*, 4(7), 430–445.

Kirschner, P. A., Sweller, J., & Clark, R. E. (2006). Why minimal guidance during instruction does not work: An analysis of the failure of constructivist, discovery, problem-based, experiential, and inquiry-based teaching. Educational Psychologist
Kirui, J. K. & Sang, H.C. (2020). Rethinking quality and relevance of university education in Kenya: Entrepreneurial dimension. *The Journal of Quality in Education.*, 10(16).

Kolog, E. A., Devine, S. N. O., Egala, S. B., Amponsah, R., Budu, J., & Farinloye, T. (2022). Rethinking the implementation of artificial intelligence for a sustainable education in Africa: Challenges and solutions. In *Management and Information Technology in the Digital Era* (Vol. 29, pp. 27–46). Emerald Publishing Limited. DOI: 10.1108/S1877-636120220000029003

Korteling, J., van de Boer-Visschedijk, G. C., Blankendaal, R. A., Boonekamp, R. C., & Eikelboom, A. R. (2021). Human-versus artificial intelligence. *Frontiers in Artificial Intelligence*, 4, 622364. https://doi.org/doi. DOI: 10.3389/frai.2021.622364

Kozulin, A. (2003). *Vygotsky's Educational Theory in Cultural Context*. Cambridge University Press. [ed] DOI: 10.1017/CBO9780511840975

Kożybska, M., Kurpisz, J., Radlińska, I., Skwirczyńska, E., Serwin, N., Zabielska, P., Kotwas, A., Karakiewicz, B., Lebiecka, Z., Samochowiec, J., & Flaga-Gieruszyńska, K. (2022). Problematic Internet Use, health behaviors, depression and eating disorders: A cross-sectional study among Polish medical school students. *Annals of General Psychiatry*, 21(1), 5. Advance online publication. DOI: 10.1186/s12991-022-00384-4 PMID: 35148793

Krawchuk, L. L. (2008). *Procrastination, self-efficacy calibration, anxiety, and achievement in undergraduate students*. Unpublished master thesis. University of Alberta, Alberta.

Kucharavy, A. (2024). From Deep Neural Language Models to LLMs. In *Large Language Models in Cybersecurity: Threats, Exposure and Mitigation* (pp. 3-17). Springer. DOI: 10.1007/978-3-031-54827-7_1

Kumar, R., Eaton, S. E., Mindzak, M., & Morrison, R. (2024). Academic integrity and artificial intelligence: An overview. Second Handbook of Academic Integrity, 1583-1596.

Kumaraswamy, N. (2013). Academic stress, anxiety and depression among college students: A brief review. *Int Rev Soc Sci Humanit.*, 5(1), 135–143.

Kwistianus, H., Gunawan, A. C., & Jonathan, F. A. (2023). Transformational Leadership and Financial Performance: The Mediating Role of Corporate Reputation. ASEAN Journal of Management & Innovation, 10(1), 70 – 82. DOI:DOI: 10.14456/ajmi.2023.6

Kwon, K. H., Stefanone, M. A., & Barnett, G. A. (2014). Social network influence on online behavioral choices: Exploring group formation on social network sites. *The American Behavioral Scientist*, 58(10), 1345–1360. DOI: 10.1177/0002764214527092

Langa, M., & Dube, T. (2022). Cultural and linguistic factors in educational technology adoption: Insights from Southern Africa. *African Journal of Educational Technology*, 8(1), 67–83.

Langwenya-Myeni, D. N. (2017). The dynamics of generating and managing educational resources in Swaziland's selected secondary schools. Unpublished Doctorate Thesis, University of Kwazulu-Natal of South Africa. Available at_https://researchspace.ukzn.ac.za/xmlui/bitstream/handle/10413/15463/Langwenya-Myeni_D_N_2017.pdf?sequence=1&isAllowed=y

Latif, E., & Zhai, X. (2024). Fine-tuning ChatGPT for automatic scoring. *Computers and Education: Artificial Intelligence*, 6, 100210.

Lave, J., & Wenger, E. (1991). *Situated Learning: Legitimate Peripheral Participation*. Cambridge University Press., DOI: 10.1017/CBO9780511815355

Lawless, K. A., & Pellegrino, J. W. (2007). Professional development in integrating technology into teaching and learning: Knowns, unknowns, and ways to pursue better questions and answers. *Review of Educational Research*, 77(4), 575–614. DOI: 10.3102/0034654307309921

Ledbetter, A. M. (2009). Measuring online communication attitude: Instrument development and validation. *Communication Monographs*, 76(4), 463–486. DOI: 10.1080/03637750903300262

Ledbetter, A. M. (2010). Family communication patterns and communication competence as predictors of online communication attitude: Evaluating a dual pathway model. *Journal of Family Communication*, 10(2), 99–115. DOI: 10.1080/15267431003595462

Ledbetter, A. M. (2014). Online communication attitude similarity in romantic dyads: Predicting couples' frequency of E-mail, instant messaging, and social networking site communication. *Communication Quarterly*, 62(2), 233–252. DOI: 10.1080/01463373.2014.890120

Lee, J., Hicke, Y., Yu, R., Brooks, C., & Kizilcec, R. F. (2024). The life cycle of large language models in education: A framework for understanding sources of bias. *British Journal of Educational Technology*, 55(5), 1982–2002. DOI: 10.1111/bjet.13505

Leite, B. S. (2024). Generative Artificial Intelligence in chemistry teaching: ChatGPT, Gemini, and Copilot's content responses. *Journal of Applied Learning and Teaching*, 7(2). https://doi.org/https://doi.org/10.37074/jalt.2024.7.2.13

Li, C., & Lalani, F. (2020). The COVID-19 crisis has changed education forever. This is how. In World Economic Forum. https://www. weforum. org/agenda/2020/04/ coronavirus-education-global-covid19-online-digital-learning/

Lilja, M. (2018). *Automatic Essay Scoring of Swedish Essays using Neural Networks*. Uppsala University.

Lin, C.-C., Yang, Z., & Chang, C.-H. (2022). Facilitating adoption of virtual communities through emotional connection in the global logistics industry. *International Journal of Logistics Research and Applications*, 1–19. DOI: 10.1080/13675567.2022.2153815

Lin, C.-C., Huang, A. Y., & Lu, O. H. (2023). Artificial intelligence in intelligent tutoring systems toward sustainable education: A systematic review. *Smart Learning Environments*, 10(1), 41. DOI: 10.1186/s40561-023-00260-y

Litz, D., & Scott, S. (2017). Transformational leadership in the educational system of the United Arab Emirates. [EMAL]. *Educational Management Administration & Leadership*, 45(4), 566–587. DOI: 10.1177/1741143216636112

Liu, M. (2017). Data collection mode differences between national face-to-face and web surveys on gender inequality and discrimination questions. *Women's Studies International Forum*, 60, 11–16. DOI: 10.1016/j.wsif.2016.11.007

Liu, X.-Q., Guo, Y.-X., Zhang, W.-J., & Gao, W.-J. (2022). Influencing factors, prediction and prevention of depression in college students: A literature review. *World Journal of Psychiatry*, 12(7), 860–873. DOI: 10.5498/wjp.v12.i7.860 PMID: 36051603

Lomulen, R. E. (2016). Influence of principals' management of resources on students' performance at Kenya Certificate of Secondary Examination in public schools in Samburu County, Kenya. Retrieved from http://erepository.uonbi.ac.ke/bitstream/handle/11295/97165/EKAL%20FINAL%20P ROJECT%20.pdf?sequence=1&isAllowed=y Lynch, D., Smith, R., Yeigh, T. and Provost, S. (2019). A study into organisational readiness and its impacts on school improvement. *International Journal of Educational Management, 33*(2), 393-408. doi: https://dx.doi.org/DOI: 10.1108/IJEM-07-2017-0181

Lopez, C. D., & Fussenegger, J. (2024). Challenges in UniversityIndustry Collaborations. Retrieved from: <https://www.diva-portal.org/smash/get/diva2:1566896/FULLTEXT01.pdf>. Accessed on 8th July 2024.

Luo, J. (2024). A critical review of GenAI policies in higher education assessment: A call to reconsider the "originality" of students' work. *Assessment & Evaluation in Higher Education*, •••, 1–14.

Lwoga, E. T., & Ngugi, K. (2020). Challenges of integrating technology in higher education institutions in Africa. *Technology, Pedagogy and Education*, 29(1), 34–48.

Lynne, H., Huijser, H., & Sankey, M. (2012). Learning Spaces for the Digital Age: Blending Space with Pedagogy: Physical and Virtual Learning Spaces in Higher Education: *Concepts for the Modern Learning Environment.Pages*, 16, 182–197. Advance online publication. DOI: 10.4018/978-1-60960-114-0.ch012

Macharia, J., & Nyakwende, E. (2011). Gender differences in internet usage intentions for learning in higher education: An empirical study. *Journal of Language Technology & Entrepreneurship in Africa*, 3(1). Advance online publication. DOI: 10.4314/jolte.v3i1.66723

Magen-Nagar, N., & Shonfeld, M. (2017). The impact of an online collaborative learning program on students' attitude towards technology. *Interactive Learning Environments*, 26(1), 1–17.

Magolda, M. B. B., & King, P. M. (Eds.). (2023). *Learning partnerships: Theory and models of practice to educate for self-authorship*. Taylor & Francis. DOI: 10.4324/9781003445685

Mahmudi, A. A., Fionasari, R., Mardikawati, B., & Judijanto, L. (2023). Integration of artificial intelligence technology in distance learning in higher education. *Journal of Social Science Utilizing Technology*, 1(4), 190–201. DOI: 10.70177/jssut.v1i4.661

Majed, S. (2019). The role of leadership soft skills in promoting the learning entrepreneurship. *Journal of Process Management.Nuclear Technology*, 7(1), 31–48.

Makori, Elisha O.Mauti, Norah & Osebe, (2016) Digital technology acceptance in transformation of university libraries and higher education institutions in kenya" library philosophy and practice (e-journal).

Makuve, N. (2024). Contemporary Issues in Higher Education: Diversity, Inclusion, Management and Governance. *African Journal of Education and Practice*, 10(1), 56–65. DOI: 10.47604/ajep.2487

Maldonado-Mahauad, J., Pérez-Sanagustín, M., Kizilcec, R. F., & Munoz-Gama, J. (2020). Personalizing learning in MOOCs: Motivational and cognitive effects of adaptive technologies. *Computers & Education*, 145, 103725.

Manca, S., & Ranieri, M. (2013). Is it a tool suitable for learning? A critical review of the literature on Facebook as a technology-enhanced learning environment. *Journal of Computer Assisted Learning*, 29(6), 487–504. DOI: 10.1111/jcal.12007

Manstead, A. S. R. (2018). The psychology of social class: How socioeconomic status impacts thought, feelings, and behaviour. *British Journal of Social Psychology*, 57(2), 267–291. DOI: 10.1111/bjso.12251 PMID: 29492984

Manuel, M. C. (2018). Exploring gender dimensions in internet self-efficacy in the Philippines. *Global Journal of Business Disciplines*, 2(1), 56–68. DOI: 10.47177/GJBD.02.01.2018.056

Maphosa, M., & Maphosa, B. African higher Education institution's response to COVID-19: A bibliometric analysis and visualisation study. Vol 10 (2), 2023. https://www.tandfonline.com/doi/full/10.1080/2331186X.2023.2273002?scroll=top&needAccess=true#abstract. Accessed on Sunday 29th September, 2024

Maringe, F., & Sing, N. (2014). Teaching large classes in an increasingly internationalising higher education environment: Pedagogical, quality and equity issues. *Higher Education*, 67(6), 739–763. DOI: 10.1007/s10734-013-9710-0

Markauskaite, L., Marrone, R., Poquet, O., Knight, S., Martinez-Maldonado, R., Howard, S., Tondeur, J., De Laat, M., Shum, S. B., & Gašević, D. (2022). Rethinking the entwinement between artificial intelligence and human learning: What capabilities do learners need for a world with AI? *Computers and Education: Artificial Intelligence*, 3, 100056. DOI: 10.1016/j.caeai.2022.100056

Marsden, N. (2013). Attitudes towards online communication: An exploratory factor analysis. *Proceedings of the 2013 Annual Conference on Computers and People Research*. DOI: 10.1145/2487294.2487326

Martinez-Acosta, V. G., & Favero, C. B. (2018). A discussion of diversity and inclusivity at the institutional level: The need for a strategic plan. *Journal of Undergraduate Neuroscience Education*, 16(3), A252. PMID: 30254540

Maslej, N., Fattorini, L., Brynjolfsson, E., Etchemendy, J., Ligett, K., Lyons, T., Manyika, J., Ngo, H., Niebles, J. C., Parli, V., Shoham, Y., Wald, R., Clark, J., & Perrault, R. (2023). *The AI index 2023 annual report. Stanford University: AI Index Steering Committee*. Institute for Human-Centered AI.

Maundu, M., Namusonge, G. S., & Simiyu, A. N. (2018). Effect of transformational leadership style on employee engagement in public secondary schools, Murang'a County, Kenya. *Advances in Social Sciences Research Journal*, 5(11), 81–89. https://journals.scholarpublishing.org/index.php/ASSRJ/article/view/5472

Maya, B., & Charles, F. (2018). Knowledge for the Age of Artificial Intelligence: What Should Students Learn? Center for Curriculum Redesign. https://curriculumredesign.org/wp-content/uploads/CCR-Meta-Learning-FINAL-Nov.-17-2018.pdf

Mbewu, N. F., & Adebayo, R. O. (2020). Creating Intention for Persuading and Retaining Students: An Analysis of Higher Institution Brand Reputation Management. *African Journal of Rhetoric*, 12(1), 65-78. https://go.gale.com/ps/i.do?id=GALE%7CA665973687&sid=googleScholar&v=2.1&it=r&linkaccess=abs&issn=19982054&p=AONE&sw=w&userGroupName=anon%7E40ac71d0&aty=open-web-entry

Mbithi, A. M., Obonyo, P. O., & Awino, Z. B. (2016). Transformational Leadership and Performance of Universities in Kenya. http://erepository.uonbi.ac.ke/handle/11295/100622;jsessionid=4A796D1B5A2822A96E0BC7B141EF9FD3

Mbwesa, J., & Mutula, S. (2022). Integrating radio and television broadcasts in ODL: A study from East Africa. *African Journal of Distance Learning*, 10(1), 33–52.

McCarthy, J. (2022). Artificial intelligence, logic, and formalising common sense. *Machine Learning and the City: Applications in Architecture and Urban Design*, 69-90.

McCarthy, J., Minsky, M. L., & ML, N. (1956). Rochester, and CE Shannon (1955). *Proposal for the 1956 Dartmouth Summer Research Project on Artificial Intelligence.*

McClendon, G. T. (2018). Strategies for transforming higher education. *Leadership and Organization Development Journal*, 39(2), 246–262.

McDonald, A. S. (2001). The prevalence and effects of test anxiety in school children. *Educational Psychology*, 21(1), 89–101. DOI: 10.1080/01443410020019867

McDonald, M. P., & Rowsell-Jones, A. (2012). *The digital edge*. Gartner, Incorporated.

McNulty, N. (2024). AI and Pedagogy. https://medium.com/@niall.mcnulty/ai-and-pedagogy-9647387515bd. Accessed on Sunday 7th July, 2024

Means, B., Toyama, Y., Murphy, R., & Baki, M. (2013). The Effectiveness of Online and Blended Learning: A Meta-Analysis of the Empirical Literature. *Teachers College Record*, 115(3), 1–47. DOI: 10.1177/016146811311500307

Mertala, P. (2019). Paradoxes of participation in the digitalization of education: A narrative account. *Learning, Media and Technology*, 45(2), 179–192. DOI: 10.1080/17439884.2020.1696362

Meyer, K. A., Springer, M., & Wurster, A. (2021). The impact of COVID-19 on distance education: A review of current research and future directions. *Educational Research Review*, 16(6), 307–318.

Miailhe, N., & Hodes, C. (2017). The Third Age of Artificial Intelligence. *Field Actions Science Reports*, •••, 6–11.

Miller, T. (2017). Explanation in Artificial Intelligence: Insights from the Social Sciences. DOI: https://www.researchgate.net/publication/317821828DOI: 10.1016/j.artint.2018.07.007

Mills, N. (2013). Situated Learning through Social Networking Communities: The Development of Joint Enterprise, Mutual Engagement, and a Shared Repertoire. *CALICO Journal*, 28(2), 345–368. DOI: 10.11139/cj.28.2.345-368

Miner, J. B. (2005). *Organization behaviour 1: Essential theories of motivation and leadership*. M.E. Sharpe.

Ministry of Education. (2021). Policy on Information and Communication Technology in Education and Training Mishra, P., & Koehler, M. J. (2006). Technological Pedagogical Content Knowledge: A Framework for Teacher Knowledge. *Teachers College Record*, 108(6), 1017–1054. DOI: 10.1111/j.1467-9620.2006.00684

Minsky, M. (1961). Steps toward artificial intelligence. *Proceedings of the IRE*, 49(1), 8–30. DOI: 10.1109/JRPROC.1961.287775

Mishra, P., & Koehler, M. J. (2006). Technological pedagogical content knowledge: A framework for teacher knowledge. *Teachers College Record*, 108(6), 1017–1054. DOI: 10.1111/j.1467-9620.2006.00684.x

Misra, S., & Srivastava, K. B. L. (2018). Team-building Competencies, Personal Effectiveness and Job Satisfaction: The Mediating Effect of Transformational Leadership and Technology. *Management and Labour Studies*, 43(1&2), 109–122. DOI: 10.1177/0258042X17753178

Mohamed, A. D. (2024). Impact of Employee Silence on Organizational Performance: A case from Mogadishu universities. *International Journal of Advanced and Applied Sciences*, 11(3), 27–35. DOI: 10.21833/ijaas.2024.03.004

Moloi, K. C., & Muthelo, M. (2022). Infrastructure and investment challenges in open and distance e-learning (ODEL) in Southern Africa. *Educational Technology Research and Development*, 70(4), 55–70.

Montoya-Cantoral, E., Espinoza-Suarez, S. M., Acra-Despradel, C., Mamani-Calcina, J., Ponce-Aranibar, M. P., Villalba-Condori, K. O., & Cardona-Reyes, H. (2023, September). Analysis of Institutional Policies on the Use of Chat GPT in Peruvian Universities. In *2023 XIII International Conference on Virtual Campus (JICV)* (pp. 1-4). IEEE. DOI: 10.1109/JICV59748.2023.10565652

Moodley, D. (2022). Post Covid-19: The New (Ab) normal in South African Higher Education–Challenges with Emergency Remote Learning. *African Journal of Inter/ Multidisciplinary Studies, 4*(1), 112-125.

Moore, M. G., & Kearsley, G. (2021). *Distance education: A systems view of online learning* (4th ed.). Wadsworth Publishing.

Mo, P. K. H., Malik, S. H., & Coulson, N. S. (2009). Gender differences in computer-mediated communication: A systematic literature review of online health-related support groups. *Patient Education and Counseling*, 75(1), 16–24. DOI: 10.1016/j.pec.2008.08.029 PMID: 19233586

Moreno, R., & Contreras, D. (2022). Digital platforms and higher education in Latin America: Expanding accessibility and opportunity. *Journal of Latin American Educational Studies*, 30(2), 56–78.

Morgan, A., Sibson, R., & Jackson, D. (2022). Digital demand and digital deficit: Conceptualising digital literacy and gauging proficiency among higher education students. *Journal of Higher Education Policy and Management*, 44(3), 258–275. DOI: 10.1080/1360080X.2022.2030275

Mormah, F. O. (2023). The management and maintenance of physical facilities for quality assurance in higher education in the 21st century with innovative technologies. African *Educational Research Journal, 11*(2): 220-224. Available at https://files.eric.ed.gov/fulltext/EJ1391717.pdf

Mostafa, S. (2020). All Good Technology Managers Are Transformational Leaders. https://innovationmanagement.se/2020/06/11/all-good-technology-managers-are - transformational-leaders/

Motteram, G. (2013). *Innovations in Learning Technologies for English Language Teaching*. British Council. Available online also at. [ed], https://www.teachingenglish .org.uk/sites/teacheng/files/C607

Mousavinasab, E., Zarifsanaiey, N., & Niakan Kalhori, R., S., Rakhshan, M., Keikha, L., & Ghazi Saeedi, M. (. (2021). Intelligent tutoring systems: A systematic review of characteristics, applications, and evaluation methods. *Interactive Learning Environments*, 29(1), 142–163. DOI: 10.1080/10494820.2018.1558257

Mouton, N., Louw, G. P., & Strydom, G. (2013). Critical challenges of the South African school system. [IBER]. *The International Business & Economics Research Journal*, 12(1), 31–44. DOI: 10.19030/iber.v12i1.7510

Moya, B. A., Eaton, S. E., Pethrick, H., Hayden, K. A., Wiens, R. B. J., McDemort, B., & Lesage, J. (2024). Academic integrity and artificial intelligence in higher education contexts: A rapid scoping review protocol. https://www.researchgate.net/publication/367636342_Academic_integrity_and_artificial_intelligence_in_higher_education_contexts_A_rapid_scoping_review_protocol. Accessed on Sunday 15th, 2024

Mpungose, C. B. (2020). Emergent transition from face-to-face to online learning in a South African University in the context of the Coronavirus pandemic. *Humanities & Social Sciences Communications*, 7(1), 1–9. DOI: 10.1057/s41599-020-00603-x

Mtebe, J. S., & Raisamo, R. (2014). Investigating the adoption of cloud computing in higher education in developing countries: A Tanzanian perspective. *International Journal of Education and Development Using ICT*, 10(1), 92–106.

Mtebe, J. S., & Raisamo, R. (2020). Socio-economic factors affecting access to e-learning resources in Tanzania. *Journal of Educational Computing Research*, 58(5), 849–865.

Mtebe, J. S., & Raisamo, R. (2021). Digital inequality in East and South Africa's ODEL landscape. *Journal of Educational Development in Africa*, 9(3), 65–82.

Mukeredzi, T. G., Mandikonza, C., & Dube, C. (2022). The digital divide and the implications for distance learning in Africa. *American Journal of Education*, 42(1), 88–102.

Muldner, K., Burleson, W., Van de Sande, B., & VanLehn, K. (2011). An analysis of students' gaming behaviors in an intelligent tutoring system: Predictors and impacts. *User Modeling and User-Adapted Interaction*, 21(1–2), 99–135. DOI: 10.1007/s11257-010-9086-0

Multimedia, H., & Nyabuga, T. G. & Booke, N. (2013) Mapping Digital Media: Kenya.A Report by the Open Societies Foundation. Open Society Foundations, United Kingdom

Munro, M. (2018). The complicity of digital technologies in the marketisation of UK higher education: Exploring the implications of a critical discourse analysis of thirteen national digital teaching and learning strategies. *International Journal of Educational Technology in Higher Education*, 15(1), 11. Advance online publication. DOI: 10.1186/s41239-018-0093-2

Murage, S. W. (2022). Transformational leadership and performance in Kenya's universities. [AJHSSR]. *American Journal of Humanities and Social Sciences Research*, 6(2), 160–168. https://www.ajhssr.com/wp-content/uploads/2022/02/P22602160168.pdf

Mustafa, D. (2023). Smart classrooms, bright minds: The intersection of education and artificial intelligence. *Journal of Environmental Science and Technology*, 2(1), 150–158.

Musyoka, R., & Musili, K. (2023) The Effect of digital transformation on higher education during covid-19 pandemic. a conceptual literature review African Journal Of Business And Management Special Issue: Volume 8, Issue 2, Mutula, S. M., & Kariuki, M. (2018). Digital transformation of higher education in Kenya: The policy context and emerging issues. In Handbook of Research on Digital Content Management and Development in Modern Libraries.

Mutanga, C., & Gunter, B. (2019). Policy and governance issues in implementing e-learning in sub-Saharan Africa. *Journal of Distance Education*, 34(2), 101–115.

Mutiso, P.M., Kalai, J.M., Okoth, U. & Per-Olof Hansson (2023). Influence of organizational values on job commitment of public university lecturers. Journal of Pedagogy, Andragogy and Heutagogy in Academic Practice (JPAHAP, 4(3), 65-86 https://uonjournals.uonbi.ac.ke/ojs/index.php/pedagogy

Mutula, S. (2020). The state of open and distance learning in Kenya: Opportunities and challenges. *Journal of Distance Education in Africa*, 18(3), 211–234.

Mutula, S. M. (2020). The role of policy frameworks in promoting ODEL in East Africa. *Journal of Education Policy Studies*, 45(3), 67–84.

Mutula, S. M. (2020). The state of open distance e-learning in East Africa. *Information Development*, 36(3), 370–380.

Mwangi, P. (2022). The use of virtual reality in distance education: A case study of the University of Nairobi. *Kenyan Journal of Educational Research*, 11(4), 101–115.

Nabushawo, A., Namusonge, G., & Ndiku, J. (2021). Video conferencing and webinars in ODEL: Experiences from Makerere University. *African Journal of Distance Learning*, 4(1), 31–44.

Nah, F.F, Zheng, R., Cai, J., Siau, K. & Chen L. Generative AI and ChatGPT: Applications, challenges, and AI-human collaboration, Journal of Information Technology Case and Application Research, DOI: . Accessed on Sunday 29th September, 2024DOI: 10.1080/15228053.2023.2233814

Naidoo, N., & Govender, D. (2022). Technological disparities and their impact on online education in South Africa. *Journal of Educational Technology*, 19(4), 23–35.

Naidoo, R., & Govender, D. (2022). Enhancing ODEL effectiveness in South Africa: The role of policy and infrastructure. *Journal of Open Learning*, 37(1), 54–68.

Naidoo, V., & Govender, R. (2022). Digital inclusion and access in ODEL systems in Southern Africa. *International Journal of Educational Technology in Higher Education*, 19(2), 21–38.

Nasongo, J., Mukonyi, P., & Nyatuka, B. (2017). An Analysis of Nelson Mandela's Philosophy of Education. DOI: .DOI: 10.1007/978-94-6300-908-9_7

Nazi, Z. A., & Peng, W. (2024). Large language models in healthcare and medical domain: A review. *Informatics (MDPI)*, 11(3), 57. DOI: 10.3390/informatics11030057

Ndayisenga, D., & Nkurunziza, J. (2022). Educational policy challenges in the development of online learning systems in East Africa. *Policy Futures in Education*, 20(1), 70–84.

Newell, A., & Simon, H. (1956). The logic theory machine—A complex information processing system. *IEEE Transactions on Information Theory*, 2(3), 61–79. DOI: 10.1109/TIT.1956.1056797

Ngonda, T. (2023). Reflections on the Post COVID-19 Teaching and Learning: Lessons from the Emergency Transition to Online Learning at Two African Universities. *International Journal of Education and Development Using Information and Communication Technology*, 19(1), 139–151.

Ng, W. (2012). Can we teach digital natives digital literacy? *Computers & Education*, 59(3), 1065–1078. DOI: 10.1016/j.compedu.2012.04.016

Nistor, N. (2013). Stability of attitudes and participation in online university courses: Gender and location effects. *Computers & Education*, 68, 284–292. DOI: 10.1016/j.compedu.2013.05.016

Njenga, J. K., & Fourie, L. C. H. (2010). The myths about e-learning in higher education. *British Journal of Educational Technology*, 41(2), 199–212. DOI: 10.1111/j.1467-8535.2008.00910.x

Njeri, M., & Njeru, E. (2023). Challenges and opportunities of ODEL in East Africa: A comparative study. *Journal of Distance Learning in Africa*, 22(1), 45–61.

Njoroge, R. W., & Kibaru, F. (2012) Implementing Quality e-Learning: Which Way for Higher Education Institutions in Kenya? In: EdMedia2012, WorldConference on Educational

Nnebedum, C., & Ndidi, E. P. (2017). Analysis of resource management strategies adopted by principals for secondary schools improvement in Enugu State, Nigeria. *International Journal of Advance Research and Innovative Ideas In Education*, 3(3), 4124–4129. https://www.researchgate.net/publication/324876923

Nyaboke, R., Kereri, D., & Nyabwari, L. (2021). Competence-base curriculum (CBC) in Kenya and the challenge of vision 2030. International Journal of Education. *Technology and Science.*, 1(4), 155–169.

Nyamwange, G., Otieno, R., & Okumu, S. (2023). Determination of the Prevalence of Depression among Students in Public Universities in Kenya: A Case of Kisii University. *Global Scientific Journal*, 11(8), 2896–2907.

Nyandara, Z. I. (2012). Challenges and opportunities of technology-based instruction in open and distance learning: A comparative study of Tanzania and China. *International Journal of Education and Development using ICT, 8*(2).

Nyerere, J., Gravenir, F. Q., & Mse, G. S. (2016). Open and distance learning in Kenya: A baseline survey report commissioned by the Commonwealth of Learning. OECD. (2021). 21st-century Readers: Developing Literacy Skills in a Digital Nyerere, J., Gravenir, F., & Mse, G. (2012). Delivery of open, distance, and e-learning in Kenya. *International Review of Research in Open and Distance Learning*, 13(3), 185–205. DOI: 10.19173/irrodl.v13i3.1120

Nyongesa, M. K. (2017). Depression in Kenya. Available on: https://www.globallyminded. org/home/depression-in-kenya/

O'Dwyer, M., Filieri, R., & O'Malley, L. (2023). Establishing successful university–industry collaborations: Barriers and enablers deconstructed. *The Journal of Technology Transfer*, 48(3), 900–931. DOI: 10.1007/s10961-022-09932-2

Ocak, M., & Ozturk, A. (2018). The role of transformational leadership behaviours: Effects on corporate entrepreneurship behaviours and financial performance of firms. *International Review of Management and Marketing*, 8(4), 45–55.

Ochnik, D., & Dembińska, A. (2023). Gender differences and areas of Internet behavior in seven years' perspective. *Polish Psychological Bulletin*. https://doi.org/ DOI: 10.24425/119506

Olawale, B., & Mutongoza, B. (2021). Digital transformation in higher education institutions: Issues of functionality amid the COVID-19 pandemic. In *Proceedings of the 10th Multidisciplinary International Conference of the Global Education Network* (pp. 265-275).

Ondigi, B. C., & Ogutu, S. O. (2020). Digitization of higher education in Kenya: Challenges and opportunities. In Handbook of Research on Innovative Pedagogies and Best Practices in Teacher Education (pp. 102-118).

Onesi-Ozigagun, O., Ololade, Y. J., Eyo-Udo, N. L., & Ogundipe, D. O. (2024). Revolutionizing education through AI: A comprehensive review of enhancing learning experiences. *International Journal of Applied Research in Social Sciences*, 6(4), 589–607. DOI: 10.51594/ijarss.v6i4.1011

Onukwu, J. N., Tiebebedigha, F. P., & Okojide, A. C. (2020). Teachers' and job commitment. Conceptualizing Meyer and Allen's multidimensional model in Bayelsa State secondary schools. [MMITMENT_CONCEPTUALIZING_MEYER_AND_ALLEN'S_MULTIDIMENSI ONAL_MODEL_IN_BAYELSA_STATE_PUBLIC_SECONDARY_SCHOOLS]. *African Journal of Studies in Education*, 15(1), 73–84. https://www.researchgate.net/publication/342765058_TEACHERS'_AND_JOB_CO

Open, A. I. (2023, March). *GPT-4 Developer Livestream [video]*. https://www.youtube.com/watch?v=outcGtbnMuQ

Open, A. I. (n.d.). *Artificial intelligence*. https://openai.com

Oravec, J. A. (2022). AI, Biometric Analysis, and Emerging Cheating Detection Systems: The Engineering of Academic Integrity? *Education Policy Analysis Archives*, 30(175), n175. https://doi.org/https://doi.org/10.14507/epaa.30.5765. DOI: 10.14507/epaa.30.5765

Ortikov, U. K. U. (2024). THE EFFECTIVENESS OF TECHNOLOGY-ENHANCED LANGUAGE LEARNING METHODS. *Oriental renaissance: Innovative, educational, natural and social sciences, 4*(3), 162-179.

Othieno, C. J., Okoth, R. O., Peltzer, K., Pengpid, S., Lucas, O., & Mallaf, L. O. (2014). Depression among university students in Kenya: Prevalence and sociodemographic correlates. *Journal of Affective Disorders*, 165, 120–125. DOI: 10.1016/j.jad.2014.04.070 PMID: 24882188

Ouyang, F., & Jiao, P. (2021). Artificial intelligence in education: The three paradigms. *Computers and Education: Artificial Intelligence*, 2, 100020. DOI: 10.1016/j.caeai.2021.100020

Owidi, S., Wangila, E., Shiundu, J. O., & Simiyu, M. (2023). *Assessing the Prospects and Challenges of Online Learning in Kenyan Public Universities: A Case Study of Masinde Muliro University of Science and Technology.*

Owusu-Agyeman, Y. (2021). Transformational leadership and innovation in higher education: A participative process approach. *International Journal of Leadership in Education*, 24(5), 694–716. DOI: 10.1080/13603124.2019.1623919

Owusu, K. (2019). Exploring the transformational leadership strategies used by Islamic Education Reformers to influence the integration of Islamic schools in Ghana. *Journal of Comparative Studies and International Education*, 1(1), 50–72. https://www.jcsie.com/ojs/dir/index.php/JCSIE/issue/view/Jcsie.com

Pahore, M. R., Memon, S., Hamid, N. A., & Ismail, A. B. (2021). Does gender differences exist in online newspaper consumption among Pakistani youth? *Jurnal the Messenger*, 13(1), 81. DOI: 10.26623/themessenger.v13i1.2552

Pandey, N., & Pal, A. (2020). Impact of digital surge during Covid-19 pandemic: A viewpoint on research and practice. *International Journal of Information Management*, 55, 102171. DOI: 10.1016/j.ijinfomgt.2020.102171

Panigrahi, A., & Joshi, V. (2020). Use of Artificial Intelligence in Education. *The Management Accountant Journal*, 55(5), 64–67. DOI: 10.33516/maj.v55i5.64-67p

Pappachan, P., & Rahaman, M. (2024). Conceptualising the Role of Intellectual Property and Ethical Behaviour in Artificial Intelligence. In *Handbook of Research on AI and ML for Intelligent Machines and Systems* (pp. 1–26). IGI Global.

Papyshev, G. (2024). Situated usage of generative AI in policy education: Implications for teaching, learning, and research. *Journal of Asian Public Policy*, •••, 1–18. DOI: 10.1080/17516234.2024.2370716

Park, J., Caltabiano, N. J., & Hajhashemi, K. (2019). The role of user demographics, self-efficacy and interpersonal competence on communication style preferences of rural university students. *Australian and International Journal of Rural Education*, 29(2), 41–52. DOI: 10.47381/aijre.v29i2.206

Parrila, J. M. (2024). AI levels the playing field for researchers applying for grants. https://www.universityworldnews.com/post.php?story=20240508134752792. Accessed on Sunday 7th July, 2024

Pedrelli, P., Nyer, M., Yeung, A., Zulauf, C., & Wilens, T. (2015). College students: Mental health problems and treatment considerations. *Academic Psychiatry*, 39(5), 503–511. DOI: 10.1007/s40596-014-0205-9 PMID: 25142250

Pedro, F., Subosa, M., Rivas, A., & Valverde, P. (2019). Artificial intelligence in education: Challenges and opportunities for sustainable development.

Pedró, F., Subosa, M., Rivas, A., & Valverde, P. (2019). *Artificial intelligence in education: challenges and opportunities for sustainable development*. UNESCO.

Perju-Mitran, A., & Budacia, A. E. (2015). Gender differences in modeling the influence of online marketing communication on behavioral intentions. *Procedia Economics and Finance*, 27, 567–573. DOI: 10.1016/S2212-5671(15)01034-5

Perkins, M. (2023). Academic Integrity considerations of AI Large Language Models in the post-pandemic era: ChatGPT and beyond. *Journal of University Teaching & Learning Practice*, 20(2). Advance online publication. DOI: 10.53761/1.20.02.07

Persico, D., Manca, S., & Pozzi, F. (2014). Adapting the Technology Acceptance Model to evaluate the innovative potential of e-learning systems. *Computers in Human Behavior*, 30, 614–622. DOI: 10.1016/j.chb.2013.07.045

Peter, J., & Valkenburg, P. M. (2006). Research note: Individual differences in perceptions of internet communication. *European Journal of Communication*, 21(2), 213–226. DOI: 10.1177/0267323105064046

Peters, O. (2010). *Distance education in transition: Developments and issues* (5th ed.). BIS-Verlag der Carl von Ossietzky Universität Oldenburg.

Phind. (n.d.). *Phind: AI-powered search for developers*. https://phind.com

Picciano, A. (2009). Blending with Purpose: The Multimodal Model. *Journal of Asynchronous Learning Networks*, 13, 7–18.

Pohekar, D. (2018). Role of ICT on universities administrative services and management. International Research Journal of Engineering and Technology, 5(11).

Pokkakillath, S., & Suleri, J. (2023). ChatGPT and its impact on education. *Research in Hospitality Management*, 13(1), 31–34. DOI: 10.1080/22243534.2023.2239579

Poth, D. R. (2023). 7 Tools that Help Teachers Work More Effectively. https://www.edutopia.org/article/7-ai-tools-that-help-teachers-work-more-efficiently/. Accessed on Sunday 8th July, 2024

Pradipta, K. D. (1999). *Artificial Intelligence Lecture Notes for Bachelor of Technology in Computer Science and Engineering & Information Technology Department of Computer Science and Engineering & Information Technology*. Veer Surendra Sai University of Technology Burla.

Prashanta, K. P. (2020). *Lecture Notes on Artificial Intelligence*. College of Engineering and Technology.

Prinsloo, P., & Slade, S. (2017). An elephant in the learning analytics room - The obligation to act. *ACM International Conference Proceeding Series*.https://doi.org/ DOI: 10.1145/3027385.3027406

Priyadarshini, A and Kumar, D (2024). Examining the Advantages, Limitations, Opportunities, and Challenges of AI Implementation in Libraries. Journal of Electrical Systems. file:///C:/Users/admin/Downloads/Examining_the_Advantages_Limitations_Opportunities.pdf. Accessed on Thursday 11th July, 2024

Putra, I. G. P. D. D. (2022). Gender communication difference between students in online learning. *The Art of Teaching English as a Foreign Language*, 3(1), 1–8. DOI: 10.36663/tatefl.v3i1.143

Qadhi, S. M., Alduais, A., Chaaban, Y., & Khraisheh, M. (2024). Generative AI, Research Ethics, and Higher Education Research: Insights from a Scientometric Analysis. *Information (Basel)*, 15(6), 325. DOI: 10.3390/info15060325

Qazi, A., Hasan, N., Abayomi-Alli, O., Hardaker, G., Scherer, R., Sarker, Y., Kumar Paul, S., & Maitama, J. Z. (2022). Gender differences in information and communication technology use & skills: A systematic review and meta-analysis. *Education and Information Technologies*, 27(3), 4225–4258. DOI: 10.1007/s10639-021-10775-x PMID: 34697533

Qolamani, K., & Mohammed, M. M. (2023). The Digital Revolution in Higher Education: Transforming Teaching and Learning. QALAMUNA: *Jurnal Pendidikan, Sosial. Dan Agama*, 15(2), 837–846. DOI: 10.37680/qalamuna.v15i2.3905

Rajbhandari, M. M. S., Rajbhandari, S., & Loock, C. (2016). Relations- and task-oriented behaviour of school leaders: Cases from primary schools in Finland. *South African Journal of Childhood Education*, 6(1), 1–10. DOI: 10.4102/sajce.v6i1.360

Raman, A., Mey, C. H., Don, Y., Daud, Y., & Khalid, R. (2015). Relationship between principals' transformational leadership style and secondary school teachers' commitment. *Asian Social Science*, 11(15), 221–228. DOI: 10.5539/ass.v11n15p221

Rambe, P., & Moeti, T. (2021). Navigating digital divides in higher education: Strategies and solutions. *Online Learning Journal*, 25(3), 100–115.

Rane, N., Choudhary, S., & Rane, J. (2024). Artificial Intelligence-driven corporate finance: enhancing efficiency and decision-making through machine learning, natural language processing, and robotic process automation in corporate governance and sustainability. *Natural Language Processing, and Robotic Process Automation in Corporate Governance and Sustainability (February 8, 2024).* https://doi.org/https://doi.org/10.48185/sebr.v5i2.1050

Rane, N., Choudhary, S., & Rane, J. (2023). Education 4.0 and 5.0: Integrating artificial intelligence (AI) for personalized and adaptive learning. *Available atSSRN* 4638365. DOI: 10.2139/ssrn.4638365

Rasheed, R. A., Kamsin, A., & Abdullah, N. A. (2020). Challenges in the online component of blended learning: A systematic review. *Computers & Education*, 144, 103701. DOI: 10.1016/j.compedu.2019.103701

Ratanya F & Muthee D, (2018) An Exploratory Study on Access and Utilization of the Institutional Repositories Among Academic Staff at Egerton University, Kenya East Africa journal of Information science

Ratnam, M., Sharma, B., & Tomer, A. (2023). ChatGPT: educational artificial intelligence. *International Journal, of advanced trends in computer science and engineering, 12*(2). DOI: 10.30534/ijatcse/2023/091222023

Rayelle, D. (2021). The Top Mental Health Challenges Facing Students. Available on: https:// www.bestcolleges.com/resources/top-5-mental-health-problems-facing -college-students/

Reddick, C. G., Enriquez, R., Harris, R. J., & Sharma, B. (2020). Determinants of broadband access and affordability: An analysis of a community survey on the digital divide. *Cities (London, England)*, 106(102904), 102904. DOI: 10.1016/j.cities.2020.102904 PMID: 32921864

Reddy, S., & Sailakshmi, M. (2018). The School as a Social System - A Review. [IJESI]. *International Journal of Engineering and Science Invention*, 7(8), 74–77. https://www.ijesi.org/papers/Vol(7)i8/Version-5/L0708057477.pdf

Redecker, C., & Johannessen, Ø. (2013). Changing assessment—Towards a new assessment paradigm using ICT. *European Journal of Education*, 48(1), 79–96. DOI: 10.1111/ejed.12018

Regona, M., Yigitcanlar, T., Xia, B., & Li, R. Y. M. (2022). Opportunities and adoption challenges of AI in the construction industry: A PRISMA review. *Journal of Open Innovation*, 8(45), 45. Advance online publication. DOI: 10.3390/joitmc8010045

Revilla, M., & H¨öhne, J. (2020). *Comparing the participation of Millennials and older age cohorts in the CROss-National Online Survey panel and the German Internet Panel.* DOI: 10.18148/SRM/2020.V14I5.7619

Richard, M.-O., Chebat, J.-C., Yang, Z., & Putrevu, S. (2010). A proposed model of online consumer behavior: Assessing the role of gender. *Journal of Business Research*, 63(9–10), 926–934. DOI: 10.1016/j.jbusres.2009.02.027

Richardson, J. C., Maeda, Y., & Swan, K. (2020). Social presence in online learning: A meta-analysis of selected studies. *Educational Research Review*, 29, 100329.

Right to Education. (N.d.). Higher Education. Available at https://www.right-to-_education.org/issue-page/higher-education

Roehl, A., Reddy, S. L., & Shannon, G. J. (2013). The Flipped Classroom: An Opportunity to Engage Millennial Students Through Active Learning Strategies. *Journal of Family & Consumer Sciences, 105*(2), Siemens, G. (2005). Connectivism: A learning theory for the digital age. *International Journal of Instructional Technology and Distance Learning*, 2(1).

Roll, I., & Wylie, R. (2016). Evolution and revolution in artificial intelligence in education. *International Journal of Artificial Intelligence in Education*, 26(2), 582–599. https://doi.org/DOI 10.1007/s40593-016-0110-3. DOI: 10.1007/s40593-016-0110-3

Roschelle, J., & Teasley, S. (1995). The construction of shared knowledge in collaborative problem-solving. In O'Malley, C. (Ed.), *Computer-supported collaborative learning* (pp. 69–97). Springer-Verlag. DOI: 10.1007/978-3-642-85098-1_5

Rosenberg, D. (2023). Older adults' perceptions of the technology influence on interpersonal communication: A cross-sectional study. *Journal of Applied Gerontology: The Official Journal of the Southern Gerontological Society*. DOI: 10.1177/07334648231218077

Russel, S., & Norvig, P. (2010). *Artificial Intelligence: A Modern Approach.* Prentice Hall.

Sabwami, M. K. (2021). *Influence of Principals' Transformational Leadership Practices on Management of Public Secondary Schools in Trans-Nzoia County Kenya. PhD Thesis*. Kisii University., Available at http://repository.kisiiuniversity .ac.ke:8080/xmlui/discover

Sagar, R. (2020). Open-AI *releases GPT-3, the largest model so far*. Analytics India Magazine. https://analyticsindiamag.com/open-ai-gpt-3-language-modelv/

Sajjad, A., Noor, A.A., Amer, H.J., Dorothea, B., Nadine, C., & Reaz, M. (2020). Organizational Effectiveness Through Transformational Leadership and Technology Innovation: A Systematic Literature Review and Future Research Agenda. Journal of International Business and Management 3(4): 01-17. DOI:https://doi.org/DOI: 10.37227/JIBM-2020-04-44

Sánchez, O., Castañeda, K., Vidal-Méndez, S., Carrasco-Beltrán, D., & Lozano-Ramírez, N. E. (2024). Exploring the influence of linear infrastructure projects 4.0 technologies to promote sustainable development in smart cities. *Results in Engineering*, 23, 102824. DOI: 10.1016/j.rineng.2024.102824

Sandkuhl, K., & Lehmann, H. (2017). *Digital Transformation in higher education-The role of enterprise architectures and portals*. Lecture Notes in Informatics.

Santoro, A., Lampinen, A., Mathewson, K., Lillicrap, T., & Raposo, D. (2021). Symbolic behaviour in artificial intelligence. *arXiv preprint arXiv:2102.03406.*

Sarnok, K., Wannapiroon, P., & Nilsook, P. (2020). Dtl-eco system by digital story-telling to develop knowledge and digital intelligence for teacher profession students. *International Journal of Information and Education Technology (IJIET)*, 10(12), 865–872. DOI: 10.18178/ijiet.2020.10.12.1472

Sarokhani, D., Delpisheh, A., Veisani, Y., Sarokhani, M., Manesh, R., & Sayehmiri, K. (2013). Prevalence of depression among university students: *A systematic review and meta-analysis study.Depression Research and Treatment*, 2013, 1–7. DOI: 10.1155/2013/373857 PMID: 24187615

Schoenfeld, A. H. (2013). "Reflections on Problem Solving Theory and Practice" in *The Mathematics Enthusiast*, 10(1) Article 3. Available online also at: https:// scholarworks.umt.edu/tme/vol10/iss1/3

Schumacher, P., & Morahan-Martin, J. (2001). Gender, Internet and computer attitudes and experiences. *Computers in Human Behavior*, 17(1), 95–110. DOI: 10.1016/S0747-5632(00)00032-7

Seaman., ... (2018). Grade increase: Tracking distance education in the United States. Babson Park, MA: Babson Survey Research Group. *Babson Survey Research Group.* Babson Survey Research Group. https://eric.ed.gov/?id=ED580852 %0Awww.favazza.com

Selwyn, N. (2015). Minding our language: Why education and technology is full of bullshit… and what might be done about it†. *Learning, Media and Technology*, 41(3), 437–443. DOI: 10.1080/17439884.2015.1012523

Selwyn, N. (2020). What's the problem with digital technology in education? *Learning, Media and Technology*, 45(1).

Senapati, R., & Singh, S. K. (2023). National education Policy-2020 and Evaluation Reforms in Higher Education: Envisioning Transformation for 21st Century India. *University News*, 61(08), 21–26.

Şenocak, D., Bozkurt, A., & Koçdar, S. (2024). Exploring the Ethical Principles for the Implementation of Artificial Intelligence in Education: Towards a Future Agenda. In Transforming Education With Generative AI: Prompt Engineering and Synthetic Content Creation (pp. 200-213). IGI Global.

Serdyukov, P. (2017). Innovation in education: What works, what doesn't, and what to do about it? *Journal of Research in Innovative Teaching & Learning*, 10(1), 4–33. DOI: 10.1108/JRIT-10-2016-0007

Setiawan, P. A. (2023). The Influence of Transformational Leadership and Lecturer Motivation on Lecturer Performance Through Tacit Knowledge Sharing at the Institut Sains dan Teknologi Terpadu Surabaya. *Journal of Social Research*, 2(11), 3836–3849. https://ijsr.internationaljournallabs.com/index.php/ijsr. DOI: 10.55324/josr.v2i11.1485

Shaik, T., Tao, X., Li, Y., Dann, C., McDonald, J., Redmond, P., & Galligan, L. (2022). A review of the trends and challenges in adopting natural language processing methods for education feedback analysis. *IEEE Access : Practical Innovations, Open Solutions*, 10, 56720–56739. DOI: 10.1109/ACCESS.2022.3177752

Shaltry, C. (2013). "Situated Learning with Online Portfolios, Classroom Websites, and Facebook" in *Tech Trends*, 57(3). doi: , N. (2017). *Education and Technology: Key Issues and Debates*. Bloomsbury Publishing.DOI: 10.1007/s11528-013-0658-9.Selwyn

Shaner, K. (2023). P&G, UC celebrate partnership that accelerates innovation. Retrieved from: <https://www.uc.edu/news/articles/2023/03/pg-uc-celebrate-partnership-that-accelerates-innovation.html>. Accessed on 10th July 2024.

Sharma, R., & Garg, M. (2021). The role of technology in the evolution of distance learning: From correspondence to virtual classrooms. *Educational Technology Review*, 67(3), 155–173.

Sheng, J. S. (2021). Kim Hua Tan & Mohd Mahzan Awang. (2021). Generic Digital Equity Model in Education: Mobile-Assisted Personalized Learning (MAPL) through e-Modules. *Sustainability (Basel)*, 13(19), 11115. DOI: 10.3390/su131911115

Shields, C. M. (2020). Becoming a transformative leader: a guide to creating equitable schools. Routledge. Available at https://scholar.google.com/scholar_lookup?title=Becoming%20a%20transformative2 0leader%20a%20guide%20to%20creating%20equitable%20schools&publication_yea r=2020&author=C.M.%20Shields

Shukla, P. K., Kumar, R., & Shukla, A. (2024). Project-Based Learning (PBL), Chapter 3, Edition 19. In Teaching and Learning Techniques: A New Paradigm (pp. 17-25). Government College Zirapur under Department of Higher Education, Government of Madhya Pradesh, India. Available at https://www.researchgate.net/publication/378334128_Project-Based_Learning_PBL

Siemens, G. (2005). Connectivism: A Learning Theory for the Digital Age. *International Journal of Instructional Technology and Distance Learning*, 2(1), 3–1.

Siemens, G. (2005). Connectivism: A learning theory for the digital age. *International Journal of Instructional Technology and Distance Learning*, 2(1), 3–10.

Siemens, G. (2013). Learning analytics: The emergence of a discipline. *The American Behavioral Scientist*, 57(10), 1380–1400. DOI: 10.1177/0002764213498851

Siemens, G. (2021). The evolving nature of networked learning in a digital age. *Journal of Educational Technology*, 18(3), 15–32.

Siemens, G., & Long, P. (2011). Penetrating the Fog: Analytics in Learning and Education. *EDUCAUSE Review*, 46(5), 30–32.

Sifuna, D. N. (2023). Policies and practices of ODEL in East African universities: Challenges and prospects. *East African Journal of Education*, 13(1), 67–85.

Simon, H. A. (1995). Artificial intelligence: An empirical science. *Artificial Intelligence*, 77(1), 95–127. DOI: 10.1016/0004-3702(95)00039-H

Simonton, D. K. (2000). Creative Development as Acquired Expertise: Theoretical Issues and an Empirical Test. *Developmental Review*, 20(2), 283–318. DOI: 10.1006/drev.1999.0504

Sjölund, S., Lindvall, J., Larsson, M., & Ryve, A. (2023). Mapping roles in research-practice partnerships–a systematic literature review. *Educational Review*, 75(7), 1490–1518. DOI: 10.1080/00131911.2021.2023103

Somar, A., & Jianwei, L. (2021). Impact of Artificial Intelligence on Management and Leadership in Research & Developmen. A Case Study of Thermo Fisher Scientific. Karlskrona Sweden

Souter, D., & Kerretts-Makau, M. (2012). Internet governance in Kenya - an assessment. London: A report for the Internet Society by ICT Development Associates Ltd at: http://www. internetsociety. org/sites/default/files/ISOC% 20study% 20of% 20IG% 20in% 20Kenya.

Spreen, C. A., & Vally, S. (2010). Outcomes-based education and its (dis) contents: Learner-centred pedagogy and the education crisis in South Africa. *Southern African Review of Education with Education with Production*, 16(1), 39–58.

Srinivasa, K., Kurni, M., & Saritha, K. (2022). Harnessing the Power of AI to Education. In *Learning, teaching, and assessment methods for contemporary learners: pedagogy for the digital generation* (pp. 311–342). Springer. DOI: 10.1007/978-981-19-6734-4_13

Srinivas, T., & Varaprasad, R. (2024). Innovation through Collaboration: Advancing Higher Education Research. *Research and Reviews: Advancement in Robotics*, 7(1), 7–16.

Ssebunnya, J., Medhin, G., Kangere, S., Kigozi, F., Nakku, J., & Lund, C. (2019). Prevalence, correlates and help-seeking behaviour for depressive symptoms in rural Uganda: A population-based survey. *Global Mental Health (Cambridge, England)*, 6, E27. DOI: 10.1017/gmh.2019.25 PMID: 31807311

Stenbom, S. (2018). A systematic review of the Community of Inquiry research: When theory meets practice. *The Internet and Higher Education*, 39, 22–32. DOI: 10.1016/j.iheduc.2018.06.001

Stephenson, L. B., & Crete, J. (2011). Studying political behavior: A comparison of internet and telephone surveys. *International Journal of Public Opinion Research*, 23(1), 24–55. DOI: 10.1093/ijpor/edq025

Strauss, V. (2013). Nelson Mandela Famous Quote on Education. The Washington Post. Available at https://www.washingtonpost.com/news/answersheet/wp/2013/12/05/nelson-mandelas- famous-quote-on-education/

Strukan, E., Nikolic, M., & Sefic, S. (2017). Impact of transformational leadership on business performance. DOI: DOI: 10.17559/TV-20150624082830

Subarto, S., Solihin, D., & Qurbani, D. (2021). Determinants of Job Satisfaction and Its Implications for the Lecturers Performance. [JPEB]. *Jurnal Pendidikan Ekonomi Dan Bisnis*, 9(2), 163–178. DOI: 10.21009/JPEB.009.2.7

Subirana, B., Bagiati, A., & Sarma, S. (2017). On the Forgetting of College Academics. *Ebbinghaus Speed*, (68), 1–12.

Su, C. H., & Cheng, C. H. (2015). A mobile gamification learning system for improving the learning motivation and achievements. *Journal of Computer Assisted Learning*, 31(3), 268–286. DOI: 10.1111/jcal.12088

Suleiman, S., Olen, D., & Bezuidenhout, M. (2024). AI regulation and policy in Africa. https://www.dentons.com/en/insights/articles/2024/june/13/ai-regulation-and-policy-in-africa. Accessed on Sunday 7th July, 2024

Supermane, S. (2019). Transformational leadership and innovation in teaching and learning activities: The mediation effect of knowledge management. *Information Discovery and Delivery*, 47(4), 242–250. DOI: 10.1108/IDD-05-2019-0040

Tait, A. (2003). Reflections on student support in open and distance learning. *International Review of Research in Open and Distance Learning*, 4(1), 1–15. DOI: 10.19173/irrodl.v4i1.134

Talwar, P. (2023). *The Strategic Use of Virtual Teacher Assistants to Increase Faculty Engagement and Job Satisfaction*. Trident University International.

Tan, D.-P., Ji, S.-M., & Jin, M.-S. (2012). Intelligent computer-aided instruction modeling and a method to optimize study strategies for parallel robot instruction. *IEEE Transactions on Education*, 56(3), 268–273. DOI: 10.1109/TE.2012.2212707

Taneja, S. (2014). DreamBox: An adaptive, personalized learning platform for early math education. *Forbes*, 20(October), •••. https://doi.org/https://www.forbes.com/sites/sungardas/2014/10/20/dreambox-adaptive-personalized-learning-platform-early-math-education/

Tapalova, O., & Zhiyenbayeva, N. (2022). Artificial intelligence in education: AIEd for personalised learning pathways. *Electronic Journal of e-Learning*, 20(5), 639–653. DOI: 10.34190/ejel.20.5.2597

Tapper, J. (2023). Authors shocked to find AI rip-offs of their books being sold on Amazon. https://www.theguardian.com/technology/2023/sep/30/authors-shocked-to-find-ai-ripoffs-of-their-books-being-sold-on-amazon. Accessed on Sunday 7th July, 2024

Tarhini, A., Hone, K., Liu, X., & Tarhini, T. (2017). Examining the adoption of digital technologies in higher education. Computers & Education, Tenya A. N. Maina J. C.& Awuor F. M (2024) Digital Literacy as a tool for enhancing access and utilization of information in digital resource platforms among academic staff in University libraries, kenya. *International Journal of Scientific Research.*

Tarus, J. K., Gichoya, D., & Muumbo, A. (2015). Challenges of implementing e-learning in Kenya: A case of Kenyan public universities. *International Review of Research in Open and Distance Learning*, 16(1). Advance online publication. DOI: 10.19173/irrodl.v16i1.1816

Tarver, W. L., Menser, T., Hesse, B. W., Johnson, T. J., Beckjord, E., Ford, E. W., & Huerta, T. R. (2018). Growth dynamics of patient-provider internet communication: Trend analysis using the health information national trends survey (2003 to 2013). *Journal of Medical Internet Research*, 20(3), e109. DOI: 10.2196/jmir.7851 PMID: 29599107

Terstegen, S., Lennings, F., Suchy, O., Schalter, K., & Suarsana, D. (2018). *Leistung & Entgelt Arbeits- und Betriebsorganisation kompakt - Künstliche Intelligenz in der Arbeitswelt der Zukunft – Ansichten und Standpunkte*. Joh. Heider Verlag GmbH.

Tess, P. A. (2013). The role of social media in higher education classes (real and virtual) – A literature review. *Computers in Human Behavior*, 29(5), A60–A68. DOI: 10.1016/j.chb.2012.12.032

Thayer, S. E., & Ray, S. (2006). Online communication preferences across age, gender, and duration of internet use. *Cyberpsychology & Behavior*, 9(4), 432–440. DOI: 10.1089/cpb.2006.9.432 PMID: 16901247

Thomas, A. P. (2024). Balancing Innovation and Integrity: Addressing Concerns of AI in Classroom Environments. https://scholarworks.gvsu.edu/gradprojects/451

Thomas, J. W. (2000). *A Review of Research on Project-Based Learning*. Retrieved from http://www.bobpearlman.org/BestPractices/PBL_Research.pdf

Thomas, J., & Achutha Menon, V. (2023). Studying in online environment: Students' attitude towards online open electives in Karnataka. [IJET]. *International Journal of Emerging Technologies in Learning*, 18(20), 114–125. DOI: 10.3991/ijet.v18i20.39541

Thompson, S. (2024). What is innovation in education and why it's important? Available at: https://corp.kaltura.com/blog/what-is-innovation-in-education/

Toosi, A., Bottino, A. G., Saboury, B., Siegel, E., & Rahmim, A. (2021). A brief history of AI: How to prevent another winter (a critical review). *PET Clinics*, 16(4), 449–469. https://doi.org/https://doi.org/10.1016/j.cpet.2021.07.001. DOI: 10.1016/j.cpet.2021.07.001

Tran, B. X., Latkin, C. A., Vu, G. T., Nguyen, H. L. T., Nghiem, S., Tan, M.-X., Lim, Z.-K., Ho, C. S. H., & Ho, R. C. M. (2019). The current research landscape of the application of artificial intelligence in managing cerebrovascular and heart diseases: A bibliometric and content analysis. *International Journal of Environmental Research and Public Health*, 16(15), 2699. DOI: 10.3390/ijerph16152699

Treiman, D. J. (2007). Inequality and equality under Chinese socialism: The hukou system and intergenerational occupational mobility. *American Journal of Sociology*, 113(2), 415–445. DOI: 10.1086/518905

Trocchia, P. J., & Janda, S. (2000). A phenomenological investigation of Internet usage among older individuals. *Journal of Consumer Marketing*, 17(7), 605–616. DOI: 10.1108/07363760010357804

Tsai, Y.-S., Poquet, S., Gašević, D., Dawson, S., & Pardo, A. (2019). Complexity leadership in learning analytics: Drivers, challenges, and opportunities. *British Journal of Educational Technology*, 50(6), 2839–2854. DOI: 10.1111/bjet.12846

Tungpantong, C., Nilsook, P., & Wannapiroon, P. (2021, March). A conceptual framework of factors for information systems success to digital transformation in higher education institutions. In 2021 9th International Conference on Information and Education Technology (ICIET) (pp. 57-62). IEEE. DOI: 10.1109/ICIET51873.2021.9419596

Turi, J. A., Khastoori, S., Sorooshian, S., & Campbell, N. (2022). Diversity impact on organizational performance: Moderating and mediating role of diversity beliefs and leadership expertise. *PLoS One*, 17(7), e0270813. DOI: 10.1371/journal.pone.0270813 PMID: 35877610

Turing, A. M. (1950). Computing Machinery and Intelligence. https://redirect.cs.umbc.edu/courses/471/papers/turing.pdf

Tyler-Wood, T. L. (2020). The Role of Digital Fabrication in Today's Society. In Handbook of Research on Tools for Teaching Computational Thinking in P-12 Education (pp. 377-391). DOI: 10.4018/978-1-7998-4576-8.ch015

U.S. Department of Education, Office of Educational Technology. (2023). *Artificial Intelligence and Future of Teaching and Learning: Insights and Recommendations*, Washington, DC, 2023. https://tech.ed.gov

Uko, E. S. (2015). Principalship and effective management of facilities in secondary schools in Cross River State, Nigeria. *International Journal of Academic Research and Reflection*, 3(1), 64–76. http://www.idpublications.org/wpcontent/uploads/2014/10/PRINCIPALSHIP-AND-EFFECTIVE-MANAGEMENT-OF-FACILITIES-IN-SECONDARY-SCHOOLS-IN-CROSS-RIVER-STATE-NIGERIA.pdf

UNESCO (2023). Education in the age of artificial intelligence. UNESCO Courier, 7 place de Fontenoy, 75352 Paris 07 SP, France UNESCO 2023.

UNESCO. (1998). World Conference on Higher Education in the Twenty-first Century: Vision and Action, Paris. https://unesdoc.unesco.org/ark:/48223/pf0000141952

UNESCO. (2011). *ICT Competency Framework for Teachers*. UNESCO. https://unesdoc.unesco.org/ark:/

UNESCO. (2015). [*Incheon Declaration and Framework for Action – Towards inclusive and equitable quality education and lifelong learning for all.* UNESCO.]. *Education*, •••, 2030.

UNESCO. (2021). *Artificial intelligence in education: Guidance for policy-makers*. https://unesdoc.unesco.org/ark:/48223/pf0000374802

UNESCO. (2021). The role of digital technologies in education during the COVID-19 pandemic. *UNESCO Education Report*.

Usman, Y. D. (2016). Educational resources: An integral component for effective school administration in Nigeria. *Research on Humanities and Social Sciences, 6*(13), 28-39. Available at https://files.eric.ed.gov/fulltext/ED578024.pdf

Varga, A., Vitez, K., Orsos, I., Fodor, B. & Gergely, H. (2021). Diversity and Inclusion in Higher Education. KÉPZÉS ÉS GYAKORLAT / TRAINING AND PRACTICE, 19 (1-2),70-81. https://doi.org/DOI: 10.17165/TP.2021.1-2.7

Vaswani, A. (2017). Attention is all you need. *Advances in Neural Information Processing Systems*.

Veletsianos, G. (2021). Learner engagement in digital learning environments: What we know and what we need to know. *Distance Education*, 42(1), 5–17.

Venable, M. (2021). Gender Differences in Online Learning: Insights from recent graduates. *ELearn, 2021*(6). DOI: 10.1145/3473344.3460821

Venkatesh, V., & Davis, F. D. (2000). A theoretical extension of the technology acceptance model: Four longitudinal field studies. *Management Science*, 46(2), 186–204. DOI: 10.1287/mnsc.46.2.186.11926

Verdugo-Castro, S., García-Holgado, A., & Sánchez-Gómez, M. C. (2019). Age influence in gender stereotypes related to Internet use in young people: A case study. *Proceedings of the Seventh International Conference on Technological Ecosystems for Enhancing Multiculturality*. DOI: 10.1145/3362789.3362846

Verma, M., & R, S. (2014). Role of gender in influencing consumers' attitude towards online advertising. *Indian Journal of Marketing*, 44(12), 32. DOI: 10.17010/ijom/2014/v44/i12/80009

Vygotsky, L. S. (1978). *Mind in society: The development of higher psychological processes*. Harvard University Press.

Waham, J. J., Asfahani, A., & Ulfa, R. A. (2023). International Collaboration in Higher Education: Challenges and Opportunities in a Globalized World. *EDUJAVARE: International Journal of Educational Research*, 1(1), 49–60.

Wahyudi (2018). The influence of job satisfaction and work experience on lecturer performance of Pamulang University. *Scientific Journal of Reflection: Economic, Accounting, Management and Business, 1*(2), 221-230. ISSN 2615-3009

Wainaina, D. (2021). The role of blockchain in secure credentialing for e-learning in Kenya. *East African Journal of Information Technology*, 7(2), 28–40.

Wall, P., Saxena, D., & Brown, S. (2021). Artificial intelligence in the Global South (AI4D): Potential and risks. *arXiv preprint arXiv:2108.10093*.

Walton Family Foundation. (2023). Teachers and students embrace ChatGPT for education. https://www.waltonfamilyfoundation.org/learning/teachers-and-students-embrace-chatgpt-for-education

Wang, D., Ma, X., & Wang, A. Y. (2021). *Human-centered AI for data science: A systematic approach*. http://arxiv.org/abs/2110.01108

Wanjiku Wang'ang'a, A. (2024). Consequences of Artificial Intelligence on Teaching and Learning in Higher Education in Kenya: Literature Review. *East African Journal of Education Studies*, 7(1), 202–215. DOI: 10.37284/eajes.7.1.1718

Warschauer, M., Tseng, W., Yim, S., Webster, T., Jacob, S., Du, Q., & Tate, T. (2023). The affordances and contradictions of AI-generated text for second language writers.. Accessed on Sunday 7th July, 2024DOI: 10.2139/ssrn.4404380

Washington, J. (2023). Comparing and Contrasting How Humans and AI Learn. https://www.linkedin.com/pulse/comparing-contrasting-how-humans-ai-learn-jerry-washington-ed-d--qmbxc. Accessed on Sunday 7th July, 2024

Wekullo, C. S., Kabindio, B., & Juma, I. (2023). Faculty and students' perspectives of online learning during COVID-19 crisis: Constraints and opportunities for Kenyan universities. *E-Learning and Digital Media*, •••, 20427530231156483.

Wekullo, C. S., Shiundu, J. O., Ouda, J. B., & Mutevane, A. (2022). COVID-19 crisis and the future of higher education: Perspectives from Kenya. In McKeown, J. S., Bista, K., & Chan, R. Y. (Eds.), *Global higher education during COVID-19: Policy, society, and technology* (pp. 73–91). STAR Scholars., https://starscholars.org/product/global-education/

White House Office of Science and Technology Policy. (October 2022), *Blueprint for an AI bill of rights: Making automated systems work for the American people.* The White House Office of Science and Technology Policy. https://www.whitehouse.gov/ostp/ai-bill-of-rights/

Whitley, B. E.Jr. (1997). Gender differences in computer-related attitudes and behavior: A meta-analysis. *Computers in Human Behavior*, 13(1), 1–22. DOI: 10.1016/S0747-5632(96)00026-X

Whitty, M., & Gavin, J. (2001). Age/sex/location: Uncovering the social cues in the development of online relationships. *Cyberpsychology & Behavior*, 4(5), 623–630. DOI: 10.1089/109493101753235223 PMID: 11725656

WHO (2017). Depression and Other Common Mental Disorder: Global Health Estimates

Wilson, D., Warton, C., & Louw, G. (1998). Stress, anxiety and academic performance among medical students at the University of Cape Town. *Southern African Journal of Child and Adolescent Mental Health*, 10(1), 23–31. DOI: 10.1080/16826108.1998.9632343

World Bank. (2021). *Internet penetration in Sub-Saharan Africa: Opportunities and challenges*. World Bank.

World Bank. (2024). Tertiary Education. Available at https://www.worldbank.org/en/topic/tertiaryeducation#:~:text=Tertiary%20education%20refers%20to%20all,poverty%2C%20and%20boosting%20shared%20prosperity.

Xiong, W. (2023). AI and Leadership New Changes of Leadership Under the Development of Artificial Intelligence Business School, The University of Hong Kong, Pokfulam, Hong Kong 999077, China wenjinxiong1998@163.com C. F. Peng et al. (Eds.): MMET 2022, ASSEHR 703, pp. 497–503, 2023. https://doi.org/DOI: 10.2991/978-2-494069-51-0_69

Xu, W., Dainoff, M. J., Ge, L., & Gao, Z. (2022). Transitioning to human interaction with AI systems: New challenges and opportunities for HCI professionals to enable human centered AI. *International Journal of Human-Computer Interaction*, 1(25). Advance online publication. DOI: 10.1080/10447318.2022.2041900

Yambo, J. M. O. (2012). *Determinants of KCSE Examination Performance in SDA Sponsored Schools: A Key to Academic Promotion to the next Level of Learning*. Lambert Academic Publishing.

Yambo, J. M. O. (2023). Dynamics of Teaching in the Era of Climate Change Education. In Sagini, J. K., & Nyatuka, B. O. (Eds.), *Handbook of Research on Climate Change Education for Sustainable Development*. IGI Global., Available at https://www.igiglobal.com/book/handbook-research-climate-change-culture-, DOI: 10.4018/978-1-6684-9099-0.ch013

Yang, K. C. C. (2004). A comparison of attitudes towards Internet advertising among lifestyle segments in Taiwan. *Journal of Marketing Communications*, 10(3), 195–212. DOI: 10.1080/1352726042000181657

Yannick, P., Tim, J., & Sven, H. (2022). Artificial Intelligence and its Impact on Leaders and Leadership. 3rd International Conference on Industry 4.0 and Smart Manufacturing www.sciencedirect.com*Procedia Computer Science*www.elsevier .com/locate/procedia

Yanti, H. S., Iim, W., Hanafiah, H., & Deti, R. (2022). Transformational Leadership in Improving Lecturer Performance in Higher Education. International Journal of Science Education and Technology Management, 1(2). 1-19. https://www.neliti .com/publications/558973/transformational-leadership-in- improving-lecturer-performance-in-higher-education

Ye, L., Shuai, W., Jun, L., & Shaohui, Q. (2024). The Innovative Path of Intelligent Teaching in the Age of Artificial Intelligence ICAIE 2023. *AHCS*, 15, 116–124. DOI: 10.2991/978-94-6463-242-2_15

Yeo, M. A. (2023). Academic integrity in the age of artificial intelligence (AI) authoring apps. *TESOL Journal*, 14(3), e716. DOI: 10.1002/tesj.716

Youssef, J., & Deane, F. (2006). Factors influencing mental-health help-seeking in Arabic-speaking communities in Sydney, *Australia.Mental Health, Religion & Culture*, 9(1), 43–66. DOI: 10.1080/13674670512331335686

Yufeia, L., Salehb, S., Jiahuic, H., & Syed, S. M. (2020). Review of the application of artificial intelligence in education. *Integration (Amsterdam)*, 12(8), 1–15.

Yusuf, A., Pervin, N., Román-González, M., & Noor, N. M. (2024). Generative AI in education and research: A systematic mapping review. *Review of Education*, 12(2), e3489. DOI: 10.1002/rev3.3489

Zacamy, J., & Roschelle, J. (2022). Navigating the tensions: How could equity-relevant research also be agile, open, and scalable? Digital Promise. http://hdl.handle.net/20.500.12265/159

Zawacki-Richter, O., Alturki, U., & Aldraiweesh, A. (2020). The role of open and distance education in fostering educational equity. *International Journal of Educational Technology*, 27(1), 45–65.

Zawacki-Richter, O., & Jung, I. (2019). Online learning engagement strategies in global education. *Journal of Educational Technology & Society*, 22(2), 12–29.

Zerkowska, A. M. (2024). PERSONALIZED LANGUAGE LEARNING IN THE AGE OF AI. Leveraging Large Language Models for Optimal Learning Outcomes.

Zhao, W. X., Zhou, K., Li, J., Tang, T., Wang, X., Hou, Y., Min, Y., Zhang, B., Zhang, J., & Dong, Z. (2023). A survey of large language models. *arXiv preprint arXiv:2303.18223.*

Zhou, D., Peng, L., & Dong, Y. (2020). The impact of Internet usage on gender role attitudes. *Applied Economics Letters*, 27(2), 86–92. DOI: 10.1080/13504851.2019.1610692

About the Contributors

George Ngwacho Areba, Ph.D, (Kabarak University); MED (Kenyatta University) & BED Arts(Egerton University) is the immediate former Dean and Postgraduate Coordinator, at the School of Education & Human Resource Development (SEDHURED), Kisii University & Senior lecturer at the Department of Education Foundations, Educational Administration, Planning and Economics (EDFO/EAPE). He is an accomplished researcher, writer, supervisor, examiner, and reviewer with several institutions of higher learning. Before joining higher education as a lecturer, he served as a high school tutor teaching English Literature in several institutions. He is also an experienced thespian in Drama and music as a trainer, facilitator, and adjudicator at all levels. His research appears in a range of international peer-reviewed scholarly journals and books like Global IGI among others

Billiah Gisore PhD (The Catholic University of Eastern Africa), M.ED (University of Nairobi), B.ED (Kenyatta University) is a lecturer in the school of education at Kisii University, Kenya. Dr Billiah is the coordinator, Teacher Education in the Faculty of Education. She is an instructor, researcher, and examiner in the university and an external examiner in other universities. She is co-author of the books: Understanding Sustainability with Pedagogical Practice: A Contribution from Geography Education Toward Sustainability Competence Based Curriculum: A Handbook for Teachers, Handbook of Research on Innovative Digital Practices and Globalization in Higher Education, Pre-Service Teachers' Pedagogical Knowledge and Perceptions of Climate Change Education, Pedagogical Strategies to Enhance Climate Change Education Outcomes among others. Her professional background is in Educational Research and Evaluation. Her interests are in Education Administration, Teacher Education, Classroom Assessments, Equity, Sustainability Education, and lately, Climate Change Education and Virtual Learning.

Evelyn Wanjiru Njurai B.Ed. Sci (Hons), MSc (Pure Maths), PhD (Mathematics Education) is currently a lecturer of Curriculum Studies and Mathematics Education courses in the Department of Curriculum, Instruction, and Media and Coordinator of Teaching Practice in the School of Education at Kisii University, Kenya. She has a wide experience in qualitative research in and out of academia. Her research interests include Mathematics education in the context of language diversity, Curriculum, E-learning, and STEM Education. Evelyn has published internationally and locally in peer-reviewed journals and book chapters and is the author of Dictionary of Mathematics for Secondary Schools, Kenya (2019). She is a co-editor of a handbook for the Competency-Based Curriculum in Kenya and co-author of two book chapters in the book. Evelyn is a member of various professional bodies and is involved in community work through volunteer service in teaching mathematics to marginalized communities in Kenya.

***

Vishnu Achutha Menon is an independent journalist, writer, researcher, and an Indian percussionist. He is a recipient of the Junior Scholarship the Ministry of Culture awarded. His research interests are film studies, verbal & nonverbal communication, south Asian performances, Natyasastra, media studies, media analysis techniques, Laban Movement Analysis, and Ethnomusicology.

Laith Shlash Ismail, a Jordanian humanitarian worker, is recognized for his leadership in diverse humanitarian and development interventions, spanning WASH (Water, Sanitation, and Hygiene), SWM (Solid Waste Management), livelihoods, agriculture, MHPSS (Mental Health and Psychosocial Support), and operations management. He holds a degree in Logistics Sciences from the German Jordanian University and a Master's in European Studies from the University of Düsseldorf. Laith has also conducted research in the circular economy, showing a keen interest in sustainable development and climate resilience. Currently, he serves as the Field Coordinator for ACTION AGAINST HUNGER in Jordan, overseeing interventions across various sectors in the country. He is set to advance his career as the Country Representative for ACTION AGAINST HUNGER in Libya. Laith is a senior member of the Arab Trainers Union, a dedicated organization working to advance the training profession in

lFredrick Mtenzi - Prof. Fredrick Mtenzi holds a PhD in Management Information Systems from the University College Dublin – Ireland. His main research interests are integrating technology in education and systems security. Specifically, identifying and customizing Open-Source software that can be used in low-cost devices with theview of increasing acceptability and utility of technology in teaching, learning and research. He has also been working on an Open-Source software designed to enable children who are out of the formal education system to learn on their own so that they can join the formal education system with their age group. He has been involved in three major national projects on quality teacher professional development that were funded Global Affairs Canada and Results for Development(R4D).

Henry Onderi is an Associate Professor of Education at Jaramogi Oginga Odinga University of Science and Technology. He is Director of Institutional Advancement and International Office and former Director, Kisii campus and Chairman, County Education Board- Kisii. His interest is in Professional Development andworking on " Identification of and Intervention in Gambling Effects Among Vulnerable Groups in Public Universities in Kenya" funded by the Bristol Hub Research Innovation Fund Seedcon

Rose Atieno Opiyo, is a passionate behavioral scientist -practitioner, who skillfully divides her time between training, consulting, scholarly mentorship, writing, research, and teaching, spanning from fields of: Behavioral Science, Teacher Education and Implementation Research She is a Senior Lecturer in department of Educational Psychology School of Education at Masinde Muliro University of Science and Technology (MMUST), Kenya. She sits in various Academic, Scientific, Technical and Advisory Boards shaping education and behavioral research scholarship mentorship and Intervention in Kenya and beyond. Opiyo affiliates to professional bodies, is a recipient of several Fellowship award – among them, the German Exchange Services (DAAD) In country Scholarship Award. She is the current recipient of Carnegie African Diaspora Fellow, International Society for the Study of Behavioral Development (ISSBD) Post-Doctoral Research Fellowship. She has coauthored two books and over 35 articles in refereed journals and book Chapters. She is an editor of several books and journals. She has penchant for multi-institutional and multi-disciplinary behavioral intervention science and evaluation res

Silyvier Tsindoli-PhD (Education Communication and Technology), M.Ed. in Education and B.Ed in Education from Moi University. She is involved in teaching/training, research, and community service. She is a lecturer in the School of Education, Deputy Director of, the Institute of Open Distance and E-Learning (IODEL), Technical Editor for 'The Educator' a journal of the School of Education, Course Coordinator and Teaching Practice Coordinator, Moi University. She has served as an examination coordinator and curriculum developer and review at the University. Tsindoli has been engaged in both local and international workshops and trainings. Her research interest and training are in educational technology, research methodology, transformative instruction, curriculum design, early childhood education and development, teacher education, gender studies and emergency education. In addition, she has supervised and examined postgraduate students to completion and published several papers in refereed journals. She has attended and presented articles in both local and international conferences. She is a member of African Network for Internationalization of Education (ANIE), Education Leadership and Research Association (ELRA) and Inter-Agency Network for Education in Emergencies (INEE).

Index

A

B

C

D

T

U

V

www.ingramcontent.com/pod-product-compliance
Lightning Source LLC
LaVergne TN
LVHW061549290926
849162LV00004B/959
* 9 7 9 8 3 3 7 3 0 0 2 5 2 *